BERENSON'S
ITALIAN PICTURES
OF THE RENAISSANCE

PHAIDON PRESS

ITALIAN PICTURES OF THE RENAISSANCE

A LIST OF THE PRINCIPAL ARTISTS
AND THEIR WORKS
WITH AN INDEX OF PLACES

BY

BERNARD BERENSON

FLORENTINE SCHOOL
IN TWO VOLUMES

VOL. I

WITH 590 ILLUSTRATIONS

THE PHAIDON PRESS

© 1963 PHAIDON PRESS LTD · LONDON SW7

PRINTED IN GREAT BRITAIN

THIS VOLUME

HAS BEEN PRODUCED

IN COLLABORATION WITH

THE SAMUEL H · KRESS FOUNDATION

AS A TRIBUTE TO

BERNARD BERENSON

AND IN APPRECIATION OF

MORE THAN A QUARTER CENTURY

OF FRIENDSHIP AND CO-OPERATION

IN THE FIELD OF RENAISSANCE PAINTING

BETWEEN BERNARD BERENSON AND

SAMUEL H · KRESS

PREFACE

The purpose of this revised and illustrated edition of Bernard Berenson's Florentine Lists is the same as that of the Venetian Lists published in 1957. Berenson himself set out this purpose in his own preface to that edition. Although published after his death (in 1959) the present text is based on Berenson's own changes, additions and corrections, noted in his copy of the 1936 edition, and on the annotated photographic files at I Tatti, in which many additional observations and changes were made.

The work of preparing the text for publication was done between September 1959 and January 1961 by Michael Rinehart. This involved correlating B.B's notes, and verifying and amplifying factual information such as locations, descriptions of subject matter, etc. Luisa Vertova Nicolson has selected the illustrations and has made a number of valuable suggestions based on her intimate knowledge of the library and the photographic material. My special thanks are due to them for the care and devotion with which they fulfilled their tasks. My own contribution has consisted in taking responsibility for various decisions where B.B. had left ambiguous or conflicting instructions, and particularly for the addition of some new lists, based partly on B.B's annotations, partly on my personal recollections of opinions expressed by him and partly on recent publications that B.B. would certainly have taken into account during a final revision.

These new lists are Cenni di Francesco, Cristiani, Benedetto Ghirlandajo, Master of the Arte della Lana Coronation, Master of the Barberini Panels, Master of the Lathrop tondo, Master of the Rinuccini Chapel, Michelangelo's early follower, Michele di Ridolfo, Paolo Schiavo, Parri Spinelli, Pietro di Miniato, Tommaso di Stefano Lunetti. I also take the responsibility of adding three paintings unknown to B.B., as I felt sure that he would have included them: the Angelico fresco at San Domenico di Fiesole (discovered by Ugo Procacci), the homeless early Bachiacca tondo, and the Giovanni del Biondo fragments of the Liverpool Coronation (found by Zeri).

As in the Venetian School, the reader will find a few groups of signed and documented works by artists not otherwise included, where they amplify some of the questions of attribution raised by the lists. These artists are: Alvaro Portoghese, Amedeo da Pistoia, the two Antonio da Firenze, Bocchi, Bonsi, Lippo di Benivieni, Mariotto di Cristofano, Pacino di Bonaguida, Puccio di Simone, Zanobi Strozzi.

In the earlier editions of the lists B.B. could not include homeless pictures, as their identity would have remained uncertain without illustrations; for this reason he published some of the many he knew, with reproductions, in the series of articles 'Quadri senza Casa' in *Dedalo* 1932. In the present edition most of the homeless pictures are reproduced but in a very few cases a reference to 'Dedalo' or other publications has seemed sufficient.

*   *   *

When in the spring of 1958 Bernard Berenson fell seriously ill he had already gone over most of these Florentine lists adding his annotations to them. At first he fully expected to recover his health and his capacity to work for a limited number of hours each day. Gradually it became clear to us that he was losing ground and that any sustained work was no longer possible. Only now and then and especially in the mornings he enjoyed looking at new books and illustrated magazines or at photos and could be asked for his opinion on some special problem.

In the summer of 1959, a few months before his death, B.B. insisted on devoting 15 to 20 minutes every day to looking at photos of the great Quattrocento Florentines. He was no longer able to speak very clearly, but his expression of contentment while gazing at these masterpieces, especially at the Botticellis, is to me unforgettable. May those who will consult his book feel some of the joy he got to the very end of his life from his work on the Florentine painters of the Renaissance.

*   *   *

In B.B's name I express my thanks to the Samuel H. Kress Foundation for its continued generous support of this publication, to the President and Fellows of Harvard University for allowing us to use the Berenson Library and its photographic archives at I Tatti, and to the Phaidon Press for making every effort to produce and publish the work to their high standard. But above all for honouring the agreement which Bela Horovitz had made with B.B. more than ten years ago about this new and lavishly illustrated edition of the lists. I hope it will be completed, but even if that is not possible, the four volumes already published will help to keep the memory of these two men alive.

Florence, 1963.   NICKY MARIANO

PREFACE TO THE EDITION OF 1932

THE Lists comprising this book differ from those originally appended to the four volumes of my *Renaissance Painters*, not only by bringing all the schools together under one alphabetical order, not only by including many more artists and a great many more pictures than I knew thirty-five years ago, but in being inspired by a different principle.

The Lists in previous editions, although revised from time to time, were all based on the conviction that the hand of the artist never faltered, even if his head did occasionally nod. The execution, on this theory, tended to weigh more than the creative mental effort. The question of questions was whether a painting was autograph. If it was not, it did not count, unless indeed it betrayed the hand of another painter, in which case it was included in that painter's work. An artistic personality thus shrank to a composite of those pictures only where hand and mind were one.

Would that hand and mind were always one! that the artist himself never worked with the makeshift of an inferior self, or with the help of apprentices!

This former exclusiveness was perhaps a necessary and salutary discipline. It enabled one to reach the heart of an artistic personality before starting to put out to its limits; it made one so familiar with his ways that one became able to recognize him even in his uninspired moments.

But now, fortified with this experience of the artist at his highest, one may well afford to relax from the earlier severity, and include every work that shows the distinct trace of his creative purpose, whether largely or only in small part by his own hand, whether done in his studio on his indications, or whether mere copies of lost works.

Indeed, it now seems that to confine interest to what looks like perfect achievement is dandiacal aestheticism. One who dedicates his whole life to art, and not merely his week-ends, holidays, and leisure moments, cannot remain satisfied with such an adolescent attitude. Mature interest leads one at least as much to the mind of the artist as to his hand. An artistic personality includes not only all that the artist did in his best moments, but all that his mind conceived in the terms of his art, in whatever shape it has been recorded, no matter how inadequate, nor how unsatisfactory.

It might indeed seem that long experience has brought me back to the old days when everything that looked like Leonardo or Raphael produced the appropriate sentiment in the soul of the beholder. 'What then,' it may be asked, 'has been the use of all this business about renaming pictures, distinguishing originals from copies, and masters from pupils, if now we are invited to get once more our Raphael or Leonardo thrill from inferior works? What has become of the touchstone of Quality, if we admit that the hand of a great artist can falter, and if we insist on tracing his genius through the works of his assistants and followers, and value even the humble achievements of copyists whose hands never vibrated with the master's touch? We are once again in the old uncharted regions where no compass pointing to quality any longer guides us, and where the only clue is the familiar one of the conception, the idea, the suggestion, that led us into so many bogs. The naive sightseer and the connoisseur join hands!'

True! But though they acclaim together 'the Master', it is with a difference. The plain sightseer can undoubtedly be deeply stirred by a work of art, but it is nearly always the literary, the romantic, the associative ideas that move him. The connoisseur who has learnt to distinguish between the poetry suggested by the picture and its specific qualities as painting, is affected in another way.

In my writings on Renaissance Painters I attempted to distinguish between the Illustrative and the Decorative elements in pictures, and it may be that I over-emphasized the latter, for I have been amused and sometimes distressed to find many subsequent writers dwelling only on the decorative elements in art, which, vitalizing as they are, do their noblest service only when they convey great human ideals.

The instructed lover of art, who has learnt to distinguish the individual touch of the artist he is studying, can perceive the creative intention even in his less happy achievements, but he does not stop at the mere thought, the suggestions given by the illustration; in his disciplined imagination he recreates the design as a whole in the exact decorative terms of the artist. And who shall say that the pleasures of a trained imagination thus stimulated are not genuine aesthetic pleasures?

In the Lists now published I have therefore been led to include not only pictures which the artists painted with more or less assistance, but such as were turned out in their studios from their designs, and even copies as well, providing they faithfully transcribe lost works. To distinguish such works from absolutely autograph pictures, I have adopted a series of signs which I enclose in brackets after the subject of the picture. These I must explain.

EXPLANATIONS

A question-mark does not mean that I expect the picture necessarily to turn out to be by the painter in whose list it is included. The intention is rather to provoke a discussion which might not arise if the picture were relegated to the limbo of anonymity, and to point out, as far as I can, the most fruitful line of inquiry.

It would have been easy to omit the pictures I have attributed with a question-mark, casting them out from the garden like worthless weeds, and my reputation would perhaps gain in certain circles had I done so. But it seems more generous to expose one's self to the risk of disparagement than to fail to call attention to the most likely affiliations of uncertain pictures. Abstention is safe, but sterile. Care must be taken, of course, to reject without mercy those attributions which are merely happy thoughts or bright guesses, and to admit only such as, even if not entirely satisfactory, are based on the fullest information, and on the truest idea of the artist available at the moment.

Even unquestioned attributions are not trademarks, although collectors and dealers would like them to be. They are stepping-stones rather than goals. None of my lists give me complete satisfaction. More and more work will be required for two or even three generations before this task will be adequately accomplished. And when it is, let us hope our successors will show their gratitude by using the material gathered by their forerunners as a foundation for their finished structure. Should their edifice prove impermanent, our ghosts may have the satisfaction of knowing that foundations at times outlast what is built upon them. To justify my attributions would not be possible in this volume, for it would require a running commentary on each of the lists, and long essays on certain items.

So much for actual attributions, questioned or unquestioned. For pictures in which the hand of assistants is traceable I have used the letters *p.* (in part by the artist) or *g.p.* (in great part). During the period with which we are concerned, no considerable work was likely to be carried through without assistance. It was seldom that a painter much in demand could indulge himself in executing with his own hand the minor parts of a picture, such as the walls or columns of buildings, furniture, obscurer bits of drapery and so on, but it is only when the more manifest parts of a picture betray another hand that I use a sign to indicate it.

For pictures done on a master's indications in his studio the letters *st.* (studio) are used, and for copies of lost works *c.* (copy).

It remains to explain the ominous letter *r.*, which means ruined, repainted, or restored. This unhappy sign might indeed be placed after almost every old picture, for no work four or five, and still less six or seven centuries old, is likely to have escaped unhurt. Even the few painters who used an impeccable technique, almost as hard as enamel, could not hinder the fading of colours, the 'mellowing', as we call it, of time. Indeed, thus 'mellowed', they please our taste, as colourless sculpture, unknown in antiquity, pleases it. The pictures as they left the Old Masters' hands would horrify most people with their bright tints. But we seldom see them thus; for time and the over-zealous restorer have usually combined to reduce them in pitch. From the filling-in of cracks and of bare spots from which the paint has flaked off, to the making over of the whole picture according to the restorer's taste and fancy, there are many gradations. I have indicated with the letter *r.* only those restorations which actually change the character of the work in colour, types, or drawing. Even in these, a good deal of the original design persists, something of the structure of the figures and of the distribution of the masses betrays the original creation. Thorwaldsen worked his will and wreaked his taste upon the Aeginetan Marbles, but the archaic Greek artist triumphs over the conventionalizing hand. And in my depressing flock of Restored Pictures the old Masters contrive still to make their genius felt.

As to the sources upon which I have based my views of the influences that formed the painters, I need scarcely say that we have next to no information in the matter, and little reliable tradition, so that the influences given in these lists are derived almost entirely from observed resemblances between the works of a given painter and those of his predecessors. Personal contact is not necessarily implied. A man may owe almost everything to another, without ever having seen him.

Certain influences are so widespread that one wearies of repeating them. Such are Giotto and Simone Martini and the Lorenzetti in the Trecento; the Antique in the fifteenth and sixteenth centuries, not only in architecture and sculpture, but in painting as well; Donatello, who is behind so much Florentine and nearly all north Italian painting; Mantegna in all the schools of the north, and still more his brother-in-law, Giovanni Bellini, from whose influence no Venetian working between 1470 and 1520 is free; while Leonardo, Michelangelo, and Raphael, in obvious as well as subtle ways, affected all their younger contemporaries.

NOTE

A number after the name of a town means that the picture is in the principal public gallery of that town, e.g. Berlin (Staatliche Museen), Paris (Louvre), London (National Gallery), Perugia (Pinacoteca), etc. Where honours are even between public collections, as between the Ashmolean and Christ Church at Oxford, or the Pitti and the Uffizi in Florence, both are mentioned.

ABBREVIATIONS

(see in Preface under Explanations)

c.: copy.
d.: dated (*i.e.* the date appears on the picture
     itself; wherever a date is given without
     this prefix, it is drawn from documents
     or other sources).
fr.: fragment.
g.p.: in great part autograph.
p.: partly autograph.
r.: ruined, restored, repainted.
st.: studio work.
st.v.: studio version.
u.: unfinished.
E.: early.
L.: late.
Sd.: signed.
* Detached frescoes, which may still be kept
   in storage by one of the Soprintendenze.
† Pictures not traced at the time of the
   present revision.

ACKNOWLEDGEMENTS

The paintings in the Royal Collection are reproduced by gracious permission of Her Majesty the Queen. Gratitude is due to all private owners who have given permission for their paintings to be reproduced and in many cases have provided new photographs.

Grateful acknowledgement is also made to the authorities of numerous Museums and Institutions for providing information and photographs and for permission to reproduce pictures in their collections, in particular:

Musée Granet, Aix-en-Provence; Lindenau Museum, Altenburg; Rijksmuseum, Amsterdam; University Museum, Ann Arbor, Mich.; Walters Art Gallery, Baltimore; Museum of Art, Barcelona; Musée Bonnat, Bayonne; Staatliche Museen, Berlin-Ost; ehem. Staatliche Museen, Berlin-Dahlem; Museum of Fine Arts, Boston, Mass.; Isabella Stewart Gardner Museum, Boston, Mass.; Herzog Anton Ulrich Museum, Braunschweig; Kunsthalle, Bremen; Museum, Brooklyn, N.Y.; Bowdoin College, Brunswick, Maine; Museum, Bucharest; Museum of Fine Arts, Budapest; Fitzwilliam Museum, Cambridge; Fogg Art Museum, Cambridge, Mass.; Musée des Beaux-Arts, Chambéry; Musée Condé, Chantilly; Musée des Beaux-Arts, Chartres; Art Institute, Chicago; Art Museum, Cincinnati; Museum of Art, Cleveland; Wallraf-Richartz Museum, Cologne; Statensmuseum, Copenhagen; Czartoryski Museum, Cracow; Museum of Art, Denver, Col.; Institute of Arts, Detroit, Mich.; Musée des Beaux-Arts, Dijon; Musée, Douai; Gemäldegalerie, Dresden; National Gallery of Ireland, Dublin; Keresteny Museum, Esztergom; Staedel Institute, Frankfurt; Bob Jones University, Greenville, S. C.; Museum of Fine Arts, Houston, Texas; John Herron Art Institute, Indianapolis; William Rockhill Nelson Gallery, Kansas City, Mo.; Kunsthalle, Karlsruhe; Museum, Kiev; Hermitage, Leningrad; Walker Art Gallery, Liverpool; National Gallery, London; Courtauld Institute of Art, London; National Trust, London; County Museum, Los Angeles; Schloß Rohoncz Collection, Lugano; Musée des Beaux-Arts, Lyon; Prado, Madrid; Musée Ingres, Montauban; Musée Fabre, Montpellier; Museum of Fine Arts, Montreal; Alte Pinakothek, Munich; Yale University Gallery, New Haven, Conn.; Metropolitan Museum, New York; Historical Society, New York; Frick Collection, New York; Samuel H. Kress Foundation, New York; Christ Church Library, Oxford; Ashmolean Museum, Oxford; National Gallery of Canada, Ottawa; Louvre, Paris; Musée de Cluny, Paris; Musée Jacquemart-André, Paris; Musée des Arts Décoratifs, Paris; John G. Johnson Collection, Philadelphia; Museum, Poznan; National Gallery, Prague; Rhode Island School of Design, Providence, R.I.; Museum of Art, Raleigh, N.C.; Museum Boymans-van Beuningen, Rotterdam; Fine Arts Gallery, San Diego, Cal.; M. H. de Young Memorial Museum, San Francisco; City Art Museum, St. Louis, Mo.; Huntington Museum, San Marino, Cal.; Museu de Arte, São Paulo; University of California, Santa Barbara, Cal.; J. Paul Getty Museum, Santa Monica, Cal.; John & Mable Ringling Museum of Art, Sarasota, Fla.; National Museum, Stockholm; Musée des Beaux-Arts, Strasbourg; Museum of Art, Toledo, Ohio; Archiepiscopal Museum, Utrecht; Akademie, Vienna; Kunsthistorisches Museum, Vienna; Museum, Warsaw; National Gallery of Art, Washington, D.C.; Sterling and Francine Clark Art Institute, Williamstown, Mass.; Art Museum, Worcester, Mass.; Martin von Wagner Museum, Würzburg.

xiv

ACKNOWLEDGEMENTS

For repeated help and advice, special thanks are due to Sydney J. Freedberg; to the Soprintendenza in Florence, who provided information on paintings in Tuscany; to M. Michel Laclotte, Inspector des Musées de Province, for locating pictures in the Campana Collection still scattered in French provincial museums; and to Professor Ellis Waterhouse, who gave valuable information on paintings in private collections in Great Britain.

FLORENTINE PICTURES
OF THE RENAISSANCE

ALBERTINELLI, Mariotto

*1474–1515. Pupil of Cosimo Rosselli and Piero di Cosimo; worked in collaboration with
Fra Bartolommeo.*

Bergamo. 325. Crucifixion with three Dominicans. (?)

    534. Two panels: SS. John Baptist and Mary Magdalen. E.

Berlin. 249. Assumption with SS. John Baptist, Peter, Dominic, Peter Martyr, Paul
and Mary Magdalen (lower part by Fra Bartolommeo). ca 1508. (Destroyed
1945.)

Cambridge. FITZWILLIAM. 162. Madonna and Child with Infant S. John (c.). 1509.

Cambridge (Mass.). 1906.5. Sacrifice of Cain and Abel.

Chartres. MUSÉE. 251 (CAMPANA 221). Portable triptych: Madonna and Child with
Angels and SS. Lucy and Apollonia. Lunette: God the Father: Wings:
Annunciation, S. Michael, S. Luke, Crucifixion, S. Dominic and a Bishop
Saint. E. *Plate* 1310.

Columbia (S.C.). MUSEUM OF ART, KRESS COLLECTION. K 148. Tondo: Madonna and
Child with Infant S. John and S. Francis.

Detroit (Mich.). 32.89. Tondo: Nativity.

Florence. ACCADEMIA. 8643. Annunciation. Sd. and d. 1510. *Plate* 1313.

    8645. Madonna and Child with SS. Julian, Dominic, Nicholas and Jerome. Sd.
    8660. Trinity (on cartoon by Fra Bartolommeo).

    PITTI. 365. Tondo: Nativity.

    UFFIZI. 1586. Predella (to 1587): Annunciation, Nativity, Circumcision. 1503. *Plate*
    1311.

        1587. Visitation. d. 1503. *Plate* 1312.

    S. MARCO (MUSEO), REFECTORY. Fresco (from S. Maria Nuova): Last Judgement
    (begun by Fra Bartolommeo in 1499, completed by Albertinelli in 1501).
    Plate 1318.

    S. MARIA DEGLI INNOCENTI. Annunciation (with Sogliani). d. 15 (17? 26?).

    (Environs) CERTOSA DEL GALLUZZO, SALA DEL CAPITOLO. Fresco: Crucifixion. Sd.
    and d. 1506.

Geneva. 1870–6. Diptych: Annunciation (head of the Virgin by Fra Bartolommeo).
Sd. by both artists and d. 1511.

Genoa. ALESSANDRO BASEVI. Madonna and Child with Infant S. John (r.). Sd. and d.
1509.

Gosford House (Longniddry, Scotland). EARL OF WEMYSS AND MARCH. Madonna
and Child (r.). *Plate* 1309.

The Hague. 306. Holy Family with Infant S. John (on Fra Bartolommeo's cartoon). (Destroyed).

Harewood House (Yorks.). EARL OF HAREWOOD. Madonna and Child with Infant S. John. Sd. and d. 1509. *Plate 1317.*

Highnam Court (Glos.). GAMBIER-PARRY COLLECTION. Nativity. *Plate 1314.*
      Creation and Temptation of Adam and Eve (see Zagreb). E. *Plate 1306.*

London. W. H. WOODWARD (EX). Adam and Eve. E.
      Sacrifice of Isaac. E. *Plate 1305.*

Madrid. DUKE OF ALBA. Madonna and Child.

Milan. MUSEO POLDI-PEZZOLI. 477. Portable triptych: Madonna nursing the Child. On back: Death's Head. Wings, outside: Annunciation. Wings, inside: SS. Catherine and Barbara. d. 1500. *Plate 1307.*

Munich. 1070. Annunciation with SS. Sebastian and Lucy.

Paris. See Toulouse.

      COMTE DE POURTALÈS (EX). Annunciation with SS. Zenobius and Francis.

Philadelphia (Pa.). MUSEUM OF ART, JOHNSON COLLECTION. 1168. Predella panel: Nativity.

Rome. GALLERIA BORGHESE. 310. Holy Family with Infant S. John (on Fra Bartolommeo's cartoon). d. 1511.
      421. The Redeemer.

Sarasota (Fla.). 26. Tondo: Holy Family with Infant S. John (with Fra Bartolommeo).

Siena. 451.564. Two panels: S. Mary Magdalen, S. Catherine. d. 1512.

Toulouse. MUSÉE DES AUGUSTINS (DEP. LOUVRE 1114). Madonna and Child with SS. Jerome and Zenobius (begun by Filippino Lippi, who laid in the S. Jerome. Albertinelli must have assisted in the execution of the rest, especially in the Child and landscape). Sd. and d. 1506. *Plate 1316.*

Turin. MUSEO CIVICO (PALAZZO MADAMA). Madonna and Child with Infant S. John (p).

Udine. MUSEO CIVICO. Crucifixion. E. (?)

Venice. SEMINARIO. 3. Madonna and Child. *Plate 1315.*

Volognano (Pontassieve). S. MICHELE. Madonna and Child with SS. Paul, George, Apollonia and Peter. Sd. and d. 1514.

Volterra. DUOMO, 2nd ALTAR L. Annunciation. d. 1497.

Zagreb. 80. Expulsion from Paradise (see Highnam Court). E. *Plate 1304.*

Homeless. Crucifixion. E. *Plate 1308.*

ALUNNO DI BENOZZO

Temporary name for a close follower of the mature Benozzo Gozzoli (also called 'Maestro Esiguo', but not identical with Amedeo da Pistoia).

Boston (Mass.). ISABELLA GARDNER MUSEUM. Crucifixion.

Chambéry. 190. See Paris, Musées Nationaux.

Columbia (Mo.). UNIVERSITY OF MISSOURI. KRESS STUDY COLLECTION. K 372. Small Crucifix.

Denver (Col.). MUSEUM OF ART, KRESS COLLECTION. K 1025. Trinity with S. Francis and a Bishop Saint.

Edinburgh. 953. Way to Calvary.

Fiesole. CONTE COMM. RIGOLI. Madonna and Child with six Angels, SS. John Baptist and Francis, and a Donor.

Florence. MUSEO NAZIONALE DEL BARGELLO, CARRAND COLLECTION. 2029. Madonna and Child with four music-making Angels and SS. Sebastian, Catherine, Ursula and Lawrence. *Plate 903.*

   MUSEO DEL BIGALLO. Madonna and Child with four Angels and SS. John Baptist, Catherine, Ursula and Blaise (r.).

   MRS. C. H. COSTER. Lamentation. *Plate 908.*

Geneva. M.F.3832. Man of Sorrows.

Kaliningrad. See Königsberg.

Königsberg (EX?). Way to Calvary.

London. HENRY HARRIS (EX). Deposition.

Lyons. EDOUARD AYNARD (EX). Man of Sorrows with two Angels. *Plate 905.*

Melbourne Hall (Derbyshire). LADY KERR. Predella panel: Lamentation.

Montefalco. S. FRANCESCO (MUSEO). Crucifixion (r.).

New York. ROBERT LEHMAN. Marriage of S. Catherine with SS. Mary Magdalen, Ursula and Agnes. Predella: Man of Sorrows, and SS. Onuphrius, Jerome, Dominic and Peter Martyr.

   Annunciation. *Plate 904.*

Paris. MUSÉES NATIONAUX (CAMPANA 252, DEP. CHAMBÉRY). S. Michael Archangel with SS. Francis, Jerome, Catherine and Clare.

   PAUL DELAROFF (EX). Lamentation. *Plate 906.*

Pisa. 191. Tobias and the Archangel.

Princeton (N.J.). 55–3252. Man of Sorrows.

Rome. VATICAN, PINACOTECA. 264. Predella panel: Lamentation. E.

Siena. 383. Assumption. (?)

Tulsa (Okla.). PHILBROOK ART CENTER, KRESS COLLECTION. K 1024. Lamentation.

Vienna. DR. HERMANN EISSLER (EX). Agony in the Garden.

Worcester (Mass.). 1913. 46–48. Cassone: Three Scenes from the Coronation of Frederick III. (?)

Homeless. Tondo: Man of Sorrows. (*Dedalo* xii, 844.)

ALUNNO DI DOMENICO
see Bartolomeo di Giovanni

ALVARO PORTOGHESE

Alvaro di Pietro, Alvaro Pirez d'Evora, active in the earliest decades of the fifteenth century, is documented in Prato with other Florentine artists in 1411. Formed his style under the influence of Lorenzo Monaco and the Sienese School.

Brunswick. HERZOG ANTON ULRICH MUSEUM. Portable Triptych: Madonna and Child with SS. John Baptist and Anthony Abbot; Wings: Crucifixion, Resurrection. Sd. and d. 1434. *Plate 468.*

Pisa. S. CROCE A FOSSABANDA. Madonna and Child with eight Angels. Sd. *Plate 467.*
(Environs). NICOSIA, CHIESA DEI FRANCESCANI. Madonna and Child with two Angels. Sd.

Volterra. PINACOTECA. Triptych: Madonna and Child with SS. Nicholas, John Baptist, Christopher and Michael; Spandrels: SS. Cosmas and Damian. Sd. and d. 1423. *Plate 466.*

AMEDEO DA PISTOIA

Close imitator of Alunno di Benozzo, with whom he is sometimes identified.

Homeless. Madonna and Child with SS. Simon and Thaddeus. Sd. *Plate 909.*

ANDREA DEL CASTAGNO
see Castagno

ANDREA DI CIONE
see Orcagna

ANDREA (Bonaiuti) DA FIRENZE

Active ca 1343–1377. Must have been in touch with Andrea Orcagna and Nardo, and later with Giovanni da Milano.

Berkeley (Cal.). EPISCOPAL STUDENT CENTER, W. H. CROCKER LOAN. Blessed Peter Petroni of Siena. *Plate 244.*

Berlin. VON BECKERATH COLLECTION (EX). S. Mary Magdalen. *Plate 242.*

Cracow. 226. Triptych: Madonna and Child with a Deacon Martyr and S. Dorothy (r.). *Plate 246.*

Florence. ACCADEMIA. 455. Annunciation (predella by Lorenzo di Niccolò). E. 3145. Two panels: SS. Agnes and Domitilla (r.). *Plate 240.*

S. MARIA DEL CARMINE, SACRISTY. Polyptych: Madonna and Child with two Angels and SS. Leonard, Nicholas, John Baptist and the Prophet Elijah.

S. MARIA NOVELLA, SPANISH CHAPEL. Frescoes. Vault: *Navicella*, Resurrection, Ascension, Pentecost. Walls: Dominican Allegories and Scenes from the Passion and the Life of S. Peter Martyr. [Left wall: Triumph of S. Thomas Aquinas. Altar wall: Way to Calvary, Crucifixion, Descent into Limbo. Right wall: Way of Salvation (*Via veritatis*). Entrance wall: Investiture of S. Peter Martyr, Preaching of S. Peter Martyr, Death of S. Peter Martyr, The Sick healed at his Tomb, Healing of a paralysed Girl, Healing of Rufino of Canapuccio]. ca 1366–68. [*Plates* 127–128]. *Plates* 235–239, 241, 243, 245.

New York. ROBERT LEHMAN. *Pietà.*

Notre Dame (Ind.). UNIVERSITY. KRESS STUDY COLLECTION. K 263. Crucifixion (Companion to Worcester). (?)

Pisa. CAMPOSANTO. Three frescoes: Scenes from the Life of S. Raynerius [Vocation of S. Raynerius, Restoration of his Eyesight; Pilgrimage and Poverty of S. Raynerius, Vision of the Virgin; S. Raynerius tormented by Devils and Beasts, Vision of Christ, Miracle of the Bread] (r.). L. (See also Antonio Veneziano). *Plates* 247–249.

Worcester (Mass.). 1940.34. Adoration of the Magi. (Companion to Notre Dame). (?)

ANDREA DI GIUSTO (MANZINI)

Died 1455. Pupil of Lorenzo Monaco, worked with Bicci di Lorenzo and Masaccio; strongly influenced by Fra Angelico and somewhat by Domenico Veneziano.

Allentown (Pa.). ART MUSEUM, KRESS COLLECTION. K 420. Predella panel: Nativity.

Altenburg. 95. Agony in the Garden and Communion of S. Jerome.

Baltimore (Md.). WALTERS ART GALLERY. 643. Madonna and Child. L.

Berlin. 57. Last Judgement (completed by Domenico di Michelino). *Plate* 635.
58E. Predella panel (to Masaccio, London 3406): S. Julian murdering his Parents, and S. Nicholas and the three Maidens (on Masaccio's design). 1426. *Plate* 583.

Boston (Mass.). 03.563. Madonna and Child with SS. John Baptist, James, Peter and a fourth Saint.

Cambridge (Mass.). 1938.95. Madonna and Child with eight Angels and SS. Anthony Abbot and John Baptist (r.).

Copenhagen. 1750. Madonna of Humility with SS. John Baptist and Francis.

Edinburgh. 1540a, b. Predella panel: Stigmatization of S. Francis and S. Anthony Abbot exorcizing a possessed Woman. (?)

Fiesole. MUSEO BANDINI. 1, 5. Madonna and Child with twelve Angels (c. of Fra Angelico at Frankfurt).

Figline (Valdarno Superiore, Environs). S. ANDREA A RIPALTA. Triptych: Adoration of the Magi, and SS. Andrew, John Baptist, James and Anthony Abbot. Pinnacles: Annunciation. Interstices of pinnacles: Six Prophets and Saints Predella: Donors, Calling of SS. Peter and Andrew, S. Andrew preaching and baptizing, and the Judgement and Crucifixion of S. Andrew. d. 1436. *Plate 642.*

Florence. ACCADEMIA. 3160. Madonna and Child with two Angels (r.).

3236. *Madonna della Cintola*, with SS. Catherine and Francis. Spandrels: Annunciation, Moses, David. Pilasters: Eight Saints. Predella: Donors, Martyrdom of S. Catherine, Dormition of the Virgin, Stigmatization of S. Francis. Sd. and d. 1437. *Plate 643.*

6004. Madonna of Humility with two Angels and the Man of Sorrows in roundel above. *Plate 644.*

BIBLIOTECA LAURENZIANA. COD. COR. LAUR. 3. *Diurno Domenicale* fol. 1v, 15, 23v, 41v, 57v, 80v. Six illuminated initials: Resurrection, Christ and the Elect, Christ and the Apostles, Monks in Choir, David before the Ark, Pentecost. (?)

MUSEO STIBBERT. 3590. Madonna and Child with six Angels.

S. MARCO (MUSEO), HOSPICE. 8499. Man of Sorrows and Adoration of the Magi. (In Fra Angelico's studio?)

BERENSON COLLECTION. Madonna of Humility. (Version of Fra Angelico, Turin 105).

CHARLES LOESER (EX). Madonna and Child with four music-making Angels.

Helsinki. ATENEUM. Predella panel: Adoration of the Shepherds.

Leningrad. 2442, 2443. Two panels from a triptych: Pope Silvester showing the Portraits of Peter and Paul to Constantine, Baptism of Constantine. *Plate 645.*

London. PETER FULD. Predella panel: Marriage of the Virgin. (?).

Montauban. 349. See Paris, Musées Nationaux.

Montecastello (Pontedera). CANONICA. Crucifixion.

Narbonne. 243. Lamentation. (Based on Lorenzo Monaco at Prague).

Paris. MUSÉES NATIONAUX (CAMPANA 332, DEP. MONTAUBAN). Crucifixion. (?)

(CAMPANA 358, 359, DEP. RENNES). Two cassone panels: Story of Susanna. L.

LOUVRE. 1294A. Resurrection. (?)

CHARLES PERRIOLAT (EX). Madonna and Child with four Angels.

Philadelphia (Pa.). MUSEUM OF ART, JOHNSON COLLECTION. 17. Christ and the Apostles in the Temple.

18, 19. Two predella panels: Circumcision, Christ among the Doctors.

21. Madonna and Child with SS. Lucy, John Baptist, Bartholomew and Dorothy.

Poggio di Loro (Loro Ciuffenna, Valdarno). S. MARIA ASSUNTA, L. WALL. Triptych: Madonna and Child with SS. Luke, Matthew, John and Mark. Pinnacles:

Christ blessing and four Prophets. Predella: S. Luke painting the Virgin, Calling of S. Matthew, Nativity, Martyrdom of S. John Evangelist, Martyrdom of S. Mark.

Prato. 8. Triptych: Madonna and Child with two Angels and SS. Bartholomew, John Baptist, Benedict and Margaret. Pinnacles: Christ blessing, Annunciation. Predella: Martyrdom of S. Bartholomew, Naming of the Baptist, S. Maurus, Nativity, S. Placidus, Death of S. Benedict, Abduction of S. Margaret. d. 1435. *Plates 639, 640.*

DUOMO, 1st CHAPEL R. OF CHOIR (CAPPELLA DELL'ASSUNTA). Frescoes. Right wall: Marriage of the Virgin. Left wall: Martyrdom of S. Stephen, Burial of S. Stephen. L. (See also Giovanni di Francesco). *Plates 646, 647.*

Rennes. 3450, 3451. See Paris, Musées Nationaux.

Stia (Casentino). (Environs). S. LORENZO A PORCIANO (GALL. FIOR. 3458). S. Lawrence.

Tulsa (Okla.). PHILBROOK ART CENTER, KRESS COLLECTION. K 234. Assumption with SS. Jerome and Francis.

Turin. GUALINO COLLECTION (EX). Portable triptych: Madonna and Child with four Angels. Left Wing: Angel of the Annunciation, SS. Francis and Clare. Right wing: Virgin Annunciate, SS. Margaret and George. *Plate 641.*

Vienna. 6686, 6687, 6690. Wings of an altarpiece: S. John Baptist and a Bishop Saint, SS. Nicholas and Francis (r.).

ANDREA DEL SARTO

1486–1530. Pupil of Piero di Cosimo; influenced by Leonardo, Fra Bartolommeo and Michelangelo.

Allentown (Pa.). ART MUSEUM, KRESS COLLECTION. K 253. Madonna and Child. E. (?).

Ascott (Bucks.). NATIONAL TRUST. Madonna and Child with Infant S. John.

Berlin. 240. Portrait of a Woman.

246. Madonna and Child with SS. Bruno, Peter, Onuphrius, Celsus, Julia, Catherine, Mark and Anthony of Padua. d. 1528. (See Florence, Pitti 163). (Destroyed 1945). *Plate 1392.*

Birmingham. BARBER INSTITUTE OF FINE ARTS. Madonna and Child with Infant S. John against Walls (c. of lost fresco in Tabernacle of Porta a Pinti).

Budapest. 66. Madonna and Child with Infant S. John (c.).

Cleveland (Ohio). 37.577. Sacrifice of Isaac (u.).

44.92. Portrait of a Lady in French Costume. 1518–19. *Plate 1384.*

Coral Gables (Fla.). UNIVERSITY OF MIAMI. JOE AND EMILY LOWE ART GALLERY, KRESS COLLECTION. K 1081. 'Benson' Tondo: Madonna and Child with Infant S. John.

Dresden. 76. Marriage of S. Catherine, with S. Margaret and Infant S. John. Sd. E. *Plate 1379.*

Dresden (contd.). 77. Sacrifice of Isaac. Sd. L. *Plate* 1396.

Florence. GALLERIE. 516. *Noli me tangere.* E.

 PITTI. 58. Lamentation, with the Virgin and SS. John Evangelist, Peter, Paul, Mary Magdalen and Catherine. Sd. 1524.

 62. Holy Family with Infant S. John.

 66. Self-Portrait as a young Man. (Version of Uffizi, 1486).

 81. Madonna and Child with S. Elisabeth and Infant S. John (for Ottaviano de' Medici). 1529–30.

 87, 88. Two Borgherini panels: Episodes from the Boyhood of Joseph. Episodes from the Life of Joseph in Egypt. Sd. 1515–20.

 97. Annunciation with SS. Michael and Gaudentius (st.).

 123. The Poppi altarpiece: Virgin in Glory with SS. Bernardo degli Uberti, Fedele, Catherine and John Gualbert (u. at the artist's death; completed by Bonilli, and d. 1540).

 124. The San Gallo Annunciation. Sd. E. *Plate* 1377.

 163. Lunette (to Berlin 246): Annunciation. 1528. *Plate* 1392.

 172. Disputation of the Trinity, with SS. Sebastian, Augustine, Lawrence, Peter Martyr, Francis and Mary Magdalen. Sd.

 191. 'Panciatichi' Assumption (u.). 1517–22.

 225. 'Passerini' Assumption, with SS. Nicholas and Margaret of Cortona. ca 1526. *Plate* 1391.

 272. S. John Baptist.

 292. Tobias and the Archangel (st.).

 307. The 'Gambassi' Madonna and Child with SS. Onuphrius, Lawrence, John Baptist, Mary Magdalen, James and Sebastian.

 476. Madonna and Child. L.

 UFFIZI. 783. Portrait of a Woman with a Volume of Petrarch. [*Plate* 224.]

 1486. Self-Portrait as a Young Man (Version of Pitti, 66). *Plate* 1382.

 1577. *Madonna of the Harpies*, with SS. Francis and John Evangelist. Sd. and d. 1517. [*Plate* 222.]

 1583. S. James with two Children in the Habit of the *Confraternita del Nicchio*.

 1694. Fresco on tile: Self-Portrait. *Plate* 1393.

 8394. Two Angels (central fragment of Vallombrosa altarpiece). 1528.

 8395. SS. Michael, John Gualbert, John Baptist and Bernardo degli Uberti (side fragments of Vallombrosa altarpiece joined together). d. 1528.

 8396. Predella (to 8395): S. Michael Archangel and Lucifer, S. John Gualbert at the Ordeal by Fire of Bd. Peter Igneus, Beheading of S. John Baptist, S. Bernardo degli Uberti seized at the Altar and imprisoned. 1528. *Plate* 1395.

 GABINETTO DEI DISEGNI. 91460, 91461, 91462, 91464. Monochrome friezes of figures with armour and musical instruments. ca 1515.

 SS. ANNUNZIATA, ATRIUM. Seven frescoes: Bd. Philip Benizzi giving his Shirt to a Leper. 1509–10.

Destruction of Bd. Philip's Mockers by Lightning. 1509–10. *Plate* 1375.

Bd. Philip healing a possessed Woman. 1509–10.

Death of Bd. Philip. 1509–10.

Healing of a Child by a Relic of Bd. Philip. d. 1510.

Arrival of the Magi. Sd. 1511. *Plate* 1376.

Birth of the Virgin. Sd. and d. 1514. *Plate* 1381.

—1st CHAPEL L. The Redeemer.

—CHIOSTRO DEI MORTI. Fresco: *Madonna del Sacco.* d. 1525. [*Plate* 223.]

S. MARCO (MUSEO), FORESTERIA. Fresco: Annunciation (r).

CENACOLO DI SAN SALVI. Fresco roundels in vault: The Trinity and four Vallom-
brosan Saints. 1515.

    Fresco: Last Supper, begun 1519. [*Plate* 226].

  8675. Detached fresco: Man of Sorrows.

CHIOSTRO DELLO SCALZO. Thirteen monochrome frescoes (see also Franciabigio):

Charity. 1512–15. *Plate* 1378.

Justice. 1515.

S. John Baptist preaching, 1515.

Baptism of the People. 1517. *Plate* 1388.

Capture of S. John. 1517.

Dance of Salome. 1522.

Beheading of S. John. 1523. *Plate* 1389.

Head of S. John brought before Herod. 1523.

Hope. 1523.

Faith.

Annunciation to Zacharias. (d. 1522 or 1523.) [*Plate* 227.]

Visitation. 1524.

Birth of S. John. 1526.

GALLERIA CORSINI. 241. Apollo and Daphne, and Narcissus. E. (?)

(Environs) POGGIO A CAIANO, VILLA MEDICEA. Fresco: Tribute to Caesar. 1521. (Enlarged and completed by Alessandro Allori, 1582).

Hampton Court. 1450. Madonna and Child with Infant S. John. (?)

Leningrad. 62. Madonna and Child with SS. Elizabeth, Catherine and Infant S.
John. Sd. *Plate* 1387.

Lisbon. 542. Self-Portrait (r.). Sd.

London. 17. Madonna and Child with S. Elizabeth and Infant S. John.

690. Portrait of a Man called the 'Sculptor'. Sd. [*Plate* 225.]

WALLACE COLLECTION. 9. Madonna and Child with Infant S. John and two Angels.
Sd.

Madrid. 332. Portrait of a Woman, called the Artist's Wife. *Plate* 1383.

334. Holy Family with an Angel ('Madonna della Scala'). Sd. *Plate* 1390.

335. Holy Family (st. replica of Rome, Barberini.)

336. Sacrifice of Isaac (p., replica of Dresden 77).

Madrid (contd.). 337. Madonna and Child (st.).

    579. Infant S. John with a Lamb.

Muncie (Indiana). BALL STATE TEACHERS COLLEGE. Portrait of an Architect. (?)

Munich. 501. Madonna and Child with SS. Elizabeth and Infant John and two
    Angels. (Variant of Paris, 1515).

Naples. 138. Portrait of Leo X with Cardinals Giulio dei Medici and Luigi de' Rossi.
    (copy after Raphael.)

New York. 22.75. Holy Family with Infant S. John.

    W. R. HEARST (EX). Madonna and Child with Infant S. John against landscape (c. of
    lost fresco in Tabernacle of Porta a Pinti). *Plate* 1380.

    JACK LINSKY. Portrait of a Man with a Book (st.).

Paris. 1514. *Caritas.* Sd. and d. 1518. *Plate* 1386.

    1515. Madonna and Child with S. Elizabeth, Infant S. John and two Angels.

    1516. Tondo (enlarged to an oval): Holy Family with S. Elizabeth and Infant S.
    John. Sd.

Petworth House (Sussex). NATIONAL TRUST. Madonna and Child with Infant S.
    John and three Angels. Sd.

Philadelphia (Pa.). MUSEUM OF ART, JOHNSON COLLECTION. 81. Portrait of a young
    Man. *Plate* 1385.

Pisa. DUOMO, CHOIR. Five panels: SS. Agnes, Catherine, Margaret, John Baptist and
    Peter. 1528–29.

Raleigh (N.C.). MUSEUM OF ART. Madonna and Child with Infant S. John (st.).

Richmond (Surrey). COOK COLLECTION (EX). 36. S. Sebastian (c.).

Rome. GALLERIA BORGHESE. 334. Madonna and Child with Infant S. John. Sd.

    336. Madonna and Child with Infant S. John. E.

    375. Predella: *Pietà*, with four Saints. E.

    GALLERIA DORIA PAMPHILJ 203 (F.N. 72). Holy Family with Infant S. John (st.).

    GALLERIA NAZIONALE (PALAZZO BARBERINI). Holy Family. L.

Vienna. 39. *Pietà*, with two Angels. Sd.

    42. Tobias and the Angel with S. Leonard and a Donor.

Washington (D.C.). 1483 (KRESS COLLECTION 1992). *Caritas.*

Windsor Castle. 146. Portrait of a Woman (u.). *Plate* 1394.

ANGELICO (Fra Giovanni da Fiesole)

1387–1455. Influenced by Ghiberti, Lorenzo Monaco and Masaccio.

Altenburg. 91. Predella panel (to 'Bosco ai Frati' altarpiece): S. Francis before the
    Sultan (p.).

    92. Three panels (from pilasters of 'San Marco' altarpiece?): SS. James, Benedict,
    and a third Saint (g.p.; companions to Venice, Cini).

Amsterdam. 17–BI. Madonna and Child with a Lily. (see Hartford).

Antwerp. 3. Predella panel: S. Romuald and Otto III (st., r.).

Berlin. 60. Madonna and Child with SS. Dominic and Peter Martyr.

    60A. Triptych: Last Judgement (g.p.).

    61, 61A, 62. Three predella panels (to 'Bosco ai Frati' altarpiece): Meeting of SS. Francis and Dominic, Death of S. Francis, Apparition of S. Francis at Arles. (r.).

    DEPOT. Head of Saint.

Berne. 875. Madonna and Child (st.).

Boston (Mass.). 14.416. Octagonal panel: Madonna and Child with SS. Peter, Paul and George, four angels and a Donor.

    ISABELLA GARDNER MUSEUM. Reliquary panel: Dormition and Assumption of the Virgin.

Brooklyn (N.Y.). MICHAEL FRIEDSAM (EX). Lunette: Annunciation. (Stolen 1933.)

Cambridge (Mass.). 1921.34. Crucifixion, with Cardinal Giovanni Torquemada as Donor. L. *Plate 625.*

Chantilly. 4, 5. Two panels (from pilasters of S. Domenico di Fiesole altarpiece): SS. Mark and Matthew (st.).

    6. Predella panel: S. Benedict in the *Sacro Speco* (st.).

Cortona. MUSEO DIOCESANO. Annunciation. Predella: Birth of S. Dominic, Marriage of the Virgin, Visitation, Adoration of the Magi, Presentation in the Temple, Death of the Virgin, S. Dominic receiving the Dominican Habit from the Virgin. *Plates* 602, 604, 605.

    Triptych from S. Domenico: Madonna and Child with four Angels and SS John Evangelist, John Baptist, Mark and Mary Magdalen. Pinnacles: Crucifixion, Annunciation. Predella: Dream of Pope Honorius III and Meeting of SS. Dominic and Francis, SS. Peter and Paul appearing to S. Dominic, Raising of Napoleone Orsini, Disputation of S. Dominic and the Miracle of the Book, S. Dominic and his Companions fed by Angels, Death of S. Dominic. *Plates* 601, 603.

    S. DOMENICO, WEST PORTAL. Fresco lunette: Madonna and Child with SS. Dominic and Peter Martyr (r.).

Detroit (Mich.). 56.32. Madonna and Child with four Angels. E. *Plate 598.*

    MRS. EDSEL FORD. Two panels: Annunciation.

Dublin. 242. Predella panel (to 'San Marco' altarpiece): Attempted Martyrdom of SS. Cosmas and Damian by Fire. 1438–40.

Florence. UFFIZI. 143 (Dep. from Pontassieve). Madonna and Child (st.).

    1612. 'S. Maria Nuova' Coronation of the Virgin. [*Plate 132*].

    S. MARCO (MUSEO), CLOISTER. Fresco: Christ on the Cross adored by S. Dominic. Fresco lunettes: S. Thomas Aquinas, Christ as Pilgrim received by two Dominicans, Man of Sorrows, S. Dominic (r.), S. Peter Martyr enjoining Silence.

Florence. S. MARCO (contd.). HOSPICE. 'Bosco ai Frati' altarpiece: Madonna and
Child with two Angels and SS. Anthony of Padua, Louis of Toulouse,
Francis, Cosmas, Damian and Peter Martyr. (Predella panels at Altenburg,
Berlin and Rome). *Plate 621.*

Predella: Man of Sorrows with SS. Peter, Paul, Bernardino and three other
Saints (fr.).

'San Marco' altarpiece: Madonna and Child with eight Angels and SS. Lawrence, John Evangelist, Mark, Cosmas, Damian, Dominic, Francis and Peter
Martyr. (Predella panels at Dublin, Munich, Paris and Washington, as well
as Florence, S. Marco). 1438–40. *Plates 609, 610.*

Predella panels (to 'San Marco' altarpiece): Dream of the Deacon Justinian.
Burial of SS. Cosmas and Damian. 1438–40. *Plate 615.*

Madonna and Child (Trinity in pinnacle by another hand). E.

'Annalena' altarpiece: Madonna and Child with SS. Peter Martyr, Cosmas,
Damian, John Evangelist, Lawrence and Francis. *Plate 611.*

Predella (to 'Annalena' altarpiece): S. Damian receiving Money from Palladia,
SS. Cosmas and Damian before Lycias, SS. Cosmas and Damian thrown into
the Sea and rescued by an Angel, Attempted Martyrdom of SS. Cosmas and
Damian by Fire, Attempted Martyrdom of SS. Cosmas and Damian with
Arrows, Beheading of SS. Cosmas and Damian (g.p.; see also Northwick
Park). *Plate 613.*

The 'S. Trinita' Deposition. Pilasters of frame: Sixteen Saints. (Pinnacles by
Lorenzo Monaco). [*Plate 136.*] *Plate 608.*

Triptych: Madonna and Child with SS. Dominic, John Baptist, Peter Martyr
and Thomas Aquinas. Pinnacles: Christ blessing, Annunciation. Interstices of
pinnacles: Preaching and Martyrdom of S. Peter Martyr (st.).

Predella panel: Naming of S. John Baptist.

Two predella panels to 'S. Maria Nuova' Coronation (Uffizi 1612): Marriage
and Burial of the Virgin.

Reliquary panel: Annunciation and Adoration of the Magi. Predella: Madonna
and Child with ten female Saints.

Reliquary panel: Coronation of the Virgin. Predella: Nativity and six Angels.

Reliquary panel: *Madonna della Stella.* Frame: Christ in Glory and eight Angels.
Predella: SS. Peter Martyr, Dominic and Thomas Aquinas.

Lamentation, with S. Dominic, S. Catherine and Beata Villana (from S. Maria
della Croce al Tempio; r.).

Last Judgement (the Damned and Hell, at the right, by another hand). *Plate 597.*

Six panels (doors of silver chest of SS. Annunziata): Scenes of the Life of Christ
and the Virgin (except three by Baldovinetti; Vision of Ezechiel and *Lex
Amoris* by Domenico di Michelino) (g.p., r.). From 1448. *Plate 626.*

Two roundels: Coronation of the Virgin, Crucifixion.

Tabernacle of the *Arte dei Linaiuoli*: Madonna and Child, Frame: Twelve music-making Angels. Wings, inside: SS. John Baptist and John Evangelist. Wings, outside: SS. Mark and Peter. Predella: S. Peter Preaching, Adoration of the Magi. Martyrdom of S. Mark. 1433. *Plates 591, 599, 600.*

— SALA DEL CAPITOLO. Fresco: Crucifixion with Saints. [*Plate 133.*]

— UPPER CORRIDOR. Fresco: Annunciation. [*Plate 135.*]

Fresco: Christ on the Cross adored by S. Dominic.

Fresco: Madonna and Child with SS. Dominic, Cosmas, Damian, Mark, John Evangelist, Thomas Aquinas, Lawrence and Peter Martyr. *Plate 619.*

— CELLS. Frescoes (ca 1439–45):

1. *Noli me tangere.* [*Plate 134.*]
2. Lamentation.
3. Annunciation. *Plate 616.*
4. Crucifixion.
5. Nativity.
6. Transfiguration. *Plate 617.*
7. Mocking of Christ. *Plate 618.*
8. Three Maries at the Sepulchre.
9. Coronation of the Virgin.
10. Presentation in the Temple.
11. Madonna and Child with two Saints.
15–23. Crucifixions. (Some ruined.)
24. Baptism of Christ.
25. Crucifixion.
26. Man of Sorrows.
28. Christ bearing the Cross.
31. Descent into Limbo.
32. Sermon on the Mount.
33. Betrayal of Christ.
34. Agony in the Garden.
35. Institution of the Eucharist.
36. Christ nailed to the Cross.
37. Crucifixion.
39. Adoration of the Magi. *Pietà.*
42. Crucifixion.
43. Crucifixion.

(Environs) S. DOMENICO DI FIESOLE, 1st CHAPEL L. Madonna and Child with eight Angels and SS. Thomas Aquinas, Barnabas, Dominic and Peter Martyr. (r.; formerly a triptych, later framed in with pilasters by Rossello di Jacopo Franchi, transformed around 1501 into oblong panel with architecture and landscape by Lorenzo di Credi; see also Chantilly and Sheffield). E. *Plate 594.*

—CONVENTO. Fresco: Madonna and Child (fr.). E. [See Preface, p. vii.] *Plate 596.*

— SALA DEL CAPITOLO. Fresco: Christ on the Cross.

Frankfurt am Main. 838. Madonna and Child with twelve Angels (p.).

Hampton Court. 1208. Pinnacle: Christ blessing (r.).

    1209. Panel from the pilaster of an altarpiece: S. Peter Martyr.

Hartford (Conn.). 1928.321. An Angel (fr. of Amsterdam; r.).

Houston (Texas). 44–550. Predella panel: Temptation of S. Anthony Abbot.

Leningrad. 253. Detached fresco: Madonna and Child with SS. Dominic and Thomas Aquinas (r.). E. *Plate 595*.

    283. Ciborium: God the Father and six Angels.

London. 663. Predella (to S. Domenico di Fiesole altarpiece): Christ glorified in the Court of Heaven (g.p.). E.

    2908. Roundel from the frame of an altarpiece: A Bishop Saint (p.; companion to New York, Moses).

    3417. Vision of the Dominican Habit (st.).

    SIR THOMAS BARLOW. Predella panel: Disputation of S. Dominic and the Miracle of the Book (r.).

Lugano. THYSSEN COLLECTION. 8. Madonna and Child with five Angels.

Madrid. 15. Annunciation. Predella: Birth and Marriage of the Virgin, Visitation, Adoration of the Magi. Presentation in the Temple, Burial of the Virgin.

    DUKE OF ALBA. Madonna and Child with two Angels (r.).

Montecarlo (Valdarno Superiore). S. FRANCESCO, 1ST ALTAR R. Diptyh: Anncunciation. Predella: Marriage of the Virgin, Visitation, Adoration of the Magi, Circumcision, Burial of the Virgin (st.).

Munich. WAF 36–38, 38A. Four predella panels (to 'San Marco' altarpiece): SS. Cosmas and Damian before Lycias, Lycias possessed by Devils, Crucifixion of SS. Cosmas and Damian, Entombment of Christ. 1438-40.

Neviges (Rheinland). FRAU F. SCHNIEWIND. Madonna of Humility with four Angels and S. Catherine.

New York. 24.22. Nativity (st.).

    14.40.628. Crucifixion with Saints (r.).

    HENRY L. MOSES. Roundel (from the frame of an altarpiece): A Bishop Saint (p.; companion to London 2908).

Northwick Park (Oxon.). CAPT. E. G. SPENCER-CHURCHILL. Predella panel (to 'Annalena' altarpiece): Dream of the Deacon Justinian (p.). *Plate 612*.

Orvieto. DUOMO, CAPPELLA DI S. BRIZIO. Frescoes (vault): Christ in Judgement and sixteen Prophets. (Assisted by Benozzo Gozzoli). 1447. *Plate 622*.

Oxford. ASHMOLEAN. 42. Portable triptych: Madonna and Child adored by S. Dominic. Wings: SS. Peter and Paul (st.).

Paris. 1290. Coronation of the Virgin. Predella: Dream of Pope Honorius III, SS. Peter and Paul appearing to S. Dominic, Raising of Napoleone Orsini, Man of Sorrows, Disputation of S. Dominic and the Miracle of the Book, S. Dominic and his companions fed by Angels. Death of S. Dominic (from S. Domenico di Fiesole).

1291. Predella panel: Dance of Salome (st.).

1293. Predella panel (to 'San Marco' altarpiece): Beheading of SS. Cosmas and Damian. 1438-40. *Plate* 614.

1294. Fresco: Crucifixion, with S. Dominic (r.).

1294b. Angel of the Annunciation (r.).

Parma. 429. Madonna and Child with SS. John Baptist, Dominic, Francis and Paul (p.).

Perugia. 91. Triptych: Madonna and Child with four Angels and SS. Dominic, Nicholas, John Baptist and Catherine. Pinnacle: Annunciation. Pilasters: Twelve Saints. Predella panel: S. Nicholas saving three Men condemned to Execution and Death of S. Nicholas. (See also Rome, Vatican 251-52). 1437. *Plate* 606.

Philadelphia (Pa.). MUSEUM OF ART, JOHNSON COLLECTION. 14. S. Francis (fr.). E.

Pisa. 118. The Redeemer.

Princeton (N.J.). 33.16, 17. Two panels: Virgin, and S. John Evangelist (st.).

Rome. GALLERIA NAZIONALE (PALAZZO BARBERINI). 723. Triptych: Last Judgement, Ascension and Pentecost.

VATICAN, PINACOTECA. 251, 252. Two predella panels (to Perugia 91): Birth of S. Nicholas, Vocation of S. Nicholas, and S. Nicholas and the three Maidens; S. Nicholas addressing an Imperial Embassy, and S. Nicholas saving a Ship at Sea. 1437. *Plate* 607.

253. Madonna and Child with nine Angels and SS. Dominic and Catherine.

258. Predella panel (to 'Bosco ai Frati' altarpiece): Stigmatization of S. Francis.

—CHAPEL OF NICHOLAS V. Frescoes. Vault: Four Evangelists. Window embrasure: Prophets. Walls: Scenes from the Lives of SS. Stephen and Lawrence flanked by eight Doctors of the Church [Upper row: Ordination of S. Stephen, S. Stephen distributing Alms, S. Stephen preaching, S. Stephen addressing the Council, Expulsion of S. Stephen, Stoning of S. Stephen; SS. Augustine, Ambrose, Leo the Great, Gregory the Great. Lower row: Ordination of S. Lawrence, S. Lawrence receiving the Treasure of the Church, S. Lawrence distributing Alms, S. Lawrence before Decius, Martyrdom of S. Lawrence; SS. Bonaventura, Thomas Aquinas, Athanasius, John Chrysostomos.] (Assisted by Benozzo Gozzoli). 1447-49. *Plates* 623, 624.

San Francisco (Cal.). DE YOUNG MEMORIAL MUSEUM, KRESS COLLECTION. K. 289. Predella panel: Meeting of SS. Francis and Dominic (r.).

Sheffield (Yorks.). REV. A. HAWKINS-JONES (EX). Two panels (from frame of San Domenico di Fiesole altarpiece): SS. Nicholas and Michael. *Plates* 592-593.

Turin. 103, 104. Two panels (from the frame of an altarpiece): Two angels.

105. Madonna of Humility (p.). L. *Plate* 620.

Venice. CONTE VITTORIO CINI. Panel (from pilaster of 'San Marco' altarpiece?): S. Thomas Aquinas (g.p.; companion to Altenburg 92).

Washington (D.C.). 5 (MELLON COLL.). Madonna of Humility with two Angels.

Washington (contd.). 371 (KRESS COLLECTION 477). Entombment (r.). L. (?)
    790 (KRESS COLLECTION 1387). Predella panel (to 'San Marco' altarpiece): Healing
      of Palladia by SS. Cosmas and Damian. 1438–40.
    1085 (KRESS COLLECTION 1425). 'Cook' Tondo: Adoration of the Magi (finished
      by Filippo Lippi). [Plate 156.]
Zagreb. 34. Predella panel: Stigmatization of S. Francis and Martyrdom of S. Peter
    Martyr (r.).

ANTONIO DA FIRENZE

*Follower of Andrea del Castagno, active in Venice as a mosaicist in the middle of the
fifteenth century.*

Leningrad. 8280. *Gonfalone:* Front: Madonna and Child with two Angels and SS.
    Liberius and John Baptist; Christ Blessing in pinnacle; Back: Crucifixion;
    Annunciation in pinnacle. Sd. *Plate* 747.

ANTONIO DA FIRENZE

*Follower of Domenico Ghirlandajo. Mentioned in Tuscany in 1474, in Udine (Friuli) from
1484 until his death (1503–6). First teacher of Pellegrino da S. Daniele.*

Venice. ACCADEMIA. 1008–1011. Four panels from the dismembered altarpiece of
    S. Maria dei Servi in Venice: SS. Zenobius and the Blessed Philip Benizzi;
    S. Martin of Todi and the Blessed Pellegrino of Forlì; S. Jerome, S. Ambrose.
    Sd. on both the first and the second panel. *Plate* 748.

ANTONIO VENEZIANO

*Antonio di Francesco da Venezia, worked in Siena with Andrea Vanni 1369–70, is docu-
mented in Florence in 1374 and in Pisa from 1384 to 1388. Must have come under the
influence of Orcagna's following in Florence, of Traini in Pisa, and of Vanni in Siena.*

Altenburg. 19. Wing of an altarpiece (Assumption, or Ascension): Six Apostles. (?).
    Plate 258.
Altomonte (Calabria). DUOMO. Triptych: S. Ladislas and four other Saints. (?)
Boston (Mass.). 84.293. Madonna nursing the Child. (Companion to Florence, ex-
    Loeser; Vienna, ex-Eissler; and Homeless.) *Plate* 264.
Figline (Valdarno Superiore). CONVENTO DI S. FRANCESCO (MISERICORDIA), CHIOSTRO.
    *Fresco: Crucifixion.

Florence. CHARLES LOESER (EX). Two panels from a polyptych: SS. Paul and Peter. (See Boston.) *Plates 260–261.*

(Environs) TORRE DEGLI AGLI.* Tabernacle fresco: Deposition, Christ blessing and four Evangelists, Last Judgement, Death of the Virgin (r.). *Plate 252.*

Göttingen. 181. Panel from an altarpiece: S. James.

Hanover. 3. Madonna and Child with four Angels.

New York. KARL F. LANDEGGER. Panel from an altarpiece: S. Nicholas.

MRS. FRANKLIN LAWRENCE (EX?). Coronation of the Virgin (r.). *Plate 251.*

Palermo. S. NICCOLÒ REALE, MUSEO DIOCESANO. Panel dedicated to the members of the *Confraternita di S. Niccolò*: Flagellation of Christ; Virgin, S. John, Evangelists and Prophets. Sd. and d. 1388. *Plate 259.*

Pisa. CAMPOSANTO. Three frescoes: Scenes from the Life of S. Raynerius [Voyage to Pisa, Miracle of the watered Wine, S. Raynerius and the Canons of Pisa; Healing of the Archbishop, Death of S. Raynerius; Miracle of the Fish, Miraculous Capture of the Saracen Ship] (r.; see also Andrea da Firenze). 1384–86. *Plates 249, 254–256.*

Fresco: Assumption (r.; begun by Traini). (?)

CONVENTO DI S. TOMMASO. Assumption. *Plate 257.*

Rome. VATICAN, PINACOTECA. 16, 19. Two panels from an altarpiece: S. James and S. Mary Magdalen.

STERBINI COLLECTION (EX). S. Lawrence.

San Francisco (Cal.). DE YOUNG MEMORIAL MUSEUM, KRESS COLLECTION. K 429. S. Paul.

Siena. 110. Four panels: Four Evangelists. E. *Plate 250.*

Toledo. CATEDRAL, CAPILLA DEL SEPULCRO. Two panels: SS. Peter and Paul.

—CAPILLA DEL BAUTISMO. Four panels: Navicella, Christ in Temple, Christ and the Adultress, Transfiguration (r.).

—CAPILLA DE S EUGENIO. Retablo: Scenes of the Life of Christ (some panels only; r.). (?)

Vienna. HERMANN EISSLER (EX). Panel from a polyptych: S. Bartholomew. (See Boston). *Plate 263.*

Homeless. Panel from a polyptych: S. Andrew or Philip. (See Boston.) *Plate 262.* Lunette: S. Matthew. *Plate 253.*

APOLLONIO DI GIOVANNI
(Master of the Jarves Cassoni)

1415–1465. With Marco del Buono (1402–1489), head of a cassone workshop whose activities are recorded between 1446 and 1463–5. The following list is far from complete.

Balcarres (Fife, Scotland). EARL OF CRAWFORD AND BALCARRES. Two cassone panels: Journey of the Queen of Sheba, Solomon and the Queen of Sheba.

Birmingham (Ala.). MUSEUM OF ART (KRESS COLLECTION 251). Cassone panel: Journey of the Queen of Sheba.

Cambridge. M. 20. Cassone: Triumph of Aemilius Paullus. *Plate 746.*

Chicago (Ill.). 33.1006. Cassone panel: Scenes from the Odyssey. *Plate 736.*
      33.1036. Cassone panel: A Wedding Celebration.

Cincinnati (Ohio). 1933.9 Cassone. Front: A Battle. *Testate:* Hercules and the Lion, Rape of Deianeira.

Edinburgh. 1974. Cassone panel: Rape of the Sabines (fr.; possibly companion to Oxford 270).

Florence. BIBLIOTECA RICCARDIANA. COD. RICC. 492. *Virgilii Opera:* Drawings for four of the eighty-six miniatures (of which twenty are unfinished) illustrating the Bucolics, the Georgics, and the Aeneid: 94 recto, 97 recto, 101 recto and verso. *Plate 740–742.*

Hanover. 186, 187. Two cassone panels: Story of Dido and Aeneas.

London. 4906. Cassone. Front: A Tournament. *Testate:* Two Horsemen. *Plates 734, 735.*

   VICTORIA AND ALBERT MUSEUM. 4639–1858. Cassone. Front: Triumph of Love, Chastity and Time. *Testate:* Pyramus and Thisbe, Narcissus. Inside: Nude Woman asleep.
      5804–1859. Cassone panel: Continence of Scipio.
      7852–1862. Cassone: Solomon and the Queen of Sheba.

Modena. 496. Cassone panel: Story of Griselda (*Decamerone*, X, 10).

New Haven (Conn.). 1871.33. Cassone panel: A Tournament.
      1871.34, 35. Two cassone panels: Scenes from the Aeneid. *Plates 737–739.*
      1871.36. Cassone panel: Solomon and the Queen of Sheba. *Plates 743–744.*

Oberlin (Ohio). 43.293. Cassone panel: Xerxes' Invasion of Greece. 1463.

Oxford. ASHMOLEAN. 31. Cassone panel: A Tournament. *Plate 745.*
      269. Cassone panel: Murder of Julius Caesar.
      270. Cassone panel: Romans entertaining the Sabines (fr.; possibly companion to Edinburgh).

Paris. MUSÉE DE CLUNY. 1710 (CAMPANA 172). Cassone panel: Duel between Turnus and Aeneas and the Wedding of Lavinia and Aeneas.

Raleigh (N.C.). MUSEUM OF ART, KRESS COLLECTION. K 491. *Desco da Nozze:* Triumph of Chastity.

Turin. 107. *Desco da Nozze:* Triumph of Love.

Venice. MUSEO CORRER. 5, 6. Cassone panels: Story of Alatiel (*Decamerone*, II, 7).

Vienna. LANCKORONSKI COLLECTION (EX). Two cassone panels: Scenes from the Odyssey.

BACHIACCA (Francesco Ubertini)

1494–1557. Pupil of Perugino; influenced by Andrea del Sarto, Michelangelo and the graphic art of Lucas van Leyden and Dürer.

Amsterdam. 394-B1. Florentine street scene.

Baltimore (Md.). MUSEUM OF ART. 59.87. Madonna and Child.

Bergamo. 564. Death of Abel.

Berlin. 267A. Portrait of a Woman with a Cat.

(BERLIN-OST). 267. Baptism of Christ.

1539. Beheading of S. John Baptist. *Plate* 1248.

EDUARD SIMON (EX). Tobias and the Angel. *Plate* 1246.

Boston (Mass.). ISABELLA GARDNER MUSEUM. Portrait of a Woman.

Bremen. 301. S. John Baptist in the Wilderness.

Brocklesby Park (Lincs.). EARL OF YARBOROUGH. Madonna and Child with S. Anne and Infant S. John.

Budapest. 2317. Preaching of S. John Baptist.

Cassel. 484. Portrait of an old Man with a Skull, or *Trionfo della morte.* (Companion to New Orleans and Homeless fragment). E. *Plate* 1237.

Coral Gables (Fla.). UNIVERSITY OF MIAMI, JOE AND EMILY LOWE ART GALLERY, KRESS COLLECTION. K 308. *Desco:* Allegory.

Cornbury Park (Charlbury, Oxon.). OLIVER VERNON WATNEY. Portrait of a Lady with a Music-book. E. *Plate* 1235.

Dijon. 1471. Resurrection. E.

Dresden. 80. Legend of the Dead King. (Companion to Franciabigio, Dresden 75, dated 1523). *Plate* 1244.

80A. Madonna and Child with Infant S. John. *Plate* 1239.

Florence. GALLERIE. 468. Holy Family with S. Elizabeth and Infant S. John (from Castello). L.

4336. Tobias and the Angel.

(501). Tapestry: *Grottesche.* 1549. *Plate* 1251.

PITTI. 102. S. Mary Magdalen.

351. Portrait of a Woman.

UFFIZI. 511. Deposition (after Perugino's of 1517 at Città della Pieve).

877. Predella (to Sogliani, Florence, S. Lorenzo): Baptism, Victory, and Martyrdom of S. Acacius and his Companions. ca 1521. *Plate* 1243.

8407. Christ before Caiaphas.

(39). Tapestry: *Grottesche.* 1549.

(524–27). Four tapestries: Months of the Year. 1552–53. *Plate* 1252.

PALAZZO DAVANZATI. (38), (499). Two tapestries: *Grottesche.* 1549.

PALAZZO VECCHIO (MEZZANINO), SCRITTOIO. Frescoes: *Grottesche* (r.).

SAN FIRENZE, SACRAMENT CHAPEL. Martyrdom of the Ten Thousand. L. *Plate* 1250.

Florence (contd.). BERENSON COLLECTION. Leda.

    CONTINI BONACOSSI COLLECTION. Portrait of a young Woman with a Lute.

    MARCHESE NICCOLINI. Madonna and Child with S. Elizabeth and Infant S. John.

    SERRISTORI COLLECTION (EX). Madonna and Child with S. Elizabeth and Infant S. John. *Plate 1241.*

Hartford (Conn.). 1930.79. Tobias and the Angel.

Locko Park (Derbyshire). COL. J. PACKE-DRURY-LOWE. Christ bearing the Cross.

London. 1218, 1219. Two Borgherini panels: Benjamin brought before Joseph, Joseph receiving his Brothers. 1515–20.

    1304. Marcus Curtius. (?)

    HENRY DOETSCH (EX). Madonna and Child with Infant S. John. (Version of Wiesbaden).

    CAPT. LANGTON DOUGLAS (EX). Holy Family with Infant S. John.

    VISCOUNT LEE OF FAREHAM (EX). Predella panel: Stigmatization of S. Francis. (Companion to Rome, Palazzo Venezia).

    LORD MELCHETT (EX). Baptism of Christ.

Memphis (Tenn.). BROOKS MEMORIAL ART GALLERY, KRESS COLLECTION. K 1620. Last Supper.

Mestre (Venice). CASARIN COLLECTION. Madonna and Child with S. Elizabeth and Infant S. John.

Munich. W.A.F. 303. Tondo: Madonna and Child with Infant S. John.

New Orleans (La.). I. DELGADO MUSEUM OF ART, KRESS COLLECTION. K 1729. Portrait of a young Man with a Lute, or *Trionfo d'amore*. (Companion to Cassel and to Homeless fragment). E. *Plate 1236.*

New York. 38.178. *Caritas.*

    BLUMENTHAL COLLECTION (EX). Madonna and Child. (?)

    JACK LINSKY. Leda. *Plate 1247.*

Oxford. CHRIST CHURCH LIBRARY. 59. Christ preaching (r.).

    60. *Noli me tangere* (r.). E.

Philadelphia (Pa.). MUSEUM OF ART, JOHNSON COLLECTION. 80. Adam and Eve.

Potsdam. NEUES PALAIS. Creation of Eve.

    S. Lawrence.

Poughkeepsie (N.Y.). VASSAR COLLEGE. Baptism of Christ.

Richmond (Surrey). COOK COLLECTION (EX). 39. Holy Family with Infant S. John. *Plate 1242.*

    40. Crucifixion. L.

Rochester (N.Y.). MEMORIAL ART GALLERY. Conversion of S. Paul.

Rome. GALLERIA BORGHESE. 425, 427, 440, 442. Four Borgherini panels: Arrest of Joseph's Brothers, Joseph sold into Egypt, Search for the stolen Cup, Discovery of the stolen Cup. 1515–20. *Plate 1240.*

    MUSEO DI PALAZZO VENEZIA. Predella panel: Vision of S. Bernard. (Companion to London, Lee of Fareham).

— (HERTZ COLLECTION). 4187. S. Mary Magdalen.

Rotterdam. 2539. Leda.

Springfield (Mass.). ART MUSEUM. S. Mary Magdalen.

Troyes. 175. Leda.

Venice. PRINCIPE GIOVANNELLI (EX). Moses striking Water from the Rock.

Washington (D.C.). 791 (KRESS COLLECTION 1362). Gathering of Manna. *Plate* 1249.

Wiesbaden. STÄDTISCHES MUSEUM (EX). Madonna and Child with Infant S. John.

York. 775. Tondo: Agony in the Garden.

Homeless. Madonna and Child with Infant S. John. *Plate* 1245.

Tondo: Holy Family (after Michelangelo's 'Doni' tondo). E. [See Preface p. vii]
Plate 1238.

Triumph of Time (fr.; companion to Cassel and New Orleans). E. *Plate* 1235-a.

BALDOVINETTI, Alessio

ca 1426–99. *Pupil of Domenico Veneziano: influenced by Uccello.*

Bergamo. 528. Fresco fragment from Florence, S. Trinita: Self-Portrait. 1471.

Fiesole. S. MARIA PRIMERANA, SACRISTY. Intarsia: Annunciation. (?)

Florence. ACCADEMIA. 8637. Trinity, and SS. Benedict and John Gualbert. 1471.
Plate 804.

UFFIZI. 483. Annunciation. *Plate* 795.

487. Madonna and Child with SS. Cosmas and Damian, John Baptist, Francis,
Peter Martyr, Lawrence, Julian and Anthony Abbot. *Plate* 802.

S. AMBROGIO, L. WALL. Eight Angels and SS. Catherine, John Baptist, Lawrence
and Ambrose around a Madonna in Glory adoring the Child, executed by
Graffione in 1485 to replace the original tabernacle. 1470–73.

SS. ANNUNZIATA, ATRIUM. Fresco: Nativity (r.). 1460–62. [*Plate* 175.] *Plate* 793.

S. MARCO (MUSEO), HOSPICE. 8491. Part of doors of silver chest of SS. Annunziata
begun by Fra Angelico: Marriage at Cana, Baptism of Christ and Transfiguration. From 1448. *Plate* 791.

— FORESTERIA. Christ on the Cross, with S. Antoninus.

S. MARIA DEL FIORE (DUOMO), L. SACRISTY. Intarsia: Annunciation, Nativity, Circumcision, Isaiah and Amos. 1463–64. *Plate* 794.

—MUSEO DELL'OPERA. Intarsia: SS. Zenobius, Eugenius and Crescentius.

S. MINIATO AL MONTE, PORTUGUESE CHAPEL. Frescoes. Lunettes: Four Evangelists
and four Doctors of the Church. Spandrels: Eight Prophets. Window wall:
Annunciation. 1466–67. *Plates* 796–800.

S. PANCRAZIO, CAPPELLA RUCELLAI, EDICOLA DEL SANTO SEPOLCRO. Fresco: Risen
Christ with two Angels (r.). *Plate* 801.

Florence (contd.). S. TRINITA, CHOIR. Frescoes. Vault: Noah, Moses, Abraham, David. Lunettes: Sacrifice of Isaac, Moses receiving the Tables of the Law (r.). 1471. *Plate* 803.

London. 758. Profile Portrait of a Lady. E. *Plate* 792.

    VISCOUNT ROTHERMERE (EX). Portrait of a Man, called 'Francesco Datini'.

New York. 80.3.679. Fresco: S. Anthony Abbot (fr.; r.).

Notre Dame (Ind.). UNIVERSITY, KRESS STUDY COLLECTION. K 1334. Annunciation.

Paris. 1134B. Madonna adoring the Child. E. [*Plate* 170.]

    MUSÉE JACQUEMART-ANDRÉ. 1028. Madonna adoring the Child.

BANCHI
see Francesco di Antonio

BARTOLOMMEO, Fra (Baccio della Porta)

1475–1517. Pupil of Cosimo Rosselli and Piero di Cosimo; collaborated with Albertinelli. Influenced by Leonardo and Michelangelo; and, after a trip to Venice in 1508, *by Bellini and Giorgione.*

Amsterdam. 432-D1. Holy Family with Infant S. John.

Belton House (Grantham, Lincs.). EARL BROWNLOW. Madonna and Child.

Berlin. 249. Assumption with SS. John Baptist, Peter, Dominic, Peter Martyr, Paul and Mary Magdalen. (Upper part by Albertinelli.) ca. 1508. (Destroyed 1945.)

    (BERLIN–OST). 124. S. Jerome in the Wilderness (replica of Norton Hall). (?) *Plate* 1322.

Besançon. CATHEDRAL. Madonna in Glory with SS. Sebastian, Stephen, John Baptist, Anthony, Bernard, and Ferry Carondolet as Donor (see Stuttgart). 1512. *Plate* 1328.

Firle Place (Lewes, Sussex). VISCOUNTESS GAGE. Holy Family with Infant S. John. *Plate* 1326.

Florence. GALLERIE. 1477. Diptych: Nativity, Circumcision. *Verso:* Annunciation. E. *Plate* 1320.

    ACCADEMIA. 1448, 1449. Two pictures: Isaiah, Job. (Companions to Pitti 159). 1516.

        8397. Marriage of S. Catherine, with SS. George, Stephen, Lawrence, Paul, Peter, Catherine of Siena, Dominic, Bartholomew and five other Saints. d. 1512.

        8455. Vision of S. Bernard. 1507. *Plate* 1323.

        8644. S. Vincent Ferrer.

        8660. Trinity (executed by Albertinelli).

    PITTI. 64. Lamentation. (finished by Bugiardini.)

        125. S. Mark. 1514.

        159. The Redeemer and the four Evangelists. Sd and d. 1516.

256. Holy Family with S. Elizabeth and Infant S. John.

377. Fresco: Head of Christ.

SAN MARCO, 2nd ALTAR R. Madonna and Child with SS. John Baptist, Peter Martyr, Catherine, Mary Magdalen, Benedict and Nicholas. d. 1509. *Plate* 1324.

— (MUSEO), SALA DEL LAVABO. Madonna and Child with S. Anne, Infant S. John and ten other Saints (u.). 1510–15. *Plates* 1329–30.

Christ carrying the Cross. d. 1514.

Frescoes: Madonna and Child (tondo), Head of Christ, S. John Baptist, S. Thomas Aquinas, S. Mary Magdalen, S. Catherine of Alexandria, S. Catherine of Siena, S. Dominic, S. Anthony Abbot.

— REFECTORY. Fresco (from S. Maria Nuova): Last Judgement (r.; begun 1499; completed by Albertinelli 1501). *Plate* 1318.

— CORRIDOR OF THE FORESTERIA. Frescoes (over doors): SS. Dominic, Thomas Aquinas, Vincent Ferrer and Ambrogio Sansedoni.

— ORATORY OF SAVONAROLA. Profile Portrait of Savonarola.

Savonarola as S. Peter Martyr.

Three frescoes: Madonna and Child (1514), Madonna and Child, Christ on the Way to Emmaus.

CONTINI BONACOSSI COLLECTION. Holy Family. E.

(Environs) CALDINE, S. MARIA MADDALENA, ALTAR R. Fresco lunette: Annunciation. 1515.

— CHAPEL. Fresco: *Noli me tangere.* d. 1517.

Geneva. 1870–6. Diptych: Annunciation (only the head of the Virgin; the rest by Albertinelli). Sd by both artists and d. 1511.

Leningrad. 82. Madonna and Child with Angels. Sd and d. 1515. *Plate* 1331.

London. 1694. Madonna and Child with Infant S. John.

3914. Holy Family. [*Plate* 220.]

SIR ROBERT MOND (EX). Small Nativity.

Lucca. 81. *Madonna della Misericordia.* Sd. and d. 1515.

88. God the Father with SS. Mary Magdalen and Catherine of Siena in Adoration. d. 1509. [*Plate* 219.] *Plate* 1327.

DUOMO, CAPPELLA DEL SANTUARIO. Madonna and Child with SS. Stephen and John Baptist. Sd and d. 1509. *Plate* 1325.

Lugano. THYSSEN COLLECTION, 19A. Holy Family with S. John. *Plate* 1321.

Naples. 100. Assumption with SS. John Baptist and Catherine. Sd. and d. 1516.

Norton Hall (Glos.). SIR WALTER AND LADY POLLEN. S. Jerome in the Wilderness.

Nottingham. ST. MARY'S. Madonna and Child (c.).

Paris. 1115. *Noli me tangere.* 1506.

1153. Annunciation, with SS. Paul, John Baptist, Margaret, Mary Magdalen, Jerome and Francis. Sd and d. 1515.

1154. Marriage of S. Catherine, with SS. Peter, Vincent Ferrer, Stephen, Dominic, Francis, Bartholomew, and two other Saints. Sd and d. 1511.

Philadelphia (Pa.). MUSEUM OF ART, JOHNSON COLLECTION. 78. Adam and Eve (u.).

Pisa. SANTA CATERINA, R. WALL. Madonna and Child with SS. Peter and Paul (st.). d. 1511.

Ponzano (Soratte). SAN NICCOLÒ, 1st CHAPEL R. Fresco (from S. Andrea in Flumine): Madonna and Child with SS. Benedict, Dominic, Vincent Martyr and Jerome (r.).

Prato. 26. Detached fresco tondo: Madonna and Child.

Richmond (Surrey). COOK COLLECTION. 29. Madonna and Child with S. Elizabeth and Infant S. John. Sd and d. 1516.

Rome. GALLERIA NAZIONALE (PALAZZO BARBERINI). F.N.579. Holy Family with Infant S. John. Sd and d. 1516.

    VATICAN, PINACOTECA. 356, 362. Two pictures: S. Peter (head and hand by Raphael), S. Paul. 1514.

    MARCHESA VISCONTI VENOSTA. Tondo: Nativity. *Plate* 1319.

Sarasota (Fla.). 26. Tondo: Holy Family with Infant S. John (with Albertinelli).

Seattle (Wash.). ART MUSEUM, S. H. KRESS COLLECTION. K 1100. Creation of Eve.

Stuttgart. 394. Three fragments of a Coronation of the Virgin (lunette from the Besançon altarpiece). 1512. *Plate* 1328.

Vienna. 34. Madonna and Child.

    36. Rape of Dinah (finished by Bugiardini in 1531). *Plate* 1260.

    38. Madonna and Child with SS. Mary Magdalen, Dominic, Catherine of Siena, Catherine of Alexandria, Peter Martyr and Barbara (st.). d. 1510.

    41. Circumcision. d. 1516. *Plate* 1332.

BARTOLOMEO DI GIOVANNI

Flourished in the last two decades of the fifteenth century and perhaps in the first decade of the sixteenth. Assistant of Domenico Ghirlandajo; influenced by Botticelli, Perugino and Filippino Lippi. Furnished designs for most of the woodcuts appearing at Florence toward and around 1500.

Aix-en-Provence. 464. Madonna adoring the Child with Infant S. John. *Plate* 1126.

Ampugnamo (Milan). CHIESA PARROCCHIALE. Madonna and Child.

Arezzo. 31. Triptych: S. Mary Magdalen adoring the Cross. Wings: SS. Anthony of Padua and George.

Atlanta (Ga.). ART ASSOCIATION GALLERIES, KRESS COLLECTION. K 77, 79. Two panels: Tribute to Apollo, A King with his Counsellors. L. (?)

Baltimore (Md.). WALTERS ART GALLERY. 421. Cassone panel: Myth of Io. (Companion to Berchtesgaden). *Plate* 1121.

    428. Three predella panels: Last Communion of S. Jerome, Entombment, Death of S. Jerome.

Berchtesgaden. SCHLOSS, WITTELSBACHER AUSGLEICHSFOND. Cassone panel: Myth of Io. (Companion to Baltimore 421). *Plate* 1122.

Bergamo. 310. Flagellation. *Plate* 1125.

Bilbao. LAUREANO JADO. Madonna and Child with two Angels and SS. Jerome and Francis.

Bonn. STÄDTISCHE KUNSTSAMMLUNGEN. Madonna and Child with Infant S. John.

Cambridge. M 3, 4. Two cassone panels: Scenes from the Life of Joseph. E. M 52. Bust of Christ.

Cape Town (South Africa). SIR JOSEPH ROBINSON (EX). Cassone panel: Story of Jason and the Golden Fleece (companion to Piero di Cosimo at Cape Town, dated 1487). *Plate* 1117.

Cassel. 482. Crucifixion with SS. John the Evangelist, Jerome, Mary Magdalen and Francis. (Destroyed.)

Chantilly. 16A. Miniature: *Mons Sapientiae.*

Chicago (Ill.). 37.996. Scenes from the Early Life of S. John Baptist.

Detroit (Mich.). 30.279. Predella panel: Adoration of the Magi (r.).
52.229. Nativity with S. Gregory and two other Saints.

Dresden. 17, 18. Two roundels: SS. Michael and Raphael with Tobias.

Dublin. (Environs). TALLAGHT, DOMINICAN FATHERS. Herod's Feast and Beheading of S. John Baptist.

Florence. GALLERIE. 61. Crucifixion with five Saints and a Donor.

8387. Three predella panels: Raising of Napoleone Orsini, *Pietà*, School of S. Thomas Aquinas.

8658, 8659. Two pilasters: Annunciation, SS. Dominic and Vincent, two Prophets.

ACCADEMIA. 8627–29. Three predella panels: Stigmatization of S. Francis, Entombment, S. Jerome in the Wilderness.

8630. S. Jerome in the Wilderness.

UFFIZI. 1502, 3154. Two predella panels: S. Benedict blessing the poisoned Wine, Rescue of S. Placidus. *Plate* 1124.

MUSEO HORNE. 39. Mythological Subject.

507. Tondo: Madonna adoring the Child with Infant S. John.

PALAZZO VECCHIO, CAMERA DELLE SABINE. Tondo: Holy Family with S. Francis.

S. SPIRITO, L. TRANSEPT, 1st CHAPEL. L. Window: Incredulity of S. Thomas.

SPEDALE DEGLI INNOCENTI, PINACOTECA. Massacre of Innocents in background of Domenico Ghirlandajo's Adoration of the Magi. 1488. *Plate* 967.

Predella (to above): S. John Evangelist in the Cauldron of Boiling Oil, Annunciation, Marriage of the Virgin, Lamentation, Circumcision, Baptism of Christ, S. Antonino blessing the *Spedale degli Innocenti*. 1488. *Plates* 1118–19.

MARCHESE MANNELLI RICCARDI (EX). Lamentation with Saints and a Donor. *Plate* 1131.

Horsmonden (Kent). MRS. AUSTEN (EX). Two cassone panels: Marriage Feast of Pirithous and Hippodamia, Battle between the Centaurs and Lapiths.

Lille. PALAIS DES BEAUX-ARTS. Madonna and Child.

Liverpool. 2755, 2756. Two predella panels: Martyrdom of S. Sebastian, S. Andrew saving a Bishop from Seduction. *Plate* 1129.

Locko Park (Derbyshire). COL. J. PACKE-DRURY-LOWE. S. John Baptist.

London. VICTORIA AND ALBERT MUSEUM. 5–1890. Lunette (over a stucco relief of the Madonna and Child): Trinity with two Angels.

    HENRY HARRIS (EX). S. Catherine.

    ANTHONY POST. 'Graham' Madonna and Child with Infant S. John.

Longleat (Wilts.). MARQUESS OF BATH. Two cassone panels: Feast and Flight.

Lovere (Lago d'Iseo). 29. Madonna and Child with Infant S. John.

Lucca. DUOMO, SACRISTY. Predella (to altarpiece by Domenico Ghirlandajo): S. Matthew, Liberation of S. Peter, S. Clement thrown into the Sea, Man of Sorrows, Martyrdom of S. Sebastian, Conversion of S. Paul, S. Lawrence (g.p.). *Plate* 1116.

Madrid. 2838–2840. Three panels: Story of Nastagio degli Onesti (*Decamerone*, v, 8; with Botticelli; the Banquet scene g.p.; see also Botticelli, Cornbury Park). 1483. *Plate* 1115.

Narni. PINACOTECA. Two predella panels (to Coronation by Domenico Ghirlandajo): Stigmatization of S. Francis, S. Jerome in the Wilderness. 1486.

New Haven (Conn.). 1871.53. S. Jerome in the Wilderness (r.).

New York. 41.100.1. Madonna and Child.

    S. H. KRESS FOUNDATION. K 1721 A, B.: Two panels: Daphne discovered by Apollo, Metamorphosis of Daphne.

Oxford. CHRIST CHURCH LIBRARY. 39. Madonna and Child with Infant S. John.

Palermo. CHIARAMONTE BORDONARO COLLECTION. S. Jerome in the Wilderness. *Plate* 1127.

Parcieux. GEORGES CHALANDON (EX). Crucifixion with SS. Monica, Augustine, Mary Magdalen, Jerome and a female Saint. *Plate* 1130.

Paris. 1416A, B. Two cassone panels: Myth of Peleus and Thetis. *Plate* 1123.

Philadelphia (Pa.). MUSEUM OF ART. 1943–40–53. Predella panel: Nativity.

    — JOHNSON COLLECTION. 70. Predella panel: Last Communion of S. Jerome. L. 71. S. John Baptist preaching. L.

Richmond (Surrey). COOK COLLECTION (EX). 61. Madonna and Child with SS. John Evangelist, Benedict, Romuald and Jerome.

Rome. GALLERIA COLONNA. 47, 52. Two panels: Rape of the Sabines, Reconciliation of the Romans and the Sabines. *Plate* 1120.

    VATICAN, APPARTAMENTO BORGIA, SALA DEI MISTERI. Frescoes: Nativity (p.; Madonna close to Pinturicchio), Adoration of the Magi (g.p.). 1492–94.

    — PINACOTECA. 69, 72. Two predella panels: S. Justus freeing the country from snakes; Worshippers at the Tomb of S. Justus.

311. Madonna and Child with S. Anthony and other Saints.

San Francisco (Cal.). DE YOUNG MEMORIAL MUSEUM, KRESS COLLECTION. K 363. 'Wittgenstein' Tondo: Adoration of the Magi. *Plate 1128.*

Vercelli. MUSEO BORGOGNA. Madonna adoring the Child with Infant S. John. E.

Vienna. LANCKORONSKI COLLECTION. Disputation of S. Stephen.

York. 729. Predella panel: *Domine quo vadis?* and Liberation of S. Peter.

BIAGIO DI ANTONIO
see 'Utili'

BICCI DI LORENZO

1373–1452. Pupil of his father, Lorenzo di Bicci; influenced by Mariotto di Nardo, Lorenzo Monaco, Gentile da Fabriano and Fra Angelico. Close to Rossello di Jacopo Franchi.

Antwerp. 176, 177. Wings of an altarpiece: S. Paul, S. Nicholas with a Donor.

Arezzo. 25, 26. Wings of an altarpiece: SS. James and Zenobius, SS. Nicholas and John Baptist (r.).

S. FRANCESCO, CHOIR. Frescoes. Vault: Four Evangelists. Above entrance arch: Last Judgement. Entrance arch: SS. Gregory and James. L.

(Environs) S. MARIA DELLE GRAZIE, HIGH ALTAR. Fresco: *Madonna della Misericordia* (p.).

Balcarres (Fife, Scotland). EARL OF CRAWFORD AND BALCARRES (EX). S. Lawrence enthroned. Pinnacle: Madonna and Child.

Baltimore (Md.). WALTERS ART GALLERY. 448. Annunciation. Spandrel: David. Predella: Birth of the Virgin, Presentation in the Temple, Dormition of the Virgin.

Berlin. 1064A. Predella (to triptych by Daddi): S. Salvi healing the Plague-stricken, Nativity, S. Bernardo degli Uberti defending Rome. d. 1423. (Destroyed 1945). *Plate 499.*

Bibbiena (Casentino). PROPOSITURA (S. IPPOLITO), CHOIR. Triptych: Madonna and Child with SS. Hippolytus, John Baptist, James and Christopher. Pinnacles: Crucifixion, Resurrection, Pentecost, Head of Christ, Annunciation. Pilasters: Four Saints, two Angels. Predella: An Evangelist, Martyrdom of S. Hippolytus, Baptism of Christ, Nativity, Beheading of S. James, Attempted Martyrdom of S. Christopher. d. 1435. *Plate 511.*

(Environs) S. MARIA DEL SASSO, HIGH ALTAR. Fresco: Madonna and Child in Glory with two Angels.

Boston (Mass.). 43.218. Annunciation.

ISABELLA GARDNER MUSEUM. Madonna and Child with SS. Matthew and Francis.

Brunswick. 4, 5. Two wings of an altarpiece: SS. Philip and Gregory, SS. Nicholas and Bartholomew.

Cambridge (Mass.). 1920.19. Predella panel: Nativity.

Cetica (Casentino). S. MARIA, HIGH ALTAR. Triptych: Madonna and Child with a Donor and SS. John Baptist, John Evangelist, Paul and Peter. Pinnacles: Crucifixion, Annunciation. Predella: S. Christopher, Baptism of Christ, S. John in the Cauldron of boiling Oil, Nativity, Beheading of S. Paul, Crucifixion of S. Peter, S. Blaise.

Darmstadt. LANDESMUSEUM (EX). 88. Madonna and Child with Angels.

Empoli. 18. Triptych (left wing missing): Madonna and Child with a Donor and SS. John Evangelist and Leonard. 1423.

    91. S. Nicholas of Tolentino defending Empoli from the Plague. 1445. *Plate* 513.

Fabriano. 1. Madonna and Child in Glory with SS. John Baptist and James.

Fiesole. MUSEO BANDINI. I, 1–2. Two panels: Choirs of Angels (fr.).

    I, 15. Baptism of S. Pancras.

    I, 30–31. Two panels: SS. James and Helen (fr.).

    II, 7. S. Catherine disputing.

    II, 12. Triptych: Madonna and Child with four Angels and SS. Louis of Toulouse, Francis, Anthony of Padua and Nicholas.

    DUOMO, HIGH ALTAR. Triptych: Madonna and Child with two Angels and SS. Alexander, Peter, Donatus and Romulus. Pinnacles: The Holy Ghost, an Evangelist and S. John Baptist. ca 1450.

Florence. GALLERIE. 120. Wings of an altarpiece: SS. Andrew and Michael, SS. Jerome and Lawrence. Pinnacles: Annunciation.

    462. Predella panel: S. Martin and the Beggar.

    ACCADEMIA. 471. S. Lawrence. Pinnacle: Christ blessing. Predella: Martyrdom of S. Lawrence, S. Lawrence saving Souls from Purgatory.

    3462. Panel from an altarpiece: S. Bernard and a Donor.

    8611. Marriage of S. Catherine, with SS. Eustace, John Baptist and Anthony Abbot. Pinnacle: Christ blessing. Predella: Man of Sorrows and four Saints.

    EDUCATORIO DI FOLIGNO, GROUND FLOOR HALL. Frescoes: S. Onuphrius in the Wilderness, Nativity with S. Francis, S. Margaret and Scenes from her Life (p.).

    — 1ST FLOOR HALL. Frescoes: A Franciscan Saint and Friars (fr.), School of S. Thomas Aquinas, Annunciation, S. Francis. Man of Sorrows and Symbols of the Passion, S. Benedict instructing his Brothers (p.).

    PORTA S. GIORGIO. Fresco: Madonna and Child with SS. George and Leonard. d. 1430. *Plate* 505.

    S. AMBROGIO, R. WALL. Triptych: Madonna and Child with SS. Cosmas and Damian, Ansanus, Ursula and two other Saints. Pinnacles: Christ blessing, Annunciation.

    S. CROCE, SACRISTY. S. Bernardino supported by two Angels, and Worshippers. L.

    S. FELICITA, SALA DEL CAPITOLO. Fresco lunette (over door): Marriage of S. Catherine, with S. Anthony Abbot.

Two detached frescoes: Annunciation.

S. GIOVANNINO DEI CAVALIERI, CHAPEL L. OF CHOIR. Nativity. Predella: Circumcision, Trinity, Adoration of the Magi. d. 1435. *Plate* 509.

S. MARIA DEL CARMINE, SACRISTY, CHAPEL. Frescoes. Vault: SS. Urban, Tiburtius, Valerian and Cecilia. Walls: Scenes from the Life of S. Cecilia [Marriage of S. Cecilia, S. Valerian giving Alms, Pope Urban in the Catacombs, Conversion and Baptism of S. Valerian, SS. Cecilia and Valerian crowned with Flowers, Conversion and Baptism of Tiburtius, Valerian and Tiburtius distributing Alms and burying the Dead, Valerian and Tiburtius before the Prefect, Conversion and Baptism of Maximus, S. Cecilia comforting Valerian and Tiburtius, Martyrdom of Valerian and Tiburtius, S. Cecilia distributing Alms and preaching, Baptism of Converts, The Faithful gathering the Blood of S. Cecilia, Burial of S. Cecilia and Consecration of her House.] E. *Plate* 497.

S. MARIA DEL FIORE (DUOMO), L. WALL, 4th BAY. SS. Cosmas and Damian. Pinnacle: Christ blessing. Predella: Dream of the Deacon Justinian, Martyrdom of SS. Cosmas and Damian. 1430.

— MUSEO DELL'OPERA. 69, 70. Two fresco fragments: Heads of two Apostles.

S. NICCOLÒ, SACRISTY. Madonna and Child with SS. Francis, a Bishop Saint, a Deacon Saint, Lucy, Nicholas and Bartholomew.

S. TRINITA, 4th CHAPEL L. Coronation of the Virgin, with twelve Saints. Predella: Birth of the Virgin, Presentation in the Temple, Marriage of the Virgin, Annunciation, Dormition of the Virgin.

SPEDALE DI S. MARIA NUOVA. Detached fresco from the façade of S. Egidio: Pope Martin V consecrating the Church of S. Egidio in 1420. After 1424. *Plate* 510.

VIA SERRAGLI AND VIA S. MONACA. Tabernacle fresco: Madonna and Child with SS. Paul and Jerome and a donor. 1427. *Plate* 501.

(Environs) BAGNO A RIPOLI, S. MARIA DI QUARTO, HIGH ALTAR. Madonna nursing the Child with two Angels.

— CALDINE, S. MARIA MADDALENA, HIGH ALTAR. Spandrels (of altarpiece by Master of S. Cecilia): Annunciation.

— LEGNAIA, S. ARCANGELO. Annunciation. d. 1440. *Plate* 514.

— — CHOIR. Four Saints.

*— PONTE A GREVE. Tabernacle fresco: Madonna and Child with SS. Lawrence, John Baptist, Anthony Abbot and Peter.

— S. MARTINO A GANGALANDI, CHAPEL R. (BAPTISTERY). Frescoes: Christ in Glory with music-making Angels, S. Martin and the Beggar, Annunciation, Four Evangelists, Four Doctors of the Church. After 1430.

— VINCIGLIATA, CASTELLO (EX). Marriage of S. Catherine, with two Angels.

Greenville (S.C.). BOB JONES UNIVERSITY GALLERY. Madonna nursing the Child with S. Anne and two Angels. *Plate* 503.

Madonna and Child in Glory with SS. John Baptist and James.

Grottaferrata (Rome). BADIA. Left wing of an altarpiece: SS. Benedict and Nicholas. (Companion to New York, Lehman, and to Parma 456). 1433. *Plate* 506.

Indianapolis (Ind.). 24.10. S. Blaise enthroned. *Plate* 512.

    52.61. Roundel: S. Mark.

Kinnaird Castle (Brechen, Scotland). LORD SOUTHESK (EX). Ecstasy of S. Mary Magdalen.

Laon. MUSÉE (CAMPANA 187). Predella panel: Death of S. Francis.

Le Puy. MUSÉE CROZATIER 61 (CAMPANA 72 bis). Left wing of an altarpiece: SS. Lucy and Blaise. Pinnacle: Angel of the Annunciation. (Companion to Marseilles).

Levens Hall (Kendal, Westmorland). O. R. BAGOT. Marriage of S. Catherine, with nine other Saints.

Liverpool. 2759, 2760. Two roundels: SS. Peter and Paul.

    2761. Predella panel: Pentecost.

London. WESTMINSTER ABBEY. 'Crawford' Triptych: Madonna and Child with two Angels and SS. Anthony Abbot, John Gualbert, John Baptist and Catherine. Spandrels: SS. Paul and Peter. Pilasters: Six Saints.

Marseilles. 798. Madonna and Child with two Angels. Pinnacle: Christ blessing. (Companion to Le Puy).

Montepulciano. 21. Marriage of S. Catherine, with SS. Francis, John Baptist and Bernard (r.).

Nantes. 16. Baptism of Christ, with S. Francis.

New York. 16.121. Predella panel (to Parma 456?): S. Nicholas raising three young Men. (Companion to 88.389 below and to Oxford). *Plate* 507.

    41.100.16. Madonna and Child with SS. Matthew and Francis.

    88.3.89. Predella panel (to Parma 456?): S. Nicholas and the three Maidens. (Companion to 16.121 above and to Oxford).

    ROBERT LEHMAN. Right wing of an altarpiece: SS. John Baptist and John Evangelist. (Companion to Grottaferrata and Parma 456.) 1433. *Plate* 506.

    HAROLD PRATT (EX). Predella panel: Nativity.

Oxford. ASHMOLEAN. 60. Predella panel (to Parma 456?): S. Nicholas saving a Ship at Sea. (Companion to New York 16.121 and 88.3.89.)

Parma. 456. Madonna and Child with four Angels. (Companion to Grottaferrata and to New York, Lehman.) d. 1433. *Plate* 506.

    CONGREGAZIONE DI S. FILIPPO NERI, PINACOTECA STUARD. 5, 6. Wings of an altarpiece: SS. Thomas and John Baptist, SS. James the Less and Nicholas.

Perugia. 79. Triptych: Marriage of S. Catherine, with SS. Agnes and Elizabeth of Hungary, and SS. Anthony of Padua, John Evangelist, Louis of Toulouse, Herculanus, Lawrence and Constantius. Spandrels: Stigmatizaton of S. Francis, Annunciation, Three Saints in the Wilderness. Predella: *Noli me tangere*, Martyrdom of S. Agnes, S. Elizabeth of Hungary ministering to the Poor, Baptism of Christ. *Plate* 500.

    R. VAN MARLE (EX). Blessed Gerard of Villamagna.

Madonna nursing the Child, with SS. John Baptist and Francis. Spandrels: Annunciation.

Pescia. BIBLIOTECA CAPITOLARE.† Coronation with two music-making Angels.

S. ANTONIO ABATE. Frescoes. Vault: Four Evangelists. Soffits: *Agnus Dei* and eight Apostles. Walls: Scenes from the Life of S. Anthony Abbot [Conversion of S. Anthony and Distribution of his Fortune, Temptation of S. Anthony. Altar wall: Meeting of SS. Anthony and Paul Hermit, SS. Anthony and Paul fed by a Raven, Annunciation, Man of Sorrows. Right wall: Death and Burial of S. Paul, Death of S. Anthony. Pilasters: S. James and the Beheading of S. James, S. Catherine and the Martyrdom of S. Catherine, S. Jerome and S. Jerome and the Lion, S. Lawrence and the Martyrdom of S. Lawrence Above entrance: Two Prophets and Angels].

S. FRANCESCO, CHAPEL R. OF CHOIR. Frescoes. Vault: Four Evangelists. Walls: Scenes from the Life of the Virgin [Expulsion of Joachim, Annunciation to Joachim and Meeting at the Golden Gate, Birth of the Virgin. Altar wall: Dormition of the Virgin, and two other fragmentary scenes. Right wall: Presentation of the Virgin, Marriage of the Virgin]. *Plate* 502.

Pisa. 112, 113. Wings of an altarpiece: SS. Anthony Abbot, Lawrence and Louis of Toulouse; SS. Francis, Catherine and Michael. Pinnacles: Annunciation.

S. Eulalia. Pinnacle: Christ blessing. Predella: Two scenes of the Martyrdom of S. Eulalia.

Poppi (Casentino). CASTELLO, COURT. Fresco: Madonna and Child with four Saints. 1441.

Rome. GALLERIA DORIA PAMPHILJ. 173, 177. Wings of an altarpiece: SS. James and Anthony Abbot, SS. Christopher and John Baptist (fr.).

PINACOTECA CAPITOLINA. 351, 352. Baptism of Christ, Stigmatization of S. Francis.

San Donato in Poggio (Val di Pesa). PIEVE, BAPTISTERY. Left wing of an altarpiece: SS. Lucy, Mary Magdalen and Donatus (fr.).

San Francisco (Cal.). M. H. DE YOUNG MEMORIAL MUSEUM. Wings of an altarpiece: SS. John Baptist and Miniato, SS. Anthony Abbot and Stephen. Pinnacles: Annunciation.

Sant' Agata (Scarperia, Mugello). PIEVE, CHOIR. Marriage of S. Catherine, with S. Mary Magdalen.

Stia (Casentino). PROPOSITURA (S. MARIA ASSUNTA), HIGH ALTAR. Triptych: Annunciation, with SS. Michael, James the Less, Margaret and John Evangelist. Pinnacles: Crucifixion, A Seraph and a Cherub. Predella: Miracle of the Bull of Gargano, Nativity, S. John in the Cauldron of boiling Oil. d. 1414. *Plate* 498.

Tempe (Ariz.). STATE UNIVERSITY, KRESS STUDY COLLECTION. K 1228. Predella panel: Nativity. (g.p.).

Todi. PINACOTECA. Wings of an altarpiece: SS. Francis and Fortunatus with a Donor, SS. James and Nicholas with a Donor.

Udine. MUSEO CIVICO. Madonna and Child with SS. John Baptist and Anthony Abbot.

Velletri. MUSEO DEL DUOMO. Visitation. Spandrel: David. d. 1434. *Plate 508.*

Venice. CA' D'ORO. Madonna and Child with two Angels and SS. Paul and Peter.

Vertine (Chianti). S. BARTOLOMEO. Triptych: Madonna and Child with two Angels and SS. Bartholomew, John Evangelist, Mary Magdalen and Anthony Abbot. Pinnacles: Christ blessing, Annunciation. Predella: Martyrdom of S. Bartholomew, S. John in the Cauldron of boiling Oil, Nativity, Ecstasy of S. Mary Magdalen, Temptation of S. Anthony. d. 1430. *Plate 504.*

Vienna. LANCKORONSKI COLLECTION. Madonna nursing the Child, with two Angels and a Donor.

Wing of an altarpiece: SS. Francis and Mary Magdalen.

Homeless. Two panels from the pilasters of an altarpiece: SS. Catherine and Mary Magdalen. (See *Rassegna d'Arte* 1915, p. 214).

BOCCHI (Bartolomeo di Andrea, da Pistoia)

Mentioned from 1450 to 1465, he still carried on, with provincial backwardness, the late Gothic tradition.

Serravalle (Pistoia). S. MICHELE, 1ST ALTAR R. Triptych: Madonna and Child with Angels; SS. Hippolytus, James, Michael and Stephen. Pinnacles: Christ blessing, Annunciation. Sd. and d. 1439. *Plate 648.*

Warsaw. 73403. Triptych: *Madonna della Cintola* with SS. James, John Evangelist, Peter and Paul. Sd. *Plate 649.*

BONSI (Giovanni, da Firenze)

Documented from 1351 to 1371. Belongs to the Gaddi school.

Rome. VATICAN, PINACOTECA. 9. Polyptych from S. Miniato al Tedesco: Madonna and Child with SS. Onuphrius, Nicholas, Bartholomew and John Evangelist. Pinnacles: Christ blessing and four Dominican Saints. Sd. and d. 1371. *Plate 306.*

BOTTICELLI (Sandro Filipepi, called)

ca 1445–1510. *Pupil of Filippo Lippi; influenced by Pollajuolo, Andrea del Castagno and Verrocchio.*

Ajaccio (Corsica). 55. Madonna and Child with an Angel. E. *Plate* 1071.

Altenburg. 100. Profile Portrait of a Woman as S. Catherine. E.

Amsterdam. 597–B1. Judith. *Plate* 1091.

Balcarres (Fife, Scotland). EARL OF CRAWFORD AND BALCARRES. S. Lawrence and female Donor (r.).

Baltimore (Md.). MUSEUM OF ART. 38.226. Tondo: Madonna adoring the Child with five Angels (st.).

Barcelona. DOÑA HELENA CAMBO DE GUARDANS. Portrait of a Man, called 'Marullus'.

Bayonne. 965. Madonna and Child with two Angels (c.).

Bergamo. 524. Portrait of Giuliano de' Medici.

    525. Story of Virginia. (Companion to Boston, Gardner Museum). *Plate* 1093.

    526. The Redeemer. *Plate* 111.

Berlin. 102. Tondo: Madonna and Child with seven Angels (st.). (Destroyed 1945).

    102A. 'Raczynski' Tondo: Madonna and Child with eight Angels (st. v.).

    106. Madonna and Child with SS. John Baptist and John Evangelist. 1485. *Plate* 1113.

    106A. Profile Portrait of a young Woman (st. v.).

    106B. Portrait of Giuliano de' Medici (g.p.; version of Bergamo 524).

    1117. Annunciation (st. v.). (Destroyed 1945).

    1128. S. Sebastian. 1473–74. *Plate* 1074.

    KUPFERSTICH KABINETT. Illustration to Canto XVIII of Dante's Inferno.

Besançon. 896.1.157. Portrait of a Boy (r.). (?)

Birmingham. BARBER INSTITUTE. Madonna and Child with young S. John.

    CITY ART GALLERY. P.31'59. Pentecost (st.). L.

Boston (Mass.). 95.1372. Madonna and Child with young S. John (st.).

    ISABELLA GARDNER MUSEUM. 'Chigi' Madonna and Child with an Angel. E.

    Story of Lucretia (Companion to Bergamo 525).

    Tondo: Nativity (g.p.).

Buscot Park (Faringdon, Berks.). LORD FARINGDON. Tondo: Nativity with young S. John (st.).

Cambridge (Mass.). 1924.27. Mystic Crucifixion (r.). L. *Plate* 1095.

    1930.2. *Salvator Mundi* (st. v.).

    1943.105. Madonna and Child (st.).

Cherbourg. 12. Entombment. E.

Chicago (Ill.). 37.1009. Madonna and Child with two Angels (c.). E.

Columbia (S.C.). MUSEUM OF ART, KRESS COLLECTION. K 1410. Fresco: Nativity (st.).

Cornbury Park (Charlbury, Oxon.). OLIVER VERNON WATNEY. Banquet of Nastagio degli Onesti (*Decamerone*, V, 8.; st; companion to Madrid). 1483.

Detroit (Mich.). 27.3. The Redeemer.

Dijon. 1184. Adoration of the Magi, with SS. Catherine and Andrew (c.).

Dresden. 8. Madonna and Child with young S. John (st. v.).

    9. Scenes from the Life of S. Zenobius. (Companion to London 3918–19 and New York 11.98). L. [*Plate* 214.]

    10. Tondo: Madonna and Child with five Angels. (st.; r.).

Edinburgh. 1536. Nativity with young S. John (g.p.).

El Paso (Texas). MUSEUM OF ART, KRESS COLLECTION. K 1240. Tondo: Madonna and Child.

Florence. GALLERIE. 4346. Adoration of the Magi (u.).

    8362. Coronation of the Virgin, with SS. John Evangelist, Augustine, Jerome and Eligius. 1488–90.

    8389. Predella (to 8362): S. John on Patmos, S. Augustine in his Study, Annunciation, S. Jerome in the Wilderness, S. Eligius restoring the Horse's Leg. 1488–90.

    ACCADEMIA. 3166. Madonna and Child with young S. John and two Angels. E.

    4344. Madonna and Child with SS. Dominic, Cosmas, Damian, Francis, Lawrence and John Baptist (st.).

    8623. Man of Sorrows, with the Virgin and S. John (st.).

    PITTI. 348. Tondo: Madonna and Child with young S. John and two Angels (st. v.).

    353. Profile Portrait of a Woman.

    357. Madonna and Child with young S. John (st.).

    372. Portrait of a young Man (g.p.). E.

    580. Tondo: Madonna adoring the Child with four Angels (c.).

    UFFIZI. 8 Dep. Madonna and Child (p.).

    29 Dep. Pallas and the Centaur. [*Plates* 199–200.]

    504. Madonna and Child with Cherubim. E.

    878. Birth of Venus. [*Plates* 204–205.]

    882. 'Medici' Adoration of the Magi. *Plate* 1077.

    1473. S. Augustine in his Study.

    1484. Judith. E. *Plate* 1075.

    1487. Holofernes found Dead. (Companion to 1484). E.

    1488. Portrait of a Man with a Medal, called 'Giovanni di Cosimo de' Medici'.

    1496. Calumny. L. *Plate* 1092.

    1601. Madonna and Child against Rose-hedge under Arch. E.

    1606. Fortitude. (Companion to Piero Pollajuolo, Uffizi 495–99, 1610). 1470. [*Plate* 213.]

    1607. Tondo: 'Madonna of the Pomegranate', with six Angels. 1487. *Plate* 1086.

    1608. Annunciation. Predella: Man of Sorrows (st.).

    1609. Tondo: 'Madonna of the Magnificat', with five Angels.

    8360. *La Primavera*. [*Plates* 203, 206.] *Plate* 1079.

8361. 'S. Barnaba' altarpiece: Madonna and Child with four Angels and SS. Catherine, Augustine, Barnabas, John Baptist, Ignatius and Michael. ca 1483. *Plate* 1084–5.

8390–93. Four predella panels (to 8361): S. Augustine's Vision of the Child on the Shore, Man of Sorrows, Salome with the Head of S. John, Extraction of the Heart of S. Ignatius. ca 1483.

8657. Madonna and Child with SS. Mary Magdalen, John Baptist, Cosmas, Damian, Francis and Catherine (heads of Madonna and Child repainted). ca 1471.

GALLERIA CORSINI. 167. Tondo: Madonna and Child with six Angels holding Instruments of the Passion (st. v.).

210. Portrait of a Man holding a Ring.

350. Two roundels: Annunciation. L.

PALAZZO VECCHIO, CAMERA VERDE. Tondo: Madonna and Child with a Book (c.).

— SALA DI PENELOPE. Madonna and Child with young S. John (st. v.).

SPEDALE DEGLI INNOCENTI, PINACOTECA. 107. Madonna and Child with an Angel (r.). E.

SS. ANNUNZIATA, SAGRESTIA DELLA MADONNA. Fresco: Madonna and Child (fr.). E. (?).

S. FELICE, 1ST ALTAR L. Triptych: SS. Anthony Abbot, Roch and Catherine. Predella: Annunciation, Temptation of S. Anthony, S. Roch discovered by Gothardus, Martyrdom of S. Catherine. (st., S. Anthony perhaps by Bartolomeo di Giovanni).

S. MARIA NOVELLA, ABOVE CENTRAL DOOR. Fresco lunette: Nativity. E.

S. MARTINO ALLA SCALA.* Fresco: Annunciation. 1481. *Plate* 1080.

OGNISSANTI, R. WALL. Fresco: S. Augustine in his Study. 1480. [*Plates* 201–202.]

CONTINI BONACOSSI COLLECTION. Predella: Communion of S. Jerome, and SS. Vincent Ferrer, Dominic, Francis and Peter Martyr (st.).

(Environs) CORBIGNANO, CAPPELLA VANELLA. Fresco: Madonna and Child enthroned (r.). E.

— LA QUIETE. Coronation of the Virgin with eighteen Saints (st.).

— LE SIECI, S. GIOVANNI A REMOLE. Crucifixion (st.).

— S. DOMENICO DI FIESOLE, 1ST CHAPEL R. (FORMERLY CENACOLO DI S. APOLLONIA). Crucifixion with the Virgin and S. Jerome (st.).

Frankfurt am Main. 764. Tondo: Crucifixion (c.).

936. Profile Portrait of a Woman (st. v.).

Glasgow. 174. Annunciation (g.p.).

Glen Falls (N.Y.). MRS. LOUIS HYDE (EX?). Predella panel: Annunciation. *Plate* 1073.

Gosford House (East Lothian, Scotland). EARL OF WEMYSS AND MARCH. Madonna adoring the Child (st.v.).

Granada. CAPILLA REAL, ALTAR R., ISABELLA'S RELIQUARY. Agony in the Garden. L. *Plate* 1094.

Hamburg. GALERIE WEBER (EX). Madonna and Child with two Angels (st.). E.

Hanover. 25. Annunciation, with a Donor. L.

Kaliningrad. See Königsberg.

Königsberg. (EX? FORMERLY BERLIN 1425). Man of Sorrows with SS. Francis and Jerome (st.).

Leningrad. 4076, 4077. Two panels: SS. Dominic and Jerome (g.p.; companions to Moscow).

Lockinge House (Wantage, Berks.). CHRISTOPHER LOYD. Madonna and Child (st. v.).

London. 226. Tondo: Madonna and Child with young S. John and two Angels (c.).

   275. Tondo: Madonna nursing the Child with young S. John and an Angel (st.).

   589. Madonna and Child with an Angel (st.). E.

   592. Adoration of the Magi. E.

   598. S. Francis, with music-making Angels (c. of early original).

   626. Portrait of a young Man.

   782. Madonna and Child. (c.).

   915. Venus and Mars.

   1033. Tondo: Adoration of the Magi. E.

   1034. Mystic Nativity. Sd. and d. 1500 (Florentine style). *Plate* 1096.

   2082. Profile Portrait of a Woman. *Verso:* An Angel (st.).

   2497. Madonna adoring the Child with young S. John (st.).

   2508. Madonna and Child with two Angels. E.

   2906. Madonna and Child with a Pomegranate (st., r.).

   3101. Portrait of a young Man.

   3918, 3919. Two panels: Scenes from the Life of S. Zenobius. (Companions to Dresden 9 and New York 11.98). L.

COURTAULD GALLERIES, LEE OF FAREHAM COLLECTION. 59. Trinity with SS. Mary Magdalen, John Baptist, Tobias and the Angel (g.p.).

VICTORIA AND ALBERT MUSEUM. C.A.I.100. Portrait of a Woman, called 'Esmeralda Bandinelli'. E. [*Plate* 211.]

VISCOUNT ROTHERMERE (EX). Profile Portrait of a Woman.

Madrid. 2838–2840. Three panels: Story of Nastagio degli Onesti. (*Decamerone*, V, 8; p., with Bartolomeo di Giovanni; companions to Cornbury Park). 1483. *Plate* 1115.

Milan. MUSEO POLDI PEZZOLI. 155. Embroidery: Coronation of the Virgin.

   156. Madonna and Child.

   552. Lamentation (st.).

PINACOTECA AMBROSIANA. Tondo: Madonna adoring the Child with three Angels. *Plate* 1089.

COMM. MARIO CRESPI. Portrait of a young Man.

   Madonna and Child (st.).

Montelupo (Florence). S. GIOVANNI, R. WALL. Madonna and Child with SS. Sebastian, Lawrence, John Evangelist and Roch. Predella: Man of Sorrows, S. Lawrence distributing the Treasure of the Church, Martyrdom of S. Lawrence, Four Saints (st.).

Montpellier. MUSÉE 676 (CAMPANA 231). Tondo: Madonna and Child with young S. John (st.).

Montreal. 14. Madonna and Child (st.).

Moscow. 1610, 1612. Two panels: Annunciation (st.; companions to Leningrad).

Munich. 1075. Lamentation, with SS. Jerome, Paul and Peter (g.p.).

Naples. 46. Madonna and Child with two Angels. E.

MUSEO FILANGERI. 1506B. Portrait of a young Man with a Glove. E. (Destroyed).

New Haven (Conn.). 1871.50. Madonna and Child (st.).

New York. 11.98. Scenes from the Life of S. Zenobius. (Companion to Dresden 9 and London 3918–19). L. *Plate* 1090.

14.40.642. Communion of S. Jerome. *Plate* 1087.

32.100.68. Portrait of a young Man.

41.109.9. Madonna and Child with two Angels (after Fra Filippo Lippi, Uffizi 1598; fr., r.). E.

49.7.4. Coronation of the Virgin, with SS. Anthony Abbot, John Baptist, Julian and Francis.

JOHN BASS. Coronation of the Virgin with Saints and Donors (st., r.; lower part perhaps by Bartolomeo di Giovanni; from S. Giusto, Volterra).

W. R. HEARST (EX). Portrait of Youth. (?)

ROBERT LEHMAN. Predella panel: Annunciation. *Plate* 1088.

MRS. JOHN D. ROCKEFELLER, JR. Madonna and Child with young S. John (r.).

Orvieto. DUOMO, MUSEO DELL'OPERA. Embroideries: Circumcision, Resurrection, Assumption.

Ottawa. 3524. Two Putti (st., r.).

Palermo. CHIARAMONTE BORDONARO COLLECTION. Tondo: Madonna and Child with S. Sebastian (st.).

Paris. MUSÉES NATIONAUX (CAMPANA 201). Madonna and Child (st.). E.

LOUVRE. 1296. Madonna and Child with young S. John (r.).

1297, 1298. Two frescoes (from Villa Lemmi): Lorenzo Tornabuoni presented to the Seven Liberal Arts; Giovanna degli Albizi and the Graces. ca 1486. [*Plate* 207.]

1298A. Madonna and Child. E. *Plate* 1072.

1300. Predella panel: S. Peter Martyr, Visitation, *Noli me tangere*, David, Meeting of SS. Francis and Dominic, S. Onuphrius (st.).

1300A. Madonna and Child with two Angels (c. by Sellaio).

1345. Madonna of Humility with five Angels (st.). E.

1657. Madonna and Child (st., r.).

1663. Portrait of a Man.

MUSÉE JACQUEMART-ANDRÉ. 739. Flight into Egypt (st.).

1048. S. Catherine of Siena (st.).

Parma. 56. *Madonna della Cintola* with SS. Benedict and Julian (st.).

Périgueux. See Paris, Musées Nationaux.

Philadelphia (Pa.). MUSEUM OF ART, JOHNSON COLLECTION. 44–47. Predella: S. Mary Magdalen attending Christ's preaching, Feast in the House of Simon, *Noli me tangere*, Ecstasy and Last Communion of S. Mary Magdalen. *Plate* 1076.

    48. Portrait of Lorenzo Lorenzano.

    50. Portrait of a young Man in a red Cap. E.

Piacenza. MUSEO CIVICO. Tondo: Madonna adoring the Child with Infant S. John (p.).

Pistoia. MUSEO CIVICO. Holy Family (g.p.).

Portland (Ore.). MUSEUM OF ART, KRESS COLLECTION. K 8917. Small cut-out Crucifix.

Raleigh (N.C.). MUSEUM OF ART, KRESS COLLECTION. K 2155. Tondo: Holy Family (st.).

Richmond (Surrey). COOK COLLECTION (EX). Allegorical Portrait of a Woman pressing Milk from her Breast (st.).

Rome. GALLERIA BORGHESE. 348. Tondo: Madonna and Child with young S. John and six Angels (g.p.). L.

    GALLERIA COLONNA. 218. S. James (st., fr.).

    PALAZZO ROSPIGLIOSI, PALLAVICINI COLLECTION. *La Derelitta*.

    Portable triptych: Transfiguration, and SS. Jerome and Augustine in their Studies (r.).

    VATICAN, SISTINE CHAPEL. Three frescoes: Moses and the Daughters of Jethro, Destruction of the Children of Korah, Purification of the Leper and Temptation of Christ. 1482. [*Plates* 208–209.] *Plates* 1081–2.

    Frescoes (between windows): Fourteen Popes. [Stephen (g.p.), Marcellinus (g.p.), Cornelius (p.), Lucius (p.), Sixtus II (p.), Evaristus (?), Soter (st.), Voius (st.), Telesphorus (st.), Anicetus (st.), Anterus (st.), Eutychian (st.), Callistus (st.), Fabian (st.)] (See also Domenico Ghirlandajo).

    — BIBLIOTECA. COD. URB. LAT. 508. Miniature: Federico da Montefeltro and a friend. 1482?

    — — COD. REG. LAT. 1896 B. Illustrations to Dante's Inferno: Canto I, X (u.), XV (see also Berlin).

Strasbourg. 215. Madonna and Child with two Angels (st. v.). E.

Turin. 110. Tondo: Madonna nursing the Child with young S. John and an Angel (st.).

Vienna. AKADEMIE. 1133. Tondo: Madonna and Child with two Angels.

Washington (D.C.). 19 (MELLON COLLECTION). Portrait of a Youth in a red Cap. [*Plate* 210.]

    21 (MELLON COLLECTION). Madonna and Child.

    22 (MELLON COLLECTION). Adoration of the Magi. [*Plate* 212.]

    714 (KRESS COLLECTION 1311). Madonna and Child with two Angels. E.

    1087 (KRESS COLLECTION 1432). Tondo: Madonna adoring the Child.

1135 (KRESS COLLECTION 1644). Portrait of Giuliano de' Medici. *Plate* 1078.
Zurich. ANNIE ABEGG-STOCKAR. Portrait of a Man as S. Augustine. *Plate* 1083.

BOTTICINI, Francesco

1446–98. Pupil of Neri di Bicci. Follower of Andrea del Castagno and Cosimo Rosselli; worked with Verrocchio; influenced by Botticelli, and, after 1480, by Filippino Lippi.

Amsterdam. 1478 B–I (FORMERLY OLDENBURG). Portrait of a young Man (r.).
Ashburnham Place (Sussex). LADY ASHBURNHAM (EX). Tondo: Madonna adoring the Child with Infant S. John. *Plate* 1067.
Autun. MUSÉE ROLIN (CAMPANA 345). Madonna adoring the Child with an Angel (r.).
Balcarres (Fife, Scotland). EARL OF CRAWFORD AND BALCARRES. Madonna and Child with S. Francis, Tobias and the Angel and a female Donor. *Plate* 1065.
Baltimore (Md.). MUSEUM OF ART. 38.224. Madonna and Child (r.).
Bergamo. 535. Tobias and the Angel.
Berlin. 70A. Crucifixion with SS. Anthony Abbot, Lawrence, Peter Martyr, Tobias and the Angel. d. 1475. (Destroyed 1945). *Plate* 1066.
28 72. Coronation of the Virgin with Saints and Angels. (Destroyed 1945).
Boston (Mass.). ISABELLA GARDNER MUSEUM. Madonna and Child with Infant S. John.
QUINCEY SHAW (EX). Tondo: Madonna and Child with Infant S. John.
Cambridge. M 10. Madonna adoring the Child.
Carrara. ACCADEMIA (GALL. FIOR. 8476). S. Sebastian.
Castle Ashby (Northants.). MARQUESS OF NORTHAMPTON. Tondo: Madonna adoring the Child with Infant S. John.
Chicago (Ill.). 37.997. Tondo: Adoration of the Magi. L.
Cincinnati (Ohio). 1948.201. Tondo (formerly Panciatichi and Benson): Madonna and Child. L. *Plate* 1068.
Cleveland (Ohio). 16.788. Madonna and Child.
Empoli. 25. Two panels: Annunciation.
26. Wings of tabernacle containing Rossellino's S. Sebastian: Two Angels with Donors. Predella: S. Sebastian at the Execution of Mark and Marcellinus, Condemnation of S. Sebastian, Attempted Martyrdom of S. Sebastian, Clubbing of S. Sebastian.
27. Tabernacle of the Holy Sacrament. Wings: SS. Andrew and John Baptist. Predella: Crucifixion of S. Andrew, Betrayal of Christ, Last Supper, Agony in the Garden, Feast of Herod and Beheading of S. John. 1484–91. *Plate* 1070.
28. Predella (?) panel: Music-making Angels.
Florence. GALLERIE. 8676. Tobias and the Angel with young Donor. *Plate* 1063.
ACCADEMIA. 8625, 8626. Two panels: SS. Augustine and Monica.
8656. Martyrdom of S. Andrew.

Florence (contd.). PITTI. 347. Tondo: Madonna adoring the Child with infant S. John and five Angels.

UFFIZI. 8359. Archangels Michael, Raphael with Tobias, and Gabriel. *Plate* 1062.

S. SPIRITO, L. TRANSEPT, 2nd CHAPEL R. S. Monica enthroned surrounded by Augustinian Nuns. Predella: Marriage of S. Monica, S. Monica praying for S. Augustine's Conversion, S. Augustine's Departure for Rome, S. Monica conversing with her son at Ostia and having a vision of Christ while receiving Last Communion, Funeral of S. Monica. *Plate* 1069.

(Environs) S. ANDREA A BROZZI, 2nd ALTAR R. Madonna and Child with SS. Sebastian, Bartholomew, James and Anthony Abbot (r.).

Fresco lunette: God the Father and two Angels (st.). d. 1480.

— BADIA FIESOLANA, 1st CHAPEL L. Lamentation with SS. Bernard and Sebastian.

Göttingen. 16. Madonna adoring the Child with Infant S. John (r.).

Kaliningrad. See Königsberg.

Königsberg (EX?). Madonna and Child with SS. Benedict, Martin, Jerome and a Bishop Saint. Predella: S. Benedict raising a Monk from the Ruins of Montecassino, S. Martin and the Beggar, Man of Sorrows, S. Jerome in the Wilderness.

Lille. 667. Ecstasy of S. Mary Magdalen (r.). (?)

London. 227. 'Rucellai' altarpiece: S. Jerome in the Wilderness and SS. Eusebius, Damasus, Paula and Eustochium. Predella: S. Jerome and the Lion, Vision of S. Jerome, Death of S. Jerome, S. Augustine's Vision of SS. Jerome and John Baptist.

781. Tobias and the Angel (on Verrocchio's design). (?)

1126. 'Palmieri' Assumption, with Saints and the Angelic Hierarchies. Before 1475. *Plates* 1060–1.

VISCOUNT ROTHERMERE (EX?). Madonna and Child.

Modena. 497. Madonna adoring the Child with Infant S. John and two Angels. E.

Montefortino (Amandola). PINACOTECA. Madonna adoring the Child.

Montreal. 1154. Madonna adoring the Child.

Panzano (Chianti). S. MARIA, 3rd CHAPEL L. Panel surrounding an earlier Image of the Madonna: SS. John Baptist, Jerome, Francis, a female Saint and two Angels holding a Crown.

Paris. 1482. Madonna and Child in Glory with Angels and SS. Mary Magdalen and Bernard. *Plate* 1064.

1683. Tondo: Madonna adoring the Child with Infant S. John and two Angels.

MUSÉE JACQUEMART–ANDRÉ. 763. Madonna and Child with SS. John Baptist, Pancras, Sebastian and Peter. d. 1471. *Plate* 1058.

944. *Pietà*, with SS. Louis of Toulouse, Dominic, James and Nicholas.

MUSÉE DE CLUNY. 1698. Triptych: Madonna and Child. Wings: S. Dominic and a Bishop Saint, SS. Thomas Aquinas and Nicholas.

HEUGEL COLLECTION (EX?). Nativity with Infant S. John.

Prato. 22. Madonna nursing the Child, with SS. Jerome, Francis, Anthony of Padua and Louis of Toulouse.

Richmond (Surrey). COOK COLLECTION (EX). 25. Portrait of a young Man.

Stockholm. ROYAL PALACE. Tondo: Portrait of a young Man (r.).

Turin. 119. Coronation of the Virgin.

GUALINO COLLECTION (EX). Madonna adoring the Child.

Venice. CA' D'ORO. Madonna adoring the Child.

Homeless. Madonna and Child with two Angels and SS. Benedict, Francis, Silvester and Anthony Abbot. 1470-75. *Plate* 1059.

BRONZINO (Angelo Allori)

1503-1572. Pupil of Pontormo; influenced by Michelangelo.

Antwerp. MAYER VAN DEN BERGH MUSEUM. 474. Full-length Portrait of a Man in Armour, called 'Francesco de' Medici'. (?)

Bergamo. 567. Portrait of Alessandro de' Medici (st.).

Berlin. 338. Portrait of a young Man with a Letter.

338A. Portrait of Ugolino Martelli. Sd. [*Plate* 231.]

338B. Portrait of Eleonora da Toledo.

Besançon. 799.1.29. *Pietà* (central panel of triptych already finished in 1545; companion to Lima). Sd. *Plate* 1448.

Bignor Park (Pulborough, Sussex). VISCOUNTESS MERSEY. Portrait of a Man with a Book and a Statue of Bacchus. [*Plate* 232 (*sic*).]

Boston (Mass.). 29.786. Portrait of a young Man writing.

ISABELLA GARDNER MUSEUM. Portrait of a Woman. L.

Budapest. 161. Adoration of the Shepherds. Sd. *Plate* 1441.

163. Venus, Cupid and Jealousy. Sd. *Plate* 1453.

4222. Portrait of (Bianca Cappello?).

Chicago (Ill.). 33.1002. Portrait of (?) Alessandro de' Medici.

Cincinnati (Ohio). 1927.381. Portrait of Eleonora da Toledo with Don Ferdinando. *Plate* 1446.

Detroit (Mich.). 35.8. Portrait of a Woman, called 'Costanza da Somaia' (st.).

42.57. Portrait of Eleonora da Toledo with her Son (p., replica of Uffizi 784).

Faenza. PINACOTECA. Portrait of Luca Martini, with a Basket of Fruit.

Fiesole. VILLA LIMONAIA, MAX RUDOLF VON BUCH. 'Crawford' Portrait of Eleonora da Toledo.

Florence. GALLERIE. 1554. Lamentation. Sd.

1613. Half-length Portrait of Cosimo I in Armour.

5959. Portrait of the Dwarf Morgante (front view and back view).

8739. Three-quarter length Portrait of Cosimo I in Armour.

BRONZINO

Florence (contd.). ACCADEMIA. 3941. Deposition from Cosmopoli, Elba (p.). 1565.

PITTI. 149. Portrait of Guidobaldo da Montefeltro, Duke of Urbino. 1531.

206. Portrait of Francesco I de' Medici (st.).

380. Bust of old Lady.

434. Portrait of Luca Martini, with a Map. L.

(539). Tapestry: Truth, Time, Innocence and Justice. 1546.

(541). Tapestry: Flora. 1546.

(721). Tapestry: Coat of Arms of Cosimo I and Eleonora da Toledo.

UFFIZI. 28 Dep. Portrait of Cosimo I in Armour (p.).

736. Portrait of Lucrezia Panciatichi.

741. Portrait of Bartolomeo Panciatichi. *Plate* 1442.

748. Portrait of Eleonora da Toledo with her Son. [*Plate* 233.]

770. Portrait of a Girl with a Prayerbook.

793. Portrait of a Woman, with a Statuette of Michelangelo's Rachel. L.

1472. Portrait of Pia de' Medici. Before 1542.

1475. Portrait of Don Garzia de' Medici as a Child. *Plate* 1449.

1543. Allegory of Felicity. L.

1571. Portrait of Don Ferdinando de' Medici.

1572. Portrait of Maria de' Medici. [*Plate* 234.]

1575. Portrait of a young Man with a Lute.

8377. 'Panciatichi' Holy Family with Infant S. John. Sd. *Plate* 1447.

8545. Lamentation. E.

MUSEO NAZIONALE DEL BARGELLO. (732; Old Inv. 19). Tapestry: Death of Jacob. (See Palazzo Vecchio, Sala dei Dugento). 1553.

MUSEO STIBBERT. 12718. Portrait of Francesco de' Medici. L.

PALAZZO RICCARDI, MUSEO MEDICEO. Eight of the twenty-four miniature portraits of members of the Medici family, from the *Scrittoio delle Muse* in the Palazzo Vecchio (p.).

PALAZZO VECCHIO, CAPPELLA DI ELEONORA DA TOLEDO. Frescoes. Ceiling: Trinity and SS. Michael, Francis, Jerome and John Evangelist (1540–41). Walls: Crossing of the Red Sea (1541–42), The Brazen Serpent (1542), Moses striking Water from the Rock, Fall of Manna (1542–45). *Plates* 1454, 1456. Triptych: Pietà; Annunciation. Sd. 1553–64.

— SALA DEI DUGENTO. Nine tapestries: (723; Old Inv. 17). Meeting of Joseph and Jacob in Egypt. 1553.

(724; Old Inv. 15). Joseph making himself known to his Brothers. 1553.

(725; Old Inv. 11). Benjamin received by Joseph. Sd. 1553.

(726; Old Inv. 16). Joseph receiving his Brothers. 1553.

(727; Old Inv. 9). Joseph selling Corn to his Brothers. 1546.

(728; Old Inv. 7). Joseph explaining Pharaoh's Dreams. 1549.

(729; Old Inv. 6). Joseph and Potiphar's Wife. Sd. 1549. *Plate* 1455.

(730; Old Inv. 1). Joseph's Dream of the Sheaves of Wheat. 1549.

(731; Old Inv. 2). Joseph's Dream of the Sun, Moon and Stars. 1549. (Companions to Bargello; to Rome, Palazzo Quirinale; and to Pontormo, Rome, Palazzo Quirinale. 1546–53).

—STUDIOLO. Tondi: Portraits of Cosimo I and Eleonora da Toledo (st.).

— (LOESER BEQUEST). Portrait of Laura Battiferri Ammannati. L. *Plate* 1460.

SS. ANNUNZIATA, CHOIR, 4th CHAPEL (GUADAGNI). Resurrection. 1548–52.

BADIA, CLOISTER. Fresco: S. Benedict in the Wilderness. E. *Plate* 1439.

S. CROCE, MUSEO DELL'OPERA. Descent into Limbo. Sd and d. 1552. *Plate* 1457.

S. FELICITA (CAPPELLA CAPPONI). Tondi (in spandrels): Four Evangelists (assisting Pontormo). E.

S. LORENZO. L. WALL. Fresco: Martyrdom of S. Lawrence. Sd. 1565–69.

S. MARIA NOVELLA, 2nd CHAPEL L. OF CHOIR (GADDI). Raising of the Daughter of Jairus (p.). 1571–72. *Plate* 1458.

REGINA DELLA PACE. Immaculate Conception (finished by assistants after his death). 1572.

(Environs) CERTOSA DEL GALLUZZO, OVER DOOR TO CLOISTER. Two fresco lunettes: Martyrdom of S. Lawrence, Man of Sorrows (r.). E.

Kansas City (Mo.). 49.28. Portrait of a Man with a Sword.

Leningrad (Environs). PAVLOVSK PALACE. Madonna and Child with Infant S. John (c. ?).

Lima. NEUHAUS COLLECTION. S. John Baptist (companion to Besançon). Before 1545.

London. 651. Venus, Cupid, Folly and Time.

1323. Portrait of Piero de' Medici.

5280. Madonna and Child with S. Elizabeth and Infant S. John.

Lucca. 23. Portrait of Don Garzia de' Medici.

25. Portrait of Ferdinando de' Medici.

Milan. BRERA. 565. Portrait of Andrea Doria as Neptune. *Plate* 1451.

Montreal. ROBERT W. REFORD. Portrait of a young Man. (Partial replica of Bignor Park).

Moscow. PUSHKIN MUSEUM. 2699. 'Stroganoff' Holy Family with Infant S. John.

New York. 29.100.16. Portrait of a young Man with a Book.

FRICK COLLECTION. 123. Portrait of a young Man, called 'Ludovico Capponi'.

Ottawa. 3717. Portrait of a Man (Cosimo I?) with a Statuette of Venus.

Oxford. ASHMOLEAN. 77. Portrait of Don (Garzia? Giovanni?) de' Medici. *Plate* 1450.

Paris. 1183. *Noli me tangere.* L.

1183A. Holy Family with S. Elizabeth and Infant S. John. (Replica of Vienna).

1184. Portrait of a Man with a Statuette, called the 'Sculptor'.

Philadelphia (Pa.). MUSEUM OF ART. 50–86–1. Orpheus. *Plate* 1444.

Pisa. S. STEFANO, 2nd ALTAR L. Nativity. 1564–65.

Pittsburgh (Pa.). EDGAR KAUFMANN. Portrait of a Man with a Medal, called 'Francesco de' Medici'.

Portland (Ore.). ART MUSEUM. KRESS COLLECTION. K 1730. Madonna and Child with
Infant S. John.

Rome. GALLERIA BORGHESE. 444. S. John Baptist. Sd.

   GALLERIA COLONNA. 56. Venus, Cupid and a Satyr. Sd.

     155. Madonna and Child with S. Elizabeth and Infant S. John.

   GALLERIA DORIA PAMPHILJ, PRIVATE APARTMENTS. Portrait of Don Giannettino Doria.
Portrait of Andrea Doria as Neptune (replica of Milan).

   GALLERIA NAZIONALE (PALAZZO BARBERINI). F.N.2171. Portrait of Stefano Colonna.
Sd and d. 1546. *Plate* 1452.

   PALAZZO QUIRINALE. Six tapestries from the Joseph series, after his designs, but of
Flemish workmanship (see Florence, Palazzo Vecchio, Sala dei Dugento):

     (Old Inv. 3). Joseph sold by his Brothers. Sd. Before 1549.

     (Old Inv. 10). Simon held captive. 1547.

     (Old Inv. 12). Joseph's Feast. d. 1549.

     (Old Inv. 13). Discovery of the Cup in Benjamin's Sack. 1549.

     (Old Inv. 18). Jacob and his Tribes welcomed by Pharaoh. Sd. 1553.

     (Old Inv. 20). Burial of Joseph. 1553.

San Francisco (Cal.). M. H. DE YOUNG MEMORIAL MUSEUM, KRESS COLLECTION. K 61.
Portrait of an Old Woman with a Book. *Plate* 1443.

Stockholm. 37. Portrait of Isabella de' Medici (st.).

Strasbourg. 261. Portrait of a Man, called 'Antonio Bandini', and his Wife.

Toledo (Ohio). 13.232. Portrait of Cosimo I in Armour (p.). *Plate* 1445.

Vienna. 49. Holy Family with S. Elizabeth and Infant S. John. Sd.

Washington (D.C.). 602 (WIDENER COLLECTION). Portrait of a Woman with a Child.
1364 (KRESS COLLECTION 2068). Portrait of Eleonora da Toledo. *Plate* 1459.

Worcester (Mass.). 1910.20. Portrait of a Woman, called 'Donna Chevara', with a
Child. L.

Homeless. Madonna and Child with Infant S. John. *Plate* 1440.

BUGIARDINI, Giuliano

*1475–1554. Pupil of Domenico Ghirlandajo and Piero di Cosimo; friend of Michelangelo;
assistant of Albertinelli; influenced by Perugino, Francia, Franciabigio and Giorgione.*

Allentown (Pa.). ART MUSEUM, KRESS COLLECTION. K162. Madonna and Child with
Infant S. John. Sd. *Plate* 1259.

Balcarres (Fife, Scotland). EARL OF CRAWFORD AND BALCARRES (EX). Madonna and
Child with Infant S. John.

Bergen.† Tondo: Holy Family with Infant S. John. (?)

Berlin. 285 (EX BONN). Madonna and Child with Infant S. John. (Destroyed 1945).
(BERLIN-OST). 142, 149. Two cassone panels: Story of Tobias.

283. Madonna adoring the Child with SS. Philip, John Evangelist, Jerome and Joseph. Sd. *Plate 1264.*

KUNSTGEWERBE MUSEUM. Cassone: Story of S. Lucy. (Destroyed).

COUNT SAURMA (EX). Madonna and Child with Infant S. John.

Bologna. 25. S. John Baptist in the Wilderness.

26. Marriage of S. Catherine, with S. Anthony of Padua and Infant S. John. Sd.

745. Tondo: Madonna and Child with Infant S. John.

Bonn. 35. See Berlin 285.

Copenhagen. 3919. *Caritas.*

Figline (Valdarno Superiore). (Environs) S. PIERO AL TERRENO, HIGH ALTAR. Madonna and Child with SS. Peter, Jerome, Francis and Paul. ca 1532.

Florence. GALLERIE. 789. Madonna nursing the Child.

3121. Madonna and Child with Infant S. John Sd and d. 1520. *Plate 1258.*

8380. Portrait of a Woman, called *La Monaca. Plate 1256.*

PITTI. 64. Lamentation (begun by Fra Bartolommeo).

CASA BUONARROTI. Portrait of Michelangelo in a Turban. *Plate 1261.*

MUSEO BARDINI. 1160. Madonna and Child (r.). (?)

S. CROCE, MUSEO DELL'OPERA. Four panels: SS. Nicholas, John Baptist, Anthony Abbot and Bartholomew (st.).

S. MARIA NOVELLA, CAPPELLA RUCELLAI. Martyrdom of S. Catherine. *Plate 1263.*

Keir (Dunblane, Scotland). LT.-COL. W. STIRLING, Madonna and Child with Infant S. John.

Leipzig. 21. Madonna and Child with Infant S. John. Sd.

Leningrad. 66. Tondo: Holy Family with Infant S. John.

London. LORD NORTHBROOK (EX). S. John Baptist in the Wilderness. *Plate 1254.*

Milan. PINACOTECA AMBROSIANA. 24. Madonna and Child with Infant S. John.

S. MARIA DELLE GRAZIE, SACRISTY. S. John Baptist in the Wilderness. Sd.

Modena. 506. Birth of S. John Baptist (version of Stockholm).

Naples. S. MARIA DEL POPOLO (OSPEDALE DEGLI INCURABILI). Pietà. Sd.

New Haven (Conn.). 1959.15.20. Portrait of (Francesco Guicciardini?). After 1534.

New Orleans. ISAAC DELGADO MUSEUM OF ART, KRESS COLLECTION. K 1172. S. Sebastian.

New York. 30.83. Madonna and Child with SS. Mary Magdalen and John Baptist.

30.95.270. Madonna and Child with Infant S. John and an Angel.

Nivaagaard (Copenhagen). HAGE COLLECTION. Madonna and Child with Infant S. John. *Plate 1255.*

Paris. MUSÉE DES ARTS DÉCORATIFS, LEGS PEYRE. Portrait of a Woman with a Prayerbook.

MUSÉE JACQUEMART-ANDRÉ. 672. Portrait of a Woman.

LUCIEN COTTREAU (EX). Fall of Man. *Plate 1262.*

DUC DE GRAMMONT (EX?). Tondo: Madonna and Child with Infant S. John.

Portland (Ore.). MUSEUM OF ART, KRESS COLLECTION. K X–3. Portrait of a Man called 'Taddeo Taddei'. (?)

Rome. GALLERIA COLONNA. 215. Madonna and Child. Sd. E.

MUSEO DI PALAZZO VENEZIA. Portrait of Leo X, Cardinal Giulio de' Medici and
Cardinal Cybo. (Copy after Raphael, with identity of right figure changed).

Stockholm. UNIVERSITY GALLERY. 216. Birth of S. John Baptist. Sd and d. 1512.
Plate 1253.

Turin. 114. Tondo: Madonna and Child with Infant S. John.

MUSEO CIVICO (PALAZZO MADAMA). Madonna and Child with Infant S. John (after
Albertinelli). (?)

Venice. CA' D'ORO. Sleeping Venus. *Plate* 1257.

Vienna. 36. Rape of Dinah (begun by Fra Bartolommeo). 1531. *Plate* 1260.

Volterra. 47–49. Three fragments of an altarpiece: Heads of the Virgin, a Saint and
a *Putto*.

CASTAGNO, Andrea del

Castagno, ca 1421–Florence, 1457. Influenced by Donatello and Uccello.

Berlin. 47A. Assumption with SS. Julian and Miniato (from S. Miniato fra le Torri).
1449–50. *Plates* 757–758.

Florence. MUSEO DEL CASTAGNO (CENACOLO DI S. APOLLONIA). Frescoes: Last Supper,
Resurrection, Crucifixion, Entombment. 1445–50. [*Plate* 149]. *Plate* 753–756.

Eleven frescoes from the Villa Carducci Pandolfini at Legnaia: Pippo Spanoi
Farinata degli Uberti, Niccolò Acciauoli, the Cumaean Sibyl, Esther, Thomy-
ris, Dante, Petrarch, Boccaccio and two fragments of decorative frieze of putt,
with garlands. [*Plate* 146]. *Plate* 759.

Fresco lunette: Man of Sorrows supported by two Angels. 1445–50.

Fresco lunette (from the Convento degli Angioli): Crucifixion with the Virgin,
S. John and SS. Benedict and Romuald. L. *Plates* 762, 764.

SS. ANNUNZIATA, 1st CHAPEL L. Fresco: Christ the Redeemer and S. Julian.
[*Plate* 148].

—2nd CHAPEL L. Fresco: Trinity and SS. Mary of Cleophas, Jerome, and Mary
Magdalen.

S. MARIA DEL FIORE (DUOMO), L. WALL, 2nd BAY. Fresco: Equestrian Portrait of
Niccolò da Tolentino. 1456. *Plate* 761.

—CUPOLA. Circular window: Deposition. 1444.

S. MINIATO AL MONTE, SACRISTY. Fresco over lavabo: Isaiah (r.).

SPEDALE DI S. MARIA NUOVA. Fresco: Crucifixion with the Virgin, Mary Magdalen, S. John and SS. Benedict and Romuald. E.

CONTINI BONACOSSI COLLECTION. Fresco (from Castello del Trebbio): Madonna
and Child with Angels and SS. John Baptist and Jerome, and two children.
E. *Plate* 749.

(Environs) SOFFIANO, VILLA CARDUCCI PANDOLFINI A LEGNAIA. Frescoes: Madonna and Child under a Baldacchino supported by two Angels, Adam and Eve (fr., r.; see Florence, Museo del Castagno). *Plate 760.*

London. 1138. Predella panel: Crucifixion. (Companion to New York, Frick).

New York. 48.78. S. Sebastian (r.). (?).

FRICK COLLECTION. S.19. Predella panel: Resurrection. (Companion to London).

Venice. S. MARCO, CHIESETTA DI S. TEODORO. Mosaic over entrance: S. Theodore.

S. ZACCARIA, CAPPELLA DI S. TARASIO. Frescoes. Vault: God the Father and SS. John Baptist, Matthew, Mark, John Evangelist, Luke and Zacharias. Entrance arch: Decoration of Putti, Garlands and Prophets (g.p., with Francesco da Faenza). Sd. by both artists and d. 1442. *Plates 750–752.*

Washington (D.C.). 17 (MELLON COLLECTION). Portrait of a young Man. [Formerly listed as by Pollajuolo. *Plate 169.*]

604 (WIDENER COLLECTION). A shield: David. L. [*Plate 147*].

Westport House (County Mayo, Ireland). MARQUESS OF SLIGO (EX). Portrait of a young Man.

CENNI DI FRANCESCO DI SER CENNI

Follower of Agnolo Gaddi, documented 1415.

Florence (Environs). S. MARTINO A SESTO. Pentecost. Predella: Dormition. (?)

Lawrence (Kansas). UNIVERSITY OF KANSAS, KRESS COLLECTION. K 268. Madonna and Child. *Plate 361.*

Little Rock (Arkansas). FINE ARTS CLUB, KRESS COLLECTION. K 1016. Predella panel: Martyrdom of S. Stephen. (?)

San Miniato al Tedesco. PALAZZO COMUNALE, SALA DEL CONSIGLIO. Fresco: Madonna and Child with the Cardinal and the Theological Virtues. d. 1393. *Plate 359.*

S. DOMENICO, CHAPEL LEFT OF CHOIR. S. Jerome in his Study. (?)

Volterra. PINACOTECA. Triptych; Madonna of Humility with SS. Nicholas, James, Christopher and Anthony Abbot. d. 1408. (?)

S. FRANCESCO, ORATORIO DELLA COMPAGNIA DELLA CROCE DI GIORNO. Frescoes. Vault of 2nd bay: SS. Francis, Anthony of Padua, Bonaventura. Pilasters dividing the two bays: S. Francis receiving Stigmata, S. John Baptist. Soffit: ten busts of Saints. Walls: Life of Virgin [Nativity, Massacre of Innocents, Flight into Egypt, Circumcision, Angel bringing warning of death to Mary, Holy Sepulchre, Dormition] and Legend of the True Cross [Seth receiving a branch of the Tree of Knowledge and planting it on Adam's grave, the Queen of Sheba recognizing the Holy Wood, Recovery of the Wood and Manufacture of the Cross, Invention of the True Cross, S. Helena taking the Cross to Jerusalem, Theft of the Cross by King Cosroes, Throne of Cosroes, Dream of Heraclius, Cosroes is beheaded and Heraclius returns the Cross to Jerusalem]. Window embrasures: Busts of Angels. Sd and d. 1410. *Plates* 360, 362.

CIMABUE

Active ca 1272–1302. Completed the revolution in Tuscan painting inaugurated earlier in the thirteenth century by Byzantine artists, apparently of popular monastic tendencies, who migrated to Pisa, Lucca and Florence.

Arezzo. S. DOMENICO, HIGH ALTAR. Crucifix. E. *Plates* 1–3.

Assisi. S. FRANCESCO, LOWER CHURCH, R. TRANSEPT. Fresco: Madonna and Child enthroned with four Angels, and S. Francis. *Plates* 7, 71.

    S. FRANCESCO, UPPER CHURCH, VAULT OF CROSSING. Frescoes: Four Evangelists. *Plates* 8–9.

— APSE. Frescoes: Scenes from the Life of the Virgin [Left wall, reading from the top: Annunciation to Joachim, Presentation in the Temple, Madonna flanked by two Angels, Gallery with three Bishop Saints, The Virgin taking leave of the Apostles. Middle walls: Dormition (below left window), Assumption (below right window). Right wall, reading from the top: Birth of the Virgin, Marriage of the Virgin, Madonna and Child flanked by two figures, Gallery with three Bishop Saints, Coronation. Window embrasures and soffits: Saints] (r.). *Plate* 13.

— RIGHT TRANSEPT. Frescoes: Scenes illustrating the Apostolic Mission [Reading from the top, left wall: Christ in Glory with Symbols of the Evangelists, Gallery with six Apostles, SS. Peter and John healing the Lame, S. Peter healing the Sick. Window wall: two Saints, Fall of Simon Magus, Crucifixion of S. Peter. Right wall: Transfiguration, Gallery with six Apostles, Crucifixion] (r.). *Plate* 17.

— LEFT TRANSEPT. Frescoes: Scenes from the Apocalypse [Right wall, reading from the top: Triumph of S. Michael, Galleries and soffits with Angels, S. John on Patmos and Fall of Babylon. Window wall, lower register: Christ the Judge, Four Angels of the Apocalypse, Adoration of the Mystic Lamb. Left wall, lower register: Crucifixion] (r.). *Plates* 11–12, 15, 19.

— NAVE, VAULT OF SECOND BAY FROM TRANSEPT. Frescoes: Christ the Redeemer, Virgin, SS. John Baptist and Francis, Angels (st., r.). *Plate* 18.

— THREE BAYS NEAREST TRANSEPT, UPPER REGISTER. Frescoes: Scenes from the Old and New Testament. [Right wall: Creation of the World, Creation of Adam, Creation of Eve, Fall of Man, Expulsion from Paradise, Building of the Ark, Sacrifice of Isaac, Animals entering the Ark, Sacrifice of Isaac, Abraham and the Angels. Left wall: Annunciation, Visitation, Nativity, Adoration of Magi, Presentation in the Temple, Flight into Egypt, Marriage at Cana, Raising of

Assisi, San Francesco: Naves of the Upper Church and of the Lower Church. Pen drawing by L. Carpinelli and G. B. Mariani (early nineteenth century).

Assisi, San Francesco: Apse and Transept of the Upper Church. Pen drawing by L. Carpinelli and G. B. Mariani (early nineteenth century).

Lazarus, Betrayal of Christ, Christ before Pliate, Way to Calvary, Crucifixion]
(st. r.; Presentation, Way to Calvary and Crucifixion by a Roman artist
following the scheme laid out by Cimabue). *Plates* 14, 16, 20, 21.

— NAVE, SOFFITS. Frescoes: Saints and Prophets (st., r.).

Bologna. S. MARIA DEI SERVI, AMBULATORY, CHAPEL L. Madonna and Child enthroned
with two Angels. *Plate* 23.

Chambéry. MUSÉE. Panel from a polyptych: S. John Baptist. (Companion to
Washington and Paris, Artaud de Montor.) E. *Plate* 4.

Florence. UFFIZI. 8343. Madonna and Child enthroned with eight Angels and four
Prophets. L. [*Plates* 105–6.] *Plate* 6.

PALAZZO VECCHIO (LOESER BEQUEST). Crucifix.

BAPTISTERY. Mosaic: Birth of S. John Baptist (p.).

S. CROCE, MUSEO DELL'OPERA. Crucifix.

S. MARIA NOVELLA, 1st CHAPEL R. OF CHOIR. Two fresco lunettes: Christ in Glory
with two Angels, S. Gregory enthroned with two Acolytes (r.). (?)

CONTINI BONACOSSI COLLECTION. Madonna and Child enthroned with two Angels
and SS. Francis and Dominic (st.).

(Environs) PATERNO, S. STEFANO. Crucifix (st.).

Mosciano. PARISH CHURCH. Madonna enthroned. E.

New York. FRICK COLLECTION. S.15. Flagellation (p.).

Paris. 1260. Madonna and Child enthroned with six Angels. *Plate* 5.

ARTAUD DE MONTOR (EX). Panel from a polyptych: S. Ursula. (Companion to
Chambéry and Washington). E. *Plate* 4.

Pisa. DUOMO, APSE. Mosaic: Christ enthroned with the Virgin and S. John (p.).
1301. *Plate* 22.

Turin. GALLERIA SABAUDA. 'Gualino' Madonna. E.

Washington (D.C.). 2 (MELLON COLLECTION). Three panels from a polyptych:
Salvator mundi, with SS. Peter and James. (Companions to Chambéry and
Paris, Artaud de Montor). E. *Plate* 4.

1139 (KRESS COLLECTION K 1549). Madonna and Child with two Angels and
SS. John Baptist and Peter (st.).

CRISTIANI, Giovanni di Bartolomeo

Pistoiese. Active in the second half of the fourteenth century.

Berea (Ky.). COLLEGE, KRESS STUDY COLLECTION. K 108. Madonna and Child with
two Angels and SS. Julian and Anthony Abbot.

Biella. ORESTE RIVETTI. Triptych: Madonna and Child with SS. Nicholas and John
Baptist. Pinnacles: Christ blessing, Annunciation. Sd.

Fiesole. MUSEO BANDINI. Two panels: SS. Dominic and Bartholomew. (?)

Florence. ACCADEMIA. 8704–05, 8708–09. See (Environs) Bagno a Ripoli.

S. AMBROGIO, R. OF HIGH ALTAR. Tabernacle: Madonna and Child with a Donor and SS. Anthony Abbot and James. Pinnacle: Christ blessing. *Plate* 334.

ACTON COLLECTION. Triptych: Madonna and Child with four angels and SS. James, John Baptist, Anthony Abbot and a Bishop Saint. Above: Annunciation, S. Ursula and S. Margaret. *Plates* 331, 333.

H. BLAKISTON WILKINS (EX). Triptych: Madonna and Child with SS. Leonard, Michael, John Baptist and Paul. Above: Christ blessing, Two Angels, Two Prophets.

(Environs) BAGNO A RIPOLI, S. MARIA DI QUARTO, CHOIR (ACCADEMIA 8704–05, 8708–09). Four panels: SS. Jerome, John Baptist, Peter and Paul. (?)

Kansas City (Mo.). 35.25. Annunciation.

Lewisburg (Penna.). BUCKNELL UNIVERSITY, KRESS STUDY COLLECTION. K 1161. Predella panel: Annunciation.

London. 4208. Baptism of Christ.

Moscow. 176. Madonna and Child with four Angels.

New Haven (Conn.). 1943.215. S. Lucy enthroned, with six Angels. *Plate* 328.

New York. 12.41.1–4. Four panels: SS. Lucy and Eustachia at the Tomb of S. Agatha, S. Lucy distributing her Fortune, S. Lucy before the Prefect, S. Lucy standing fast against the Oxen. *Plate* 329–330.

Pistoia. MUSEO CIVICO. Madonna and Child with six Angels. Sd. *Plate* 335.
S. John Evangelist.

S. GIOVANNI FUORCIVITAS. S. John Evangelist and eight Scenes from his Life [Arrival at Ephesus, Raising of Drusiana, Drusiana serving S. John, Crato's Followers destroying their Patrimony, Conversion of Crato and his Followers, Acteus and Eugenius meeting their former Servants, S. John restoring their Wealth, Raising of Satheus]. Sd and d. 1370. *Plates* 325–327.

Ponce (Puerto Rico). MUSEO DE ARTE, KRESS STUDY COLLECTION. K 1119. Madonna and Child.

Rome. BARONE ALBERTO FASSINI (EX). Two panels: SS. Paul and Elizabeth of Hungary.

Vienna. AUSPITZ COLLECTION (EX). Madonna and Child with SS. Stephen, John Baptist, Lawrence and Anthony Abbot. Above: Christ blessing. (?)

Homeless. *Salvator Mundi* (fr.). *Plate* 332.

DADDI, Bernardo

Active ca 1312–1348. Pupil of Giotto, influenced by the S. Cecilia Master, Ambrogio Lorenzetti and thirteenth-century French sculpture.

Ajaccio (Corsica). 67. Last Judgement. (?)
Altenburg. 13. Coronation of the Virgin.

Altenburg (contd.). 14. Crucifixion.

> 15. Portable triptych: Madonna and Child with four Angels and six Saints. Wings: Annunciation, Nativity, Crucifixion.

Altomonte (Calabria). S. MARIA DELLA CONSOLAZIONE. Two panels from an altarpiece: SS. John Baptist and Mary Magdalen, A Bishop Saint and S. James. Pinnacles: Two Evangelists (st.).

Baltimore (Md.). WALTERS ART GALLERY. 553. Madonna and Child.

> 734. Portable triptych: Madonna and Child with four Saints. Wings: Nativity, Crucifixion (st.).

Bayonne. 2. Crucifixion (r.).

> 971. Virgin Annunciate.

Berlin. 1064. Triptych: Coronation of the Virgin, Nativity, and Crucifixion. Pinnacles: Christ blessing and two Evangelists.

> 1064A. Triptych: Madonna and Child with SS. Salvius and Bernardo degli Uberti. Pinnacles: SS. Benedict, Paul and Peter. (Predella by Bicci di Lorenzo). (Destroyed 1945).

> 1094. Predella panel: S. Thomas Aquinas resisting Seduction with the Aid of Angels (companion to New Haven 1871.6; Paris, Musée des Arts Décoratifs; and Poznan; from S. Maria Novella, 1338?). *Plate* 173.

> VON GOLDAMMER COLLECTION (EX). Madonna and Child with four Angels and SS. John Baptist and Peter (st.).

Berne. 871. Portable triptych: Crucifixion. Wings: Annunciation, SS. Paul and Peter, Madonna and Child (st., r.).

> 880. Two panels (joined): SS. Thomas Aquinas and Paul. (Companions to Rome, Vatican 174).

> 883. Crucifixion.

Boston (Mass.). 23.211. Crucifixion (st.).

> ISABELLA GARDNER MUSEUM. Madonna and Child. Pinnacle: Christ blessing. (Companion to Florence, ex-Loeser?)

Brussels. MLLE. MICHÈLE STOCLET. Left wing of a triptych: Arrival of S. Ursula at Basle (companion to Zurich).

> MME. PAUL PECHÈRE. Predella panel: S. Reparata in Prison. (Companion to Cologne, New York 41.190.15 and 43.98.3–4, and Rome, Principe Borghese).

> VAN GELDER COLLECTION. Three fragments of a predella (to Highnam polyptych?): SS. Lucy and Catherine, S. John Evangelist and a Bishop Saint. (Companions to London, Jones; and to Strasbourg).

Cambridge (Mass.). 1918.33. Portable triptych: Crucifixion. Wings: Agony in the Garden, SS. Peter, Paul, Catherine, Margaret, James and Benedict. d. 1334.

1923.35. Madonna and Child. Pinnacle: Christ blessing.

1929.234. Stigmatization of S. Francis.

1936.56. Panel from a polyptych: S. Gregory. Pinnacle: A Prophet. (Companion to Sherborn, Mrs. Pickhardt; and to Philadelphia). 1334.

Chicago (Ill.). 33.1032. Crucifixion.

Cologne. 878. Predella panel: Martyrdom of S. Reparata by Fire. (See Brussels, Pechère).

Columbia (S.C.). MUSEUM OF ART, KRESS COLLECTION. K 1089. Madonna and Child with twelve Saints. Pinnacle: Christ blessing (st.).

Cracow. 169. Predella panel: Baptism of S. Tiburtius (fr.; companion to Essen and Pisa).

Crespina (Pisa). S. MICHELE. S. Michael Archangel.

Dijon. 1470. Predella panel: Nativity (st.).

Edinburgh. 1904. Portable triptych: Crucifixion. Pinnacle: Christ blessing. Wings: Crucifixion of S. Peter, Nativity, S. Nicholas and the three Maidens, Madonna and Child with four Saints (g.p.). d. 1338.

Essen. MUSEUM FOLKWANG, PRIVATE LOAN. Predella panel: Marriage of S. Cecilia (companion to Cracow and Pisa).

Fiesole. MUSEO BANDINI. I, 10. Panel from a polyptych: S. John Evangelist (companion to Florence, Serristori and to Munich).

Florence. GALLERIE. 4668. Madonna and Child with two Angels and SS. John Baptist and John Evangelist (r.). d. 1333.

6165. The Virgin, called *La Ninna*, crowned by two Angels.

ACCADEMIA. 442. Crucifix (p.).

3449. Coronation of the Virgin with Angels and Saints. Pinnacles: Christ blessing and four Cherubim (p.).

3466. Madonna and Child enthroned (r.).

8563. Crucifixion; on back, S. Christopher (g.p.).

8564. Madonna and Child with eight Angels and SS. Peter and Paul. Sd. and d. 1334.

8566, 8567, 6152, 6153. Diptych: Madonna and Child with four Saints, Crucifixion. Predella: Three Living Kings and three Dead Kings.

8570. Crucifixion. Pinnacle: Christ blessing. d. 1343.

UFFIZI. 3073. Triptych: Madonna and Child with SS. Matthew and Nicholas. Pinnacles: Christ blessing and two Angels. Sd. and d. 1328. *Plate 164.*

8345. Panels from 'S. Pancrazio' polyptych: Madonna and Child with Angels and SS. Pancras, Zenobius, John Evangelist, John Baptist, Reparata and Miniato. Spandrels: Four Angels. Pinnacles: Ten Apostles and four Prophets. Predella: Joachim expelled from the Temple, Annunciation to Joachim, Meeting at the Golden Gate, Birth of the Virgin, Presentation of the Virgin, Annunciation, Nativity (see also Hampton Court). *Plates 177–179.*

MUSEO DEL BIGALLO. Portable triptych: Madonna and Child, and fourteen Saints. Pinnacle: Christ blessing. Wings, inside: S. Nicholas rescuing Adeodatus from the Service of the Pagan King, Nativity, S. Nicholas restoring Adeodatus to his Parents, Crucifixion. Wings, outside: SS. Margaret, Martin, Catherine and Christopher. d. 1333. *Plates 166, 167.*

Florence (contd.). MUSEO HORNE. 42, 43. Diptych: Madonna and Child with SS. Francis, John Baptist, James and Margaret. Crucifixion.

S. CROCE, 4th CHAPEL L. OF CHOIR (PULCI E BERALDI). Frescoes: Martyrdom of S. Lawrence, Martyrdom of S. Stephen.

S. MARIA DEL FIORE (DUOMO), L. OF ENTRANCE. S. Catherine, and a Donor. Pinnacle: Christ blessing.

— MUSEO DELL'OPERA. Madonna of the 'Magnificat', with SS. Catherine and Zenobius; above, Christ blessing; below, two female Donors. d. 1334. *Plate 165.*

S. MARIA NOVELLA, SPANISH CHAPEL. Polyptych: Madonna and Child with SS. Peter, John Evangelist, John Baptist and Matthew. Pinnacles: Christ blessing and four Prophets (p.). Sd and d. 1344. *Plates 235, 236.*

ORSANMICHELE. Madonna and Child with eight Angels in Tabernacle by Orcagna. 1347. *Plate 184.*

S. TRINITA, 1st CHAPEL L. (STROZZI). Fresco lunette: *Noli me tangere* (r.).

BORGO PINTI AND VIA DEGLI ALFANI. Tabernacle fresco: Madonna and Child with SS. John Baptist and Peter (r.).

ACTON COLLECTION. Madonna and Child (st.).

BERENSON COLLECTION. Madonna and Child with a Bird. Spandrels: Two Angels. *Plate 182.*

Crucifixion; on back, S. Christopher.

CHARLES LOESER (EX). Panel from an altarpiece: S. Dominic. (Companion to Boston, Gardner?)

SERRISTORI COLLECTION. Panel from a polyptych: S. Catherine. (Companion to Fiesole and Munich).

(Environs) BAGNO A RIPOLI, S. MARIA DI QUARTO, HIGH ALTAR. Two panels from a polyptych: SS. Bartholomew and Lawrence. (Companions to New York, ex-Hirsch; and to Vienna, ex-Lanckoronski).

— S. GIORGIO A RUBALLA, ALTAR R. Madonna and Child with four Angels and SS. Matthias and George. d. 1336.

— SIGNANO, S. GIUSTO, 1st ALTAR R. Madonna and Child with two Angels and SS. Peter and Paul.

Ghent. 1903A. Coronation of the Virgin with six music-making Angels. (Companion to Göttingen). L. (?)

Göttingen. 61. Two panels from an altarpiece: S. Catherine, S. Lawrence. (Companions to Ghent). L. (?)

Hamburg. KUNSTHALLE, WEDELLS COLLECTION (EX). Madonna and Child with SS. Francis and Mary Magdalen (r.).

Hampton Court. 1210. Predella panel to Florence, Uffizi 8345: Marriage of the Virgin (fr.).

Highnam Court (Glos.). GAMBIER-PARRY COLLECTION. Polyptych: Crucifixion, and SS. Lawrence, Andrew, Bartholomew, George, Paul, Peter, James and

Stephen. Pinnacles: Christ blessing and four Evangelists. Sd. and d. 1348. *Plate* 183.

Kansas City (Mo.). 39.14. Panel from a polyptych: S. John Evangelist. Pinnacle: A Prophet. (Companion to Radensleben).

46.1952 (KRESS COLLECTION 1300). Madonna and Child with eight Angels and eight Saints. Pinnacle: Christ blessing.

London. COURTAULD GALLERIES, LEE OF FAREHAM COLLECTION. 5. Madonna and Child with SS. Peter and Paul (st.).

WALLACE COLLECTION. 549. Nativity; on back, a Saint (fr.).

MRS. LAWRENCE JONES. Predella panel (to Highnam polyptych?): Madonna and Child with four Angels. (Companion to Brussels, van Gelder and to Strasbourg.)

COUNT SEILERN. Portable triptych: Madonna and Child with eight Angels and eight Saints. Pinnacle: Christ blessing. Wings, inside: Annunciation, Nativity, Crucifixion. Wings, outside: Two Bishop Saints, Adoration of the Magi. d. 1338. *Plates* 170–171.

ST. AUBYN COLLECTION (EX). The Centurion and four other figures from a Crucifixion (fr.; companion to Zagreb). *Plate* 168.

Lucarelli (Chianti). S. MARTINO. Polyptych: Madonna and Child with SS. Lucy, Nicholas, Gregory and Mary Magdalen. Pinnacles: Christ blessing and four Evangelists. (st.).

Lucca. CONTE CENAMI-SPADA. Coronation of the Virgin with eight music-making Angels (st.; companion to Parma 427 and 433).

Lugano. THYSSEN COLLECTION. 115. Madonna and Child.

Malines (Belgium). 23/39. Panel from an altarpiece: S. Peter. (Companion to San Francisco).

Milan. MUSEO POLDI PEZZOLI. Inv. 3195. Processional Crucifix (*recto* and *verso*).

BARONE ANREP. Fragment of predella: Nativity.

COMM. ALDO CRESPI. Coronation of the Virgin (st.). d. 1338.

Minneapolis (Minn.). 34.20. Portable triptych: Madonna and Child with four Saints. Wings: Annunciation, Stigmatization of S. Francis, Crucifixion. d. 1338.

Monterinaldi (Chianti). PARROCCHIALE. Polyptych: Madonna and Child with SS. Nicholas, Silvester, Catherine and Mary Magdalen. Pinnacles: Christ and the four Evangelists.

Munich. 10828. Panel from a polyptych: A Bishop Saint. (Companion to Fiesole and Florence, Serristori).

Nantes. 72. Madonna and Child with four Saints (st.).

Naples. 31. Madonna and Child.

39. Virgin, from a Coronation (fr.).

41. Left panel of diptych: Madonna and Child with SS. Bernard (?), Francis, Augustine and John Baptist. *Plate* 169.

New Haven (Conn.). 1871.6. Predella panel: S. Dominic's Vision of SS. Peter and Paul (from S. Maria Novella, 1338? See Berlin 1094). *Plate* 172.

—(EX). 1943.207. Crucifixion.

New Orleans (La.). I. DELGADO MUSEUM OF ART, KRESS COLLECTION. K 204. Polyptych: Madonna and Child with SS. John Gualbert, Pancras, Michael and Benedict. Pinnacles: Four Prophets or Evangelists (st.).

New York. 32.100.70. Portable triptych: Madonna and Child with four Angels and SS. Nicholas and Bartholomew. Wings: Annunciation, Stigmatization of S. Francis, Crucifixion.

41.100.15. Madonna and Child with eight Saints (st.).

41.190.12. Crucifixion.

41.190.15. Predella panel: S. Reparata tortured by hot Irons. (See Brussels, Pechère).

43.98.3. Predella panel: S. Reparata before Decius. (See Brussels, Pechère).

43.98.4. Predella panel: S. Reparata shorn of her Hair. (See Brussels, Pechère).

HISTORICAL SOCIETY. B–6, 7. Diptych: Madonna and Child with six Angels, Last Judgement (st.).

MORGAN LIBRARY (EX). Madonna and Child with SS. John Gualbert, John Baptist, Nicholas and Francis.

DR. JAKOB HIRSCH (EX). Panel from a polyptych: S. Cecilia. (Companion to Florence, Bagno a Ripoli and to Vienna, ex-Lanckoronski).

ROBERT LEHMAN. Madonna and Child enthroned.

Diptych: Madonna and Child with four Saints, Crucifixion.

North Mimms (Herts.). MRS. WALTER BURNS. S. Catherine.

S. Louis of Toulouse, with two Angels and a Donor (st.).

Oxford. ASHMOLEAN. 271. Entombment.

Paris. 1301. Predella panel: Annunciation.

1667. Triptych: Madonna and Child with Angels and four Saints, Nativity, Crucifixion. Pinnacles: Christ blessing and Annunciation.

MUSÉE DES ARTS DECORATIFS, LEGS PEYRE. Predella panel: Preaching of S. Peter Martyr (from S. Maria Novella, 1338? See Berlin 1094). *Plate* 174.

Parma. 427, 433. Wings of a triptych: SS. Catherine, Ursula, Reparata, Mary Magdalen and other female Saints and Angels: SS. Peter, James, John Evangelist, John Baptist and other male Saints and Angels (st.; companion to Lucca).

446. Triptych: Madonna and Child with SS. Peter and Paul. E. *Plate* 163.

Philadelphia (Pa.). MUSEUM OF ART, JOHNSON COLLECTION. Inv. 344. Three panels from a polyptych: Madonna and Child with SS. John Baptist and Giles. Pinnacles: Christ blessing and two Prophets. (Companions to Cambridge 1936.56 and Sherborn, Mrs. Pickhardt). d. 1334.

Pisa. 39, 41. Two predella panels: S. Cecilia urging Valerian to Conversion, Martyrdom of S. Cecilia. (Companions to Cracow and Essen).

Pistoia. MUSEO CIVICO. Crucifixion (st.).

Poznan. Mo 11. Predella panel (from S. Maria Novella, 1338?): S. Dominic saving a Ship at Sea (see Berlin 1094). *Plate 175.*

Prague. DO 876–878. Portable triptych: Madonna and Child with four Angels and SS. Bartholomew and Benedict. Wings: Annunciation, four Saints, Crucifixion.

   DO 869–871. Portable triptych: Madonna and Child with four Angels and eight Saints. Wings: Annunciation, Nativity, Crucifixion.

Prato. 2. Predella: Seven Scenes from the Legend of the Holy Girdle [Apostles at the Virgin's Tomb, S. Thomas consigning the Girdle to a Priest, Betrothal of Michele Dagomari, Dagomari receiving the Girdle, Voyage to Italy, Dagomari moved by Angels in his Sleep, Consignment of the Girdle to the Provost of the Duomo]. *Plate 176.*

   4. Polyptych: Madonna and Child with SS. Francis, Bartholomew, Barnabas and Catherine.

Radensleben. W. VON QUAST (EX). Two panels from a polyptych: S. Helena and a Bishop Saint. Pinnacles: Two Prophets. (Companions to Kansas City 39.14).

Rome. PRINCIPE BORGHESE (EX). Predella panel: Beheading of S. Reparata (see Brussels, Pechère).

   PRINCIPE COLONNA. Burial of S. Benedict.

   MARCHESA VISCONTI VENOSTA. Portable triptych: Madonna and Child with six Saints. Wings: Annunciation, Nativity, Crucifixion (central panel repainted by ?Defendente Ferrari). 1336.

   VATICAN, PINACOTECA. 147–50, 158–61. Eight predella panels: Martyrdom of S. Stephen and the Legend of his Relics [Stoning of S. Stephen, Dream of Lucian, Lucian before the Patriarch, Recovery of the Body of S. Stephen and other Saints, Translation of the Bodies, Exorcism of the Emperor's Daughter and Burial of S. Stephen with S. Lawrence, Second Translation of the Saints, Cripples and Paupers at the Saint's Tomb]. *Plates 180–181.*

   174. Madonna of the *Magnificat* (fr., p.; companion to Berne 880).

   177. Small triptych: Madonna and Child with four Saints.

   180. Madonna and Child.

San Francisco (Cal.). DE YOUNG MEMORIAL MUSEUM, KRESS COLLECTION. K 198. Panel from an altarpiece: Female martyr Saint. (Companion to Malines).

San Godenzo (Mugello). BADIA DI S. GODENZO, HIGH ALTAR. Polyptych: Madonna and Child with SS. John Baptist, Benedict, Nicholas, and John Evangelist. Pinnacles. Christ blessing and four Prophets (st.). d. 1333.

São Paulo. 019. Madonna and Child.

Seattle (Wash.). ART MUSEUM, KRESS COLLECTION. K 1290. Madonna and Child enthroned, with female Donor.

Sherborn (Mass.). MRS. CARL PICKHARDT. Panel from a polyptych: S. Francis. Pinnacle: A Prophet (r.; companion to Cambridge 1936.56 and to Philadelphia). 1334.

Siena. 60. Portable triptych: Madonna and Child with sixteen Angels and four Saints. Pinnacle: Christ blessing. Wings: S. Nicholas rescuing Adeodatus from the Service of the Pagan King, Nativity, S. Nicholas restoring Adeodatus to his Parents, Crucifixion. d. 1336.

 73. Madonna and Child with six Angels and ten Saints (r.).

Strasbourg. 204. Predella panel (to Highnam polyptych?): SS. Margaret and Agnes. (Companion to Brussels, van Gelder and to London, Jones).

Turin. 102. Coronation of the Virgin. Pinnacle: Christ blessing (fr.).

 MUSEO CIVICO (PALAZZO MADAMA). 3500. Predella panel: Last Supper. (st.; r.)

Upton House (Banbury, Oxon.). NATIONAL TRUST. Predella panel: Last Supper (st.).

Utrecht. 18A, 19A. Two pinnacles: Archangels Michael and Gabriel (st.).

Venice. CONTE VITTORIO CINI. Crucifixion. Pinnacle: Christ blessing.

Verona. 2162. Crucifixion. (Stolen 1957).

Vienna. LANCKORONSKI COLLECTION (EX). Madonna and Child with two music-making Angels (st.; companion to Florence, Bagno a Ripoli and to New York, ex-Hirsch).

Washington (D.C.). 3 (MELLON COLLECTION). S. Paul. d. 133(3?). *Plate* 162.

 795 (KRESS COLLECTION 1369). Crucifixion.

 1140 (KRESS COLLECTION 1718). Madonna and Child with six Angels and ten Saints. [*Plate* 130.]

 DUMBARTON OAKS. 36.57. Madonna and Child with four Angels and four Saints. Pinnacle: Christ blessing. d. 1337.

Zagreb. 9. The Virgin and other figures, from a Crucifixion (fr.; see London, St. Aubyn).

Zurich. LM 7253. Right wing of a triptych: Martyrdom of S. Ursula. (Companion to Brussels, Stoclet).

Homeless. Fragment of a Crucifixion, see London, St. Aubyn.

Fra DIAMANTE

1430– after 1498. Pupil and assistant of Filippo Lippi from 1452 to 1469; strongly influenced by Baldovinetti.

Athens (Ga.). UNIVERSITY OF GEORGIA, KRESS STUDY COLLECTION. K 503A, B. Two panels: Two Saints. (See London, Sir John Leslie).

Budapest. 45. Madonna and Child with SS. Lawrence and Anthony Abbot and a Donor. *Plate* 866.

Cassel. 479. S. Francis enthroned giving the Rule of the Order to S. Clare, with SS. Louis of Toulouse and Stephen.

Frankfurt am Main. 1181, 1182. Two cassone panels (*grisailles*): Horatius Cocles defending the Sublician Bridge against Porsenna, History of Mucius Scaevola. L. (?)

Göttingen. 11. Madonna adoring the Child with two Angels.

Honolulu. ACADEMY OF ARTS, KRESS COLLECTION. K 441A–D. Four panels: Four male Saints. (See London, Sir John Leslie.) *Plate 863.*

London. 248. Vision of S. Bernard (possibly with Fra Filippo). 1447.

4868 B, D. Predella panels (to Pesellino, London 727): Beheading of S. James, S. Jerome and the Lion (with Filippo Lippi). After 1457. *Plate 833.*

6266. Madonna and Child (after Pesellino, Boston). *Plate 862.*

COURTAULD GALLERIES, LEE OF FAREHAM COLLECTION. 73. Four panels: S. Dominic, S. Peter and two other Saints. (See London, Sir John Leslie).

SIR JOHN LESLIE (EX). Four panels: Four Saints. (Companions to Athens; Honolulu; London, Courtauld; New York, Lehman; and Worcester). *Plate 863.*

Lucca. PINACOTECA. Madonna and Child. (?)

Milan. COMM. PAOLO GERLI. 'Benson' Madonna and Child with three Angels.

New York. ROBERT LEHMAN. Two panels: Two Saints. (See London, Sir John Leslie.) *Plate 863.*

Paris. 1269D. Madonna and Child with two Angels. (?)

1343. Nativity (after Pesellino?).

Pisa. 186, 187. Two cassoni: Battles of Romans and Gauls at the Gates of Rome (st.).

Prato. 9. *Madonna del Ceppo*, with SS. Stephen and John Baptist, Francesco Datini and other Donors (the whole design and the head of the Virgin by Fra Filippo Lippi). 1453. *Plate 864.*

10. *Madonna della Cintola*, with S. Margaret, two Bishop Saints, Tobias and the Angel and a Donor.

12. Predella: Adoration of the Magi, Circumcision, Massacre of the Innocents. *Plate 867.*

18. Nativity, with SS. George and Vincent Ferrer (execution by Fra Diamante, except the Madonna, the Child, the head and hand of S. Vincent by Filippo Lippi). Commissioned in 1450.

DUOMO, R. TRANSEPT. Death of S. Jerome (only the upper part, on Lippi's design).

— SACRISTY. Annunciation with a Saint (st.).

S. SPIRITO, ALTAR R. Circumcision (on Lippi's design). 1466–68.

Spoleto. DUOMO, APSE. Frescoes. Vault: Coronation of the Virgin. Wall:Annunciation, Death of the Virgin, Nativity (with Lippi). 1467–69. *Plate 865.*

Vienna. LANCKORONSKI COLLECTION. S. Christopher.

Worcester (Mass.). 1940.37 a, b. Two panels: S. Catherine and a male Saint. (See London, Sir John Leslie).

DOMENICO DI MICHELINO

1417–91. Follower of Fra Angelico; influenced by Baldovinetti and Pesellino. His only certain work is the 'Dante' in the Duomo of Florence.

Bergamo. 324. Madonna of Humility with four Angels. E. (?)

Berlin. 57. Last Judgement (begun by Andrea di Giusto; group of Damned, perhaps by Francesco del Chierico). d. 1456. (Destroyed 1945). *Plate 635.*

Cape Town (South Africa). SIR JOSEPH ROBINSON (EX). Last Judgement.

Chambéry. 214. Portable triptych: Man of Sorrows. Wings: Annunciation, Visitation, Meeting of SS. Francis and Dominic.

Chartres. MUSÉE (DEP. LOUVRE 1924C, CAMPANA 155). Madonna and Child with Angels and SS. Cosmas, Damian, Jerome, John Baptist, Francis and Lawrence. Predella: Dream of S. Jerome, Death of S. Jerome, Man of Sorrows, S. Jerome appearing to S. Augustine, S. Silvanus rescued by S. Jerome. *Plate 632.*

Dublin. 861. Assumption with SS. Jerome and Francis. (Predella at Prato). *Plate 636.*

Florence. S. MARCO (MUSEO), HOSPICE. Madonna and Child enthroned with four Angels. (?). *Plate 629.*

Allegorical Wheel or Vision of Ezechiel; *Lex Amoris* (on doors of silverchest from SS. Annunziata; see Angelico). After 1448. *Plate 626.*

— LIBRARY. Two overdoors: School of S. Albertus Magnus, School of S. Thomas Aquinas.

— — In various choirbooks, miniatures: e.g. Trinity, Youthful Saint reading, Annunciation, Nativity, David praying, etc.

S. MARIA DEL FIORE (DUOMO), L. WALL, 4th BAY. Dante, and Illustrations of the *Divina Commedia*. 1465. *Plate 638.*

Leningrad. 135. Madonna and Child. (?)

London. 582. Predella panel: Adoration of the Magi. E.

1406. Annunciation.

BUCKINGHAM PALACE, ROYAL COLLECTION. B.P.14. Madonna of Humility with two Angels.

COUNT SEILERN. Madonna and Child with S. Dominic and another Saint.

Milan. COMM. MARIO CRESPI. Madonna of Humility with two music-making Angels. *Plate 630.*

Montreal. 1181. S. Jerome in the Wilderness. (?)

New Haven (Conn.). 1871.31. Fragment of an altarpiece: A Bishop Saint and SS. Francis and Anthony of Padua.

Paris. LOUVRE. See Chartres.

MUSÉE JACQUEMART-ANDRÉ. 1050 bis. God the Father enthroned with two Angels.

Philadelphia (Pa.). MUSEUM OF ART, JOHNSON COLLECTION. 22. Annunciation. *Plate 631.*

Prato. 15, 16, 17. Predella (to Dublin 861): S. Jerome in the Wilderness, Dormition of the Virgin, Stigmatization of S. Francis.

Providence (R.I.). RHODE ISLAND SCHOOL OF DESIGN (EX). Madonna and Child with SS. John Baptist, Francis and two other Saints. *Plate 637.*

Rome. VATICAN, PINACOTECA. 255–57, 259, Four predella panels: Nativity, Adoration of the Magi, Christ among the Doctors and Transfiguration, Entry into Jerusalem.

Strasbourg. 212. Journey of the Magi. *Plate 634.*

Tucson (Ariz.). UNIVERSITY OF ARIZONA, KRESS COLLECTION. K.1720. Madonna of Humility.

Williamstown (Mass.). CLARK ART INSTITUTE. John Paleologus setting out for Venice. *Plate 633.*

Worcester (Mass.). 1940.40. Madonna of Humility (r.).

Homeless. Madonna of Humility with two Angels (*Dedalo* XII, 523).

DOMENICO VENEZIANO

ca 1400–1461. *A native of Venice active in Florence at least after 1438; influenced by Pisanello, Fra Angelico, Masaccio and Uccello.*

Berlin. 64. Predella panel (to Florence, Uffizi): Martyrdom of S. Lucy. *Plate 710.*

95A. Tondo. Adoration of the Magi. E. *Plate 701.*

Boston (Mass.). ISABELLA GARDNER MUSEUM. Profile Portrait of a Woman. *Plate 702.*

Bucharest. 4. Madonna and Child against a Hedge of Roses. *Plate 707.*

Cambridge. 1106, 1107. Two predella panels (to Florence, Uffizi): Annunciation, Miracle of S. Zenobius. [*Plate 152.*] *Plate 709.*

Florence. UFFIZI. 884. Madonna and Child with SS. Francis, John Baptist, Zenobius and Lucy. (Predella panels at Berlin, Cambridge and Washington). [*Plates 150, 153, 154.*]

s. CROCE, MUSEO DELL'OPERA. Detached fresco: SS. John Baptist and Francis. L.

BERENSON COLLECTION. Madonna and Child. [*Plate 155.*]

Glasgow. 35–634. Judgement of Paris (st.; companion to Vienna, Lanckoronski).

Houston (Texas). 44–574. *Desco:* Solomon and the Queen of Sheba (g.p.). *Plate 700.*

London. 585. Profile Portrait of a Lady. *Plate 703.*

766, 767. Two fresco fragments: Heads of two Saints (r.; companions to 1215 below).

1215. Fresco (from the Canto de' Carnesecchi tabernacle): Madonna and Child (fr., r.). Sd. *Plate 706.*

PETER FULD. Diana and Actæon (st.).

Lugano. THYSSEN COLLECTION. 12C. Kneeling Monk holding Cross. (?)

Münster i/W. SEMINARY. *Desco:* Triumph of Charity (st.). (Destroyed.)

New York. 19.87. Crucifixion (r.).

    49.7.6. Profile Portrait of a Woman.

    HISTORICAL SOCIETY. B–5. *Desco da parto* (for Lorenzo de' Medici): Triumph of Fame (executed by Francesco di Antonio). 1449. *Plate* 732.

    MRS. JOHN D. ROCKEFELLER, JR. Profile Portrait of Michele Olivieri. (Companion to Washington 15). *Plate* 705.

Vienna. LANCKORONSKI COLLECTION. Two panels: June, Venus and Minerva approaching Paris; Rape of Helen (st.; companions to Glasgow).

Washington (D.C.). 15 (MELLON COLLECTION). Profile Portrait of Matteo Olivieri. (Companion to New York, Rockefeller). *Plate* 704.

    251 (KRESS COLLECTION 278). Predella panel (to Florence, Uffizi): Stigmatization of S. Francis.

    332 (KRESS COLLECTION 410). Madonna and Child against a Hedge of Roses. *Plate* 708.

    715 (KRESS COLLECTION 1331). Predella panel (to Florence, Uffizi): S. John Baptist in the Wilderness. [*Plate* 151.]

FRANCESCO DI ANTONIO
(di Bartolomeo, erroneously read 'Banchi')

Born 1394. Pupil of Lorenzo Monaco, influenced by Masaccio and Masolino. (His activity after 1433 is not documented, but the late works here attributed to him show the influence of Domenico Veneziano; his work as a cassone painter is problematic).

Arezzo. 28. Madonna and Child with two music-making Angels.

Assisi. MRS. F. M. PERKINS. Madonna and Child.

Baltimore (Md.). WALTERS ART GALLERY. 733. S. Lawrence. E. (?)

Barcelona. MUSEO DE ARTE. Two cassone panels: Seven Liberal Arts, Seven Virtues.

Birmingham (Ala.). MUSEUM OF ART, KRESS COLLECTION. K 1108. Predella panels: Temptation of S. Anthony and S. Bernardino preaching.

Bourges. See Paris, Musées Nationaux.

Budapest. 1288. Diptych: Nativity, Crucifixion and eight Saints (st.).

Cambridge. M33. Triptych: Madonna and Child with SS. Lawrence and John Gualbert. Pinnacles: A Prophet, Annunciation. Sd and d. 1415. *Plate* 713.

Carcassonne. See Paris, Musées Nationaux.

Cherbourg. MUSÉE (CAMPANA 76). Madonna and Child with two Angels.

Cologne. 731. Madonna and Child with ten Angels. *Plate* 712.

Copenhagen. 4785, 4786. Two cassoni: Feud and Reconciliation of two Florentine Families. *Plates* 728, 730.

Denver (Col.). MUSEUM OF ART, KRESS COLLECTION. K 543. Madonna and Child with a Swallow. Pinnacle: Christ blessing. (Companion to Pisa?)

Durham. USHAW COLLEGE. Madonna and Child with Angels. (?)

Figline (Valdarno Superiore). S. FRANCESCO (MISERICORDIA), R. OF ENTRANCE. Fresco: Crucifixion, with the Virgin and SS. John, James, Francis and two Bishop Saints. E.

— L. OF ENTRANCE. Frescoes: A Franciscan Saint, Annunciation with donor, Coronation of the Virgin. Sd. E. *Plate 711.*

Florence. ACCADEMIA. 8457. 'Adimari' cassone panel. *Plate 733.*

9271. Organ shutter from Orsanmichele. Outside: Evangelists John and Matthew. Inside: Four singing Angels. 1429.

9272. Organ shutter from Orsanmichele. Outside: Evangelists Luke and Mark. Inside: Four singing Angels. 1429. (Lost). *Plates 718, 719.*

MUSEO HORNE. 50. Madonna and Child with two Angels. L.

PALAZZO DAVANZATI. Tondo: *Giuoco del Civettino.* L. *Plate 731.*

1611. Round chest: Triumphs of Petrarch.

S. FELICITA, SACRISTY. Adoration of the Magi. (?)

S. NICCOLÒ OLTRARNO.* Fresco: S. Ansanus. *Plate 726.*

S. TRINITA, SACRISTY. Madonna and Child with four Angels.

PIAZZA S. MARIA NOVELLA.* Tabernacle fresco: Madonna and Child with two Angels, S. John Baptist and a Bishop Saint (r.). *Plate 724.*

MRS. C. H. COSTER. Madonna and Child in Glory.

Fucecchio (Valdarno Inferiore). COLLEGIATA. Madonna and Child appearing to SS. Lazarus, Mary Magdalen and Martha on the Voyage to Marseilles, with S. Sebastian. *Plate 723.*

Grenoble. 544 (CAMPANA 106). Madonna and Child with six Angels and SS. John Baptist and Jerome. Spandrels: God the Father, Annunciation, Two Prophets. (See also Paris, Musées Nationaux). *Plate 714.*

Highnam Court (Glos.). GAMBIER-PARRY COLLECTION. Madonna and Child with SS. Anthony Abbot and Julian and a Donor.

Kansas City (Mo.). 35.26. Two panels: Eight music-making Angels (st.).

Lewisburg (Penna.). BUCKNELL UNIVERSITY, KRESS STUDY COLLECTION. K 1148. Madonna and Child with SS. Stephen and Lawrence. L. (?)

London. 1456. Madonna and Child with six Angels.

VICTORIA AND ALBERT MUSEUM. 398–1890. *Desco da Nozze:* Triumph of Love.

Loppiano (Incisa Valdarno). S. VITO. *Madonna della Cintola* with six Angels.

Los Angeles (Cal.). A.5141.45–292. Cassone panel: A Triumph. (Companion to Milan).

Milan. CHIESA COLLECTION (EX). Three cassone panels: Triumphs. (Companions to Los Angeles). *Plate 729.*

Montgomery (Ala.). MUSEUM OF ART, KRESS COLLECTION. K 1046. Annunciation, Crucifixion, and nine Saints.

New York. HISTORICAL SOCIETY. B–5. *Desco da parto* (for Lorenzo de' Medici): Triumph of Fame (on Domenico Veneziano's design?). 1449. *Plate 732.*

Paris. MUSÉES NATIONAUX (CAMPANA 159, 210, 160). Three predella panels (to Grenoble 544): Dream of S. Jerome, Vision of S. Benedict and Prophecy of his Death, Death of S. Benedict, *Plate* 715–717.

BIBLIOTHÈQUE NATIONALE, MS. IT. 545. Triumphs of Petrarch. 1456.

Pisa. 114, 115. Wings of an altarpiece: SS. Dominic and Michael, SS. Catherine and another Saint. Pinnacles: Annunciation. (Companions to Denver?).

Prague. DO 1272, 1273. Two panels: SS. John Baptist and Bartholomew. (?)

Rome. COMM. ARDUINO COLASANTI. Nativity. *Plate* 725.

San Giovanni Valdarno. 5–9. Five panels: Madonna and Child, S. Ansanus, S. Blaise, two Choirs of Angels (p.). L. *Plates* 721, 722.

Seattle (Wash.). MUSEUM OF ART, KRESS COLLECTION. K 1145 A, B. Two panels: Annunciation.

Strasbourg. 211. Risen Christ.

Tucson (Ariz.). ST. PHILIP'S IN THE HILLS, KRESS STUDY COLLECTION. K 1015A, B. Two panels: SS. John Baptist and Anthony Abbot.

Vienna. AKADEMIE. A24. Madonna and Child with two Angels.

Homeless. Madonna nursing the Child with two Angels. *Dedalo* XII, 533.
Madonna and Child eating grapes. *Plate* 720.
Madonna and Child enthroned. *Plate* 727.

FRANCHI, see Rossello di Jacopo

FRANCIABIGIO

ca 1482–1525. *Pupil of Piero di Cosimo and Mariotto Albertinelli; influenced by Andrea del Sarto, with whom he worked.*

Barnard Castle (Durham). BOWES MUSEUM. 45. Portrait of a Man (r.).

Berlin. 235. Portrait of a Man.
245. Portrait of a Man writing. Sd and d. 1522. *Plate* 1371.
245A. Portrait of a Man.
EUGEN SCHWEITZER (EX). Madonna and Child with Infant S. John (p.).

Birmingham (Ala.). MUSEUM OF ART, KRESS COLLECTION. K 1110. Madonna holding Child on parapet (replica of Rome, Galleria Nazionale 580).

Bologna. 294. Madonna and Child.

Brocklesby Park (Lincs.). EARL OF YARBOROUGH (EX). Portrait of a Jeweller. Sd. and d. 1516. *Plate* 1365.

Brussels. 415. Leda.

Chantilly. 41. Portrait of a Man.

Detroit (Mich.). 89.7. Portrait of a Man. (?)

    28.133. Portrait of a Man (r.). Sd.

Dijon. T.I. Madonna and Child with Infant S. John.

Dresden. 75. Benintendi panel (companion to Bachiacca, Dresden 80): Story of Bathsheba. Sd and d. 1523. *Plate 1374.*

Florence. GALLERIE. Fresco (from Villa Dani): Nativity (r.). 1510. *Plate 1358.*

    517. Tondo: Madonna with Infant S. John. E.

    1593. Madonna with SS. John Baptist and Job. Sd and d. 1516. *Plate 1364.*

    2178. Tondo: Madonna and Child with Infant S. John. E. (?)

    ACCADEMIA. 888. Tondo: Holy Family with Infant S. John E.

    1445. *Madonna del Pozzo*, with Infant S. John.

    PITTI. 427. Calumny of Apelles. E.

    UFFIZI. 8381. Portrait of a Man with a Glove. Sd and d. 1514.

    MUSEO HORNE. 3242. Fresco: *Noli me tangere* (fr.). 1510. *Plate 1359.*

    PALAZZO DAVANZATI. 1600. Temple of Hercules.

    SS. ANNUNZIATA, ATRIUM. Fresco: Marriage of the Virgin. 1513. *Plate 1362.*

    SAN GIOVANNINO DELLA CALZA, REFECTORY. Fresco: Last Supper. Sd.

    CHIOSTRO DELLO SCALZO. Three monochrome frescoes: Baptism of Christ (after 1514), S. Zacharias giving his Blessing to the young S. John (1518–19), Meeting of Jesus and the young S. John (1518–19). *Plate 1369.*

    MARCHESE SERLUPI-CRESCENZI. Madonna and Child with Infant S. John (r.).

    DR. BLAKISTON WILKINS (EX). Tondo: Half-length Madonna and Child with Infant S. John.

    (Environs) POGGIO A CAIANO, VILLA MEDICEA. Fresco: Triumph of Cicero. 1521. *Plate 1370.*

Genoa. PALAZZO BIANCO, MAGAZINE. 273. Tondo: Madonna and Child with Infant S. John.

Hamburg. GALERIE WEBER (EX). Portrait of a Man.

Hampton Court. 1168. 'Piero de' Medici's Gardener.' Sd. *Plate 1367.*

Lisbon. 1611. Portrait of a Man.

London. 1035. Portrait of a Knight of Rhodes. Sd and d. 1514. *Plate 1366.*

Munich. 8886. Madonna and Child.

New York. 32.100.89. Head of the Virgin.

    HUNTER COLLEGE, S. H. KRESS COLLECTION. K1060. Portrait of an Artist. (r.). (?)

Oxford. ASHMOLEAN. 164. Predella panel: Nicholas of Tolentino performing miracles.

Paris. 1644. Portait of a Man.

Rome. GALLERIA BORGHESE. 177. Marriage of S. Catherine. *Plate 1360.*

    458. Tondo: Madonna and Child with Infant S. John. E.

    GALLERIA NAZIONALE (PALAZZO BARBERINI). F.N.570. Madonna and Child holding Apple.

    F.N.580. Madonna and Child. Sd and d. 1509. *Plate 1361.*

Rome (contd.). GALLERIA COLONNA. Tondo: Madonna and blessing Child with an Angel. E. (?)

MARCHESA MANCINFORTE (EX). Tondo: Full-length Madonna and Child with Infant S. John.

Turin. 112. Annunciation. E. *Plate* 1363.

Vaduz. LIECHTENSTEIN COLLECTION. 254. Madonna and Child with Infant S. John. Sd. *Plate* 1372.

851. Portrait of a Man. d. 1517. *Plate* 1368.

Vienna. 46. Holy Family. *Plate* 1373.

52. Madonna and Child with Infant S. John. (?).

Wiesbaden. M32. Cassone panel: Story of Lucretia.

GADDI, Agnolo

First mentioned 1369, died 1396. Pupil and follower of his father, Taddeo Gaddi.

Amsterdam. 2228–B1. Madonna of Humility with four Angels.

Berlin. 1118. Madonna of Humility with ten Angels and Christ blessing. (Destroyed 1945).

(BERLIN–OST). 1039. Triptych: Madonna and Child with six Angels and SS. John Evangelist, John Baptist, James and Bartholomew. Above: Holy Ghost and two Angels, Two Bishop Saints.

Birmingham (Ala.). MUSEUM OF ART, KRESS COLLECTION. K 261. Madonna and Child in Glory with SS. Catherine, Peter, James, Anthony Abbot, Paul and Lucy (p.).

Empoli. 19. Triptych: Madonna and Child with SS. Anthony Abbot, Catherine, Jerome and John Baptist. Pinnacles: Annunciation. Predella: Man of Sorrows with the Virgin, S. John and four other Saints (r.).

Fiesole. MUSEO BANDINI. I, II. Madonna and Child with two Angels and SS. John Baptist, Catherine, Mary Magdalen and Anthony Abbot (st.).

Florence. GALLERIE. Triptych (from Antella): Madonna and Child with SS. Philip and Lawrence. Pinnacles: Christ blessing, Annunciation. Predella: Miracle of S. Philip, Dead Christ with Virgin and S. John Evangelist, Martyrdom of S. Lawrence. *Plate* 349.

ACCADEMIA. 461. Madonna of Humility with six Angels.

MUSEO BARDINI. 1148. Madonna of Humility with two Angels (st.).

MUSEO NAZIONALE DEL BARGELLO, CARRAND COLLECTION. 2013–15. Three fragments: Madonna nursing the Child, Heads of two Saints.

S. AMBROGIO, SECOND ALTAR R. Madonna nursing the Child with two Angels and SS. John Baptist, Catherine, Mary Magdalen and Anthony Abbot.

— L. OF ENTRANCE. Fresco: Martyrdom of S. Sebastian (fr., r.). *Plate* 342.

s. CROCE, CHOIR. Frescoes. Above entrance: Two Prophets. Vault: Christ, S. Francis and the four Evangelists. Walls: Legend of the True Cross. [Right wall: Seth receiving a Branch of the Tree of Knowledge and planting it on Adam's Grave, Recognition and Burial of the Holy Wood, Recovery of the Wood and Manufacture of the Cross, Invention of the True Cross. Left wall: S. Helen taking the Cross to Jerusalem, Theft of the Cross by King Cosroes, Throne of Cosroes, Dream of Heraclius and Defeat of Cosroes, Beheading of Cosroes and Entry of Heraclius into Jerusalem. Entrance arch, pilasters and window walls: Saints.] *Plates* 343–348.

— IST CHAPEL L. OF CHOIR. Fresco above entrance: Assumption (r.).

— CASTELLANI CHAPEL (SACRAMENT CHAPEL). Frescoes: Scenes from the Lives of SS. Nicholas, John Baptist, Anthony Abbot and John Evangelist [Pier to right: SS. Lawrence and Stephen, Martyrdom of S. Apollonia, S. Nicholas preventing the Execution of three Innocent Men. S. Nicholas raising three Boys from Barrels. Right wall, first bay: S. Nicholas and the three Maidens, Story of the deceitful Creditor and the Jew, Miracle of the drowned Child and the golden Chalice. Right wall, second bay: Annunciation to Zacharias, Baptism of Christ and the People, Disciples of Baptist following Christ (fr.). Altar wall, right: S. John Baptist in the Wilderness, Preaching of S. John Baptist. Altar wall, left: S. Anthony Abbot entering the Wilderness, S. Anthony stoned by a Devil, Meeting of SS. Anthony and Paul Hermit. Left wall, second bay: Vocation of S. Anthony and Distribution of his Fortune, Temptation of S. Anthony, Death of S. Anthony. Left wall, first bay: S. John Evangelist on Patmos, Baptism of Crato and Miraculous Transformation of Pebbles and Sticks into Gold. Above entrance: Two Prophets. Vault: Doctors of the Church and Evangelists. Entrance arch and pilasters: Saints] (p.). L. *Plate* 351.

s. MARIA NOVELLA, EX-REFECTORY. Fresco: Madonna and Child with SS. Thomas Aquinas, Dominic, John Baptist and Peter Martyr and Donor (r.).

s. MINIATO AL MONTE, CAPPELLA DEL CROCEFISSO. Eleven panels: S. John Gualbert, S. Miniato, and Scenes from the Life of Christ. [Annunciation, Last Supper, Washing of Feet, Betrayal of Christ, Mocking of Christ, Flagellation, Resurrection, Ascension.] (Series unfinished at the artist's death.) L. *Plate* 354.

CONTINI BONACOSSI COLLECTION. Madonna and Child with eight Angels. Pinnacle: Two Angels with a Crown. (Predella at New Haven, 1943.213.) (Companion to Munich 7818–19?). *Plate* 336.

Two panels from an altarpiece: Bishop Saint and S. Peter, SS. John Baptist and Miniato.

(Environs) s. MARTINO A SESTO. Crucifix. *Plate* 341.

Highnam Court (Glos.). GAMBIER-PARRY COLLECTION. Madonna of Humility with six Angels.

Indianapolis (Ind.). G. H. A. CLOWES. Four panels: SS. Mary Magdalen, Benedict, Bernard and Catherine.

London. 568. Coronation of the Virgin with four Angels (?)

COURTAULD GALLERIES, LEE OF FAREHAM COLLECTION. Madonna and Child with SS. Julian and Catherine (r.).

Munich. 7818, 7819. Wings of an altarpiece: S. Nicholas and Donor; S. Julian. Predella panels: S. Nicholas and the three Maidens, S. Nicholas saving a Ship at Sea, S. Julian murdering his Parents, S. Julian assisting a Pilgrim across a River. (Companions to Florence, Contini Bonacossi?). *Plates 337–338.*

New Haven (Conn.). 1871.20. SS. Julian, James and Michael (fr?).

1871.30. Predella panel: Miraculous Conversion of S. John Gualbert.

1943.213. Predella panel (to Florence, Contini Bonacossi): S. Michael dividing the Sea before a Pilgrim, Miracle of the Bull of Gargano. *Plate 336.*

New York. 41.100.33. Trinity.

HAROLD I. PRATT (EX). Madonna of Humility with six Angels. *Plate 356.*

Paris. 1302. Predella: Feast of Herod, Crucifixion, Hermogenes brought to S. James, Beheading of S. James (p). *Plates 339–340.*

ROUART COLLECTION (EX). Madonna and Child with two Angels and SS. Catherine, John Baptist, Anthony Abbot and Mary Magdalen.

Parma. 435. Madonna and Child with Angels and SS. Dominic, John Baptist, Peter Martyr, Thomas Aquinas, Paul, Lawrence and female Donor (Madonna only, Saints by another hand).

Perugia. DUOMO, MUSEO DELL'OPERA. 16. Triptych: Madonna and Child with six Angels and SS. James and Andrew, and SS. John Baptist, Peter, Paul and a Bishop Saint (g.p.).

Prague. DO 795, 793. Two predella panels: Descent into Limbo, Heraclius entering Jerusalem.

Prato. DUOMO, CHAPEL L. (CAPPELLA DEL SACRO CINGOLO). Frescoes: Scenes from the Life of the Virgin and the Legend of the Holy Girdle. [Above entrance arch (inside): Expulsion of Joachim from the Temple, Annunciation to Joachim. Left wall: Meeting at the Golden Gate, Birth of the Virgin, Presentation in the Temple, Marriage of the Virgin, Annunciation, Nativity. Window wall: Dormition of the Virgin and *Madonna della Cintola* (r.), Coronation of the Virgin. Right wall: S. Thomas consigning the Girdle to a Priest, Marriage of Michele Dagomari, Voyage to Prato, Arrival at Prato, Dagomari moved by Angels in his Sleep, Death of Dagomari and Consignment of the Girdle to the Provost of the Duomo, Procession to the Duomo. Vault: Four Evangelists and four Doctors of the Church. Pilasters: SS. Lawrence, Dominic, Anthony Abbot, Bartholomew and three other Saints (r.). Soffits: Saints. Two small lunettes (overdoors): Madonna and Child, Christ blessing.] *Plate 353.*

— 1st CHAPEL L. OF CHOIR (CAPPELLA MANASSEI). Frescoes. Vault: Four Evangelists. Soffits: Eight Saints. Walls: Scenes from the Lives of SS. James and Margaret. [Left wall: S. Margaret rejecting Olybrius' Proposal, S. Margaret before Olybrius, Beheading of S. Margaret. Right wall: Hermogenes before S.

James, Conversion and Baptism of Hermogenes, Arrest and Beheading of
S. James. Altar wall: Christ blessing, Annunciation, SS. Joachim and Anne
(r.).] (execution in part by Pietro di Miniato). *Plate* 352.

Santa Barbara (Cal.). MUSEUM OF ART. S. Ursula. (?)

Tucson (Ariz.). UNIVERSITY OF ARIZONA, KRESS COLLECTION. K.563. Madonna of
Humility with two Angels.

Vaduz. LIECHTENSTEIN COLLECTION (EX). Madonna and Child with two music-
making Angels. L. (?)

Washington (D.C.). 4. Triptych: Madonna and Child with twelve Angels and SS.
Andrew, Benedict, Bernard and Catherine. Pinnacles: Christ blessing and
Annunciation.

314 (KRESS COLLECTION 364). Coronation of the Virgin with six Angels. *Plate* 350.

GADDI, Taddeo

Pupil and Assistant of Giotto. Died not later than 1366.

Berlin. 1073, 1074. Pentecost, S. Francis raising a Child. (See Florence, Accademia
8581–8603).

1079–81. Portable triptych: Madonna and Child enthroned, and fourteen
Saints. Wings, inside: S. Nicholas rescuing Adeodatus from the Service of the
Pagan King, Nativity, S. Nicholas restoring Adeodatus to his Parents,
Crucifixion. Wings, outside: S. Margaret, Christ recommending the Virgin
to S. John, S. Catherine, S. Christopher. Sd and d. 1334. *Plates* 116–117.

Bernay. See Paris, Musées Nationaux.

Berne. 877. Portable altarpiece: Madonna and Child with Angels and six Saints (r.).

Bloomington (Ind.). UNIVERSITY OF INDIANA, KRESS STUDY COLLECTION. K 1348.
Portable altarpiece: Madonna and Child enthroned with two Donors.

Brolio (Chianti). BARONE RICASOLI. Presentation in the Temple (r.).

Cannes. FRANK GOULD. Portable altarpiece: Madonna and Child with eight Saints.
Pinnacle. Coronation of the Virgin (r.).

Castelfiorentino (Val d'Elsa). S. VERDIANA (PINACOTECA PARROCCHIALE). Madonna
and Child enthroned.

Castiglion Fiorentino (Val di Chiana). PINACOTECA. Madonna and Child enthroned (fr.).

Fiesole. MUSEO BANDINI. I, 23. Annunciation (g.p.).

Florence. ACCADEMIA. 448. Lunette: Madonna and Child. Pinnacle: Christ blessing
and two Prophets. Predella: Man of Sorrows and eight Saints. (Pinnacle and
predella by a later artist).

8581–93. Fourteen panels with Scenes from the Life of Christ and the Virgin:
Annunciation, Visitation, Nativity, Adoration of the Magi, Circumcision,
Christ among the Doctors, Baptism of Christ, Transfiguration, Last Supper,

Crucifixion, Resurrection, *Noli me tangere*, Incredulity of S. Thomas, Ascension. (Companions to Berlin 1073; same series as 8594–8603 below). *Plate* 115.

8594–8603. Ten panels with Scenes from the Life of S. Francis: S. Francis renouncing his Inheritance, Dream of Innocent III, S. Francis preaching to Honorius, S. Francis appearing to his Brothers in a Chariot of Fire, Martyrdom at Ceuta, Confirmation of the Rule, Institution of the *Presepio* at Greccio, Apparition at Arles, Stigmatization of S. Francis, Death of S. Francis. (Companions to Berlin 1073–74 and Munich; same series as 8581–93 above). *Plate* 114.

UFFIZI. 3 Dep. Madonna and Child with four Angels and two female Saints. Sd and d. 1355.

ARCHIVIO NOTARILE. Frescoes: Annunciation, Visitation.

MUSEO HORNE. 77. Madonna and Child (r.).

MUSEO NAZIONALE DEL BARGELLO, ENTRANCE HALL. Fresco: Madonna and Child enthroned with Worshippers (r.).

S. CROCE, R. TRANSEPT. Frescoes (over door to Sacristy): Christ among the Doctors (fr.), Four Prophets.

Fresco lunette (over Baroncelli monument): Madonna and Child. ca 1328. *Plate* 112.

— BARONCELLI CHAPEL. Frescoes. Vault: Eight Virtues. Soffits: Saints. Walls: Scenes from the Life of the Virgin [Left wall: Expulsion of Joachim from the Temple, Annunciation to Joachim, Meeting at the Golden Gate, Birth of the Virgin, Presentation in the Temple, Marriage of the Virgin. Altar wall: Annunciation, Visitation, Annunciation to the Shepherds, Nativity, Annunciation to the Magi, Adoration of the Magi. Pilaster: S. Joseph and David]. 1332–38. [*Plate* 126.] *Plates* 118–124.

— 5th CHAPEL L. OF CHOIR (BARDI DI VERNIO). Frescoes (over Bardi tomb): Entombment with female donor, Two Prophets, Man of Sorrows and two Prophets. *Plates* 125, 154.

S. CROCE (MUSEO), REFECTORY. Frescoes: S. Bonaventura's Vision of the Crucifixion (*Lignum vitae*), Stigmatization of S. Francis, S. Louis of Toulouse ministering to the Sick and Poor, S. Benedict in the Sacro Speco and the Priest at his Easter Meal, Feast in the House of Simon, Last Supper. *Plate* 128.

S. FELICITA, SACRISTY. Polyptych: Madonna and Child with four Angels and SS. James, John Baptist, Luke and Philip. Spandrels: Ten Prophets. L.

S. MARCO (MUSEO), FORESTERIA. Detached fresco: Madonna and Child enthroned with SS. Nicholas and Michael. (Extensively repainted, esp. the Child and Saints, by a Ghirlandajo pupil.)

S. MINIATO AL MONTE, CRYPT. Frescoes (vault): Christ blessing, Prophets and Saints (r.). *Plate* 126.

OGNISSANTI, SACRISTY. Fresco: Crucifixion.

(Environs). S. GIORGIO A RUBALLA. Crucifix.

— S. LORENZO ALLE ROSE. Madonna and Child. L.

— S. MARTINO A MENSOLA, ALTAR R. OF CHOIR. Triptych: Madonna and Child with SS. Lucy and Margaret. Predella: Annunciation, Man of Sorrows, Beheading of S. Margaret (figures in pinnacles and spandrels by another hand). L.

Indianapolis (Ind.). 52.62. S. Anne.

Munich. 10676, 10677. Death of the Knight of Celano, Ordeal by Fire of S. Francis before the Sultan. (See Florence, Accademia 8594–8603.) *Plate* 113.

New Haven (Conn.). 1871.8. Entombment (r.).

1943.205. Madonna and Child enthroned.

New York. 10.97. Polyptych: Madonna and Child with two Angels and SS. Lawrence, John Baptist, James and Stephen (r.).

HISTORICAL SOCIETY. B–375. Madonna and Child enthroned with ten Saints.

Paris. MUSÉES NATIONAUX (CAMPANA 91, DEP. BERNAY). Madonna and Child enthroned.

Pisa. CAMPOSANTO. Frescoes: Satan before the Lord, Trials of Job (except Banquet and Hunt) (fr., r.).

S. FRANCESCO, CHOIR. Frescoes (vault): S. Francis in Glory (p.), and six other Saints (st.). 1342. *Plate* 127.

Pistoia. S. GIOVANNI FUORCIVITAS, HIGH ALTAR. Polyptych: Madonna and Child with SS. James, John Evangelist, Peter and John Baptist. Above: Christ blessing, Annunciation, Eight Saints. 1353. *Plates* 129–131.

Poppi (Casentino). CASTELLO, CHAPEL. Frescoes. Vault: Four Prophets. Right wall: Raising of Drusiana, Ascension of S. John Evangelist. Entrance wall: Circumcision, Death of the Virgin. Left wall: S. John Baptist indicating Christ to the People, Feast of Herod. Dado: Saints (st., r.).

Rome. MUSEO DI CASTEL S. ANGELO. Portable triptych: Madonna and Child with SS. Peter, Paul, Anthony Abbot and a Bishop Saint. Wings: Annunciation, Baptism and Lamentation. d. 1336.

Strasbourg. 202. Portable triptych: Madonna and Child with twelve Saints and Donors. Wings: Nativity, Two Saints, Crucifixion (st.).

Venice. MARIANO FORTUNY (EX). Madonna and Child. Pinnacle: Christ blessing (r.). *Plate* 132.

Williamstown (Mass.). WILLIAMS COLLEGE, KRESS STUDY COLLECTION. K 1372. Roundel: Isaiah.

GHIRLANDAJO, Benedetto

1458–1497. Assistant of his brother Domenico; influenced by Flemish painting.

Aigueperse (Auvergne), NOTRE-DAME. Nativity. Sd. *Plate* 998.
Balmville (Newburgh, N.Y.). MISS TESSIE JONES. Portrait of a Woman. *Plate* 992.

Florence. MUSEO STIBBERT. 834. Predella panel: S. Vincent Ferrer raising a Child on
an Altar. *Plate* 997.

    S. MARIA NOVELLA, L. WALL, 3rd BAY. S. Lucy with a Donor (despite document of
allocation to Davide, by Benedetto; only Donor by Davide). 1494. *Plate* 996.

    S. MARTINO BUONOMINI. See Davide Ghirlandajo.

    S. TRINITA. See Davide Ghirlandajo.

Philadelphia (Pa.). MUSEUM OF ART, JOHNSON COLLECTION. 68. Nativity. (?). *Plate* 995.

GHIRLANDAJO, Davide

*1452–1525. Assistant of his brother Domenico, whom he constantly helped until latter's
death in 1494. Most of the works here attributed to him are based on Domenico's designs.*

Altenburg. 102. Portrait of a Woman. *Plate* 993.

Bayonne. 7. Fresco: Head of the Virgin (fr.).

Berlin. 21. Judith. d. 1489. *Plate* 994.

    68. Madonna and Child with S. Francis and a Bishop Saint. (Destroyed 1945).

    (BERLIN–OST). 75. 'S. Maria Novella' altarpiece (back): Resurrection of Christ
(landscape with three Maries probably by Granacci). (Companion to Granacci
and Mainardi, Berlin 74, 76 and Munich 1076–78). Soon after 1494. *Plate* 972.

Cambridge. M.2. Madonna and Child with SS. Ursula and Catherine and female
Donor.

    M.44, 45. Two cassone panels: Siege of Troy, Death of Hector.

Chantilly. 14. Madonna and Child (r.). (?)

Florence. MUSEO DEL CASTAGNO (CENACOLO DI S. APOLLONIA). Fresco: Crucifixion
with SS. Benedict and Romuald.

    PALAZZO VECCHIO, SALA DEI GIGLI. Frescoes: Brutus, Mucius Scaevola, Camillus,
Decius, Scipio and Cicero. (See also Domenico Ghirlandajo). 1482–84.
Plate 963, 989.

    S. CROCE, NOVITIATE (CAPPELLA MEDICI). Fresco lunette: S. Francis in Glory wor-
shipped by Franciscan Novices, with SS. Cosmas, Damian, Louis of Toulouse
and Bernardino. (?)
Fresco lunette: Annunciation.

    S. JACOPO IN CAMPO CORBOLINI. Marriage of S. Catherine, with S. Margaret and a
Donor (p.). d. 1501.

    S. LORENZO, R. TRANSEPT, 1st CHAPEL R. Madonna adoring the Child with Infant S.
John and SS. Jerome and Francis. L.

    S. MARIA NOVELLA, CHOIR. Frescoes: Presentation of the Virgin (nearly all), Mar-
riage, Visitation (except portraits to r.); and other Scenes from the Lives of
the Virgin and S. John Baptist (p., assisting Domenico Ghirlandajo). 1486–90.
Plates 968–71.

— L. WALL, 3rd. BAY. S. Lucy with a Donor (Bust of Tommaso Cortesi only, the rest by Benedetto). *Plate 996.*

S. MARTINO BUONOMINI. Ten fresco lunettes: Dream of S. Martin, S. Martin and the Beggar, and eight Acts of Mercy of the Buonomini [giving Drink to the Thirsty, giving a Dowry, receiving a Legacy, burying the Dead, lodging Pilgrims, visiting Prisoners, visiting the Sick, clothing the Poor] (probably with Benedetto's assistance; r.). After 1479. *Plates 987–8.*

OGNISSANTI, 2nd ALTAR R. Fresco below Domenico's Mother of Mercy: Lamentation. E.

S. TRINITA, 2nd CHAPEL R. OF CHOIR (SASSETTI). Fresco: Ordeal by Fire of S. Francis (on Domenico Ghirlandajo's design, with Benedetto?). 1483–85.

(Environs) S. DONNINO DI VILLAMAGNA, ALTAR L. Madonna and Child with SS. Sebastian, Donnino, John Baptist and Nicholas. E.

London. LORD MELCHETT (EX). Profile Portrait of a Woman. E. (?)

Munich. ERWIN ROSENTHAL (EX). Two Men in Conversation. (?)

Norton Hall (Glos.). SIR WALTER AND LADY POLLEN. Two cassone panels: Scenes from the Life of Joseph. E. (?)

Oxford. ASHMOLEAN. 176. SS. Bartholomew and Julian (fr.).

Paris. MUSÉE DE CLUNY. 4763. Mosaic: Madonna and Child enthroned with two Angels. Formerly Sd and d. 1496. *Plate 991.*

Philadelphia (Pa.). MUSEUM OF ART, JOHNSON COLLECTION. 65. 'Manzi altarpiece': Madonna and Child with SS. Apollonia and Sebastian (heads of Madonna and Sebastian by Domenico).

66. Madonna and Child.

67. Four predella panels: Last Supper, Betrayal, Christ before Pilate, Way to Calvary.

Pisa. 181. Martyrdom of S. Sebastian.

Poitiers. MUSÉE 109 (CAMPANA 191). Predella panel: Investiture of a Monk (r.). (?)

Radda (Chianti). PALAZZO COMUNALE, PORCH. Fresco: Madonna and Child with SS. John Baptist and Christopher.

Rome. OSPEDALE DI S. SPIRITO, SALONE SISTINO. Frescoes: Scenes from the Life of Sixtus IV (st., r.).

VATICAN, PINACOTECA. 66, 68. Two panels: Deposition, Resurrection (st.). L.

— SISTINE CHAPEL. Fresco: Crossing of the Red Sea (with 'Utili'). 1482. *Plate 1037.*

Rotterdam. 2549. Madonna and Child with Infant S. John and two Angels. E.

Saint Louis (Mo.). 109.22. Madonna and Child with S. Louis of Toulouse, another Saint and two Donors. d. 1486.

Stia (Casentino). (Environs) S. MARIA DELLE GRAZIE, L. WALL. Fresco: Madonna and Child with two Angels and a Donor. d. 1485. *Plate 990.*

Venice. CA' D'ORO. Madonna and Child with Infant S. John. (?)

GHIRLANDAJO (Domenico Bigordi, called)

1449–94. Pupil of Baldovinetti; influenced strongly by Verrocchio and to some degree by young Leonardo and Botticelli. In nearly all his frescoes and in many of his panels assisted by his brothers Davide and Benedetto, and his brother-in-law Mainardi.

Berlin. 93. Meeting of Jesus and the young S. John in the Wilderness. E. *Plate* 962.

Cambridge (Mass.). EDWARD FORBES. Detached fresco: Virgin Annunciate (r.). E.

Chantilly. 18. Profile Portrait of a young Man (st.).

Città di Castello. 78. Coronation of the Virgin with Angels and ten Franciscan Saints. (Execution by Granacci and others).

Detroit (Mich.). 25.205. Predella panel (to Florence, Uffizi 881): Fall of Lucifer (st.).

    31.53. Fresco: Profile Portrait of an old Man (r.).

    MRS. ALFRED G. WILSON, Madonna and Child. E.

Florence. GALLERIE. 8654. Visitation (figures only; r.).

    UFFIZI. 881. Madonna and Child with four Angels and SS. Michael, Justus, Zenobius and Raphael. (Predella panels at Detroit 25.205, London 2902 and New York 13.119.1–3).

        1619. Tondo: Adoration of the Magi. d. 1487. [*Plate* 180].

        8387. Predella (to 8388): Beheading of S. Dionysius, Raising of Napoleone Orsini, Entombment, S. Clement's Vision of the Lamb, School of S. Thomas (p., with Bartolomeo di Giovanni).

        8388. Madonna and Child with two Angels and SS. Dionysius, Dominic, Clement and Thomas Aquinas.

    PALAZZO RICCARDI, MUSEO MEDICEO. Lunette: Portrait of Giovanni Bicci de' Medici.

    PALAZZO VECCHIO, SALA DEI GIGLI. Fresco: S. Zenobius enthroned with SS. Lawrence and Stephen (g.p.; see also Davide Ghirlandajo). 1482–84. *Plates* 961, 963.

    S. LORENZO, 2nd CHAPEL L. OF CHOIR. S. Anthony Abbot enthroned with SS. Leonard and Julian. Predella: S. Leonard liberating Prisoners, Temptation of S. Anthony, Murder of S. Julian's Parents (st.).

    S. MARCO (MUSEO), SMALL REFECTORY. Fresco: Last Supper. *Plate* 959.

    S. MARIA DEL FIORE (DUOMO), OVER NORTH DOOR. Mosaic: Annunciation. d. 1490.

    S. MARIA NOVELLA, CHOIR. Frescoes. Vault: Four Evangelists. Walls: Scenes from the Lives of the Virgin and of S. John Baptist [Left wall: Expulsion of Joachim from the Temple, Birth of the Virgin, Presentation of the Virgin, Marriage of the Virgin, Adoration of the Magi, Massacre of the Innocents, Death and Assumption of the Virgin. Altar wall: Francesco Tornabuoni, Francesca Pitti, Annunciation, S. John in the Wilderness, S. Dominic and the Miracle of the Book, Death of S. Peter Martyr, Coronation of the Virgin. Right wall: Annunciation to Zacharias (d. 1490), Visitation, Birth of S. John, Naming of S. John, Preaching of S. John, Baptism of Christ, Feast of Herod] (execution, save certain portrait heads, chiefly by Davide Ghirlandajo, Mainardi, Granacci and other assistants). 1486–90. [*Plate* 181.] *Plates* 968–71.

Window: *Madonna della Cintola*, Circumcision, Foundation of S. Maria Maggiore, and SS. Peter, John Baptist, Dominic, Paul, Lawrence, and Thomas Aquinas.

OGNISSANTI, L. WALL. Fresco: S. Jerome in his Study. d. 1480.

— 2nd ALTAR R. Fresco lunette: *Madonna della Misericordia*, with the Vespucci Family (g.p.). E. *Plate 957.*

— REFECTORY. Fresco: Last Supper. d. 1480. *Plate 960.*

S. TRINITA, 2nd CHAPEL R. OF CHOIR (SASSETTI). Adoration of the Shepherds. d. 1485. Frescoes. Vault: Four Sibyls. Walls: Scenes from the Life of S. Francis [Over entrance: Caesar Augustus and the Tiburtine Sibyl. Left wall: S. Francis renouncing his Inheritance, Stigmatization of S. Francis. Altar wall: Approval of the Order, Raising of a Child of the Spini Family, Nera Corsi, Francesco Sassetti. Right wall: Ordeal by Fire of S. Francis, Death of S. Francis] (g.p.). (See also Davide Ghirlandajo). d. 1485. [*Plate* 182.] *Plates 965–6.*

SPEDALE DEGLI INNOCENTI, PINACOTECA. Adoration of the Magi. (See also Bartolomeo di Giovanni). 1488. *Plate 967.*

SPEDALE DI ORBATELLO, FAÇADE. Fresco lunette: Annunciation (p.). d. 1485.

(Environs) BROZZI, S. ANDREA, ALTAR L. Frescoes: Madonna and Child with SS. Sebastian and Julian, Baptism of Christ (g.p.). E.

— S. ANDREA A CERCINA, CHAPEL R. OF CHOIR. Fresco: SS. Jerome, Barbara and Anthony Abbot. E.

Hartford (Conn.). TRINITY COLLEGE, KRESS STUDY COLLECTION. K 1147. Madonna and Child (fr.). E. (?)

Lille. 337. Madonna and Child (p.).

London. 1230. Portrait of a Girl (g.p.).

1299. Portrait of a young Man (p.).

2490. Portrait of Costanza Caetani. E.

2902. Predella panel (to Florence, Uffizi 881): S. Justus of Volterra distributing Bread (st.).

W. H. WOODWARD (EX). Virgin adoring (fr. of a Nativity; r.). E. *Plate 956.*

Lucca. DUOMO, SACRISTY. Madonna and Child with SS. Peter, Clement, Sebastian and Paul. Lunette: Man of Sorrows. Predella: S. Matthew, Liberation of S. Peter, S. Clement thrown into the Sea, Man of Sorrows, Martyrdom of S. Sebastian, Conversion of S. Paul, S. Lawrence (g.p.; see also Bartolomeo di Giovanni.)

Lugano. THYSSEN COLLECTION. 150. Profile Portrait of a young Woman, called 'Giovanna Tornabuoni'. d. 1488.

Milan. MUSEO POLDI PEZZOLI. 561. Portrait of a young Man (p.).

Munich. 1078. 'S. Maria Novella' altarpiece: Madonna and Child in Glory with SS. Dominic, Michael, John Baptist and John Evangelist (executed by Granacci and Mainardi on Domenico's design; companion to Mainardi, Munich 1076–77; and to Granacci and Davide Ghirlandajo, Berlin 74–76). Soon after 1494. *Plate 974.*

Narni. PINACOTECA. Coronation of the Virgin with Angels and Saints. Pilasters: Six
Saints. Predella: Stigmatization of S. Francis, Man of Sorrows, S. Jerome in
the Wilderness (g.p.; see also Bartolomeo di Giovanni). 1486.

New Haven (Conn.). 1871.52. Fresco: Head of a Woman (fr.).

1943.229–332. Four predella panels: Agony in the Garden, Way to Calvary,
Resurrection, *Noli me tangere* (st.).

New York. 13.119.1–3. Three predella panels (to Florence, Uffizi 881): Marriage of
the Virgin, Translation of the Body of S. Zenobius, Tobias and the Angel (st.).

32.100.71. Portrait of a young Woman of the Sassetti Family.

49.7.7. Portrait of Francesco Sassetti and his Son Teodoro.

80.3.674. Fresco: S. Christopher (g.p.). E.

Paris. 1321. Visitation, with SS. Mary of James and Mary Salome (g.p., assisted by
Mainardi). d. 1491. *Plate 976.*

1322. Portrait of an old Man and a Boy. [*Plate 183.*]

1322A. Portrait of a young Man.

1367A. Madonna and Child (g.p.). E. *Plate 954.*

Passignano (Val di Pesa). BADIA, EX-REFECTORY. Fresco: Last Supper (p.). ca 1477.

Philadelphia (Pa.). MUSEUM OF ART, JOHNSON COLLECTION. 65. Madonna and Child
with SS. Apollonia and Sebastian (only the heads of the Madonna and S.
Sebastian; the rest by Davide Ghirlandajo).

Pisa. 177. SS. Sebastian and Roch (p.).

179. Madonna and Child with SS. Catherine, Stephen, Lawrence and Fina
(g.p.). 147(9?).

180. Madonna and Child with SS. Jerome, Romuald, two other Saints and
young Donor (g.p.).

Portland (Ore.). ART MUSEUM, KRESS COLLECTION. K 487 A, B. Two panels: SS.
Michael and Dominic (r.).

Princeton (N.J.). L 130.47. Fresco: An Angel (fr., r.). E.

Rimini. PINACOTECA. S. Vincent Ferrer with SS. Sebastian and Roch and four
Donors. Lunette: God the Father blessing. Predella: S. Vincent Ferrer raising
a Child, healing Cripples and appearing from heaven to raise a dead Man
(unfinished at the artist's death, the Donors were painted by a Bolognese artist,
possible Francia). L.

Rome. TORLONIA COLLECTION. Profile Portrait of Maddalena Cybo (c.?). d. 1487.

VATICAN, SISTINE CHAPEL. Fresco: Calling of SS. Peter and Andrew (g.p.). 1482.
Plate 964.

Frescoes (between windows): Twelve Popes [Anacletus, Clement, Alexander,
Hyginus, Pius, Eleutherius, Victor, Zephyrinus, Urban, Dionysius, Felix,
Damasus] (p.).

San Gimignano. COLLEGIATA, CAPPELLA DE S. FINA. Frescoes. Right wall: S. Gregory
announcing the Death of S. Fina. Left wall: Healing of the Nurse at the Bier
of S. Fina. (See also Mainardi.) ca 1475. *Plate 958.*

Sanginesio (Macerata). PINACOTECA. Marriage of S. Catherine (st.).

Urbino. GALLERIA NAZIONALE DELLE MARCHE (PALAZZO DUCALE). Madonna and Child (u., st.). E.

Volterra. 30. Christ in Glory with SS. Benedict, Romuald, kneeling Saints Actinea and Graeciniana, and Giusto Bonvicini as Donor (p.). 1492.

Washington (D.C.). 1412. (KRESS COLLECTION 2076). Madonna and Child. E. *Plate* 955.

Zurich. ANNIE ABEGG-STOCKAR. Portrait of a young Man.

GHIRLANDAJO, Ridolfo

1483–1561. Son of Domenico Ghirlandajo, pupil of Fra Bartolommeo, Piero di Cosimo and Granacci. He was an eclectic imitator of his contemporaries, particularly Raphael.

Bergamo. 553. Portrait of a Man (r.). (?)

Berlin. 91. Nativity with two Angels. E. (Destroyed 1945).

Budapest. 68. Adoration of the Shepherds, with SS. Roch and Sebastian. Sd and d. 1510. *Plate* 1287.

Charlotte (N.C.). MINT MUSEUM, KRESS COLLECTION. K 1181. Tondo: Madonna and Child with SS. Dominic, John Baptist, Jerome and a fourth Saint.

Chicago (Ill.). 33.1009. Portrait of a Man. E.

Colle Val d'Elsa. S. AGOSTINO, R. WALL. Lamentation with SS. John Baptist, Nicholas and Jerome. Predella: S. Nicholas and the three Maidens, Beheading of S. John, Resurrection, S. John in the Wilderness, Communion of S. Mary Magdalen. 1521. *Plate* 1292.

Colle Ramole (Tavarnuzze). See Florence, Environs.

Eastnor Castle (Hereford). HON. MRS. HERVEY BATHURST. Portrait of a Man with a Book.

Firle Place (Lewes, Sussex). VISCOUNTESS GAGE. Portrait of a Man.

Florence. GALLERIE. 2155. Portrait of a Man. (?)

    4660. S. Jerome in the Wilderness. After 1520.

  ACCADEMIA. 1584, 1589. S. Zenobius raising a Child, Translation of the Body of S. Zenobius. 1517. *Plate* 1290.

    4652. Madonna and Child with SS. Francis and Mary Magdalen. d. 1503. *Plate* 1279.

    8648, 8649. Two panels: Six adoring Angels. E.

  PITTI. 207. Portrait of a Man, called the 'Goldsmith'.

    224. Portrait of a Woman. d. 1509. *Plate* 1283.

  PALAZZO RICCARDI, MUSEO MEDICEO. Portrait of Cosimo I as a Boy. 1531. *Plate* 1293.

  PALAZZO VECCHIO, CAPPELLA DEI PRIORI. Frescoes. Vault: Trinity, Four Evangelists, Putti with Passion Symbols, Dove of the Holy Ghost, Twelve Apostles.

Lunettes: Annunciation, Vision of S. Bernard. Walls: Monochrome and gilt *grottesche* and S. John Baptist. ca 1514. *Plate* 1288.

S. LORENZO, R. TRANSEPT, 2nd CHAPEL R. S. Lawrence enthroned, with SS. Stephen and Leonard (g.p.). d. 1511.

S. MARIA DEGLI ANGELI, REFECTORY. Fresco: Last Supper (after Andrea del Sarto's at S. Salvi). d. 1543.

S. MARIA NOVELLA, CAPPELLA DEL PAPA (SCUOLA SOTTUFFICIALI CARABINIERI). Fresco lunette: Coronation of the Virgin. 1515.

S. TRINITA, 2nd CHAPEL L. S. Jerome in the Wilderness. L. *Plate* 1281.

CONTINI BONACOSSI COLLECTION. Portrait of a Man.

GALLERIA CORSINI. 129. Portrait of a Man.

MARCHESA LUCIA TORRIGIANI. Portrait of a Man. *Plate* 1284.

(Environs) COLLE RAMOLE, VILLA AGOSTINI, CHAPEL. Frescoes: Madonna and Child with SS. Dominic and Benedict, Faith, Hope, and the Artist and his Family as Donors. 1515–16. *Plate* 1289.

—LA QUIETE. Marriage of S. Catherine, with SS. Dominic, James, John Evangelist and two Bishop Saints.

Four organ shutters from the Monastery of Ripoli: SS. Jerome, Cosmas, Damian and Sebastian. E. *Plates* 1278, 1280.

Genoa (Environs). PEGLI, MUSEO NAVALE. 3487. Portrait of a Man, called 'Christopher Columbus' (r.).

Leningrad. 104. Portrait of a Man.

London. 1143. Way to Calvary. *Plates* 1282, 1285.

2491. Portrait of a Man, called 'Girolamo Benivieni' or 'Bernardo del Nero'.

LADY MARGARET WATNEY (EX). Portrait of Old Man in octagonal frame.

Manchester. 1947.188. 'Beit' Tondo: Adoration of the Shepherds.

Minneapolis. INSTITUTE OF ARTS. 61–7. Portrait of a young Man with a letter.

New Haven (Conn.). 1871.73. Madonna and Child with SS. Dominic and Jerome.

New York. 06.171. Madonna and Child with Infant S. John. E. (?)

32.100.80. Portable triptych: Nativity with a Benedictine Donor. Wings: SS. Benedict, Peter, Ursula, Dorothy, Paul and John Evangelist. *Plate* 1286.

Paris. 1324. Coronation of the Virgin, with SS. Peter Martyr, John Baptist, Mary Magdalen, Francis and Thomas Aquinas, and a sixth Saint (from Ripoli). 1504.

Philadelphia (Pa.). MUSEUM OF ART, JOHNSON COLLECTION. 73. Portrait of a Man with a Letter, called 'Andrea Bandini'.

74. Portrait of an old Man with a Glove and a Letter. L.

Pistoia. MUSEO CIVICO. Madonna and Child with SS. Sebastian, James, John Baptist, Gregory and two female Saints. 1528. *Plate* 1291.

— FIRST FLOOR. Fresco: Coronation and four Saints.

S. DOMENICO, SACRISTY. S. Sebastian, with SS. Jerome and Augustine. E. (?)

S. GIOVANNI FUORICIVITAS, L. WALL. S. Sebastian in landscape.

Prato. 13. Portrait of a Man, called 'Baldo Magini'.

DUOMO, OVER ENTRANCE. *Madonna della Cintola*, with SS. Stephen, Catherine, Lawrence, Margaret and another Saint. 1514.

Reggello (Valdarno Superiore). (Environs) S. PIETRO A PITIANA. Annunciation.

Stockton (Cal.). SAN JOAQUIN PIONEER MUSEUM AND HAGGIN MEMORIAL ART GALLERIES, KRESS COLLECTION. K 1098. Portrait of a young Lady.

Washington (D.C.). 619 (WIDENER COLLECTION). Portrait of a Woman, called 'Lucretia Summaria'.

Williamstown (Mass.). CLARK ART INSTITUTE. Portrait of a Man.

Worcester (Mass.). 1914.25. Portrait of a Priest. (?)

Zagreb. 30(94). Madonna and Child with Infant S. John (c. of New York 06.171).

GIOTTO

Ca 1267-1337. Follower of Cavallini; influenced by Cimabue and Giovanni Pisano.

Assisi. S. FRANCESCO, UPPER CHURCH, NAVE, VAULT OF FOURTH BAY FROM ENTRANCE. Frescoes: Four Doctors of the Church. *Plate 24.*

— — SOFFIT OF ENTRANCE ARCH. Frescoes: Sixteen Saints.

— — WALLS, UPPER REGISTER. Frescoes: Scenes from the Old and New Testament. [Right wall, two bays nearest entrance: Isaac and Jacob, Isaac and Esau, Joseph in the Well, Joseph's Brothers in Egypt. Left wall, bay nearest entrance: Christ among the Doctors, Baptism of Christ, Lamentation, Resurrection. Entrance wall: Pentecost, Ascension] (r.). *Plate 25.* See also diagram of right wall of nave on p. 49 above.

The above frescoes are Giotto's earliest known works.

— — WALLS, LOWER REGISTER. Frescoes: Scenes from the Legend of S. Francis. [Right wall: I. S. Francis and the Simpleton (p.; with Master of S. Cecilia), II. S. Francis giving his Cloak to a Beggar, III. Vision of the Church Militant and Triumphant, IV. Miracle of the Crucifix of S. Damiano, V. S. Francis renouncing his Inheritance, VI. Dream of Innocent III, VII. Confirmation of the Rule, VIII. S. Francis appearing to his Brothers in a Chariot of Fire, IX. Vision of the Heavenly Thrones, X. Exorcism of Arezzo, XI. Ordeal by Fire, XII. Ecstasy of S. Francis, XIII. Institution of the *Presepio* at Greccio. Entrance wall: XIV. Miracle of the Spring, XV. S. Francis preaching to the Birds. Left wall: XVI. Death of the Knight of Celano, XVII. S. Francis preaching to Honorius, XVIII. Apparition at Arles, XIX. Stigmatization of S. Francis, XX. Death of S. Francis (p.), XXI. Apparitions to Fra Agostino and Bishop Guido (p.), XXII. Examination of the Stigmata (p.), XXIII. Translation of the Body of S. Francis to S. Damiano (p.), XXIV. Canonization of S. Francis (p.), XXV. Dream of Pope Gregory (p.)]. (See also Master of S. Cecilia). E. [*Plate* 109.] *Plates* 30, 31. See also diagram on p. 49.

Assisi. S. FRANCESCO, UPPER CHURCH (contd.). OVER ENTRANCE. Fresco roundel: Madonna and Child (contemporary with S. Francis legend).

    S. FRANCESCO, LOWER CHURCH, 3rd CHAPEL R. (MAGDALEN CHAPEL). Frescoes. Vault: Christ blessing, S. Mary Magdalen, Lazarus, Martha (st.). Soffits of entrance arch: Twelve Saints (st.). Walls: Scenes from the Life of S. Mary Magdalen. [Left wall: Feast in the House of Simon (g.p.), Raising of Lazarus (g.p.), Last Communion of S. Mary Magdalen (st.), S. Rufino with Tebaldo Pontano (p.), S. Clare (st.). Right wall: *Noli me tangere* (p.), Voyage to Marseilles (st.), Ecstasy of S. Mary Magdalen (st.), S. Mary Magdalen and Tebaldo Pontano (p.), a Saint (st.). Entrance wall: S. Mary Magdalen clothed by Zosimo (g.p.). Window wall: Four Saints (st.)]. (The Feast, The Raising of Lazarus and The Magdalen Clothed by Zosimus, not much later than the Paduan frescoes). *Plates* 49–51.

Berlin. 1884. Dormition of the Virgin (g.p.). L. *Plate* 52.

Boville Ernica (Frosinone). S. PIETRO ISPANO. Mosaic: An Angel (fr. of the *Navicella*; companion to Rome, Grotte Vaticane). E. *Plate* 46.

Châalis (Ermenonville). MUSÉE JACQUEMART-ANDRÉ. 10, 11. Two panels from a polyptych: SS. John Evangelist and Lawrence. Pinnacles: Two Angels (p.; companions to Florence, Museo Horne; and Washington). L.

Florence. UFFIZI. 8344. Madonna and Child enthroned, with Saints and Angels. [*Plates* 107–108.]

    MUSEO HORNE. 52. Panel from a polyptych: S. Stephen (g.p.; companion to Châalis and Washington). L.

    S. CROCE, 1st CHAPEL R. OF CHOIR (BARDI CHAPEL). Frescoes: Scenes from the Legend of S. Francis [Vault: Four Virtues. Left wall: S. Francis renouncing his Inheritance, Apparition at Arles, Death of S. Francis. Right wall: Confirmation of the Rule, Ordeal by Fire, Apparitions to Fra Agostino and Bishop Guido. Window wall: SS. Louis of Toulouse, Clare and a third Saint. Above entrance to chapel: Stigmatization of S. Francis] (r.). Not before 1317. *Plates* 56, 57, 59–62, 343.

    — 2nd CHAPEL R. OF CHOIR (PERUZZI CHAPEL). Frescoes: Scenes from the Lives of SS. John Baptist and John Evangelist [Left wall: Annunciation to S. Zacharias, Birth and Naming of S. John Baptist, Feast of Herod. Right wall: S. John on Patmos, Raising of Drusiana, Ascension of S. John Evangelist] (r.). L. [*Plate* 114.] *Plates* 55, 58.

    S. MARIA NOVELLA, SACRISTY. Crucifix. E. *Plates* 26–29.

    BERENSON COLLECTION. A Franciscan Monk.

London. LADY JEKYLL (EX). Finial (to Rimini Crucifix): Christ blessing. *Plate* 48.

Padua. MUSEO CIVICO. Crucifix (g.p.). ca 1305–06.

    ARENA CHAPEL (SCROVEGNI CHAPEL), VAULT. Frescoes: Christ blessing, Madonna and Child, Seven Prophets, S. John Baptist. Friezes: Prophets, Saints and Scenes from the Old Testament (p.; with author of frescoes in choir).

— WALLS. Frescoes: Scenes from the Lives of Christ and the Virgin. [Right wall, upper register: Expulsion of Joachim from the Temple, Joachim among the Shepherds, Annunciation to S. Anne, Sacrifice of Joachim, Dream of Joachim, Meeting at the Golden Gate. Left wall, upper register: Birth of the Virgin, Presentation in the Temple, Consignment of the Rods, Flowering of the Rods, Marriage of the Virgin, Marriage Procession of the Virgin. Altar wall: Mission to Gabriel and Annunciation, Visitation. Right wall, middle register: Nativity, Adoration of the Magi, Circumcision, Flight into Egypt, Massacre of the Innocents. Left wall, middle register: Christ among the Doctors, Baptism of Christ, Marriage at Cana, Raising of Lazarus, Entry into Jerusalem, Expulsion of the Moneychangers from the Temple. Altar wall: Judas receiving the Price of Betrayal. Right wall, lower register: Last Supper, Washing of Feet, Betrayal of Christ, Christ before Caiaphas, Mocking of Christ. Left wall, lower register: Way to Calvary, Crucifixion, Lamentation, *Noli me tangere*, Ascension, Pentecost. Entrance wall: Last Judgement. Dado: Seven Virtues (right wall), Seven Vices (left wall)]. ca 1305–06. [*Plates* 110–113, 116–117.] *Plates* 35–45.

Rimini. S. FRANCESCO. Crucifix. *Plate* 48.

Rome. S. GIOVANNI LATERANO, 1ST PILLAR R. *Fresco: Pope Boniface VIII proclaiming the Jubilee of 1300 (fr., r.). *Plate* 33.

VATICAN, GROTTE. Mosaic: An Angel (fr. of the *Navicella*; companion to Boville Ernica). E.

Washington (D.C.). 367 (KRESS COLLECTION 473). Madonna and Child (companion to Châalis and Florence, Museo Horne). L. *Plate* 54.

GIOTTO's Assistants

No attempt has been made to distinguish between the assistants who executed the following works under Giotto's orders and direction. They were so able and so well disciplined that their individuality can be detected only in their failings; and these perhaps are not worth tracing.

Assisi. S. FRANCESCO, LOWER CHURCH, VAULT OF CROSSING. Frescoes: S. Francis in Glory and Allegories of Chastity, Poverty and Obedience. *Plates* 67–69.

— R. TRANSEPT. Frescoes: Scenes from the Life of Christ, and Miracles of S. Francis. [Vault: Visitation, Nativity, Adoration of the Magi, Circumcision, Flight into Egypt, Massacre of the Innocents, Christ among the Doctors, Departure from Jerusalem, Crucifixion, Raising of a Child through the Intercession of S. Francis, S. Francis indicating a Skeleton. Wall: Annunciation, Death of the Youth of Suessa, S. Francis raising the Youth of Suessa.] *Plates* 70–71.

Berlin. 1074A. Crucifixion.

Bologna. 102. Polyptych: Madonna and Child with SS. Peter, Gabriel, Michael and
Paul. Predella: Man of Sorrows and four Saints. *Plate* 77.

Boston (Mass.). ISABELLA GARDNER MUSEUM. Circumcision. (Companion to Florence,
Berenson collection; London; Munich; and New York).

Dresden. 5. S. John Baptist in Prison (r.).

Florence. PALAZZO DEL BARGELLO, CAPPELLA DEL PODESTÀ. Frescoes: Last Judgement
and Scenes from the Life of S. Mary Magdalen [Altar wall: Last Judgement.
Entrance wall: Inferno. Right wall: Feast in the House of Simon, Raising of
Lazarus, Resurrection, *Noli me tangere*, Ecstasy of S. Mary Magdalen, her
Communion, her Last Communion and Death. Left wall: Voyage to Mar-
seilles and three other Scenes, Two Saints] (r.).

S. CROCE, BARONCELLI CHAPEL. 'Baroncelli' polyptych: Coronation of the Virgin,
with Saints and Angels (cut at top; see San Diego). Predella: Man of Sorrows
and four Saints. *Plates* 63, 111.

— MUSEO DELL'OPERA. 'Badia' polyptych: Madonna and Child with SS. Nicholas,
John Evangelist, Peter and Benedict. Pinnacles: Christ blessing and four
Angels. *Plates* 32, 34.

S. FELICE. Crucifix.

BERENSON COLLECTION. Entombment. (See Boston). *Plate* 53.

London. 5360. Pentecost. (See Boston).

Munich. 643. Last Supper. (See Boston).
     667. Crucifixion. (See Boston).
     5295. Descent into Limbo. (See Boston).

New York. 11.126.1. Adoration of the Magi. (See Boston).

Padua. S. ANTONIO, SALA DEL CAPITOLO. Frescoes: Stigmatization of S. Francis,
Martyrdom at Ceuta, Ten Saints, and two fragments of another Scene
(Crucifixion?) (fr., r.).

Paris. 1312. Stigmatization of S. Francis. Below: Dream of Innocent III, Confirmation of the Rule, S. Francis preaching to the Birds.

Rome. VATICAN, PINACOTECA. 120. 'Stefaneschi' polyptych [*Front:* Christ enthroned
with Angels worshipped by Cardinal Stefaneschi; Crucifixion of S. Peter;
Beheading of S. Paul. Pinnacles: *Salvator mundi*, Abraham and Moses. Predella: Madonna and Child with two Angels and twelve Apostles. *Back:* S.
Peter enthroned between two Angels, and at his feet Stefaneschi and a bishop,
presented by their Patron Saints, offer him a reproduction of the polyptych
and a book; SS. James, Paul, Mark and John. Pinnacles: Three Angels.
Predella (fr.): Three Saints]. *Plates* 64-66.

San Diego (Cal.). FINE ARTS GALLERY. Pinnacle (to 'Baroncelli' polyptych): God the
Father and Angels (fr.). *Plate* 63.

Strasbourg. 201. Crucifixion.

Homeless. Madonna and Child with SS. John Baptist, Francis, four other Saints and seven Virtues. *Plate 72.*

GIOTTO's Anonymous Contemporaries and Immediate Followers

Assisi. S. FRANCESCO, LOWER CHURCH, R. TRANSEPT, S. NICOLA CHAPEL. Frescoes: Scenes from the Life of S. Nicholas [Vault: S. Nicholas and the three Maidens, S. Nicholas preventing the Execution of three Innocent Men, S. Nicholas pardoning the iniquitous Consul, S. Nicholas appearing to Constantine, and two ruined scenes. Over altar: Madonna and Child with SS. Nicholas and Francis. Entrance wall: Christ blessing with SS. Francis and Nicholas and Napoleone and Gian Gaetano Orsini, SS. Mary Magdalen and John Baptist and two other Saints. Right wall: S. Nicholas raising a Child, S. Nicholas rescuing Adeodatus from the Service of the Pagan King, S. Nicholas restoring Adeodatus to his Parents, Five Saints. Left wall: A Jew beating an Image of S. Nicholas, two other ruined scenes, Two Saints. Soffits of entrance arch: Twelve Saints]. Before 1316.

Brussels. MME. FERON-STOCLET. Nativity. (Probably companion to Florence, Berenson collection; Rome, Vatican 176; and Homeless). *Plate 74.*

Capesthorne Hall (Cheshire). LT.-COL. SIR W. H. BROMLEY-DAVENPORT. Polyptych: Man of Sorrows and SS. Francis, Peter, Paul and Philip. Pinnacles: Two Angels and four Prophets. *Plate 78.*

Dublin. JAMES A. MURNAGHAN. Madonna and Child with SS. Nicholas, Lawrence and Francis (close to Pacino).

Florence. ACCADEMIA. 6146. Madonna and Child.

8698, 8699, 8700. Panels of polyptych: Bishop Saint, S. John Evangelist, S. Augustine and Bishop Saint (close to Pacino).

MUSEO HORNE. 91. Madonna and Child with SS. Francis and Lawrence.

COMPAGNIA DI S. BONIFACIO, CAPPELLA. Crucifix (close to Pacino).

S. CROCE, CHIOSTRO. Fresco: Madonna in Glory and four Angels.

S. MARCO, OVER ENTRANCE. Crucifix. *Plates 79–80.*

S. MARIA DEL FIORE (DUOMO), L. TRANSEPT, 4th CHAPEL. Polyptych. *Front:* Madonna and Child with SS. Eugenius, Miniato, Zenobius and Crescentius. *Back:* Annunciation, and SS. Reparata, John Baptist, Mary Magdalen and Nicholas.

OGNISSANTI, SACRISTY. Crucifix.

BERENSON COLLECTION. Crucifixion. (See Brussels, Feron-Stoclet). *Plate 75.*

Memphis (Tenn.). BROOKS MEMORIAL ART GALLERY, KRESS COLLECTION. K1289. Portable triptych: Madonna and Child with SS. Peter and John Baptist. Wings: Bishop Saint, Donor, Crucifixion (close to S. Cecilia Master).

Naples. S. CHIARA, SALA DEL CAPITOLO. Fresco: Miracle of the Loaves and Fishes.

New York. ROBERT LEHMAN. Madonna and Child and Holy Ghost.

Ottawa. 2023. Madonna and Child enthroned, with two Donors (close to S. Cecilia Master).

Oxford. ASHMOLEAN. 178. Madonna and Child.

Paris. 1665A. Crucifixion.

Philadelphia (Pa.). MUSEUM OF ART, JOHNSON COLLECTION. 1. Annunciation, Nativity and Crucifixion.

3. Madonna and Child.

Rome. VATICAN, PINACOTECA. 171. Lamentation.

176. Madonna and Child. (See Brussels, Feron-Stoclet).

Homeless. Annunciation. (See Brussels, Feron-Stoclet). *Plate* 73.

Lamentation. (See Brussels, Feron-Stoclet). *Plate* 76.

GIOVANNI DEL BIONDO

Active ca 1356-1399. *Probably a pupil of the Gaddi; influenced by Daddi in his early work, and later by the Orcagna brothers.*

Allentown (Pa.). ART MUSEUM, KRESS COLLECTION. K 1150. Marriage of S. Catherine and female Donor.

Arezzo. MUSEO (DEP. GALLERIE FIORENTINE 3081). Madonna and Child with two Angels. (Destroyed).

Baltimore (Md.). WALTERS ART GALLERY. 719. SS. Sebastian, Anthony Abbot, Margaret, Lucy and a Bishop Saint.

Buffalo (N.Y.). 34.71, 72. Two panels: Annunciation (fr.).

Cambridge (Mass.). 1929.314. Fresco: Madonna and Child (r.). (?)

Charlotte (N.C.). MRS. G. C. ADAMS. Two panels: Last Communion, Extreme Unction.

Detroit (Mich.). 29.315, 316. Two pinnacles: Annunciation. (Companions to S. Giovanni Valdarno 1-2).

Dublin. 943. Madonna and Child with four Angels, and Christ blessing.

Fiesole. DUOMO, SACRISTY. Coronation of the Virgin with Saints and Angels. Pinnacles: Crucifixion and Annunciation. d. 1373.

Figline (Valdarno Superiore). S. FRANCESCO (MISERICORDIA), SACRISTY. Madonna and Child (st.). Sd and d. 1392. *Plate* 305.

Florence. GALLERIE. 444. S. John Evangelist enthroned. *Plate* 292.

446. Predella (to 444 above): Ascension of S. John Evangelist.

ACCADEMIA. 8462. Triptych: Circumcision, and SS. John Baptist and Benedict. Predella: Annunciation to S. Zacharias, Birth of the Baptist, Naming of the Baptist, Feast of Herod. d. 1364. *Plates* 288-289.

8606. Triptych: Annunciation, and twenty-seven Saints. Pinnacles: Flagellation, Crucifixion, Resurrection, Angels. Pilasters: Six Saints. Predella: Man of Sorrows with the Maries and S. John, and six Doctors of the Church. ca 1378.

8707. S. Lawrence.

s. CROCE, HIGH ALTAR. Four lateral panels of polyptych: SS. Ambrose, Gregory, Augustine and Jerome (central panel by Niccolò di Pietro Gerini, predella by Mariotto di Nardo). d. 1363. *Plate 286.*

— 1st CHAPEL L. OF CHOIR (TOSINGHI). Polyptych: Madonna and Child with SS. Augustine, Anthony Abbot, Bartholomew and Lawrence. Pinnacles: Christ blessing and four Saints (predella by Neri di Bicci). d. 1372.

— 5th CHAPEL L. OF CHOIR (BARDI DI VERNIO). Triptych: S. John Gualbert and Scenes from his Life. [Pinnacles: Christ blessing and two Seraphim. Wings: Conversion of S. John, An Angel bringing Bread to the Monastery, Ordeal by Fire of Bd. Peter Igneus, Death of S. John. Predella: Man of Sorrows and six Saints]. (?)

— SACRISTY, RINUCCINI CHAPEL. Polyptych: Madonna and Child with SS. Francis, John Baptist, John Evangelist and Mary Magdalen. Above: Crucifixion, Four Prophets, Six Apostles. Predella: Stigmatization of S. Francis, Baptism of Christ, Journey of the Magi and Nativity, S. John on Patmos, Ecstasy of S. Mary Magdalen. d. 1379. *Plates 300–301, 381.*

s. FELICITA, SACRISTY. Madonna and Child.

s. MARIA DEL FIORE (DUOMO), 1st PILLAR L. S. Zenobius enthroned with two Angels and SS. Eugenius and Crescentius. Pinnacle: Christ blessing. Predella: Raising of a Dead Boy, Miracle of the flowering Tree.

— MUSEO DELL'OPERA. 84–86. Triptych: Martyrdom of S. Sebastian and Scenes from his Life [Pinnacle: Christ blessing. Wings: Annunciation, Preaching of S. Sebastian, S. Sebastian invoked against the Plague, Death of S. Sebastian and Disposal of his Body, S. Lucilla's Dream and the Recovery of the Body. *Plates 291, 293.*

90. S. Catherine enthroned with three Donors. (Surrounding scenes and two smaller of the three donors added later by another artist). ca 1370.

s. MARIA NOVELLA, STROZZI CHAPEL. Frescoes (entrance arch): SS. Jerome, Augustine, Ambrose and Gregory (assisting Nardo). E. *Plate 287.*

OGNISSANTI, L. OF ENTRANCE. Fresco: Annunciation and Donor (fr., r.).

SPEDALE DEGLI INNOCENTI, PINACOTECA. Triptych: Annunciation, and SS. Nicholas and Anthony Abbot. 1385. *Plate 303.*

CONTINI BONACOSSI COLLECTION. S. John Baptist and Scenes from his Life. [Annunciation to S. Zacharias, Visitation, Birth of S. John, Naming of S. John, S. John in the Wilderness, S. John indicating Christ to the People, Baptism of Christ, Feast of Herod, Beheading of S. John, S. John's Head brought to Salome, Descent into Limbo]. *Plate 290.*

(Environs). s. FELICE A EMA. Madonna and Child (st.). d. 1387.

Gazzada (Varese). VILLA CAGNOLA. Madonna and Child with two Angels and six Saints. Predella: Annunciation.

Hamburg. WEDELLS COLLECTION (EX?). Two panels with pairs of music-making Angels (fragment of Liverpool Coronation).

Le Mans. 1. Predella panel: Worshippers at the Tomb of a Saint.

Liverpool. 2782. Coronation of the Virgin (fr.; companion to Hamburg).

London. BUCKINGHAM PALACE, ROYAL COLLECTION. B.P.143. Two panels: Annunciation.

HENRY HARRIS (EX). Panel from an altarpiece: S. John Baptist.

Los Angeles (Cal.). L 2100.39–551 (KRESS COLLECTION 1121). Madonna and Child with two Angels and Donor (SS. John Baptist and Evangelist by another hand).

Memphis (Tenn.). BROOKS MEMORIAL ART GALLERY, KRESS COLLECTION. K 259. Madonna and Child with SS. John Baptist and Catherine. Above: Annunciation.

Montreal. 1093. Madonna and Child with four Angels. *Plate 295.*

Muncie (Ind.). BALL STATE TEACHERS COLLEGE. Coronation of the Virgin with four Angels. (?)

New Haven (Conn.). 1871.19. Christ and the Virgin enthroned, with Angels. Above: The Church and the Synagogue.

New Orleans (La.). I. DELGADO MUSEUM, KRESS COLLECTION. K 63. Madonna nursing the Child.

Philadelphia (Pa.). MUSEUM OF ART, JOHNSON COLLECTION. Inv. 1290–92. Three predella panels: Beheading of S. John Baptist and Martyrdom of S. Lawrence, Adoration of the Magi, Flaying of S. Bartholomew and Miracle of the Bull of Gargano. *Plate 302.*

Pisa. 31. Madonna and Child with two Angels and twelve Saints (r.).

Princeton (N.J.). L 6.54. Madonna and Child with S. Anne. (?)

Richmond (Surrey). COOK COLLECTION (EX). 12. Triptych: Coronation of the Virgin with four Angels and twenty-four Saints and Guglielmo Geri de Spinis, Prior of Peretola, as Donor. d. 1372. *Plate 294.*

Rome. VATICAN, PINACOTECA. 13. Right wing of an altarpiece: SS. John Evangelist, Bartholomew, Francis and nineteen other Saints. (Companion to 15).

14. Madonna and Child with eight Saints. Spandrels: Annunciation. Predella: *Imago mortis. Plate 298.*

15. Left wing of an altarpiece: SS. Nicholas, Lawrence, John Baptist and fifteen other Saints. (Companion to 13).

Romena (Casentino). PIEVE DI S. PIETRO. Madonna and Child with two Angels and SS. Peter and Paul. Pinnacle: Christ blessing (r.). 1386. *Plate 304.*

San Donato in Poggio (Val di Pesa). PIEVE, BAPTISTERY. Two panels of an altarpiece: Coronation of the Virgin with SS. Anthony Abbot and Louis of Toulouse, S. Thomas Aquinas and female Donor. d. 1375. *Plate 296.*

San Giovanni Valdarno. 1. Triptych: Coronation of the Virgin with Angels and thirty-five Saints.

2. Pinnacle (to 1). : Crucifixion. (Companion to Detroit).

3, 4. Two pinnacles: Man of Sorrows, Christ blessing.

San Miniato al Tedesco (Pisa). S. DOMENICO, CHAPEL L. OF CHOIR. Panel from an altarpiece: S. Catherine (r.).

Sant'Agata (Scarperia, Mugello). PIEVE, CHAPEL R. OF CHOIR. Madonna and Child.
— R. OF ENTRANCE. Two fragments in frame around relic: SS. Agatha and Lucy.

Sarasota (Fla.). 6. Madonna and Child with two Angels and SS. John Baptist, Peter, Paul and James.

Siena. 584. Madonna and Child. Above: Crucifixion. Sd and d. 1377. *Plate 297.*

GIOVANNI DI FRANCESCO
(Master of the Carrand Triptych)

Only documented activity in 1459. Probably a pupil of Uccello, but equally influenced by Andrea del Castagno, Domenico Veneziano, Filippo Lippi and Piero della Francesca.

Berlin. (Sculpture, 74.) Heads of three Prophets and a Sibyl (on frame of a bas-relief tondo of the Madonna and Child). (Destroyed?).
  1141. S. Nicholas of Tolentino.
  W. WEISBACH (EX). Madonna and Child with SS. Benedict and Romuald.

Boston (Mass.). ISABELLA GARDNER MUSEUM. Predella panel from Pratovecchio altarpiece (see Florence, Gallerie, and London): Dormition of the Virgin with female Donor. (?) *Plate 694.*

Chantilly. 7. S. John Baptist in the Wilderness. (?)

Detroit (Mich.). 37.37. S. John Evangelist (r.).

Dublin. HON. JAMES MURNAGHAN. Cassone panel: Scene in a Florentine Street.
  REV. J. SHINE. Madonna and Child.

Edinburgh. 1210. Predella panel: Last Supper. (Companion to Andrea del Castagno, London 1138 and New York, Frick?)

Florence. GALLERIE. Virgin in Glory with Cherubim (from S. Giovanni Evangelista at Pratovecchio; companion to Boston and London). (?) *Plate 693.*
  ACCADEMIA. 5381. Scenes of Monastic Life and Vision of S. Bernard. *Plate 679.*
  CASA BUONARROTI. Predella (to the Carrand triptych?): S. Nicholas and the three Maidens, Raising of the three Boys, S. Nicholas saving two Men from Execution. *Plate 689.*
  MUSEO NAZIONALE DEL BARGELLO. 2025. The 'Carrand' Triptych: Madonna and Child with SS. Francis, John Baptist, Nicholas and Peter. Pinnacles: Annunciation, Coronation of the Virgin, *Madonna della Cintola. Plates 687, 688, 690.*
  S. MARIA DEGLI INNOCENTI, PORTICO, Fresco lunette (over entrance): God the Father with two Angels and martyred Innocents. 1459. *Plate 686.*
  S. MARIA MAGGIORE, CHAPEL L. OF CHOIR. Fresco above Madonna in polychrome relief: Christ on the Cross.
  S. TRINITA, 5th CHAPEL L. (SPINI). Fresco: Blessed Gregory.

Florence (contd.). SEMINARIO MAGGIORE (from S. Andrea a Brozzi). Crucifix. *Plate* 685.

— (from S. Bartolomeo a Quarata). Predella: S. John in Patmos, Adoration of the Magi, SS. James and Ansanus.

CONTINI BONACOSSI COLLECTION. Madonna and Child with two Cherubim. (Companion to Lyons and Milan). L. [*Plate* 164.] *Plate* 682.

A Sainted Nun and two worshipping Children (fr.). *Plate* 674.

(Environs). PETRIOLO, S. BIAGIO. Altar frontal: S. Blaise. d. 1453. *Plate* 683.

Karlsruhe. 404. Nativity with SS. Jerome, Mary Magdalen and Eustace. *Plates* 675, 676, 678.

London. 584. Wings of Pratovecchio altarpiece: SS. Michael and John Baptist, A Bishop Saint and a female Martyr. Pinnacles: Virgin, S. John, Annunciation. Pilasters: Twelve Saints. (Companions to Florence, Gallerie, and Boston). (?) *Plate* 692.

Lucca. S. FRANCESCO, CHAPEL R. OF CHOIR. Frescoes. Left wall: Meeting at the Golden Gate (fr.). Altar wall: Annunciation. Right wall: Presentation and Marriage of the Virgin; Putti, Garlands (r.). L. (?)

Lugano. THYSSEN COLLECTION. 431. Predella panel: Crucifixion, with SS. John Baptist and Francis. *Plate* 677.

Lyons. MUSÉE. Wing of an altarpiece: S. James. (Companion to Florence, Contini Bonacossi, and Milan). *Plate* 682.

Milan. BRIZIO COLLECTION. Wing of an altarpiece: S. Anthony Abbot. (Companion to Florence, Contini Bonacossi, and Lyons). *Plate* 682.

Montpellier. MUSÉE FABRE 137 (CAMPANA 296). Predella panel: Nativity and Adoration of the Magi.

Morrocco (Tavarnelle Val di Pesa). S. MARIA. Frescoes. Entrance wall: Two Apostles. Left wall: Annunciation, Two Apostles. Right wall: Nativity, Two Apostles (fr., r.). 1459. *Plate* 684.

New York. HUGH SATTERLEE. Triptych: Madonna and Child with two Angels and SS. Bridget and Michael. (?). *Plate* 691.

Oxford. ASHMOLEAN. 268. David reproved by Nathan. (?)

Parma. CONGREGAZIONE DI S. FILIPPO NERI, PINACOTECA STUARD. 10. Christ bearing the Cross.

Philadelphia (Pa.). MUSEUM OF ART, JOHNSON COLLECTION. 59. Madonna and Child with SS. Anthony Abbot, Cosmas, Damian and Lawrence (r.).

Prato. DUOMO, 1ST CHAPEL L. OF CHOIR (CAPPELLA DELL'ASSUNTA). Frescoes. Vault: Faith, Hope, Charity, Fortitude. Soffits: SS. Jerome, Dominic, Paul and Francis. Walls: Scenes from the Lives of the Virgin and S. Stephen [Right wall: Birth of the Virgin, Presentation of the Virgin. Left wall: Disputation of S. Stephen] (See also Andrea di Giusto). E. *Plates* 672, 673.

— SALA DEL CAPITOLO. Fresco (from the Cappella Bocchineri or dell'Assunta): Blessed Jacopone da Todi. E.

GIOVANNI DA MILANO

Mentioned in Florence 1346–1366, in Rome 1369. Probably trained by Lombard Giotteschi, but influenced by Orcagna and Nardo.

Amsterdam. 981–PI. Crucifixion, with Saints.

Bordeaux. MUSÉE (CAMPANA 114). Wing of an altarpiece: S. Francis. (Companion to Williamstown?)

Florence. ACCADEMIA. 8467. *Pietà.* Sd and d. 1365.

    UFFIZI. 459. Panels from a polyptych: SS. Catherine and Lucy, Stephen and Lawrence, John Baptist and Luke, Peter and Benedict, James and Gregory. Spandrels: Scenes from the Apocalypse. Predella: Heavenly Choirs of Virgins, Martyrs, Apostles, Patriarchs and Prophets. *Plates 270–271.*

    S. CROCE, SACRISTY, RINUCCINI CHAPEL. Frescoes. Vault: Four Prophets. Entrance arch: Twelve Apostles, SS. Francis, Anthony of Padua, Louis of Toulouse and Andrew of Anagni. Walls: Scenes from the Lives of the Virgin and S. Mary Magdalen [Left wall: Expulsion of Joachim from the Temple, Annunciation to Joachim, Meeting at the Golden Gate, Birth of the Virgin. Right wall: Feast in the House of Simon, Christ in the House of Mary and Martha, Raising of Lazarus] (Four additional scenes in lower registers by the Master of the Rinuccini Chapel). Not finished in 1365. *Plates 273–276, 381.*

    — MUSEO DELL'OPERA. Madonna and Child. Predella: Man of Sorrows with the Virgin and SS. Dominic, Mary Magdalen and Catherine. *Plate 265.*

    BERENSON COLLECTION. Two fragments of portable triptych: Annunciation.

    CONTINI BONACOSSI COLLECTION. Christ enthroned with four Angels. *Plate 269.*

London. 579A. Three pinnacles from an altarpiece: God the Father, the Virgin, and Isaiah.

    H. SOMMER. Crucifixion (g.p.).

New York. 07.200. Lunette: Madonna and Child with two Donors. *Plate 278.*

Paris. MARTIN LE ROY (EX). *Pietà. Plate 277.*

Ponce (Puerto Rico). MUSEO DE ARTE, KRESS STUDY COLLECTION. K 66, 67. Two panels: Two Prophets. (?)

Prato. 5. Polyptych: Madonna and Child with SS. Catherine, Bernard, Bartholomew and Barnabas. Pinnacles: Five Prophets. First predella: Beheading of S. Catherine, Vision of S. Bernard, Annunciation, Flaying of S. Bartholomew, Martyrdom of S. Barnabas. Second predella: Nativity, Adoration of the Magi, Circumcision, Agony in the Garden, Betrayal of Christ, Way to Calvary. Sd. *Plate 266–268.*

    S. NICOLA, OVER ENTRANCE. Fresco lunette: Madonna and Child with SS. Nicholas and Dominic.

Rome. GALLERIA NAZIONALE (PALAZZO BARBERINI). F.N.695. Madonna and Child with four Angels, Annunciation, Nativity, SS. Nicholas and Lawrence, SS.

Eustace and James, Crucifixion, Lamentation, SS. Margaret and Catherine.
VATICAN, PINACOTECA. 192. Predella panel: S. Dominic raising Napoleone Orsini. (?)

Sutton Place (Surrey). DUKE OF SUTHERLAND (EX). Two predella panels: Resurrection, Incredulity of S. Thomas. *Plate 272.*

Turin. 652. Left wing of an altarpiece: SS. John Evangelist, James, Peter and eight other Saints.

Williamstown (Mass.). WILLIAMS COLLEGE, KRESS COLLECTION. K 199. Wing of an altarpiece: S. Anthony Abbot (fr.). (Companion to Bordeaux?)

GIOVANNI (di Marco, called) DAL PONTE

1385–after 1437. Probably a pupil of Spinello Aretino; strongly influenced by Lorenzo Monaco, and subsequently by Fra Angelico and Masaccio. Close to the Master of the Bambino Vispo.

Arezzo. MUSEO (DEP. GALLERIE FIORENTINE 6232, 6105). Two panels: SS. Julian and John Baptist.

Ashburnham Place (Sussex). LADY ASHBURNHAM (EX). Two fragments of 'spalliere': Two allegorical couples in a garden, facing left (companions to Cracow and Fifield). *Plate 486.*

Brussels. 631. Three predella panels: Stigmatization of S. Francis, Adoration of the Magi, Temptation of S. Anthony.

Budapest. 1139. Marriage of S. Catherine with four Angels and two Donors. Pilasters: Eight Saints. Predella: Disputation of S. Catherine and Martyrdom of the Doctors, Conversion and Martyrdom of the Empress and the Jailors, Attempted Martyrdom and Beheading of S. Catherine. *Plate 492.*

Cambridge. 551. Madonna and Child enthroned with eight Angels.

565. Two panels: SS. Jerome and Francis, SS. John Baptist and Anthony Abbot.

Cambridge (Mass.). 1919.564. Dante and Petrarch (fr.). *Plate 485.*

Chantilly. 3. Triptych: Coronation of the Virgin with four music-making Angels and SS. Anthony Abbot, Louis of Toulouse, a male Saint, Peter, John Baptist, Blaise, Nicholas and Thomas. Pinnacles: God the Father, Annunciation. Pilasters: Abraham, Moses, and six Angels. d. 1410. *Plate 483.*

Columbia (S.C.). MUSEUM OF ART, KRESS COLLECTION. K 300. Triptych: Madonna and Child with SS. Stephen, Lawrence, Michael and George. Pinnacles: Christ blessing, Annunciation.

Cracow. 231. Fragment of 'spalliera': Two allegorical couples in a garden, facing right (companion to Ashburnham Place and Fifield).

Dijon. 1182. Left wing of an altarpiece: SS. Michael and Bartholomew (r.).

Englewood (N.J.). D. F. PLATT (EX). Madonna and Child enthroned.

Fiesole. MUSEO BANDINI. II, 13–14. Wings of an altarpiece: SS. John Baptist and Peter, SS. Paul and Francis.

Fifield House (Oxon). MRS. LOUISE BISHOP (EX). Fragment of 'spalliera': Allegorical couple in a garden, facing right (r.; companion to Ashburnham Place and Cracow).

Florence. GALLERIE. 4656. Coronation of the Virgin with four music-making Angels. E. (?).

UFFIZI. 1620. Predella: SS. Thomas, James Minor, Luke and James Major; Liberation of S. Peter; *Cathedra Petri*; Martyrdom of S. Peter; SS. Andrew, Joseph, Matthew and Philip. *Plates 493–494*.

ACCADEMIA. 458. Triptych: Coronation of the Virgin with four music-making Angels and SS. Francis, John Baptist, Ives and Dominic. Pinnacles: Descent into Limbo, Annunciation. *Plate 484*.

MUSEO HORNE. 3231. Wings of a triptych: Annunciation, SS. Michael and Dorothy.

ORSANMICHELE, IST PILLAR. Fresco: Annunciation (r.). (?)

S. SALVATORE AL MONTE. Madonna and Child with SS. Michael, Cecilia, a female Donor, Domitilla, Achilleus, Nereus and another Saint. L.

S. TRINITA, IST CHAPEL R. OF CHOIR (CAPPELLA DELL'ABBACO). Fresco over entrance: Christ enthroned with Angels and SS. John Baptist, John Evangelist, Peter and Paul. 1429–30.

— IST CHAPEL L. OF CHOIR (CAPPELLA FICOZZI). Fresco over entrance: Ascension of (?) S. John Evangelist, and Saints (r.). 1429–30.

— 2nd CHAPEL L. OF CHOIR (CAPPELLA SCALI). Frescoes: Martyrdom of S. Bartholomew, Beheading of a Saint (r.). 1434–35. *Plate 496*.

VIA DEI TAVOLINI. Tabernacle: Madonna and Child with two Angels and two female Saints.

(Environs) CERTOSA DEL GALLUZZO. Madonna and Child enthroned. *Plate 490*.

Hanover. 278. Left wing of an altarpiece: SS. Nicholas and Benedict.

Highnam Court (Glos.). GAMBIER-PARRY COLLECTION. Annunciation. Adoration of the Magi.

London. 580, 580A. Triptych: Ascension of S. John Evangelist, with SS. Bernard, Scholastica, Benedict, John Baptist, Peter, Romuald, Catherine and Jerome. Spandrels: Descent into Limbo, SS. Michael and Raphael with Tobias. Pilasters: Six Saints. Pinnacles: Trinity, Annunciation. Predella: S. Apollonia, Mission of the Apostles, S. John on Patmos, S. John in the Cauldron of boiling Oil, S. Verdiana.

COURTAULD GALLERIES, LEE OF FAREHAM COLLECTION. Virgin Annunciate (fr., r.).

Madrid. 2844. Cassone panel: Seven Liberal Arts. *Plate 487*.

New Haven (Conn.). 1943.217. Cassone panel: Allegory of Love or Pleasure.

1959.15.7A, B. Wings of a triptych: SS. James and John Baptist, Crucifixion and Resurrection.

Oakly Park (Shrops.). EARL OF PLYMOUTH. Madonna nursing the Child, with SS. Lucy, John Baptist, Francis and Catherine. *Plate 489*.

Paris. 1317A. Predella panel: Heraclius entering Jerusalem. (?)

MUSÉE JACQUEMART-ANDRÉ. 1053. Cassone: Garden of Love.

BARON CASSEL (EX). Cassone panel: Seven Virtues.

Perugia. R. VAN MARLE (EX). Madonna and Child with two Angels and SS. Bartholomew and Francis.

Philadelphia (Pa.). MUSEUM OF ART, JOHNSON COLLECTION. Inv. 1739. Right wing of an altarpiece: SS. Gimignano and Francis.

Pisa. 165. Madonna and Child with SS. Cosmas and Damian and two other Saints.

Pittsfield (Mass.). MRS. LAWRENCE K. MILLER. Two predella panels: Stoning of S. Stephen, Beheading of SS. Cosmas and Damian.

Poppiena (Casentino). BADIA, ALTAR R. Annunciation, with SS. John Baptist and Mary Magdalen.

Rome. VATICAN, PINACOTECA. 11. Triptych: Annunciation, and SS. Louis of Toulouse and Anthony of Padua. Predella: Man of Sorrows, Virgin and S. John. d. 1435.

Rosano (Pontassieve). SS. ANNUNZIATA. Triptych: Annunciation, with SS. Eugenius, Benedict, John Baptist and Nicholas. Pinnacles: Christ blessing, two Prophets. d. 1430. *Plate* 495.

San Francisco (Cal.). DE YOUNG MEMORIAL MUSEUM, KRESS COLLECTION. K 1556. Madonna and Child with four Angels. *Plate* 491.

Strasbourg. 207. Mocking of Christ. (?)

Venice. CONTE VITTORIO CINI. Allegory, on back of chessboard.

Zurich. ALFRED E. STEHLI-KAUFMANN. Heraclius entering Jerusalem.

Homeless. Madonna and Child with two Angels and SS. John Baptist and Catherine. On frame: Ten Angels. *Plate* 488.

GIUSTO D'ANDREA

1440–1496. Assistant successively of Neri di Bicci (1458), *Filippo Lippi* (1462) *and Benozzo Gozzoli* (1465). *The pictures here listed which may be, but are not necessarily, by him, represent the work of a close follower of Pesellino, influenced by Domenico di Michelino and Benozzo Gozzoli.*

Anghiari. S. STEFANO, ALTAR L. Madonna and Child with SS. Peter, Stephen, Bartholomew, Paul, Lawrence and a Bishop Saint.

Arles. MUSÉE RÉATTU. 154. Madonna and Child with two Angels (r.).

Berlin. 1090. Madonna of Humility with two Angels.

Boston (Mass.). ROBERT J. EDWARDS (EX). Madonna and Child with two Angels.

Certaldo. PALAZZO DEI PRIORI, CAMERA DELLE SENTENZE. *Fresco: Crucifixion. 1478.

Dallas (Texas). ART MUSEUM, KRESS COLLECTION. K158, 159. Two panels: SS. Francis and Jerome.

Dijon. D.93. Madonna and Child with SS. John Baptist, Peter, Francis, Leonard and Donor. *Plate 927*.

Fiesole. MUSEO BANDINI. Predella panel: Man of Sorrows with the Virgin and S. John.

Firenzuola (Mugello). MUNICIPIO. Fresco over door: S. Francis receiving Stigmata. (Destroyed).

Florence. GALLERIE. Madonna and Child, with SS. Francis, Luke, Louis of Toulouse and Catherine of Siena. L.

 8621. Pilaster: SS. Michael, Vincent and Lawrence. (Companion to Benozzo Gozzoli, Florence 8620).

 ACCADEMIA. 3452. S. Bernardino of Siena with two Angels.

 3450. Madonna and Child with SS. Anthony of Padua, Louis of Toulouse, Francis, Jerome, Bernardino and Sebastian.

 8624. Archangels Michael, Raphael with Tobias, and Gabriel.

 8636. Trinity. Predella: Triumph of S. Michael, Annunciation, Tobias and the Angel.

 CONSERVATORIO DI S. MARIA DEGLI ANGELI. Madonna and Child with two Angels and SS. Sebastian and Lucy. d. 1459.

 MUSEO DEL BIGALLO. Madonna of Humility with two Angels. E.

 S. CROCE, SACRISTY. S. Bonaventura with two Angels. *Plate 926*.

 (Environs) CAREGGI, S. PIETRO. Madonna and Child.

 — PERETOLA, S. MARIA. Frescoes in niche behind second altar right: S. Leonard liberating a Prisoner; below, Two Angels, SS. Lucy and Catherine, S. Lucy standing fast against the Oxen, Martyrdom of S. Catherine.

Munich. W.A.F.1086. Madonna and Child with SS. Lawrence, Anthony Abbot, Julian, Lucy and John Gualbert. d. 1458. *Plate 924*.

Parma. 432. S. Vincent Ferrer.

Pisa. 183. Madonna and Child with SS. Paul and Benedict. (?)

San Gimignano. 23. Madonna and Child with SS. Gregory, John Baptist, Francis and Fina. *Plate 925*.

San Giovanni Valdarno. 11. Madonna and Child with SS. Anthony Abbot, John Baptist, Margaret, Mary Magdalen, James and Peter Martyr.

San Miniato al Tedesco. S. DOMENICO, R. TRANSEPT. Madonna and Child with SS. Cosmas, Damian, Thomas and another Saint. Predella: Dream of the Deacon Justinian, Adoration of the Magi, Beheading of SS. Cosmas and Damian, *Madonna della Cintola*.

Volterra (Environs). S. GIROLAMO. Madonna and Child with SS. Lawrence, Anthony of Padua, Jerome, Francis, Cosmas and Damian.

GOZZOLI (Benozzo di Lese)

1420-1497. Pupil and assistant of Fra Angelico; probably influenced by Domenico Veneziano and Pesellino.

Berlin. 60B. Madonna of Humility with SS. Mary Magdalen and Martha. (Destroyed 1945).

    60C. Predella panel (to London 283): S. Zenobius raising a Child. 1461.

Béziers. MUSÉE. 268 (CAMPANA 375). Predella panel: S. Mary Magdalen and another Saint. (Companion to Lugano).

Cambridge (Mass.). 1907.68. Madonna and Child (r.).

Castelfiorentino (Val d'Elsa). CAPPELLA DELLA VISITAZIONE. Frescoed tabernacle. [*Trompe l'œil* altarpiece: Madonna and Child with four Saints. Christ in Glory with four Evangelists and four Doctors of the Church, Expulsion from the Temple, Annunciation to Joachim, Meeting at the Golden Gate, Birth of the Virgin, Presentation in the Temple, Annunciation, Nativity.] (g.p.). L.

Castelnuovo (Val d'Elsa). (Environs). ORATORIO DELLA MADONNA DELLA TOSSE. Frescoes. Vault: Christ blessing and four Evangelists. Soffits: Twelve Saints. Central wall: Five Angels drawing back a curtain above *trompe l'œil* altarpiece. [Madonna and Child with SS. Peter, Catherine, Margaret and Paul. Predella: Man of Sorrows and four Saints]. Left wall: Dormition of the Virgin. Right wall: *Madonna della Cintola.* ca 1484.

Certaldo (Val d'Elsa).* CAPPELLA DEL PONTE DELL'AGLIENA. *Tabernaccolo dei Giustiziati.* Frescoes: Annunciation, God the Father and the four Evangelisst, SS. Thomas and John Baptist, SS. James and Anthony Abbot, Crucifixion, Deposition, Resurrection, Martyrdom of S. Sebastian. 1466.

Cracow. 213. Madonna and Child. On back: Tobias and the Angel (p.).

Detroit (Mich.). MRS. LILLIAN HENKEL HAASS. Man of Sorrows, with a Donor. E.

    MRS. EDSEL FORD. Madonna and Child with Cherubim.

Florence. GALLERIE. 8620. Pilaster: SS. Bartholomew, John Baptist and James (st.; companion to Giusto d'Andrea, Florence 8621).

    UFFIZI. 886. Predella: Marriage of S. Catherine, Man of Sorrows with SS. John and Mary Magdalen, SS. Anthony Abbot and Giles.

    MUSEO HORNE. 18. Deposition. L.

    PALAZZO MEDICI RICCARDI, CAPPELLA. Frescoes: Journey of the Magi, Garden of Paradise. 1459. [*Plate 177.*] Plates 887-891.

    — — VESTIBULE OVERDOOR. Apocalyptic Lamb.

Legoli (Peccioli, Val d'Elsa).* CAPPELLA CATANTI. Frescoes (p.).

Locko Park (Derbyshire). COL. J. PACKE-DRURY-LOWE. Crucifixion with SS. Jerome and Dominic. E.

London. 283. Madonna and Child with SS. Zenobius, John Baptist, Jerome, Francis, Peter and Dominic (predella panels at Buckingham Palace,

Berlin 60 c, Milan, Philadelphia and Washington 1086). 1461.

591. Rape of Helen. E.

5581. Madonna and Child with nine Angels. E. *Plate 880.*

BUCKINGHAM PALACE, ROYAL COLLECTION. B.P.590. Predella panel (to London 283): Fall of Simon Magus. 1461. *Plate 892.*

Lugano. THYSSEN COLLECTION. 29. Predella panel: S. Jerome and another Saint. (Companion to Béziers.)

Milan. BRERA. 475. Predella panel (to London 283): S. Dominic raising a Child. 1461. *Plate 893.*

Montefalco. S. FRANCESCO (MUSEO), 1st CHAPEL R. (CAPPELLA DI S. GIROLAMO). Frescoes. [*Trompe l'œil* polyptych: Madonna and Child with SS. Francis, Jerome, John Baptist and Louis of Toulouse. Pinnacles: Christ blessing and four Doctors of the Church. Predella: SS. Christopher and James, SS. Clare and Fortunatus, Man of Sorrows with Virgin and S. John, SS. Severus and Bernardino, SS. Rose and Clare of Montefalco. Surrounding wall: Crucifixion with four Saints, S. Jerome departing from Rome, S. Jerome and the Lion. Vault: Four Evangelists. Soffit and pilasters: Christ blessing and Angels, SS. Bernardino, Catherine, Jerome, Sebastian and Illuminata.] Sd and d. 1452. *Plates 882-3.*

— APSE. Frescoes. Vault: S. Francis in Glory and SS. Anthony of Padua, Catherine, Bernardino, Elizabeth of Hungary and Louis of Toulouse. Soffits: S. Francis and his twelve Companions. Walls: Scenes from the Life of S. Francis [Birth of S. Francis and Homage of the Simpleton, S. Francis giving the Cloak to a Beggar and the Vision of the Church Militant and Triumphant, S. Francis renouncing his Inheritance, Meeting of SS. Francis and Dominic, Dream of Innocent III and Approval of the Franciscan Order, Exorcism of Arezzo, S. Francis preaching to Birds and refusing the Bishopric, Death of the Knight of Celano, Institution of the *Presepio* at Greccio, Ordeal by Fire, Stigmatization of S. Francis, Death of S. Francis. Window embrasures: SS. Clare of Montefalco, Agnes of Assisi, Fortunatus, Severus, Eleazer and Louis of Toulouse. Dado: Twenty roundels with half-figures of illustrious Franciscans]. Sd and d. 1452. *Plates 884-6.*

(Environs) S. FORTUNATO, ENTRANCE. Fresco: Madonna and Child with Angels and SS. Francis and Bernardino. 1450.

— R. WALL. Fresco: Madonna and Child with an Angel (fr.). 1450.

— 2nd ALTAR R. Fresco: S. Fortunatus enthroned. 1450.

Narni. PINACOTECA. Annunciation. E.

New York. 15.106.1-4. Four predella panels: Fall of Simon Magus, Conversion of S. Paul, S. Zenobius raising a Child, Totila before S. Benedict. E.

Orvieto. DUOMO, CAPPELLA DI SAN BRIZIO. Frescoes (vault): Christ in Judgement and sixteen Prophets (p., assisting Fra Angelico: some of the heads, also Christ and Angels to left). 1447. *Plate 622.*

Ottawa. 6084. Madonna and Child with SS. Gregory, Dominic, John Baptist, John Evangelist, Francis and Julian. d. 1473. *Plate* 902.

Paris. 1319. Triumph of S. Thomas Aquinas.

Perugia. 124. Madonna of Humility with SS. Peter, John Baptist, Jerome and Paul. Pilasters: Six Saints. Predella: Man of Sorrows with the Virgin, S. John and four other Saints. 1456.

Philadelphia (Pa.). MUSEUM OF ART, JOHNSON COLLECTION. 38. Predella panel (to London 283): Circumcision. 1461.

Pisa. 109. Madonna and Child with S. Anne, and female Donors.

    111. Madonna and Child with SS. Benedict, Scholastica, Ursula and John Gualbert.

    ARCIVESCOVADO. Madonna and Child with SS. Lawrence, Lazarus, Anthony Abbot and Bernardino and two Donors. Predella: Man of Sorrows with the Virgin and S. John, and SS. Peter and Stephen. d. 1470.

    CAMPOSANTO. Frescoes: Annunciation, Adoration of the Magi, Nine kneeling Saints, and twenty-three Scenes from the Old Testament. [Drunkenness of Noah, Curse of Ham, Construction of the Tower of Babel, Abraham and the Worshippers of Bel, Journey of Abraham and Lot into Egypt, Abraham victorious over the Assyrians, Story of Hagar and Abraham, Destruction of Sodom, Sacrifice of Isaac, Story of Isaac and Rebecca, Jacob and Esau, Marriage of Jacob, Reconciliation of Jacob and Esau and the Rape of Dinah, Joseph and his Brothers, Joseph in Egypt, Infancy of Moses, Passage of the Red Sea, Moses and the Tables of the Law, Story of Korah and Dathan and Abiram, Rod of Aaron, Death of Aaron and Moses, Fall of Jericho and David and Goliath, Solomon and the Queen of Sheba.] (fr., largely destroyed in 1944). 1467–84. [*Plates* 176, 178.] *Plates* 898–901.

    REFETTORIO DI SAN DOMENICO, RICOVERO DI MENDICITÀ. Frescoes: Crucifixion with Saints, S. Dominic with two Angels (g.p.). L.

Rome. MUSEO DI PALAZZO VENEZIA. Detached fresco: Head of Christ (fr.).

    S. ANGELO IN PESCHERIA, L. OF HIGH ALTAR. Fresco: Madonna and Child with Angels (p.).

    SS. DOMENICO E SISTO, 3rd ALTAR R. Fresco: Madonna and Child with two Angels. (r.). E.

    S. MARIA IN ARACOELI, 3rd CHAPEL L. (CAPPELLA CESARINI). Fresco: S. Anthony of Padua with two Angels and two Donors.

    VATICAN, PINACOTECA. 262. *Madonna della Cintola.* Pilasters: Six Saints. Predella: Birth of the Virgin, Marriage of the Virgin, Annunciation, Nativity, Circumcision, Dormition of the Virgin. 1450. *Plate* 881.

    — CHAPEL OF NICHOLAS V. Frescoes: Scenes from the Lives of SS. Lawrence and Stephen, etc. (p., assisting Fra Angelico, esp. Prophets in window embrasure.) E.

San Gimignano. PALAZZO DEL POPOLO (MUSEO CIVICO), SALA DEL CONSIGLIO. Fresco:

Restoration of Lippo Memmi's *Maestà*, with addition of two figures at the right. Sd and d. 1467.

24. Madonna and Child with two Angels and SS. John Baptist, Mary Magdalen, Augustine and Martha. Sd and d. 1466.

25. Madonna and Child with two Angels and SS. Andrew and Prosper. Predella: Man of Sorrows with the Virgin and S. John, and SS. Jerome and William. Sd and d. 1466.

26. Detached fresco: Crucifixion with SS. Jerome and Francis (st.).

S. AGOSTINO, CHOIR. Frescoes. Vault: Four Evangelists. Walls: Scenes from the Life of S. Augustine [S. Augustine entrusted to his Tutor, S. Augustine admitted to the University of Carthage, S. Monica blessing her Son, Voyage to Italy (r.), Disembarkation in Italy, S. Augustine reading Rhetoric and Philosophy, Departure for Milan (Sd and d. 1465), S. Augustine welcomed by Theodosius and S. Ambrose, S. Augustine hearing the Homily of S. Ambrose and disputing the Manichean Heresy, S. Augustine reading the Epistles of S. Paul, Baptism of S. Augustine, S. Augustine and the Christ Child and the Divulgation of the Augustinian Order, Death of S. Monica, S. Augustine consecrated Bishop, Conversion of Fortunatus, S. Augustine in Ecstasy, Death of S. Augustine]. Soffit: Christ and Apostles. Left pilaster: SS. Monica, Sebastian, Gimignano and Bartolo. Right pilaster: SS. Fina, Tobias and the Angel, Nicholas of Bari and Nicholas of Tolentino. (The children's heads and the putti in the purely ornamental parts are by assistants). 1465. *Plates* 895-896.

— 3rd ALTAR L. Fresco: S. Sebastian as Intercessor. d. 1464. *Plate* 894.

COLLEGIATA, ENTRANCE WALL. Frescoes: Martyrdom of S. Sebastian. Left pilaster: SS. Anthony Abbot, Jerome and Bernardino. Right pilaster: Assumption and SS. Augustine and Bernard. Sd and d. 1465.

(Environs) CONVENTO DI MONTE OLIVETO, CLOISTER. Fresco: Crucifixion. d. 1466.

Sermoneta (Lazio). S. MARIA ASSUNTA, 1st CHAPEL R. Madonna and Child in Glory. E.

Terni. PINACOTECA. Marriage of S. Catherine with SS. Bartholomew, Lucy and Francis. Sd and d. 1466. *Plate* 897.

Vienna. 26. Altar frontal: Madonna of Humility with SS. Francis and Bernardino and a Donor. E.

Volterra. DUOMO, CAPPELLA DEL SANTO NOME. Fresco background to terracotta Nativity: Arrival of the Magi.

Washington (D.C.). 376 (KRESS COLLECTION 482). S. Ursula with two Angels and a Donor.

620 (WIDENER COLLECTION). Raising of Lazarus.

1086 (KRESS COLLECTION 1648). Predella panel (to London 283): Feast of Herod. 1461. [*Plate* 179.]

GRANACCI, Francesco

1469–1543. Pupil first of Credi and then of Domenico Ghirlandajo, whom he assisted; influenced by Botticelli, Michelangelo, Fra Bartolommeo, Raphael and Pontormo.

Ashburnham Place. LADY ASHBURNHAM (EX). Tondo: Madonna and Child. *Plate* 1268.

Baltimore (Md.). WALTERS ART GALLERY. 436. Tondo: Holy Family. L.

Berlin. 74, 76. Wings of 'S. Maria Novella' altarpiece: S. Antoninus and S. Vincent Ferrer. (Companions to Davide Ghirlandajo, Berlin 75, and to Granacci and Mainardi, Munich 1076–78). Soon after 1494. (Destroyed 1945). *Plate 975.*

    88. Madonna and Child with SS. John Evangelist, Francis, Jerome and John Baptist (kneeling figures and landscape from his own cartoons, the rest on Ghirlandajesque design). E. (Destroyed 1945).

    Baptist. E. (Destroyed 1945.)

    229. Tondo: Trinity.

  (BERLIN–OST). 97 (DEP. HALLE). Madonna and Child with SS. John Baptist and Michael. E. *Plate* 1266.

Boston (Mass.). 03.567. Tondo: Madonna and Child with two Angels. E. (?)

Boughton House (Northants.). DUKE OF BUCCLEUCH. Rest on the Flight with Infant S. John (version of Dublin 98). L. *Plate* 1270.

Budapest. 1208. Tondo: S. John on Patmos.

Cape Town (South Africa). SIR JOSEPH ROBINSON (EX). Two cassone panels: Annunciation to Zacharias, Visitation and Birth of S. John Baptist; S. John Baptist preaching in the Wilderness. (Companions to Liverpool). E. *Plate* 1265.

Castelfiorentino (Val d'Elsa). S. VERDIANA, PINACOTECA PARROCCHIALE. Madonna and Child with SS. Francis and Sebastian (not the predella). L.

Charlotte (N.C.). MINT MUSEUM OF ART, KRESS COLLECTION. K298. Tondo: Madonna and Child. E.

Città di Castello. 78. Coronation of the Virgin (on Ghirlandajo's design).

Corsham Court (Wiltshire). LORD METHUEN. Annunciation.

Darmstadt. G K 93. Crucifixion.

Dublin. 98. Rest on the Flight with Infant S. John. *Plate* 1269.

Florence. ACCADEMIA. 1596. *Madonna della Cintola*, with S. Michael.

    3247. 'Covoni' altarpiece: Madonna and Child with SS. Francis and Zenobius.

    8650. Assumption with SS. Bernardo degli Uberti, Fidelis, John Gualbert and Catherine. *Plate* 1275.

    8690–95. Six panels from S. Apollonia: Scenes from Legends of female Martyrs. (Companions to Berenson collection and Rossie Priory). L. *Plate* 1276.

    PITTI. 345. Holy Family with Infant S. John.

    UFFIZI. 2152. 'Borgherini' panel: Joseph with Jacob and his Brothers before Pharaoh. (Companion to Palazzo Davanzati). 1515–20. *Plate* 1271.

MUSEO STIBBERT. 11591. Predella: Man of Sorrows, and SS. Catherine of Siena, John Baptist, Mary Magdalen, and Catherine of Alexandria.

PALAZZO DAVANZATI. 2150. 'Borgherini' panel: Joseph taken to Prison. (Companion to Uffizi). 1515-20. *Plate 1272.*

PALAZZO RICCARDI, MUSEO MEDICEO. Entry of Charles VIII into Florence. *Plate 1273.*

S. GIOVANNINO DEI CAVALIERI, R. WALL. S. Michael (r.). (?)

S. MARTINO (ISTITUTO DEI MINORENNI CORRIGENDI, VIA DELLA SCALA). Madonna and Child with SS. Sebastian and Julian (r.). (?)

S. SPIRITO, L. TRANSEPT, 4th CHAPEL. Trinity with SS. Mary Magdalen and Catherine. Predella: Communion of S. Mary Magdalen, Nativity, and Martyrdom of S. Catherine. (?)

BERENSON COLLECTION. Two panels from S. Apollonia: Legends of female Martyrs. (Companions to Florence, Accademia 8690-95, and Rossie Priory).

(Environs) S. DONNINO DI VILLAMAGNA. Madonna and Child with SS. Gerard of Villamagna and Donnino. *Plate 1274.*

— S. PIETRO A QUINTOLE. *Pietà*, with SS. Peter and Lawrence. L.

Honolulu (Hawaii). ACADEMY OF ARTS, KRESS COLLECTION. K 532. Tondo: Holy Family with Infant S. John.

Leningrad. 89. Holy Family with SS. Francis and Jerome.

Lisbon. GULBENKIAN FOUNDATION. Portrait of a young Woman. E.

Litchfield (Conn.). STANLEY MORTIMER. Return of Ulysses. (Companion to Poughkeepsie). (?)

Liverpool. 2783. Cassone panel: Naming of S. John Baptist, Leavetaking of S. John, Meeting of S. John and Christ, S. John in the Wilderness. (Companion to Cape Town). E.

London. 2489. Portrait of a young Man. E.

   HON. MRS. DONNELL POST (EX). 'Graham' Tondo: Holy Family with Infant S. John.

Montemurlo (Prato). PIEVE DI S. GIOVANNI BATTISTA. Madonna and Child with SS. John Baptist, Nicholas, Anthony Abbot and Peter. 1521.

Montreal. 1084. Christ and the Virgin as Intercessors. E.

Munich. 1065-68. Four panels from S. Apollonia altarpiece: SS. Jerome, Apollonia, John Baptist and Lucy.

   1078. 'S. Maria Novella' altarpiece (front): Madonna and Child in Glory, with SS. Dominic, Michael, John Baptist and John Evangelist (with Mainardi on Ghirlandajo's design; companion to Mainardi, Munich 1076-77; and to Granacci and Davide Ghirlandajo, Berlin 74-76). Soon after 1494. *Plate 974.*

New Haven (Conn.). 1871.74. *Pietà*, with S. Dominic. (?)

New York. S. H. KRESS FOUNDATION. K 169. Tondo: Madonna and Child with Infant S. John, a Saint and two Angels (r.). (?)

   MRS. BORCHARD. Tondo: Madonna and Child. *Plate 1267.*

Oxford. ASHMOLEAN. 181. Two panels: Angel of the Annunciation, S. Anthony of Padua. (Companions to Oxford, Christ Church).

Oxford (contd.). CHRIST CHURCH LIBRARY. 55. S. Francis. (Companion to Ashmolean).

Pagiano (Valdarno Superiore). S. MARTINO, HIGH ALTAR. Madonna and Child with SS. Jerome and Francis. E.

Portland (Ore.). ART MUSEUM, S. H. KRESS COLLECTION. K 1294. Tondo: Madonna and Child with two Angels.

Poughkeepsie (N.Y.). VASSAR COLLEGE. Two panels: Ulysses and Polyphemus, Ulysses and the Laestrygonians. (Companions to Litchfield). (?)

Reigate Priory (Surrey). LADY HENRY SOMERSET (EX). Madonna and Child enthroned.

Rome. GALLERIA BORGHESE. 463. Jacob hearing of Joseph's supposed Death. (?)

Rossie Priory (Inchture, Perthshire). LORD KINNAIRD (EX). Panel from S. Apollonia, Florence: Scene from the Legend of a female Martyr. (See Florence, Accademia 8690–95). *Plate 1277.*

San Francisco (Cal.). PALACE OF THE LEGION OF HONOR. Madonna and Child.

Santa Barbara (Cal.). UNIVERSITY OF CALIFORNIA, F. M. SEDGWICK COLLECTION. Cassone panel: Miracles of S. Nicholas of Tolentino. (?)

Sarasota (Fla.). *Madonna della Cintola* with SS. John Baptist, James, Lawrence and Bartholomew.

Warwick Castle. EARL OF WARWICK. *Madonna della Cintola*, with SS. Francis, Benedict and Paul.

Washington (D.C.). 437 (KRESS COLLECTION 1012). Three Scenes of Figures in Landscapes (?)

   HOWARD UNIVERSITY, KRESS STUDY COLLECTION. K 1152A–B. Cassone panel: Visitation, Annunciation to Joachim, Birth of S. John Baptist, Beheading of S. John, and the Head of S. John brought before Herod. (?)

Wiesbaden. M.335. Tondo: Madonna and Child.

JACOPO DEL CASENTINO

Died 1349 (or 1358?). Possibly a pupil of Meo da Siena; influenced by Bolognese artists, by the S. Cecilia Master and later by Daddi.

Ann Arbor (Mich.). UNIVERSITY OF MICHIGAN. 'Loeser' Madonna and Child with Saints and Angels. *Plate 99.*

Arezzo. MUSEO. 5. Detached fresco: Madonna and Child with two Saints (fr., r.). (DEP. GALLERIE FIORENTINE 8571–73). Three panels from a polyptych: SS. John Baptist, John Evangelist and Nicholas. Pinnacles: Three Prophets.

   OSPEDALE, CHAPEL. The Virgin and two symbolic Images of Christ, Adoration of the Magi, five adoring Figures, Annunciation. (Destroyed 1944.)

Berlin. 1091. Portable triptych: Madonna and Child with four Angels and six Saints. Wings: Nativity, Three Dead Kings and three Living Kings,

Crucifixion. L. *Plates* 104–105.

1096 (BONN 122). Madonna and Child with four Angels and six Saints.

Berne. 872. Portable triptych: Coronation of the Virgin with Saints and Angels. Wings: Annunciation, Last Communion of S. Mary Magdalen, S. Martin and the Beggar, Crucifixion.

Bordeaux. MUSÉE. Madonna and Child (r.).

Boston (Mass.). 10.37. S. Lucy with a Donor.

Bremen. 292. Portable triptych: Madonna and Child with six Angels and four Saints, Dormition of the Virgin. Pinnacle: Christ blessing. Wings: Annunciation, Last Judgement, Crucifixion.

Bristol. CITY ART GALLERY. 'Loeser' Crucifixion, with Deposition below.

Brussels. 794. Madonna and Child. (Companion to Houston).

Budapest. 6006. Madonna and Child with eight Angels and ten Saints. Pinnacle: An Angel. d. 1345.

Cambiano (Val d'Elsa). S. PROSPERO. Three panels from a polyptych: SS. Catherine, James and John Evangelist. (Companions to Staten Island; and to Rome, Vatican).

Cleveland (Ohio). 43.280. Processional Crucifix.

52.281. Illuminated initial: female Martyr (S. Lucy?).

El Paso (Texas). MUSEUM OF ART, KRESS COLLECTION. K 1296, 1297. Two panels: SS. John Baptist and Lucy. Spandrels: Four Angels.

Florence. ACCADEMIA. 440. S. Bartholomew enthroned with eight Angels. Pinnacle and spandrels: Christ blessing and two Prophets.

UFFIZI. 9258. 'Cagnola' portable triptych. Madonna and Child with four Angels and SS. John Gualbert and John Baptist. Wings: Stigmatization of S. Francis, two female Saints, Crucifixion. Sd. *Plate* 102.

MUSEO HORNE. 46. Madonna and Child.

PALAZZO DELL'ARTE DELLA LANA, TABERNACLE. Madonna and Child with six Angels and SS. John Baptist and John Evangelist. *Plate* 100.

S. MARIA DEL FIORE (DUOMO), MUSEO DELL'OPERA. 91. Processional panel: S. Agatha (copying XIII-century panel on back). (?)

S. MARIA NOVELLA, SACRISTY. Crucifix. (?)

S. MINIATO AL MONTE, CHOIR L. S. Miniato and Scenes from his Life [Arrest of S. Miniato, Death of the Leopard, Torture of S. Miniato in an Oven, on the Gallows, and over a Fire, Refusal of the Bribe, Beheading of S. Miniato, S. Miniato carrying his Head to the Site of his Church]. E. *Plates* 106–108.

CHARLES LOESER (EX). Annunciation. *Plate* 101.

Dormition of the Virgin.

CONTE VITTORIO DE MICHELI. Madonna and Child.

(Environs) POZZOLATICO, S. STEFANO, 3rd ALTAR R. Madonna and Child.

Frankfurt am Main. 842. Madonna and Child with fifteen Angels, SS. Peter, Paul, the Baptist, the Evangelist and two Donors.

Geneva. VILLA ARIANA. Madonna and Child. L.

Houston (Texas). ST. THOMAS UNIVERSITY. Four panels from a polyptych: SS. Catherine, John Baptist, Philip and John Evangelist. Pinnacles: Four Prophets. (Companions to Brussels).

Kansas City (Mo.). 47.1952 (KRESS COLLECTION 446). Circumcision. d. 1330. *Plate* 103.

London. HELEN GURNEY. Madonna and Child with four Angels, S. Mary Magdalen, a Deacon Saint and two Donors.

New Haven (Conn.). 1939.557. Coronation of the Virgin.
   1943.209. Madonna and Child (r.).

New York. W. R. HEARST (EX). S. Catherine and twelve Scenes from her Life [S. Catherine consulting the Hermit, Madonna and Child appearing to S. Catherine, Baptism of S. Catherine, Mystic Marriage of S. Catherine, Disputation of S. Catherine, Martyrdom of the Doctors, Scourging of S. Catherine, Conversion of the Empress, Christ appearing to S. Catherine in Prison, Attempted Martyrdom of S. Catherine, Martyrdom of the converted Soldiers, Beheading of S. Catherine.] E. (?). *Plate* 98.

Pavia. 166. Wings of a portable triptych: Stigmatization of S. Francis, two Saints, Crucifixion.

Poppi. BIBLIOTECA COMUNALE. Cod. I. Antiphonal. fol. 14, 16v, 20v, 48, 60v, 114v, 119. Seven illuminated initials: Nativity, S. Stephen, S. John Evangelist, Circumcision, Annunciation, Assumption, Birth of the Virgin.

Princeton (N.J.). MRS. DOUGLAS DELANOY. Crucifixion. Pinnacle: Christ blessing.

Rome. GALLERIA NAZIONALE (PALAZZO CORSINI). Portable triptych: Madonna and Child with SS. Peter and Paul and fourteen other Saints or Angels. Pinnacle: Christ blessing. Wings: Annunciation, Baptism of Christ, Crucifixion.

   VATICAN, PINACOTECA. 179. Madonna and Child. (Companion to Cambiano and Staten Island).

Scarperia (Mugello). MADONNA DELLE GRAZIE (ORATORIO DELLA COMPAGNIA DI PIAZZA). Madonna and Child with two Angels (r.). *Plate* 109.

Staten Island (N.Y.). INSTITUTE OF ARTS AND SCIENCES, KRESS STUDY COLLECTION. K 1138. A Bishop Saint. (Companion to Cambiano and Rome, Vatican).

Tucson (Ariz.). UNIVERSITY OF ARIZONA, KRESS COLLECTION. K 572. Portable triptych: Madonna and Child with six Angels and eight Saints. Pinnacle: Christ blessing. Wings: Annunciation, Disputation of S. Catherine, Crucifixion.

Vienna. OSCAR BONDY (EX). Portable triptych: Madonna and Child with ten Angels and four Saints. Wings: Annunciation, Nativity, Crucifixion. *Plate* 110.

   EMIL WEINBERGER (EX). Portable triptych: Madonna and Child with two Angels and four Saints. Wings: Annunciation, SS. Catherine and Elizabeth of Hungary, Crucifixion.

Homeless. Madonna and Child enthroned with two Saints. *Dedalo* xi, 272.

Four panels from a polyptych: SS. Peter, Barbara, Francis and a Bishop Saint. *Dedalo* xi, 271.

Madonna nursing Child (see Offner, *Corpus* III, vol. III, p. II, Plate LII).

JACOPO DI CIONE

Mentioned 1365–1398, but probably active considerably before the first date. Brother and assistant of Andrea Orcagna. His independent manner was based more upon Andrea's sculpture than on his paintings. Influenced overpoweringly by Maso, then by his brother Nardo and later by Niccolò di Pietro Gerini.

Allentown (Pa.). MUSEUM OF ART. KRESS COLLECTION. K 445. Roundel: Crucifixion (st.).

Altenburg. 16. Coronation of the Virgin with Angels and Saints. (?)

18. Coronation of the Virgin with Saints. Pinnacle: Christ blessing.

Bayonne. 966. Portable triptych: Madonna and Child. Wings: Twenty-four Saints. E. *Plate 222.*

Berlin. 1141A. Madonna and Child with eight Saints. E.

Boston (Mass.). ISABELLA GARDNER MUSEUM. Annunciation. (?)

Budapest. 2540. Madonna and Child with six Angels. E. *Plate 224.*

Calenzano (Prato). S. NICCOLÒ. Annunciation. *Plate 220.*

Cambridge (Mass.). 1939.103. Madonna and Child with eight Saints. Pinnacle: Christ blessing.

Chicago (Ill.). 37.1004. Madonna of Humility with two Angels.

Copenhagen. 3479. Madonna and Child with four Angels and six Saints. (Companion to Houston 44.570).

Denver (Col.). MUSEUM OF ART, KRESS COLLECTION. K 296. Predella panel: Man of Sorrows with the Virgin, S. John and a Donor.

Edinburgh. 1958. Portable triptych: Madonna and Child with four Angels and eight Saints. Wings: Annunciation, Nativity, Crucifixion.

Fiesole. MUSEO BANDINI. I, 21. Predella panel: *Pietà*, with S. Catherine and another Saint (with Niccolò di Pietro Gerini.)

I, 36. *Madonna del Parto*, with a Donor.

Florence. ACCADEMIA. 132 Dep. Madonna of Humility (on Nardo's design). *Plate 223.*

165 Dep. Triptych: Pentecost (on Orcagna's design).

456. Coronation of the Virgin with ten Saints. Spandrels: Two Prophets. 1373. *Plates* 229, 231, 232.

3152. Triptych: Crucifixion with S. Francis at foot of Cross. Wings: SS. Paul, Mary Magdalen, Luke, Bartholomew, Catherine and Peter Martyr. Pinnacles: Christ blessing and Annunciation. (Saints in wings chiefly by Niccolò di Pietro Gerini.)

Florence (contd.). 3156. Madonna of Humility with four Angels and SS. Lawrence, Francis, John Baptist, Paul, Anthony Abbot and Catherine (p.).

    3469. Polyptych: Madonna and Child with SS. Nicholas, Philip, John Baptist and John Evangelist (p., central panel in part by Orcagna). *Plate* 210.

    8562. *Madonna della Misericordia.*

    8565. Three predella panels: Stigmatization of S. Francis, Nativity, Conversion of S. Paul (p.).

    8579. Coronation of the Virgin with Saints and Angels (st.).

    8607. Polyptych: Madonna and Child with two Angels and SS. Clare and Catherine. Wings: SS. Lawrence, John Baptist, Francis and Stephen. Pinnacles: Annunciation, and SS. Peter and Paul. Predella: Adoration of the Magi, and six Saints. d. 1383. *Plate* 234.

    UFFIZI. 3163. Triptych: S. Matthew and Scenes from his Life [Vocation of S. Matthew, Subduing of the Dragons, Raising of the King's Child, Death of S. Matthew]. ca 1367–68. *Plates* 226, 228.

    MUSEO DEL BIGALLO. S. Peter Martyr consigning the Banner to the *Capitani di S. Maria.* Pinnacle: Madonna and Child with SS. Dominic and Francis.

    MUSEO STIBBERT. 3891. Madonna and Child enthroned with four Angels. Pinnacle: Christ blessing (st.). E.

    PALAZZO VECCHIO. Detached fresco: Expulsion of the Duke of Athens from Florence (fr.). *Plate* 233.

    S. CROCE. Triptych: Madonna and Child with S. Gregory and Job. Predella: Scenes from the Story of Job (with Nardo di Cione). d. 1365. *Plate* 225.

    S. MARIA NOVELLA, STROZZI CHAPEL. Frescoes (vault): Four Images of S. Thomas Aquinas with Virtues (assisting Nardo). E.

    — CHIOSTRINO DEI MORTI (STROZZI CHAPEL). Frescoes: Nativity, Crucifixion. E. [*Plate* 125.] *Plates* 216–219.

    S. TRINITA, 3rd CHAPEL L. (DAVANZATI). Fresco: Disputation of S. Catherine (r.). ca 1364. (?)

    BERENSON COLLECTION. Madonna and Child with eighteen Angels and four Saints.

Gazzada (Varese). VILLA CAGNOLA. Left wing of an altarpiece: A female Saint. E.

Geneva. M.F.3831. Madonna and Child with four Angels and eight Saints (st.).

Hampton Court. 1220. Portable triptych: Coronation of the Virgin with ten Saints. Pinnacle: Christ blessing. Wings: Annunciation, Nativity, Crucifixion.

Highnam Court (Glos.). GAMBIER-PARRY COLLECTION. Portable triptych: Madonna and Child with two Angels and eight Saints. Wings: Annunciation, Nativity, Crucifixion.

Houston (Texas). 44–556, 557, 558, 559. Four panels from a polyptych: SS. Bartholomew, Agnes, Elizabeth of Hungary and Nicholas.

    44–561. Predella panel: Meeting at the Golden Gate.

    44–570A, B. Wings of a portable triptych: Nativity, Crucifixion. (Companions to Copenhagen.)

Le Mans. 6. SS. James and Bartholomew.

Liverpool. 2857. Wings of a portable triptych: Annunciation, Nativity, Crucifixion (p.).

London. 569–578. Triptych: Coronation of the Virgin with Angels and Saints. Pinnacles: Trinity, Adoring Angels, Nativity, Adoration of the Magi, Resurrection, Maries at the Sepulchre, Ascension, Pentecost (probably planned by Andrea and executed with aid of Niccolò di Tommaso and Niccolò di Pietro Gerini). (Panels from the predella are at Philadelphia, Providence, Radensleben, and Rome). 1370–71. *Plate* 230.

    1468. Crucifixion. SS. John Baptist, Paul, James and Bartholomew. Predella: Madonna and Child and four Saints.

New Haven (Conn.). 1871.18. Trinity with the Virgin and SS. John Baptist, Mary Magdalen and John Evangelist (with Niccolò di Pietro Gerini). 1943.214. Madonna of Humility. (?)

New York. 52.229.2. Triptych: Coronation of the Virgin with two Angels and SS. Bernard, Silvester, Nicholas and Julian. Pinnacles: Christ blessing and two Prophets. Predella: Apparition of SS. Peter and Paul to Constantine, Conversion and Baptism of Constantine, Raising of the Bull, Binding of the Dragon, Raising of the two Pagan Priests. d. 1394.

    ROBERT LEHMAN. Crucifixion, with six Angels in frame. E.

    Madonna of Humility with God the Father, Angels and Holy Ghost above, red book on floor to right.

Northampton (Mass.). SMITH COLLEGE MUSEUM OF ART. Madonna and Child with four Saints.

Omaha (Neb.). JOSLYN MEMORIAL MUSEUM. Madonna and Child with four Saints. E.

Philadelphia (Pa.) MUSEUM OF ART, JOHNSON COLLECTION. 4. Predella panel: Liberation of S. Peter (p.; see London 569–78). 1370–71.

    5. Polyptych: Madonna and Child with SS. Mary Magdalen, James, Stephen and Nicholas. E. (?)

    6. Marriage of S. Catherine, with a Bishop Saint and kneeling Nun.

Poggibonsi (Environs). S. LUCCHESE, HIGH ALTAR. Polyptych: Coronation of the Virgin with six Angels and SS. John Baptist, Mary Magdalen, Francis and a Bishop Saint. Pinnacles: Christ blessing and two Prophets. E. (Destroyed 1944).

Ponce (Puerto Rico). MUSEO DE ARTE, KRESS STUDY COLLECTION. K 156. Annunciation with Donor. (?)

Providence (R.I.) RHODE ISLAND SCHOOL OF DESIGN. Predella panel: Arrest of S. Peter (p.; see London 569–78). 1370–71.

Radensleben. W. VON QUAST (EX). Predella panel: Last Meeting of SS. Peter and Paul (p.; see London 569–78). 1370–71.

Rome. MUSEO DI PALAZZO VENEZIA. Coronation of the Virgin, with two Angels and fourteen Saints.

Rome (contd.). VATICAN, PINACOTECA. 96. Predella panel: Annunciation to Joachim.
    103. Predella panel: Flight into Egypt. *Plate 227.*
    107. Predella panel: *Cathedra Petri* (p.; see London 569–78). 1370–71.
    113. Predella panel: Raising of the Son of Theophilus (p.; see London 569–78).
        1370–71.
    116. Assumption.
Rosano (Pontassieve). PARROCCHIALE. Annunciation. E. *Plate 221.*
Rotterdam. 2541. Crucifixion.
Saint Louis (Mo.). 51.26. Portable triptych: Madonna and Child with six Angels.
    Wings: Eighteen Saints.
San Francisco (Cal.). DE YOUNG MEMORIAL MUSEUM, KRESS COLLECTION. K 74.
    Madonna and Child with six Saints.
San Giovanni Valdarno. PIEVE, HIGH ALTAR. Triptych: Trinity with the Virgin
    and S. Mary Magdalen, and SS. James, John Baptist, John Evangelist and
    Anthony Abbot. Pinnacles: Two Prophets.
Tucson (Ariz.). S. PHILIP'S IN THE HILLS (KRESS COLLECTION 537). Crucifix.
Volterra. 18. *Pietà.* (?)
Washington (D.C.). 814 (KRESS COLLECTION 1363). Madonna and Child with eight
    Angels (with Andrea Orcagna).

LEONARDO (Malatesta) DA PISTOIA

1483–*after* 1518. *Follower of Fra Bartolommeo and Raphael.*

Berlin. 286 (FORMERLY MÜNSTER). Madonna and Child. Sd and d. 1516. *Plate 1340.*
Boston (Mass.). 17.3227. Madonna and Child. (Partial copy of Raphael's *Pala Dei*,
    Pitti 165).
Breslau. 198 (BERLIN 1415). Madonna and Child.
Brussels. 795. Madonna and Child. (Copy of Raphael's 'Bridgewater Madonna').
Casalguidi (Pistoia). S. PIERO, HIGH ALTAR. Madonna and Child with four Saints. Sd.
Dijon. 70. Madonna and Child with SS. Bernardino and John Baptist (r.).
Keir (Dunblane, Scotland). LT.-COL. WILLIAM STERLING. Holy Family with Infant
    S. John.
Linz. 6. Tondo: Madonna and Child with Infant S. John.
London. VICTORIA AND ALBERT MUSEUM. 770–1865. Madonna and Child. (?)
Münster. See Berlin.
New Haven (Conn.). 1871.76. Archangels Gabriel, Michael and Raphael with
    Tobias and a female Donor.
New York. MRS. BENJAMIN THAW (EX). Holy Family with S. Elizabeth and Infant S.
    John.
Paris. LOUIS FOURNIER (EX). Madonna and Child.

Philadelphia (Pa.). MUSEUM OF ART, JOHNSON COLLECTION. 79. Holy Family with S. Elizabeth and Infant S. John.

Volterra. 28. Madonna and Child with SS. Sebastian, Stephen, Lawrence and Nicholas. Sd. and d. 1516. *Plate 1338.*

Wroclaw. See Breslau.

LEONARDO DA VINCI

Florentine. 1452–1519. Pupil of Verrocchio. Left Florence for Milan in 1482 and returned to Florence only from 1500 to 1507. (The copies and versions by his Milanese followers are included in the list of North Italian pictures of the Renaissance. Only a few Tuscan copies of important lost originals are listed here.)

Cracow. 180. Portrait of a Lady with an Ermine, probably Cecilia Gallerani. ca 1481. [*Plate* 196.]

Drumlanrig (Scotland). DUKE OF BUCCLEUCH. Madonna of the Yarn-Winder (c. of lost original, 1501). *Plate 1205.*

Florence. UFFIZI. 1594. Adoration of the Magi (u.). Begun 1481. [*Plates 192–193.*] *Plate 937.*

    1618. Annunciation. E. [*Plate 191.*]

    8358. Baptism of Christ. (Angel on left, distant landscape and part of Christ by Leonardo; the rest by Verrocchio). E. [*Plate 190.*]

    PALAZZO VECCHIO. Fighting horsemen (c. from lost cartoon of the Battle of Anghiari 1503–05). Cf. *Plates 1209–10.*

Leningrad. 249. 'Litta': Madonna nursing the Child (u., r.). (?)

    2773. 'Benois' Madonna and Child. E. *Plate 932.*

London. 1093. Virgin of the Rocks (later version of Louvre 1599, made by Ambrogio De Predis under Leonardo's supervision).

    6337. 'Burlington House' cartoon for a Madonna and Child with S. Anne [*Plate 194.*]

Milan. AMBROSIANA. 19. Portrait of a Musician (u.).

    CASTELLO SFORZESCO, SALA DELL'ASSE. Frescoes. Vault: Decoration of interlaced trees and cords (r.). Wall: Trees (fr., r.). 1498.

    S. MARIA DELLE GRAZIE, REFECTORY. Fresco: Last Supper (r.). ca 1497.

    Frescoes: Donors in Crucifixion (r.). (?)

Munich. 7779. Madonna and Child. E. [*Plate 195.*]

Paris. 1597. S. John Baptist (u.). L.

    1598. Madonna and Child with S. Anne (u.). *Plate 1207.*

    1599. 'The Virgin of the Rocks'. 1483 or earlier. *Plate 940.*

    1600. Portrait of a Woman, called 'La Belle Ferronnière'.

    1601. Portrait of a Woman, called 'La Gioconda', or 'Mona Lisa'. *Plate 1206.*

Paris (contd.). 1602A. Predella panel (to altarpiece by Lorenzo di Credi at Pistoia):
Annunciation. (Lorenzo di Credi, retouched by Leonardo). E. *Plate 936*.
  MME. DE RUBLÉ (EX). Leda (c. of lost original, ca 1506). *Plate 1208*.
Rome. VATICAN, PINACOTECA. 337. Penitent S. Jerome (u.).
Vaduz. LIECHTENSTEIN COLLECTION. 32. Portrait of Ginevra dei Benci (fr.). E.
Plate 931.

LIPPI, Filippino

1457–1504. Pupil and follower of Botticelli.

Balcarres (Fife, Scotland). EARL OF CRAWFORD AND BALCARRES. Two panels: Stories
of Lucretia and Virginia. E.
Berlin. S.1. Tondo: Madonna and Child with two Angels. L. (Destroyed 1945).
  78A. Allegory of Music. L. *Plate 1153*.
  82. Madonna and Child. *Plate 1136*.
  87. Madonna and Child with two Angels and SS. Nicholas, Vincent Ferrer,
Peter Martyr and Dominic (st.). (Destroyed 1945).
  96. Crucifixion with the Virgin and S. Francis (from S. Procolo; companion to
Florence, Accademia 8651, 8653). L. (Destroyed 1945).
  98. Madonna and Child with two Angels, Infant S. John and SS. Sebastian and
Andrew (st.). (Destroyed 1945).
  101. Madonna and Child. (Destroyed 1945).
  (BERLIN-OST). 96A. Fresco: Head of a young Man (fr.).
Bologna. S. DOMENICO, CHAPEL R. OF CHOIR. Marriage of S. Catherine, with SS.
John Baptist, Peter, Paul and Sebastian. Sd and d. 1501.
Budapest. 1140. Madonna and Child, with a Franciscan Donor recommended by
S. Anthony of Padua. E.
Cambridge (Mass.). 1916.1. Madonna and Child with SS. Roch and Sebastian (c.).
  1941.133. S. John Baptist in the Wilderness. E. (?)
Chantilly. 19. Cassone panel: Esther before Ahasuerus. (Companion to Florence,
Horne and Ottawa; see also, for second cassone, Ottawa and Paris, Vogüé). E.
Cleveland (Ohio). 32.227. 'Warren' Tondo: Holy Family with Infant S. John and
S. Margaret. *Plate 1150*.
Copenhagen. ROYAL MUSEUM, SPENGLER NO. 40. Meeting at the Golden Gate. Sd and
d. 1497. *Plate 1151*.
Denver (Col.). MUSEUM OF ART, SIMON GUGGENHEIM BEQUEST. Christ on the Cross.
Edinburgh. 1758. Predella panel: Nativity with two Angels. E.
  2099. S. John Baptist in the Wilderness (fr.). E.
El Paso (Texas). MUSEUM OF ART, KRESS COLLECTION. K 1727. S. Jerome in his study.
Florence. GALLERIE. 4666. *Madonna della Cintola*, with S. Anthony of Padua (st.).

ACCADEMIA. 8370. Deposition (only the upper part, Christ excepted, was designed by Filippino Lippi; finished by Perugino).

  8651, 8653. Side panels to the 'S. Procolo' Crucifixion (Berlin 96): SS. Mary Magdalen and John Baptist. L.

PITTI. 368. Cassone panel: Story of Lucretia. E. (Companion to Paris 1662A).

UFFIZI. 1485. Fresco: Head of an old Man.

  1566. Adoration of the Magi. 1496.

  1568. Madonna and Child with SS. John Baptist, Victor, Bernard and Zenobius. d. 1485. *Plate 1147.*

  1711. Fresco: Self-Portrait. E.

  3249. Madonna adoring the Child. E.

  8378. Allegory.

  8652. S. Jerome in the Wilderness.

MUSEO FERRONI. Madonna adoring the Child with Infant S. John. E.

MUSEO HORNE. 41. Cassone panel (*testata* to Chantilly): Vasthi departing from Susa. E. (See Chantilly).

  98. Crucifixion (r.). L.

S. AMBROGIO, L. WALL. Spandrels and predella of a niche with a statue of S. Sebastian: Two Angels, Annunciation. L. (?)

BADIA, L. WALL. Vision of S. Bernard, with Piero di Francesco del Pugliese as Donor. E. [*Plate 215.*] *Plate 1144.*

S. MARIA DEL CARMINE, BRANCACCI CHAPEL. Frescoes: Scenes from the Life of S. Peter. [Left wall: Raising of the Son of Theophilus (the Son, the group of eight men and a child behind him, and the group of four figures at extreme left; the rest by Masaccio), S. Peter in Prison visited by S. Paul. Right wall: Liberation of S. Peter, SS. Peter and Paul before the Proconsul and Crucifixion of S. Peter]. E. *Plates 1139–43.*

S. MARIA NOVELLA, 1ST CHAPEL R. OF CHOIR (FILIPPO STROZZI). Frescoes. Vault: Adam, Noah, Abraham and Jacob. Walls: Scenes from the Lives of SS. John Evangelist and Philip [Left wall: Raising of Drusiana, S. John in the Cauldron of Boiling Oil. Right wall: Exorcism of the Temple of Hieropolis, Crucifixion and Stoning of S. Philip. Altar wall: *Grisaille* decoration with Allegorical Figures]. Completed in 1502. *Plate 1154.*

  Window: Madonna and Child, SS. John Evangelist and Philip.

S. SPIRITO, R. TRANSEPT, 4th CHAPEL L. Madonna and Child with Infant S. John, SS. Martin and Catherine, and Tanai de' Nerli and his Wife as Donors. *Plate 1149.*

GALLERIA CORSINI. 162. Tondo: Madonna and Child with five Angels. E.

  340. Five female Allegorical Figures. E.

(Environs) POGGIO A CAIANO, VILLA REALE, PORTICO. Fresco: Laocoon (fr., r.).

Genoa. PALAZZO BIANCO. S. Sebastian, with SS. John Baptist and Francis. Lunette: Madonna and Child with two Angels. Sd and d. 1503.

Kilburn (Yorks.). ST. AUGUSTINE'S. Madonna and Child with Infant S. John. L.

Leningrad. 287. Tondo: Madonna adoring the Child with six Angels. E. *Plate* 1137.
4079. Predella panel: 'Stroganoff' Annunciation.

Lille. PALAIS DES BEAUX ARTS 932 (CAMPANA 237). Tondo: Adoration of the Shepherds with Infant S. John (c.).

London. 293. 'Rucellai' altarpiece: Madonna and Child in landscape, with SS. Jerome and Dominic.
927. An adoring Angel (fr., r.). (Companion to Strasbourg?)
1124. Adoration of the Magi. E.
1412. Madonna and Child with Infant S. John. E.
4904, 4905. Two panels: Moses striking Water from the Rock, Adoration of the Golden Calf (st.). L.
W. H. WOODWARD (EX). Infant S. John (fr.).

Lucca. S. MICHELE, L. TRANSEPT. SS. Roch, Sebastian, Jerome and Helen.

Lugano. THYSSEN COLLECTION. 241. Madonna and Child (g.p.).

Luton Hoo (Beds.). SIR HAROLD WERNHER. Tondo: Madonna and Child. L.

Memphis (Tenn.). BROOKS MEMORIAL ART GALLERY, KRESS COLLECTION. K. 209. S. Francis in Glory with Blessed Lucchesius of Poggibonsi, S. Louis of Toulouse, S. Elizabeth of Hungary and Blessed Bona (p.).

Milan. CONTESSA RASINI. Allegory of Love. *Plate* 1138.

Montepulciano. 12. Crucifixion (c.).

Munich. 1074. Christ and the Virgin as Intercessors. Predella: Man of Sorrows with six Saints (p.).

Nancy. 159. Tondo: Madonna and Child with Infant S. John (c.).

Naples. 42. Annunciation, with SS. John Baptist and Andrew. E.
FROM THE PALAZZO REALE. Tondo: Madonna and Child with two Angels (g.p.). L.

New Haven (Conn.). 1871.56. Christ on the Cross. L.

New York. 14.40.641. Holy Family with an Angel. L.
49.7.10. Madonna and Child.
HISTORICAL SOCIETY. B-330. Madonna and Child with four Angels. E.
MRS. RUSH H. KRESS. Small portrait of Man.

Ottawa. 6085. Cassone panel (*testata* to Chantilly): Esther arriving at Susa. E. (See Chantilly). *Plate* 1133.
6086. Cassone panel (*testata* to Paris, Vogüé): Triumph of Mordecai. E. (See Chantilly). *Plate* 1134.

Oxford. CHRIST CHURCH LIBRARY. 33, 34. Two panels: Ten Sibyls (r.). E.
38. Centaur; on back, Allegorical Figures (u.).

Paris. 1416. Coronation of the Virgin with SS. Jerome, Francis, Bonaventura and Louis of Toulouse (p., finished by Alonso Berruguete and others).
1662A. Cassone panel: Story of Virginia. (Companion to Florence, Pitti). E.
HEUGEL COLLECTION. Tondo: Madonna and Child with two Angels (p.).
COMTESSE DE VOGÜÉ. Cassone panel: Revocation of the Edict against the Jews. (See Chantilly.) *Plate* 1132.

Prato. GALLERIA COMUNALE. Frescoed Tabernacle from Canto a Mercatale: Madonna and Child on pedestal, flanked by SS. Anthony Abbot and Margaret, SS. Catherine and Stephen (r.). d. 1498. *Plate* 1152.

24. Madonna and Child with SS. Stephen and John Baptist. d. 1503.

Raleigh (N.C.). MUSEUM OF ART, KRESS COLLECTION. K342A–B. Two predella panels: SS. Donatus and Augustine.

Rome. S. MARIA SOPRA MINERVA, CARAFFA CHAPEL. Annunciation, with Cardinal Caraffa as Donor recommended by S. Thomas Aquinas. 1489–93.

Frescoes. Vault: Four Sibyls. Altar wall: Assumption. Right wall: Vocation of S. Thomas Aquinas and Miracle of the Crucifix at Naples, Triumph of S. Thomas (g.p.). 1489–93. *Plate* 1148.

San Gimignano. 31, 32. Two tondi: Annunciation. 1483–84. *Plates* 1145–6.

Strasbourg. 217. Head of an Angel (fr.). (Companion to London 927?)

Toulouse. MUSÉE DES AUGUSTINS (DEP. LOUVRE 1114). Madonna and Child with SS. Jerome and Zenobius (design and S. Jerome only; finished and signed by Albertinelli). *Plate* 1316.

Turin. 113. Archangels Michael, Raphael with Tobias, and Gabriel. E.

Venice. SEMINARIO. 36, 39. Diptych: Christ and the Samaritan Woman, *Noli me tangere.* L.

Washington (D.C.). 18 (MELLON COLLECTION). Madonna adoring the Child with an Angel.

20 (MELLON COLLECTION). Portrait of a young Man. E.

340 (KRESS COLLECTION 418). Tobias and the Angel. E. [*Plate* 216.]

537 (KRESS COLLECTION 1242). Lunette: Coronation of the Virgin. *Plate* 1135.

1165 (KRESS COLLECTION 1889). Predella panel: Man of Sorrows.

Zagreb. 54. Tondo: Holy Family with S. Margaret (st. v. of Cleveland).

LIPPI, Fra Filippo

Florence ca 1406–Spoleto 1469. Pupil of Lorenzo Monaco and follower of Masaccio; influenced by Fra Angelico and Donatello.

Altenburg. 96. SS. Francis and Jerome in the Wilderness.

Balcarres (Fife, Scotland). EARL OF CRAWFORD AND BALCARRES. Four panels: The Apostles (st.). L.

Baltimore (Md.). WALTERS ART GALLERY. 429. Madonna and Child. *Plate* 854.

Berlin. 69. Madonna adoring the Child with Infant S. John and S. Bernard (from Florence, Cappella del Palazzo Medici Riccardi). Sd. 1455–60.

95. Altar frontal: *Madonna della Misericordia* (g.p.). 1467. (Destroyed 1945).

95B. Predella panel (to Uffizi 8352): Miraculous Infancy of S. Ambrose. 1441.

1700. Profile Portrait of a Lady. *Plate* 847.

Cambridge. 559. Portable triptych: Madonna and Child with four Angels and a Donor. Wings: SS. John Baptist and George (g.p.). E.

Cambridge (Mass.). 1902.7. SS. John Baptist, Jerome and Ansanus (p.).

Corsham Court (Wilts.). LORD METHUEN. Annunciation (st.).

Empoli. 24. Madonna and Child with seven Angels and SS. Bernard, Michael and Bartholomew. *Plate 844.*

Florence. PITTI. 343. Tondo: Madonna and Child, with the Birth of the Virgin in the background. 1452. *Plate 856.*

   UFFIZI. 1598. Madonna adoring the Child with two Angels. L. [*Plate 159.*]

     8350. Nativity with SS. Hilarion, Jerome and Mary Magdalen.

     8351. Predella (to Paris 1344): S. Frediano changing the course of the River Serchio, Annunciation of the Death of the Virgin, S. Augustine in his Study. 1437. *Plates 848, 850.*

     8352. Coronation of the Virgin (see Berlin 95 B). 1441. *Plates 851–2.*

     8353. 'Tornabuoni' Adoration of the Child with Infant S. John and S. Bernard. ca 1463. *Plate 861.*

     8354. 'Medici' altarpiece: Madonna and Child with SS. Francis, Damian, Cosmas and Anthony of Padua. (Predella by Pesellino at Florence, Uffizi 8355 and Paris 1414.) ca 1450. *Plate 831.*

     8356, 8357. Four panels: Annunciation, SS. Anthony Abbot and John Baptist.

   PALAZZO DELL'ARCIVESCOVADO. Man of Sorrows with SS. Francis and Jerome (r.). E. (?)

   PALAZZO RICCARDI, MUSEO MEDICEO. Madonna and Child. [*Plate 160.*]

   S. LORENZO, CAPPELLA MARTELLI. Annunciation. Predella: S. Nicholas preventing an Execution, S. Nicholas and the three Maidens, S. Nicholas raising three Boys from Barrels.

   S. MARIA DEL CARMINE, CLOISTER.* Fresco: Confirmation of the Carmelite Order (fr.). 1432. *Plate 842.*

Leningrad. 5511. Predella panel: S. Augustine's Vision of the Christ Child. L.

London. 248. Vision of S. Bernard (probably with Fra Diamante; r.). 1447.

   666. Lunette: Annunciation.

   667. Lunette: SS. Francis, Lawrence, Cosmas, John Baptist, Damian, Anthony Abbot and Peter Martyr. (Companion to 666).

   3424. Madonna and Child (g.p.).

   4868A–D. Predella (to Pesellino, London 727): S. Mamas in Prison, Beheading of S. James, S. Zeno exorcizing the Daughter of Emperor Gallienus, S. Jerome and the Lion (p., see also Fra Diamante and Master of San Miniato). 1458–60. *Plate 833, 838.*

Milan. CASTELLO SFORZESCO (TRIVULZIO COLLECTION). 551. Pinnacle: Madonna of Humility with six Angels and SS. Dominic, Peter Martyr, and a female Saint. E. *Plate 843.*

   MUSEO POLDI-PEZZOLI. 587. Entombment.

Munich. 647. Madonna and Child.

    1072. Annunciation. ca 1443.

New Orleans (La.). I. DELGADO MUSEUM OF ART, KRESS COLLECTION. K 1325. Madonna and Child enthroned (p.).

New York. 17.89. Right wing of an altarpiece: SS. Augustine, Francis, Louis of Toulouse and Benedict (p., r.). E.

    35.31.1. Three panels from the 'Alessandri' altarpiece: S. Lawrence enthroned with SS. Cosmas and Damian and three Donors, S. Benedict, S. Anthony Abbot.

    49.7.9. Madonna and Child with two Angels. (Companion to Turin). E.

    89.15.19. Portrait of a Man and a Woman at a Window (g.p.).

    FRICK COLLECTION. 125. Two panels: Annunciation. *Plate 849.*

    CARL HAMILTON (EX). Madonna and Child. *Plate 853.*

Oxford. ASHMOLEAN. 246. Predella panel: Meeting at the Golden Gate.

Paris. 1344. 'Barbadori' altarpiece: Madonna and Child with Angels and SS. Frediano and Augustine. (Predella at Florence, Uffizi 8351). 1437. [*Plates* 157–158.]

Prato. 9. *Madonna del Ceppo*, with SS. Stephen and John Baptist, Francesco Datini and other Donors. (Execution, except for head of Madonna, by Fra Diamante on Lippi's design.) 1453. *Plate 864.*

    18. Nativity with SS. George and Vincent Ferrer. (Execution, except for Madonna and Child, and head and hand of S. Vincent, by Fra Diamante).

    DUOMO, CHOIR. Frescoes (assisted by Fra Diamante). Vault: Four Evangelists. Walls: Scenes from the Lives of SS. John Baptist and Stephen [Right wall: Birth and Naming of S. John Baptist, Leavetaking and Preaching of S. John, Dance of Salome and the Presentation of the Head of S. John. Left wall: Birth and Substitution of S. Stephen, Ordination and Disputation of S. Stephen, Martyrdom and Funeral of S. Stephen (Sd. and d. 1460). Altar wall: SS. John Gualbert and Albertus Magnus]. 1452–64. *Plates 857–60.*

    — R. TRANSEPT. Death of S. Jerome, with Inghirami as Donor (upper part executed by Fra Diamante).

    S. SPIRITO, ALTAR R. Circumcision. (Executed by Fra Diamante on Lippi's design.) 1466–68.

Richmond (Surrey). COOK COLLECTION. 17. Side panels to King Alfonso's triptych: SS. Anthony Abbot and George. 1457.

Rome. GALLERIA DORIA PAMPHILJ, PRIVATE APARTMENTS. Annunciation. *Plate 855.*

    GALLERIA NAZIONALE (PALAZZO BARBERINI). F.N.19220. Annunciation with two Donors.

    — (DEP. MUSEO NAZIONALE, TARQUINIA). Madonna and Child. d. 1437. *Plate 846.*

    VATICAN, PINACOTECA. 243. Triptych: Coronation of the Virgin with Angels, four Saints and two Donors (Angels executed by an assistant).

Spoleto. DUOMO, APSE. Frescoes. Vault: Coronation of the Virgin. Wall: Annunciation, Death of the Virgin, Nativity. (Chiefly executed by Fra Diamante, who completed the series after Lippi's death). 1467–69. *Plate 865.*

Turin. ACCADEMIA ALBERTINA. 140, 141. Wings of an altarpiece: SS. Augustine and Ambrose, SS. Gregory and Jerome. (Companions to New York 49.7.9). E.

Venice. CONTE CINI. Madonna and Child with Saints, Angels and a Donor. *Plate 845.*

Washington (D.C.). 390 (KRESS COLLECTION 497). Predella panel: Nativity (p.).
    401 (KRESS COLLECTION 501). Madonna and Child.
    536 (KRESS COLLECTION 1241). Annunciation.
    804 (KRESS COLLECTION 1342). Predella panel: Miraculous Rescue of S. Placidus.
    1085 (KRESS COLLECTION 1425). 'Cook' Tondo: Adoration of the Magi. (Begun by Fra Angelico). [*Plate 156.*]

LIPPO DI BENIVIENI

Florentine open to Sienese influence, mentioned from 1296 to 1353.

Florence. ACTON COLLECTION. Three panels from the Bartolini-Salimbeni-Vivai polyptych: Madonna and Child with SS. Peter and Paul. (Companions to New York and Ottawa.) Sd. *Plate 95.*
    CONTE COSIMO DEGLI ALESSANDRI. Polyptych: Madonna and Child with SS. Zenobius, Peter, Paul and Benedict. Sd. *Plate 97.*

New York. MAURICE SALOMON. Panel from polyptych: S. John Baptist. (See Florence, Acton.)

Ottawa. 2995. Panel from polyptych: S. John Evangelist. (See Florence, Acton.) *Plate 96.*

LORENZO DI CREDI

ca 1459–1537. Pupil and assistant of Verrocchio; strongly influenced by the young Leonardo.

Ajaccio (Corsica). 48. Madonna and Child.
    177. Stigmatization of S. Francis.

Berlin. 80. Portrait of a young Woman. *Plate 945.*
    100. Nativity. (Destroyed 1945.)
    103. Ecstasy of S. Mary Magdalen.
    (BERLIN-OST). 89. Tondo: Madonna adoring the Child.

Boston (Mass.). ISABELLA GARDNER MUSEUM. Portrait of a young Man.

Brunswick. See Hanover.

Cambridge (Mass.). 1930.195. Madonna and Child with a Bird (g.p.).

Castiglion Fiorentino. COLLEGIATA, CHAPEL R. OF CHOIR. Nativity. (S. Joseph by Sogliani). L.

Cincinnati (Ohio). 1927.388. Madonna nursing the Child (r.).

Cleveland (Ohio). 16.826. Madonna and Child (r.).

Copenhagen. 3640. Tondo: Madonna adoring the Child with Infant S. John (st.).

Coral Gables (Fla.). UNIVERSITY OF MIAMI, JOE AND EMILY LOWE ART GALLERY, KRESS COLLECTION. K 1149. Madonna and Child (st.).

Dresden. 13. Madonna and Child with Infant S. John. E. *Plate 933.*

    14. Nativity (g.p.).

    15. Madonna and Child with SS. Sebastian and John Evangelist.

Esztergom. KERESTÉNY MÜZEUM. Communion of S. Mary Magdalen. *Plate 944.*

Florence. GALLERIE. 883. Tondo: Madonna adoring the Child, with an Angel (p.).

    1482. Portrait of Andrea Verrocchio. Before 1488. *Plate 946.*

    1603. Annunciation.

    1604. The Virgin and S. John Evangelist against landscape.

    1614. Christ and the Samaritan Woman.

    1616. *Noli me tangere. Plate 949.*

    ACCADEMIA. 8661. Nativity (g.p.).

    UFFIZI. 1490. Portrait of a young Man.

    1597. Annunciation; below, monochrome Scenes of Creation of Eve, Fall of Man, Expulsion from Paradise. E. *Plate 947.*

    3094. Venus. E. [*Plate 198.*]

    3244. Tondo: Madonna and Child with Infant S. John and two Angels (st.).

    8399. Adoration of the Shepherds (from S. Chiara). 1510. *Plate 950.*

    S. AGATA, L. WALL. Holy Family enthroned, with four Saints (g.p.). L.

    S. MARIA DEL FIORE (DUOMO), R. SACRISTY. S. Michael (g.p.). ca 1523. *Plate 951.*

    ORSANMICHELE, 2nd PILASTER L. S. Bartholomew. 1510.

    (Environs) S. DOMENICO DI FIESOLE, 2nd CHAPEL R. Baptism of Christ (version of Verrocchio and Leonardo, Uffizi 8358). *Plate 943.*

— VILLA SCHIFANOIA. Madonna adoring the Child with Infant S. John. E.

Forlì. 130. Portrait of a young Woman.

Göttingen. 40. Crucifixion (g.p.).

Hanover. 63. Portrait of a young Man, inscribed *Franciscu Alunus.*

Kansas City (Mo.). 39.3. Madonna and Child with Infant S. John.

Karlsruhe. 409. Tondo: Madonna adoring the Child with Infant S. John. *Plate 941.*

Liverpool. 2772. Madonna nursing the Child (p.).

London. 593. Madonna nursing the Child.

    648. Madonna adoring the Child.

    LORD ROSEBERY (EX). S. Michael.

Longleat (Wilts.). MARQUESS OF BATH. Madonna and Child.

Mainz. 220. Madonna and Child. E.

Manhassett (L.I.). MRS. NICHOLAS F. BRADY (EX?). Madonna and Child (r.).

Modena. 502. Martyrdom of S. Sebastian.

Montepulciano. S. AGOSTINO, 3rd ALTAR L. Crucifixion. (?)

Muncie (Ind.). BALL STATE TEACHERS COLLEGE. Madonna and Child.

Naples. 44. Madonna and Child with S. Leonard and another Saint (st.). E.
  48. Nativity and two Angels. L.

New Haven (Conn.). 1871.51. Crucifixion with the Virgin and S. John (r.). E.
  1871.54. Crucifixion with S. Mary Magdalen (st., r.). E.
  1871.91. S. Sebastian (st., r.). L.

New York. 09.197. Tondo: Madonna adoring the Child with Infant S. John and an
  Angel (g.p.).
  43.86.5. Portrait of a young Woman with a Ring, called 'Ginevra de' Benci'.
  CHAUNCEY STILLMAN. Portrait of a Man.

Omaha (Neb.). JOSLYN MEMORIAL ART MUSEUM. Tondo: Madonna and Child with
  Infant S. John and two Angels.

Oxford. ASHMOLEAN. 118. Madonna and Child (u.).

Palermo. GALLERIA NAZIONALE (FROM OLIVELLA). Madonna adoring the Child with
  Infant S. John and an Angel (executed by Sogliani). *Plate* 1341.

Paris. 1263. Madonna and Child with SS. Julian and Nicholas (from Cestello). Not
  before 1503. *Plate* 948.
  1264. *Noli me tangere.*
  1602A. Predella panel (to Pistoia, Duomo): Annunciation (retouched by Leonardo). E. *Plate* 936.

Philadelphia (Pa.). MUSEUM OF ART, JOHNSON COLLECTION. 75. Communion of S.
  Mary Magdalen (st.).

Pistoia. DUOMO, CHAPEL L. OF CHOIR. Madonna and Child with SS. John Baptist and
  Donatus. (Executed in Verrocchio's studio; predella panels at Paris 1602A and
  Worcester; and by Perugino at Liverpool). 1478–85. *Plate* 935.
  S. MARIA DELLE GRAZIE (MADONNA DEL LETTO). Madonna and Child with SS. John
  Baptist, Mary Magdalen, Catherine and a fourth Saint. 1510.

Rome. GALLERIA BORGHESE. 433. Tondo: Madonna and Child with Infant S. John.
  VATICAN, PINACOTECA. 340. Madonna nursing the Child (p.).

San Marino (Cal.). HUNTINGTON MUSEUM. Tondo: A Saint in Glory with two
  Angels. *Plate* 942.

Shenfield Mill (Berks.). DR. JAMES HASSON. Coronation of the Virgin with SS.
  Barbara, Ursula and two other Saints (st.).

Strasbourg. 218. Madonna and Child. E.

Turin. GALLERIA SABAUDA. 115. Madonna and Child (g.p.).
  116. Madonna and Child with a Cherry. E.
  655. GUALINO COLLECTION. Portrait of a young Man (r.).

Vaduz. LIECHTENSTEIN COLLECTION. Painted terracotta: S. Catherine.

Venice. PINACOTECA QUERINI STAMPALIA. Tondo: Madonna adoring the Child with
  Infant S. John.

Washington (D.C.). 634 (WIDENER COLLECTION). Self-Portrait. 1488. [*Plate* 197.]
Worcester (Mass.). 1940.29. Predella panel (to Pistoia, Duomo): S. Donatus and the
    Tax Collector. 1478-85. *Plate* 939.

LORENZO MONACO

*ca 1370–1425. Follower of Agnolo Gaddi; influenced by Ghiberti, the Sienese, and
possibly by fourteenth century Byzantine as well as Franco-Flemish painting.*

Altenburg. 23. Crucifixion with SS. Benedict, Francis and Romuald.
    90. Predella panel: Flight into Egypt. (Companion to Highnam Court and New
        York, Lehman). *Plate* 436.
Amsterdam. 1641–B1. S. Jerome in his Study. (Companion to Copenhagen,
    Thorwaldsen?)
    1641–B3. Madonna and Child enthroned. *Plate* 429.
    1641–B4. Stigmatization of S. Francis. (Companion to Rome, Palazzo Rospi-
        gliosi.) *Plate* 454.
Assisi. MRS. F. M. PERKINS. Madonna of Humility with two Angels.
Baltimore (Md.). MUSEUM OF ART. 51.391. S. Anthony Abbot. (?)
    WALTERS ART GALLERY. 645. Madonna and Child with two Angels and SS.
    Peter and Paul. E.
Bergamo. 515. Man of Sorrows.
Berlin. 1119. Madonna and Child with Angels and SS. John Baptist and Nicholas.
    d. MCCC [incomplete]. (Destroyed 1945).
    1123A. Madonna of Humility. Predella: Man of Sorrows with the Virgin and S.
    John (g.p.). (Destroyed 1945).
    KUPFERSTICHKABINETT. 608. Two chiaroscuro miniatures: Visitation, Journey of
    the Magi.
    Illuminated initial: Eternal in letter O.
Bologna. 501. Madonna and Child with four Angels.
Brooklyn (N.Y.). 34.842. Madonna of Humility (p.).
Brussels. MME. FERON-STOCLET. Annunciation. (1398–1400?). *Plate* 445.
Budapest. 1089. Cut-out Crucifix. *Plate* 458.
Cambridge. 555. Madonna and Child with two Angels. E.
Cleveland (Ohio). 49.536. Miniature: A Prophet.
Copenhagen. 235. Predella panel: S. Benedict, Annunciation, and a kneeling Nun
    (st., fr.). (Companion to Tulsa).
    THORWALDSEN MUSEUM. 1. Madonna of Humility. (Companion to Amsterdam
    1641–B 1?).
Empoli. 2. Triptych: Madonna of Humility with SS. Donnino, John Baptist, Peter
    and Anthony Abbot. Pinnacles: Annunciation. d. 1404. *Plate* 433.

Empoli (contd.). 21, 72. Triptych: Madonna and Child with SS. John Evangelist, Catherine, John Baptist and a Bishop Saint (st.).

Fiesole. MUSEO BANDINI. I, 32. Crucifixion, with S. Francis. L.

Florence. ACCADEMIA. 438. Agony in the Garden, with Donor. Predella: Betrayal of Christ and Disrobing of Christ. E. *Plate 432*.

467. Man of Sorrows with Virgin and S. John and Symbols of the Passion. d. 1404.

470. Madonna and Child with two Angels and SS. John Baptist and Peter. d. 1408. *Plate 438*.

2140. S. John Evangelist (fr.).

2141. Crucifixion.

2169. The Virgin (fr.). (Companion to 2140, and probably to 2141.)

3147. Cut-out Crucifix (front to Careggi.)

3153. Cut-out Crucifix.

8458. 'Badia' triptych: Annunciation, with SS. Catherine, Anthony Abbot, Proculus and Francis. Pinnacles: Christ blessing, and two Angels. *Plate 444*.

8615–17. Three predella panels: S. Nicholas saving a Ship at Sea, Nativity, Encounter of SS. Onuphrius and Paphnutius. L. *Plate 465*.

UFFIZI. 466. Adoration of the Magi. Pinnacles: Christ blessing and two Prophets. (Annunciation and two Prophets in interstices of pinnacles by Cosimo Rosselli.) L. *Plates 459–461*.

468. Triptych: Madonna and Child with two Angels and SS. Bartholomew, John Baptist, Thaddeus and Benedict. Pinnacles: Christ blessing, Annunciation, and two Prophets. d. 1410.

885. 'S. Maria degli Angeli' Coronation of the Virgin. Pinnacles: Christ blessing, and Annunciation. Pilasters of frame: Saints and Prophets. Predella: Death of S. Benedict, S. Benedict in the *Sacro Speco* and a Monk tempted from Prayer by the Devil, Nativity, Adoration of the Magi, Miraculous Rescue of S. Placidus and S. Benedict detained by S. Scholastica, Raising of a Monk from the Ruins of Montecassino. Sd and d. 1414 (*Florentine style: 1413*). *Plates 448, 450, 452–453*.

BIBLIOTECA LAURENZIANA. Cod. Cor. Laur. 3. *Diurno Domenicale*. fol. 35, 38v, 46v, 65v, 86v, 89v. 93, 96v. Eight illuminated initials: Prophets. ca 1409. *Plates 442–443*.

Cod. Cor. Laur 5. Antiphonal. fol. 138. Illuminated initial: S. Jerome. ca 1394. *Plate 430*.

Cod. Cor. Laur. 8. Antiphonal. fol. 34, 76, 163. Three illuminated initials: David, S. Romuald, S. Paul. ca 1395. *Plate 431*.

MUSEO NAZIONALE DEL BARGELLO. Illuminated initials in codices from S. Maria Nuova. Cod. E 70. Female Martyr, S. Augustine, S. Benedict, Madonna and Child, Trinity. *Plate 435*.

Cod. F 72. Prophets and holy Monks (st.).

Cod. G 73. Prophets and holy Monks (st.).

Cod. H 74. Prophets and holy Monks (g.p.). 1412–13.

MUSEO FERRONI. 126. Crucifixion.

MUSEO HORNE. 97. Small cut-out Crucifix painted on both sides.

3231. Madonna and Child with SS. Anthony Abbot, Lucy, John Baptist, Peter, Julian and a female Saint.

S. CROCE, MUSEO DELL'OPERA. S. James enthroned.

S. GIOVANNINO DEI CAVALIERI, CHOIR. Three panels: Cut-out Crucifix, Virgin and S. John. *Plates 456–457.*

S. GIUSEPPE, 2nd CHAPEL L. Cut-out Crucifix.

S. MARCO (MUSEO), HOSPICE. Three pinnacles to Fra Angelico's Deposition: *Noli me tangere*, Resurrection, and the Maries at the Tomb.

*EX-CONVENTO DELLE OBLATE. Frescoes: above, Christ praying in the Garden and Christ watching the three sleeping Apostles (r.); below, Man of Sorrows with the Virgin, S. John and two female Saints and Symbols of the Passion in background.

OGNISSANTI, REFECTORY. 4. Fresco: Man of Sorrows (fr.).

29. Fresco: Crucifixion (fr.).

S. TRINITA, 4th CHAPEL R. (BARTOLINI). Altarpiece: Annunciation. Pinnacles: Three Prophets. Pilasters of frame: Eight Saints. Predella: Visitation, Nativity, Adoration of the Magi, Flight into Egypt. 1422–25. *Plates 463–464.*

Frescoes. Vault: Four Prophets. Soffits: SS. Bartholomew, John Baptist, John Evangelist and Paul. Walls: Scenes from the Life of the Virgin [Left wall: Expulsion of Joachim from the Temple and Annunciation to Joachim, Meeting at the Golden Gate. Altar wall: Founding of S. Maria Maggiore, Birth of the Virgin, Presentation of the Virgin. Right wall: Marriage of the Virgin, Dormition of the Virgin] (r.). 1422–25. [*Plate 131.*] *Plate 462.*

BERENSON COLLECTION. Madonna of Humility. d. 1405.

Madonna and Child with SS. John Baptist and Zenobius. E.

(Environs) CAREGGI, NUOVO CONVENTO DELLE OBLATE. Crucifix (st.; back to Florence, Accademia 3147).

— S. MARTINO A GANGALANDI, 1st ALTAR R. Two panels: Annunciation. (?)

— S. ROMOLO A SETTIMO. Madonna of Humility (p.).

Göttingen. 65. Crucifixion (st.).

Highnam Court (Glos.). GAMBIER-PARRY COLLECTION. Two predella panels: Visitation, Adoration of the Magi. (Companions to Altenburg and New York, Lehman).

Houston (Texas). 44–567A, B. Wings of a tabernacle: Annunciation, SS. Michael and Francis.

Kansas City (Mo.). 35.328. Stigmatization of S. Francis (st.).

40.40. Madonna of Humility.

Leghorn. LARDEREL COLLECTION (EX). Madonna and Child with SS. Julian, Dorothy, Jerome and a female Martyr.

London. 215, 216, 1897. Three parts of altarpiece from S. Benedetto fuori Porta a
  Pinti: Coronation of the Virgin with Angels and sixteen Saints. *Plate* 447.

  2862. Predella panel: S. Benedict receiving SS. Maurus and Placidus into the
  Order (fr. belonging to Vatican 193; companion to 4062 and Lennard Loan).

  3089. Illuminated letter B, from a Choral Book: Abraham and the Angels. (?)

  4062. Predella panel: Miraculous Rescue of S. Placidus and S. Benedict detained
  by S. Scholastica (fr. belonging to the Lennard panel; companion to 2862
  and Vatican 193).

  5224. Predella panel: S. Benedict in the *Sacro Speco* at Subiaco (fr., r.).

  LOANED BY SIR RICHARD BARRETT LENNARD. Predella panel: Death of S. Benedict
  (fr. belonging to 4062; companion to 2862 and Vatican 193). *Plate* 451.

Milan. CRESPI COLLECTION (EX). Madonna of Humility with six Saints. Pinnacle:
  Christ blessing.

Monte San Savino. S. MARIA DELLE VERTIGHE. Cut-out Crucifix.

Moscow. MUSEUM OF FINE ARTS. Madonna of Humility with two Angels. d. 1400.

Münster. DIOZESAN MUSEUM. 93. Bust of Baptist.

New Haven (Conn.). 1871.24. Crucifixion.

New York. 09.91 Madonna of Humility with two Angels. E.

  GUGGENHEIM MUSEUM (EX). 1271. King David. (Companion to Parcieux). 1405–10.
  Plate 440.

  ROBERT LEHMAN. Predella panel: Nativity. (Companion to Altenburg and Highnam
  Court).

  'Loeser' Crucifixion.

Nice. 162. Predella panel: Death of S. Augustine. L.

Parcieux. HENRI CHALANDON (EX). Three panels: Abraham, Noah and Moses.
  (Companions to New York, Guggenheim Museum). 1405-10. *Plate* 441.

Paris. 1315. Madonna of Humility (g.p.; pinnacle with God the Father by another
  hand).

  1348. Triptych: S. Lawrence enthroned, with SS. Agnes and Margaret. Pinnacles: Christ blessing, and Annunciation (st.; predella at Rome, Vatican
  215–17). 1407.

  1348A. Wings of a portable triptych: Agony in the Garden, and the Maries at
  the Tomb. d. 1408.

  JOSEPH SPIRIDON (EX). Madonna and Child enthroned (st.).

Pescia. MUSEO (BIBLIOTECA COMUNALE). I. Madonna of Humility (st.).

Philadelphia (Pa.). MUSEUM OF ART, JOHNSON COLLECTION. 10. Madonna of
  Humility (g.p.).

Pisa. MUSEO (FROM S. ERMETE). Madonna of Humility with six Angels. d. 1412.

Poznan. MO 21. Predella panel: Adoration of the Magi. L.

Prague. DO 820. Lamentation. *Plate* 439.

Prato. 7. Triptych: Madonna and Child with two Angels (fr.); SS. Catherine,
  Benedict, John Gualbert and Agatha. Pinnacles: Annunciation.

Ravenna. 191. Crucifixion with Saints (g.p.; not SS. Peter and Paul).

Rome. PALAZZO ROSPIGLIOSI, PALLAVICINI COLLECTION. Death of S. Francis. (Companion to Amsterdam 1641–B4). *Plate 455.*

VATICAN, PINACOTECA. 193. Predella panel: A Monk tempted from Prayer by the Devil, and the Raising of a Monk from the Ruins of Montecassino (fr. belonging to London 2862; companion to London 4062 and the Lennard panel).

194. Predella panel: Nativity (st.). L.

214. Predella panel: SS. Anthony Abbot and Paul Hermit. L.

215–17. Predella (to Paris 1348): Martyrdom of S. Lawrence, Martyrdom of S. Agnes, S. Margaret taken Prisoner by the Governor of Antioch (st.). 1407.

San Diego (Cal.). FINE ARTS GALLERY. Madonna and Child with SS. Romuald, John Baptist, Peter and Paul. Above: Man of Sorrows with the Virgin and S. John. E.

Seattle (Wash.). MUSEUM OF ART, KRESS COLLECTION. K 1654. Crucifixion (st.). d. 1408.

Siena. 57. Portable triptych: Madonna of Humility. Above: A Bishop Saint. Wings: Annunciation, SS. John Baptist and Nicholas. E. *Plate 437.*

Toledo (Ohio). MUSEUM OF ART. 45.30. Madonna of Humility. Above: Christ blessing. Predella: Man of Sorrows and Instruments of the Passion.

Tulsa (Okla.). PHILBROOK ART CENTER, KRESS COLLECTION. K 1047. Predella panel: S. Romuald (st., fr.; companion to Copenhagen 235).

Turin. MUSEO CIVICO. 3023. Painting on glass: Madonna and Child with S. John Baptist and another Saint. d. 1408.

Vaduz. LIECHTENSTEIN COLL. 865. Madonna and Child with two Angels. *Plate 434.*

— (EX). Virgin Annunciate. *Plate 446.*

Washington (D.C.). 514 (KRESS COLLECTION 1293). Madonna of Humility. d. 1413. *Plate 449.*

LORENZO DI NICCOLÒ

Recorded 1391–1411. Pupil of his father Niccolò di Pietro Gerini; influenced by Spinello Aretino and Lorenzo Monaco. (See also Master of Arte della Lana Coronation).

Altenburg. 67. Madonna and Child with two Angels and SS. John Baptist and Anthony Abbot (with Spinello Aretino).

Assisi. MRS. F. M. PERKINS. Left wing of an altarpiece: SS. Nicholas and John Gualbert. Pinnacle: Angel of the Annunciation.

Berlin. 1063. Predella panel: Beheading and Translation of S. Catherine. (?)

1108. Predella panel: Last Supper. (?)

Brolio (Chianti). BARONE RICASOLI. Madonna and Child with Saints.

Brooklyn (N.Y.). 03.74–79. Six predella panels: Scenes from the Life of S. Lawrence [S. Lawrence giving Alms, brought before Valerian, martyred, buried with S. Stephen, saving Souls from Purgatory, and interceding on Behalf of Emperor Henry III].

Chianciano (Chiusi). MUNICIPIO. Madonna of Humility.

Cortona. S. DOMENICO, HIGH ALTAR. Triptych: Coronation of the Virgin, with SS. Lawrence, Catherine of Siena, Dominic, Thomas Aquinas, Mark, John Baptist, Benedict, John Evangelist, Catherine of Alexandria and Julian. Pinnacles: Trinity, Annunciation, Angels and Prophets. Pilasters: Twelve Saints. Predella: Martyrdom of S. Lawrence, S. Peter dictating the Gospel to S. Mark, Adoration of the Magi, Death of S. John Evangelist, Totila before S. Benedict. 1402. *Plate 393–394.*

Denver (Col.). MUSEUM OF ART, SIMON GUGGENHEIM BEQUEST. Madonna and Child with eight Angels and twenty-eight Saints. E.

Florence. GALLERIE. 3258. Pinnacle: Crucifixion (r.).

ACCADEMIA. 455. Predella (to Annunciation by Andrea da Firenze): Nativity, Adoration of the Magi, Circumcision. (?)

8461. Triptych: Madonna and Child with Angels; SS. Paolino, John Baptist, Andrew and Matthias. 1391.

8468. Triptych: Coronation (on Spinello's design) and predella [SS. Jerome. Simon, Luke, Thaddeus, James Minor, Philip, Simon (*sic*), Bartholomew, Thomas, Paul, Gregory and Lawrence]. (Side panels by Niccolò di Pietro Gerini). d. 1401. *Plate 386.*

8604, 8605. Wings of 'S. Gaggio' altarpiece: S. Catherine, S. Caius. Pinnacles: Annunciation.

8610. Triptych: Madonna and Child with two Angels and SS. Anthony Abbot, John Baptist, Lawrence and Julian. Above: SS. Peter and Paul. d. 1404.

MUSEO BARDINI. 771. Crucifix. (?)

MUSEO NAZIONALE DEL BARGELLO. 17. SS. Michael and Catherine.

S. CROCE. Triptych: Coronation of the Virgin with eight Angels and SS. Lucy, John Evangelist, Peter and Lawrence. Pinnacles: Christ blessing, Annunciation, Two Prophets. L. *Plate 396.*

— SACRISTY. Polyptych: Madonna and Child with SS. Lawrence, Anthony Abbot, Andrew, John Baptist, Louis of Toulouse, John Evangelist, Peter, Bartholomew, Christopher and Francis. Spandrels: Five Prophets. Predella: Eight Saints.

— CAPPELLA MEDICI. Madonna and Child. d. 1409.

S. FELICITA, L. TRANSEPT. Fresco: Nativity (with Niccolò di Pietro Gerini).

S. LEONARDO IN ARCETRI, HIGH ALTAR. Triptych: Madonna and Child with SS. Leonard, Anthony Abbot, James and Lawrence. *Plate 390.*

(Environs) S. LORENZO IN COLLINA. Polyptych: Madonna and Child with SS. Nicholas, Michael, Lawrence and Julian. d. 1412.

— s. maria a quinto, l. wall. Triptych: Madonna and Child with SS. Peter, Philip, Lawrence and James. Pinnacles: Christ blessing and Annunciation (with Spinello Aretino). d. 1393. *Plate* 415.

— s. martino a terenzano, l. wall. Triptych: Madonna and Child with SS. Martin and Lawrence. Pinnacles: Christ blessing and Annunciation. Sd (?) and d. 1402. *Plates* 391–392.

— — l. and r. walls. Two panels from an altarpiece: S. Clement and S. Lucy. Pinnacles: Annunciation.

Graz. 190. Madonna and Child enthroned.

Highnam Court (Glos.). gambier-parry collection. Pinnacle: Coronation of the Virgin. E.

Munich. 644. Pinnacle: *Salvator Mundi.* (?)

New Haven (Conn.). 1871.26. Wing of portable triptych: Angel of Annunciation and six Saints below (the rest by Niccolò di Pietro Gerini).

1871.27, 28. Wings of an altarpiece: SS. Augustine and Lucy, SS. Agnes and Dominic. Pinnacles: Four Prophets.

1943.204. Madonna and Child. E.

New York. 58.135. Conversion of S. John Gualbert. *Plate* 389.

Oxford. christ church library. 19. Madonna of Humility.

Parma. 445. Madonna and Child.

Pelago (Florence). (Environs) oratorio del magnale. Madonna and Child enthroned.

— s. martino a pagiano. SS. Anthony Abbot and Michael (companions to Madonna above).

Pescia. biblioteca comunale (museo). 8.† Madonna and Child.

Pisa. 129. Right wing of a triptych: SS. John Baptist, James and Anthony Abbot (with Spinello). (Companion to Duomo).

duomo, sala del capitolo. Left wing of a triptych: SS. Raynerius, Silvester and Michael (with Spinello). (See Pisa 129).

— opera primaziale. Centre panel of a triptych: Coronation of the Virgin with four music-making Angels (with Spinello). (See Pisa 129).

(Environs) cevoli, parrocchiale. Madonna and Child.

Raleigh (N.C.). museum of art, kress collection. k 1093. Crucifixion (with Spinello?).

Rennes. musée. Two predella panels: Martyrdom of S. Lawrence, Crucifixion of Bishop. (?)

Rome. vatican, pinacoteca, 1, 3. Two panels: SS. Paula and Eustochium. (?)

189–91. Three predella panels: S. John in the Cauldron of boiling Oil, S. John and the poisoned Wine and the Raising of the Pagan Priests, Ascension of S. John.

Saint Louis (Mo.). 43.37. Triptych: Madonna and Child with SS. Christopher, Blaise, Sebastian and Francis. Pinnacles: Christ blessing, Annunciation. *Plate* 395.

San Gimignano. 12. Polyptych painted on both sides: SS. Gregory and Fina, Two

Angels, and Scenes from the Life of S. Fina [S. Fina nursed by her Mother,
S. Fina's Mother pushed down the Stair by a Demon, Death of S. Fina,
Miraculous Healing of the Nurse Beldia, Exorcism of S. Fina's Tomb, S. Fina
saving a falling Workman, Fire quelled by her Shirt, S. Fina saving a Ship at
Sea]. *Plate 388.*

13. Madonna and Child enthroned.

14. Triptych: S. Bartholomew enthroned and four Scenes from his Life [Birth
and Substitution, Condemnation, Flaying and Beheading of S. Bartholomew].
Pinnacles: Annunciation. Pilasters: Six Saints. Predella: Crucifixion and six
Saints. d. 1401. *Plate 387.*

Stia (Casentino). (Environs) S. MARIA DELLE GRAZIE, HIGH ALTAR. Madonna and Child
with SS. John Baptist, Catherine, Dorothy and Anthony Abbot. Predella:
Man of Sorrows and four Saints.

Zurich. 1946.15. Crucifixion.

MACHIAVELLI, Zanobi

*1418–79. Follower of Fra Angelico and assistant of Benozzo Gozzoli; influenced by
Filippo Lippi and Pesellino.*

Amsterdam. 786 D–1. Predella panel: S. Nicholas of Tolentino saving a Man from
Hanging. *Plate 812.*

Avignon. 413. Madonna and Child enthroned.

Baltimore (Md.). WALTERS ART GALLERY. 714. Portable triptych: Madonna and
Child with SS. Catherine, Francis and Sebastian. Spandrels of frame: An-
nunciation. Lunette: Man of Sorrows. Wings: Tobias and the Angel and
SS. James, Julian, Mary Magdalen, Barbara, Lucy and Apollonia. E.

Bergamo. 317. Madonna and Child.

Berlin. 94A. Right wing of an altarpiece: S. James. Pinnacle: Virgin Annunciate.
Sd and d. 1463. *Plate 815.*

Besançon. 896.1.183. Madonna and Child.

Boston (Mass.). 48.297. Madonna and Child with SS. Sebastian, Andrew, Bernardino,
Paul, Lawrence and Augustine. *Plate 811.*

Chantilly. 11. Madonna and Child with two Saints and six Angels. *Plate 817.*

Dijon. 31. Coronation of the Virgin, with Angels and SS. John Baptist, Francis,
Mary Magdalen and Peter. Sd and d. 1473. *Plate 816.*

1312. Madonna and Child. (?)

Dublin. 108. Madonna and Child with SS. Bernardino, Mark, Louis of Toulouse
and Jerome. Sd. *Plate 808.*

Florence (Environs). S. ANDREA A BOTINACCIO, CHIESA DI S. MARIA COELI AULA.
Madonna and Child. E.

— S. MARTINO A MENSOLA, ALTAR L. OF CHOIR. Annunciation. *Plate* 814.

Fucecchio (Valdarno). MUSEO. Madonna and Child (fr.).

London. 586. Triptych: Madonna and Child with Angels and SS. Nicholas of Tolentino, a Bishop Saint, Bartholomew and Monica.

587, 588. Wings of an altarpiece: SS. John Baptist and John Evangelist, SS. Mark and Augustine. *Plate* 813.

CHARLES LIVIJN (EX). Madonna and Child with SS. James, Jerome, Anthony Abbot, Mary Magdalen and a Donor.

Lucca. PINACOTECA. Madonna and Child with SS. Bartholomew, Mary Magdalen, Louis of Toulouse and Anthony of Padua.

Minneapolis (Minn.). INSTITUTE OF ARTS (EX). 22.16.1. Panel from an altarpiece: S. James. (?)

New Haven (Conn.). 1943.224. Madonna and Child with two Angels (variant of Rome, Pallavicini collection).

New York. R. M. HURD (EX). Madonna and Child (possibly with Filippo Lippi or in his studio). E.

Pisa. 172. Madonna and Child with SS. Anthony of Padua, Silvester, John Baptist and Francis. Sd. *Plate* 809.

Rome. VATICAN, PINACOTECA. 568, 570. Two panels: SS. James and Anthony Abbot, SS. Anthony of Padua and Louis of Toulouse. (?)

PALAZZO ROSPIGLIOSI, PALLAVICINI COLLECTION. Madonna and Child with two Angels. *Plate* 810.

Vienna. 6688, 6689. Two panels: SS. Dominic and John Baptist. (?)

Homeless. Three predella panels: S. Jerome healing the Lion, S. Jerome appearing to S. Augustine, Death of S. Jerome. *Plate* 805–7.

Madonna and Child with two Angels. *Dedalo* xii, 696.

Madonna and Child. *Burl. Mag.* 1950, p. 346.

MAINARDI, Bastiano

Died 1513. Pupil and imitator of his brother-in-law Domenico Ghirlandajo.

Bagno di Romagna. S. MARIA DEL FIORE. Nativity with SS. Bartholomew, Catherine, Infant S. John, Lucy and Francis.

Balcarres (Fife, Scotland). EARL OF CRAWFORD AND BALCARRES. S. Barbara and a Donor. *Plate* 978.

Barnard Castle (Durham). BOWES MUSEUM. 40. Madonna adoring the Child. (Versions at Boston, Cracow, Zagreb, and Homeless).

Berlin. 77. Madonna and Child. (Destroyed 1945).

83. Profile Portrait of a Woman.

86. Portrait of a young Man. (Companion to 83 above). [*Plate* 184.]

Berlin (contd.). (BERLIN-OST). 84 (DEP. COLOGNE). Madonna and Child with SS. Clare, Paul, Francis and Catherine.

    1134. Tondo: Madonna and Child.

    1.203 (DEP. BONN). Tondo: Madonna and Child with Infant S. John and three Angels. (See Paris 1367).

Birmingham (Ala.). MUSEUM OF ART, KRESS COLLECTION. K267. Tondo: Madonna and Child with Infant S. John and three Angels. (See Paris 1367.)

Bonn. 128. See Berlin.

Boston (Mass.). 46.1429. Madonna adoring the Child. (See Barnard Castle).

Brooklyn (N.Y.). 32.841. Madonna adoring the Child (p.).

Budapest. 4914. S. Stephen (from S. Maria Novella altarpiece; see Munich 1078). Soon after 1494. *Plate 973.*

Cambridge. M54. Nativity (p.). (See Florence, Brozzi).

Cambridge (Mass.) RADCLIFFE COLLEGE. Madonna and Child. E.

Cherbourg. 15. Tondo: Madonna and Child with Infant S. John and three Angels. (p.). L. (See Paris 1367).

Cologne. 502. See Berlin.

Copenhagen. 3638. Resurrection.

Cracow. WAWEL MONASTERY. 67. Madonna adoring the Child. (See Barnard Castle). (?)

Denver (Col.). MUSEUM OF ART, KRESS COLLECTION. K 1726. Coronation of the Virgin with SS. John Baptist and John Evangelist (fr., r.).

Dresden. 16. Tondo: Nativity. (See Florence, Brozzi).

Enschede. RIJKSMUSEUM TWENTHE. N.K.1578. Man of Sorrows.

Esztergom. KERESTÉNY MÜZEUM. Coronation of the Virgin, with SS. Jerome and Anthony of Padua.

Florence. GALLERIE. 505. Madonna and Child with SS. Blaise, Francis, Benedict and Anthony Abbot.

    ACCADEMIA. 1621. SS. James, Stephen and Peter.

    MUSEO NAZIONALE DEL BARGELLO, CHAPEL. Fresco tondo: Madonna and Child (p.). d. 1490.

    — CARRAND COLLECTION. 2030. Profile Portrait of a Woman.

    S. CROCE, BARONCELLI CHAPEL. Fresco: *Madonna della Cintola*. *Plate 983.*

    S. MARIA NOVELLA, CHOIR. Frescoes: Scenes from the Lives of the Virgin and of S. John Baptist, esp. S. John entering the Wilderness. (p., assisting Domenico Ghirlandajo). 1486–90. *Plates 968–71.*

    SPEDALE DI ORBATELLO.* Fresco: Madonna and Child with two Cherubim (Eternal, SS. Andrew and Dionysius by Master of S. Miniato).

    MRS. C. H. COSTER. Tondo: Madonna and Child with Infant S. John and an Angel. (See Paris 1367).

    (Environs) BROZZI, VIA DI BROZZI AND VIA PISTOIESE. Tabernacle fresco: Nativity, and SS. Ansanus and Roch. (Versions at Cambridge, Dresden, Vienna, and Homeless). *Plate 984.*

Hamburg. 754. Tondo: Madonna and Child with Infant S. John and three Angels. (See Paris 1367).

Indianapolis (Ind.). 51.58. Madonna and Child with S. Justus and a female Saint. d. 1507.

Kaunas (Lithuania). MUSEUM OF RELIGIOUS ART (EX). Man of Sorrows.

Leipzig. 485. Tondo: Adoration of the Shepherds. d. 1492.

London. 2502. Madonna and Child with Infant S. John.

3937. Madonna and Child.

Longleat (Wilts.). MARQUESS OF BATH. Madonna and Child with two Angels and SS. Bernardino, John Baptist, Francis and Catherine.

Maidenhead (Berks.). SIR THOMAS MERTON. Tondo: Madonna and Child with Infant S. John. (See Paris 1367). *Plate 979.*

Mühlheim (Cologne). DR. F. THYSSEN (EX). Madonna adoring the Child.

Munich. W.A.F.543, 544. Triptych: Madonna and Child with a Donor. Wings: SS. George and Sebastian (p.).

1076, 1077. Wings of 'S. Maria Novella' altarpiece: SS. Catherine of Siena and Lawrence. Soon after 1494.

1078. Front of 'S. Maria Novella' altarpiece: Madonna and Child in Glory with SS. Dominic, Michael, John Baptist and John Evangelist (with Granacci on Ghirlandajo's design; companion to 1076–77, and to Granacci and Davide Ghirlandajo, Berlin 74–76). Soon after 1494. *Plate 974.*

Naples. 45. Tondo: Madonna and Child with Infant S. John and three Angels. (See Paris, 1367).

New York. 14.40.635. Tondo: Madonna adoring the Child with two Angels (replica of Venice; r.).

32.100.67. Portrait of a Cardinal.

Palermo. CHIARAMONTE BORDONARO COLLECTION. Madonna and Child with SS. Francis and Julian. d.1506.

Paris. 1321. Visitation with SS. Mary of James and Mary Salome (with Domenico Ghirlandajo). d. 1491. *Plate 976.*

1367. Tondo: Madonna and Child with Infant S. John and three Angels. (Replicas and variants of this composition are at Berlin 1.203; Birmingham; Cherbourg; Florence, Mrs. Coster; Hamburg; Maidenhead; Naples; San Gimignano 36; Sarasota; and Vaduz).

1367B, C. Portraits of a Man and a Woman (variants of Berlin 83 and 86).

GUSTAVE DREYFUS (EX). Profile Portrait of a Woman.

Philadelphia (Pa.). MUSEUM OF ART, JOHNSON COLLECTION. 69. Madonna and Child with Infant S. John (p.).

1167. Two panels: Male and female Worshippers. *Plates 980, 982.*

Pisa. 175. Woman carrying a Basket of Fruit on her head (replica of figure in Ghirlandajo's Birth of S. John, Florence, S. Maria Novella).

Rome. VATICAN, PINACOTECA. 344. Nativity.

San Gimignano. 34. Tondo: Madonna and Child with two Angels. L.

    35. Madonna and Child with SS. Jerome and Bernard. Predella: Birth of the Virgin. d. 1502.

    36. Tondo: Madonna and Child with Infant S. John and an Angel. L. (See Paris 1367).

    37. Madonna and Child in Glory with six Saints.

    COLLEGIATA, CAPPELLA DI S. FINA. Frescoes. Vault: Four Evangelists. Lunettes: Six Doctors of the Church. Spandrels: Six Prophets. (See also Domenico Ghirlandajo). ca 1475.

    — ORATORIO DI S. GIOVANNI BATTISTA. Fresco: Annunciation. d. 1482. *Plate* 977.

    S. AGOSTINO, CHAPEL R. OF ENTRANCE. Frescoes. Vault: Four Doctors of the Church. Wall: SS. Nicholas, Lucy and Augustine.

    — L. WALL. Fresco: S. Gimignano blessing three Men. d. 1487.

    Frescoed Monument to Fra Domenico Strambi. d. 1488.

    OSPEDALE DI S. FINA, VESTIBULE. Frescoes. Spandrel of vault: Madonna and Child. Lunettes: SS. Bartolo, Francis and two Bishop Saints.

    VIA S. GIOVANNI. 46. Tabernacle fresco: Madonna and Child with Cherubim (r.).

San Marino (Cal.). HUNTINGTON MUSEUM. Portraits of a Man and a Woman (versions of Berlin 83 and 86).

    Madonna and Child with two Angels.

Sarasota (Fla.). 20. Tondo: Madonna and Child with Infant S. John and three Angels. (See Paris 1367).

Siena. DUOMO. Two windows: SS. Francis, Blaise and Anthony of Padua; SS. Bonaventura, Bernardine and Louis of Toulouse.

Vaduz. LIECHTENSTEIN COLLECTION. 853. Tondo: Madonna and Child with Infant S. John and two Angels. (See Paris 1367).

Venice. CONTE VITTORIO CINI. Tondo: Madonna adoring the Child with two Angels. (Replica of New York 14.40.635).

Vienna. GALERIE HARRACH. Nativity. (See Florence, Brozzi).

Washington (D.C.). SMITHSONIAN INSTITUTION. 19.6.13.G. Tondo: Madonna and Child with Infant S. John and an Angel. L.

Zagreb. 92. Tondo: Madonna adoring the Child (p.). (See Barnard Castle).

Homeless. Madonna adoring the Child. (See Barnard Castle). *Plate* 985.

    Tondo: Adoration of the Shepherds. d. 1493. (Version of Leipzig). *Plate* 981.

    Tondo: Nativity, with Infant S. John. (See Florence, Brozzi). *Plate* 986.

MARIOTTO DI CRISTOFANO

S. Giovanni Valdarno 1393–Florence 1457. Brother-in-law of Masaccio, active in Florence from 1419. Influenced by Angelico and Paolo Schiavo.

Florence. ACCADEMIA. 3162, 3164. Altarpiece from the Spedale di S. Matteo. Front panel: Marriage of S. Catherine, with SS. Dorothy, Agnes, Mary Magdalen and Elizabeth of Hungary. Back panel: Resurrection. Documented 1445–47. *Plates 650, 651.*

MARIOTTO DI NARDO

Recorded 1394–1431. Close follower of Jacopo di Cione; influenced by Niccolò di Pietro Gerini, and later by Lorenzo Monaco.

Altenburg. 35. Wings of a triptych framed together (Eternal in interstice possibly by Giovanni di Francesco): Annunciation, Crucifixion, S. Cecilia.

Amherst (Mass.). COLLEGE, KRESS STUDY COLLECTION. K 93. Crucifixion.

Amiens. 420. See Paris, Musées Nationaux.

Amsterdam. ERNST PROEHL. Predella panel: Betrayal of Christ. (Companion to Paris, Campana 46–54).

Arezzo. 14. Madonna and Child.

Assisi. MRS. F. M. PERKINS. Madonna and Child enthroned with two Donors. d. 1404. *Plate 519.*

Avignon. MUSÉE CALVET 409 (CAMPANA 120). Coronation of the Virgin, with SS. Anthony Abbot, Lucy, Augustine, Lawrence, Dorothy and James.

Balcarres (Fife, Scotland). EARL OF CRAWFORD AND BALCARRES. Six octagonal predella panels: Annunciation, Nativity, Adoration of the Magi, Circumcision, Christ among the Doctors, Baptism of Christ. *Plate 523–524.*

Baltimore (Md.). WALTERS ART GALLERY. 746. SS. Lawrence, Christopher, Sebastian and a Bishop Saint. E.

Bergamo. 506, 538. Two panels: SS. Apollonia, Dorothy, Catherine, Lucy and Ursula; SS. Anthony Abbot, Lawrence, John Baptist, Bartholomew and Julian.

Berlin (EX). 1102. Two panels: Nativity, Circumcision. (Companions to Blaricum, Brunswick, Nantes, Princeton and Florence, Longhi collection.)

RICHARD VON KAUFMANN (EX). Crucifixion, Madonna and Child with two music-making Angels and eight Saints. Predella: Five Saints. *Plate 526.*

Birmingham (Ala.). MUSEUM OF ART. KRESS COLLECTION. K 333. Madonna and Child with four Angels and SS. Francis and Anthony Abbot.

Blaricum (Netherlands). DR. J. P. KLEIWEG DE ZWAAN. Two panels: Adoration of the Magi, Christ among the Doctors. (See Berlin.)

Borselli (Pontassieve). (Environs). s. MARGHERITA DI TOSINA. Triptych: Madonna and Child with four Angels and SS. Anthony Abbot, Romuald, Margaret and Francis.

Brant Broughton (Lincs.). REV. CANON SUTTON (EX). Predella panel: Crucifixion.

Brunswick. 2. Christ before Pilate. (See Berlin).

Budapest. 1442. Madonna of Humility with four Angels.

     SIMON MELLER. Madonna and Child enthroned.

Cambridge. M28. Coronation of the Virgin with Angels and SS. John Baptist and Stephen.

Cambridge (Mass.). 1938.79. Predella panel: Martyrdom of S. Lawrence (fr.).

Châteauroux (Indre). MUSÉE (CAMPANA 98). Madonna and Child with three music-making Angels and SS. Catherine, John Baptist, Francis and Lucy.

Detroit (Mich.). 25.43. Madonna of Humility.

Empoli. 5. Madonna nursing the Child with four Angels. Above: Crucifixion. E.

Esher (Surrey). LORD D'ABERNON (EX). Portable triptych: Madonna and Child with six Saints. Wings: Annunciation, Nativity, Crucifixion.

Fiesole. MUSEO BANDINI. I, 22. Trinity, with SS. Francis and Mary Magdalen.

     (Environs) ORATORIO DI FONTELUCENTE. Triptych: *Madonna della Cintola*, and SS. Jerome and John Evangelist. Pinnacle: Christ with a Crown and Angels. Formerly d. 1398. *Plate* 517.

Florence. 2212. GALLERIE. Madonna of Humility (r.).

     3163. Predella: S. Nicholas received as Bishop of Myra, S. Nicholas saving a Ship at Sea, Crucifixion, S. Nicholas preventing the Execution of an Innocent Man, Miracle of the Child and the Golden Chalice.

     3258–60. Three pinnacles: Annunciation, Crucifixion.

     ACCADEMIA. 450. Lunette: Madonna and Child (Annunciation in spandrels by a later hand). (?)

     463. Annunciation.

     473. Madonna and Child with SS. Philip and John Baptist. Pinnacle: Two crowning Angels. d. 1418.

     3460. Madonna and Child in Glory, with SS. Stephen and Reparata.

     8612. Triptych: Madonna and Child with four Angels and SS. Lawrence, John Evangelist, James and Sebastian.

     8613. Predella (to 8612): Annunciation to Joachim, Birth of the Virgin, Dormition of the Virgin, Presentation in the Temple, Marriage of the Virgin. *Plate* 528.

     COMPAGNIA DEL BIGALLO. Triptych: Madonna and Child, S. John Baptist, S. Peter Martyr. Pinnacles: Christ blessing, Annunciation. 1415–16. (Stolen.) *Plate* 525.

     MUSEO STIBBERT. 14433. Madonna of Humility.

     S. CROCE, HIGH ALTAR. Four predella panels of polyptych: Martyrdoms of four Saints. (See also Giovanni del Biondo and Niccolò di Pietro Gerini).

— L. WALL (BETWEEN IST AND 2ND ALTARS). Frescoes: Crucifixion, *Noli me tangere*, Ascension (fr.).

— SACRISTY. Madonna and Child.

S. MARIA NOVELLA, FARMACIA (VIA DELLA SCALA 16). Monochrome frescoes. Vault: Four Evangelists. Walls: Scenes from the Passion [Opposite wall: Christ in the Temple and Judas receiving the Price of Betrayal, Last Supper, Washing of Feet. Right wall: Agony in the Garden, Arrest of Christ, Christ before Caiaphas, Christ before Pilate. Entrance wall: Mocking of Christ, Flagellation of Christ, Way to Calvary. Left wall: Crucifixion, Entombment, *Noli me tangere*.] *Plate 529*.

S. MINIATO AL MONTE, L. WALL. Detached fresco: Madonna and Child in Glory with SS. Lawrence, Romuald, Jerome and Mary Magdalen (fr., r.).

Detached fresco: Crucifixion with the Virgin and S. John, and SS. Francis, Miniato, Benedict, Stephen and Anthony Abbot (r.).

S. TRINITA, HIGH ALTAR. Triptych: Trinity, and SS. Anthony Abbot, Michael, Francis and Julian. Pinnacles: Annunciation. d. 1406.

ACTON COLLECTION. Coronation of the Virgin. Spandrel: Holy Ghost and two Angels. d. 1431. *Plate 531*.

Madonna of Humility with two Angels. d. 1422.

Lunette: Madonna and Child.

Predella panel: S. Julian assisting a Pilgrim across a River.

PROF. ROBERTO LONGHI. Betrayal of Christ. (See Berlin).

SERRISTORI COLLECTION. Triptych: Madonna and Child with six Angels and SS. James, John Baptist, Andrew and Bernard. Pinnacles: Christ blessing, Annunciation, Two Prophets. Predella (r.): A Donor, Beheading of S. James, Baptism of Christ, Adoration of the Magi, Crucifixion of S. Andrew, Vision of S. Bernard. d. 1424.

Desco: Justice of Trajan. (?)

(Environs) CERTOSA DEL GALLUZZO. Coronation of the Virgin with six Angels.

— IMPRUNETA, COLLEGIATA, SACRISTY. Trinity with two Donors. d. 1418.

— LEGNAIA, S. ARCANGELO, L. WALL. Triptych: Madonna and Child with six Angels and SS. Bartholomew, Michael, Lawrence and Nicholas.

— VICCHIO DI RIMAGGIO, S. LORENZO, R. WALL. Fresco: S. Lawrence saving Souls from Purgatory (fr.).

— S. DONNINO DI VILLAMAGNA, HIGH ALTAR. Madonna and Child with two Angels and twelve Saints. Pinnacles: Annunciation. Predella: Man of Sorrows, the Virgin, S. John and four other Saints. ca 1394–95. *Plate 515*.

— VINCIGLIATA, CASTELLO. Frescoes: Life of S. Bernardo degli Uberti. (?)

Grand Rapids (Mich.). ART GALLERY. Four panels (from pilasters of the altarpiece formerly at Hatton Garden Church, London): SS. Francis, Sylvester, Dominic and a Bishop Saint. 1408.

Hampton Court. 1219. Madonna and Child, with Crucifixion above.

Kiev. 3. Adoration of Shepherds.

London. HATTON GARDEN CHURCH (EX). Triptych: Coronation of the Virgin with five Angels and SS. Lawrence, Stephen, John Baptist and John Evangelist. Spandrels: Two Angels. Pilasters: Two Saints. d. 1408. (See also Grand Rapids.) *Plate 520.*

Loro Ciuffenna. CHIESA PARROCCHIALE. Triptych: Madonna and Child with Angels; SS. Peter, John Baptist, Michael, Gabriel, Anthony Abbot, Paul, Nicholas, Francis (st.).

Los Angeles (Cal.). A.2530.31–1. Madonna of Humility.

Lutzchena (Leipzig). SPECK VON STERNBURG (EX). Martyrdom of S. Lawrence (fr.).

Munich. ERWIN ROSENTHAL (EX). Predella panel: Ordination of S. Stephen and Exorcism of a Possessed Woman. *Plate 522.*

Nantes. 73. Last Supper. (See Berlin).

Nevers. MUSÉE 23 (CAMPANA 319). Madonna and Child in Glory with six Angels and the twelve Apostles.

New Haven (Conn.). 1871.16. Madonna and Child with SS. Nicholas, Margaret, Dorothy and John Baptist. Above: Crucifixion.

    1871.17. Gable: Nativity and Resurrection.

    1871.29. Predella panel: A Woman protected from the Devil by SS. Cosmas and Damian, and Dream of the Deacon Justinian.

New York. METROPOLITAN MUSEUM, THE CLOISTERS. 53.37. Christ and the Virgin as Intercessors. (?)

    HISTORICAL SOCIETY. B–12, 13. Two pinnacles: S. Anthony Abbot and another male Saint.

Oberlin (Ohio). 43.118. Predella panel: Adoration of the Magi. (Companion to Vienna, Lanckoronski).

Oxford. CHRIST CHURCH LIBRARY. 18. Madonna and Child in Glory with two music-making Angels and six Saints.

Palermo. CHIARAMONTE BORDONARO COLLECTION. Madonna and Child with music-making Angels.

    Trinity.

Panzano (Chianti). (Environs) PIEVE DI S. LEONINO. Triptych: Madonna and Child with two Angels and SS. Francis, John Baptist, Euphrosynus and Lawrence. Pinnacles: Christ blessing, Annunciation. Predella: S. Catherine, Stigmatization of S. Francis, Beheading of S. John, S. Anthony Abbot, Man of Sorrows, S. Dominic, S. Euphrosynus healing at an Altar (?), Martyrdom of S. Lawrence, S. Lucy. d. 1421. *Plate 530.*

Parcieux. HENRI CHALANDON (EX). Madonna and Child with four Angels and SS. Nicholas and Francis. *Plate 518.*

Paris. MUSÉES NATIONAUX (CAMPANA 46–54). Nine predella panels: Man of Sorrows, Nativity, Last Supper, Flagellation, Crucifixion, Lamentation, Resurrection, *Noli me tangere*, Ascension. (Companions to Amsterdam).

LOUVRE. 1314. Madonna and Child with SS. Mary Magdalen, Bartholomew, Lucy, Anthony Abbot, Catherine and a Deacon Saint.

MUSÉE DES ARTS DÉCORATIFS, LEGS PEYRE. Coronation of the Virgin with SS. John Baptist, Peter, Paul, Anthony Abbot and six female Saints (r.). E.

Perugia. S. DOMENICO, CHOIR. Windows: Annunciation, Saints, Scene from the Life of S. James. 1404.

Pesaro. 23. Triptych: Madonna and Child with two Angels; SS. Francis and Michael. Predella: SS. Jerome, Anthony of Padua and the Baptist, Flagellation, SS. John Evangelist, Louis of Toulouse and Claire. d. 1400.

Pistoia. MUSEO CIVICO. Madonna of Humility with four Angels. Pinnacle: Christ blessing. Pilasters: Six Saints.

Triptych: Annunciation. (Lateral panels by Rossello di Jacopo Franchi). *Plate 532.*

Princeton (N.J.). 33–21. Flagellation. (See Berlin).

Providence (R.I.). 17.520, 521. Two predella panels: Martyrdom of S. Lawrence, Stigmatization of S. Francis.

Rome. VATICAN, PINACOTECA. 97. Predella panel: S. Nicholas preventing the Execution of three Innocent Men.

101, 102. Two predella panels: Annunciation, Nativity.

117–19. Three predella panels: Baptism of S. Pancras, Crucifixion, Martyrdom of S. Pancras (st.).

San Miniato al Tedesco. S. DOMENICO, CHAPEL R. OF CHOIR. Predella: Birth of S. John Baptist, S. John entering the Wilderness, S. John indicating Christ to the People, Baptism of Christ, S. John before Herod and the Dance of Salome. *Plate 516.*

— CHAPEL L. OF CHOIR. Predella panel: S. Jerome in the Wilderness. (?)

Fresco: Translation of the body of S. James to Galicia. (?)

Santa Barbara (Cal.). MRS. GEORGE F. STEEDMAN. Madonna and Child with two Angels and SS. Catherine and John Baptist (r.).

Sarasota (Fla.). 7. Madonna of Humility with six Angels. Pinnacle: Christ blessing.

Siena. 589. Madonna and Child (fr., r.).

SARACINI COLLECTION. Madonna and Child in Glory with six Angels and SS. Lawrence, John Baptist, Anthony Abbot, Nicholas, Philip and Bernard (r.).

Utrecht. ARCHEPISCOPAL MUSEUM. Madonna nursing the Child, with SS. John Baptist, Peter, Catherine and a fourth Saint.

Vaduz. LIECHTENSTEIN COLLECTION. 871. *Desco da nozze:* Garden of Love or Pleasure. *Plate 527.*

Vercelli. MUSEO BORGOGNA. Madonna and Child with two Saints.

Vienna. 6684. Madonna and Child.

LANCKORONSKI COLLECTION. Predella panel: Nativity. (Companion to Oberlin).

Homeless. Pinnacle: S. James. *Plate 521.*

MASACCIO

1401–28. Pupil of Masolino, influenced by Brunelleschi and Donatello.

Berlin. 58A, B. Two predella panels (to London 3046) : Adoration of the Magi, Crucifixion of S. Peter and Beheading of S. John Baptist. 1426. *Plates 582, 584.*

    58C. *Desco da parto*, painted on both sides (g.p.).

    58D. Four panels: SS. Augustine, Jerome, and two Carmelites. (See London
3046). 1426.

    58E. Predella panel (to London 3046): S. Julian murdering his Parents and S.
Nicholas and the three Maidens (st., execution by Andrea di Giusto). 1426.
Plate 583.

Boston (Mass.). ISABELLA GARDNER MUSEUM. Profile Portrait of a young Man in a
Turban (r.). (?)

Chambéry. 364. Profile Portrait of a young Man in a Turban, with the legend
El fin fa tutto (r.). (?)

Florence. UFFIZI. 8386. 'S. Ambrogio' altarpiece: Madonna and Child with S. Anne
and five Angels. E. *Plate 579.*

    MUSEO HORNE. 60. Predella panel: S. Julian murdering his Parents (r.).

    S. MARIA DEL CARMINE, BRANCACCI CHAPEL. Frescoes: Scenes from the Old Testa-
ment and from the Life of S. Peter [Left wall: Expulsion from Paradise,
Tribute Money, Raising of the Son of Theophilus (except the son, the group
of eight men and a child behind him, and the group of four figures at the
extreme left, all of which are by Filippino Lippi, while the fourth head of the
last group is again by Masaccio; in fresco of Paul visiting Peter in prison, the
S. Paul was probably begun by Masaccio). Altar wall: S. Peter baptizing,
S. Peter healing the Sick, S. Peter distributing Alms]. (See also Masolino).
[Plates 139–141.] *Plates 586–90.*

    S. MARIA NOVELLA, 3rd ALTAR L. Fresco: Trinity with the Virgin, S. John Baptist
and two Donors; below, *Imago Mortis. Plate 585.*

London. 3046. Madonna and Child with four Angels. (Central panel of altarpiece
from S. Maria del Carmine at Pisa, which included Berlin 58 A, B, D and E;
Naples 36; Pisa 110; and Vienna, Lanckoronski). 1426. *Plate 580.*

    5962. SS. Jerome and John Baptist. (Companion to Masolino: London 5963,
Naples 33 and 35, and Philadelphia 408–09). *Plate 566.*

Montemarciano (Valdarno Superiore). MADONNA DELLE GRAZIE. Fresco: Madonna
nursing Child between SS. Michael and John Baptist E.

Naples. 36. Crucifixion. (See London 3046). 1426. *Plate 581.*

Pisa. 110. S. Paul. (See London 3046). 1426.

Vienna. LANCKORONSKI COLLECTION. S. Andrew. (See London 3046). 1426.

Washington (D.C.). 7 (MELLON COLLECTION). Madonna of Humility.

    14 (MELLON COLLECTION). Profile Portrait of a young Man in a Turban. (?)

Zurich. 586. Two busts of Florentine Gentlemen (c.; possibly after lost fresco, formerly in S. Maria del Carmine, Florence, depicting the consecration of the church).

MASO DI BANCO

Active first half of fourteenth century. Pupil of Giotto; in a later phase strongly influenced by the Lorenzetti.

Assisi. S. CHIARA, CAPPELLA DI S. GIORGIO, L. WALL. Fresco: Madonna and Child with SS. Clare, John Baptist, George and Francis (r.). *Plate* 144.

S. FRANCESCO, LOWER CHURCH, 3rd BAY L. (TRIBUNE). Frescoes: Coronation of the Virgin, S. Stanislaus raising a Man who testifies to his Honesty, Dismembering of S. Stanislaus (r.). *Plates* 137–139.

— SALA DEL CAPITOLO. Fresco: Crucifixion with the Virgin and S. John and SS. Louis of Toulouse, Paul, Francis, Clare, Peter and Anthony of Padua. *Plate* 140.

EDUCATORIO DI S. GIUSEPPE. Frescoes: Annunciation, Crucifixion (fr., r.). *Plate* 145.

S. RUFINUCCIO. Frescoes: Flagellation (?), Crucifixion, Entombment (r.).

Berlin. 1040. Madonna and Child. (Companion to 1529–30 below and to New York). *Plate* 142.

1141B. *Madonna della Cintola.* E. *Plate* 133.

1529–30. Two panels from a polyptych: SS. Anthony Abbot and John Baptist. (Companions to 1040 above and to New York; destroyed 1945). *Plates* 141, 143.

Brooklyn (N.Y.) 34.838. Portable triptych: Madonna and Child enthroned with Saints. Pinnacle: Christ blessing. Wings: Annunciation, Nativity, Crucifixion. E. *Plate* 134.

Budapest. 7793. Coronation of the Virgin. *Plate* 135.

Chantilly. 1. Dormition of the Virgin. E. *Plate* 136.

Florence. BADIA, COVONE CHAPEL.* Frescoes: Flaying of S. Bartholomew, and fragments of another scene and of decoration (r.). *Plate* 153.

S. CROCE, 5th CHAPEL L. OF CHOIR (BARDI DI VERNIO). Frescoes: Scenes from the Life of S. Silvester. [Left wall: Constantine advised by Magicians to bathe in the Blood of Christian Infants (r.), Dream of Constantine. Right wall: Recognition of the Portraits of Peter and Paul, Baptism of Constantine, Raising of the Bull, Raising of the two Pagan Priests. Entrance arch: Eight Bishop Saints. Window wall: Four Bishop Saints. Window embrasure: Eight Virtues]. ca 1335–45. [*Plate* 124]. *Plates* 154–158.

Frescoes (over Bardi tomb): Resurrection of a Member of the Bardi Family, four Prophets and two Angels.

Florence. S. CROCE (contd.) MUSEO DELL'OPERA. Fresco lunette: Coronation of the
Virgin (fr.). *Plate 152.*
Fresco: Head of Christ (fr.).
Fresco: Head of a Saint (fr.).
S. LUCIA AL PRATO, L. WALL. Fresco: Annunciation.
S. SPIRITO, CHOIR, 2nd CHAPEL R. Polyptych: Madonna and Child with SS. Mary
Magdalen, Andrew, Julian and Catherine. Pinnacle: Crucifixion (st.).
— CENACOLO DI S. SPIRITO. Frescoes: Crucifixion, Last Supper (fr., r.). L.
Naples. CASTELNUOVO, CAPPELLA PALATINA (S. BARBARA). Twelve fresco fragments:
Heads of Saints and Angels (r.). *Plates 148–151.*
New York. 43.98.13. Panel from a polyptych: S. Anthony of Padua. (Companion to
Berlin 1040 and 1529–30).
Pistoia. S. FRANCESCO, 1st CHAPEL R. OF CHOIR. Frescoes: Six Scenes from the Lives
of SS. Louis of Toulouse and Anthony of Padua (fr.). (?)
— 2nd CHAPEL R. OF CHOIR. Frescoes: S. Donnino healing a Man bitten by a Dog,
Martyrdom of S. Donnino, and two other Scenes (r.). (?)
Raleigh (N.C.). MUSEUM OF ART, KRESS COLLECTION. K 1424, 1441–4. Polyptych:
Salvator Mundi, with the Virgin and SS. John Evangelist, Francis and John
Baptist. *Plate 146.*
Homeless. *Salvator Mundi.* (?). *Plate 147.*

MASOLINO

*Born at Panicale 1384. His visit to Hungary lasted from September 1425 to July 1427. Died
after 1435.*

Berne. 874. Part of predella: SS. Nicholas, Lawrence and Peter Martyr. (?)
Bremen. 164. Madonna of Humility. d. 1423. *Plate 553.*
Castiglione d'Olona. COLLEGIATA, APSE. Frescoes (vault): Marriage of the Virgin,
Annunciation, Nativity (Sd), Adoration of the Magi, Assumption, Corona-
tion of the Virgin. *Plate 575.*
Frescoes (walls): Life of SS. Stephen, Lawrence, etc. (execution by Paolo Schiavo
and others).
BAPTISTERY. Frescoes: Scenes from the Life of S. John Baptist. [Entrance wall:
Annunciation to Joachim, Visitation (r.). Left wall: Naming of S. John (r.).
Tribune walls: S. John preaching and indicating Christ to the People,
Baptism of Christ, S. John before Herod, S. John in Prison. Altar wall, right:
Beheading of S. John. Right wall: Feast of Herod and S. John's Head brought
to Salome. Vault: Four Evangelists. Tribune vault: God the Father and
Angels. Soffits of tribune arch: Four Doctors of the Church and a Prophet].
d. 1435. [*Plate 137*]. *Plates 576–7.*
PALAZZO CASTIGLIONE. Fresco: Landscape and friezes.

Empoli. 95. Fresco: Man of Sorrows. ca 1424.

S. STEFANO, ABOVE SACRISTY DOOR. Fresco (lunette): Madonna and Child with two Angels. ca 1424. *Plate 558.*

— IST CHAPEL R. *Fragments of fresco decoration. 1424.

Florence. SEMINARIO MAGGIORE. Side panel of Carnesecchi triptych: S. Julian. (Companion to Montauban and Novoli). *Plate 555.*

S. MARIA DEL CARMINE, BRANCACCI CHAPEL. Frescoes: Preaching of S. Peter, Resurrection of Tabitha and the Healing of a Cripple, Fall of Man. (See also Masaccio and Filippino Lippi). ca 1425. [*Plate 138.*] *Plates 559–560.*

London. 5963. A Pope and S. Matthias. (Companion to Naples and Philadelphia; and to Masaccio, London 5962). *Plate 563.*

Montauban. 116. Predella panel of Carnesecchi triptych: S. Julian murdering his Parents (r., companion to Novoli and Florence, Seminario). *Plate 556.*

Munich. W.A.F.264. Madonna of Humility. *Plate 578.*

Naples. 33, 35. Two panels: Assumption, Foundation of S. Maria Maggiore (Companions to Philadelphia and London). *Plates 562, 565.*

New York. ROBERT LEHMAN (EX). Pinnacle: Virgin Annunciate. *Plate 567.*

Novoli (Florence). S. MARIA (EX). Centre panel of Carnesecchi triptych: Madonna and Child (see Montauban and Florence, Seminario). (Stolen 1923). *Plate 554.*

Philadelphia (Pa.). MUSEUM OF ART, JOHNSON COLLECTION. Inv. 408, 409. Two panels: SS. Peter and Paul, An Evangelist and S. Martin. (Companions to Naples and London). *Plates 561, 564.*

Rome. S. CLEMENTE, CHAPEL L. Frescoes. Above entrance: Annunciation. Soffits of entrance arch: Apostles. Vault: Four Evangelists and four Doctors of the Church. Walls: Crucifixion, and Scenes from the Lives of SS. Catherine and Ambrose [Left wall: S. Catherine before the Emperor, Conversion and Martyrdom of the Empress, Disputation of S. Catherine, Attempted Martyrdom of S. Catherine, Beheading of S. Catherine. Altar wall: Crucifixion. Right wall: Miraculous Infancy of S. Ambrose, S. Ambrose designated Bishop of Milan, Miraculous Destruction of the Man without Fear of God, S. Ambrose in his Study (r.), Death of S. Ambrose. Pilaster left of entrance: S. Christopher]. ca 1428–31. *Plates 569–573.*

VATICAN, PINACOTECA. 245. Predella panel: Dormition of the Virgin (g.p.). 260. Crucifixion (g.p.).

Stockholm. 5173. Madonna crowned by Angels with SS. John Baptist and Francis (upper part only; completed by inferior hand). *Plate 568.*

Todi. S. FORTUNATO, 4th CHAPEL R. Fresco: Madonna and Child with two Angels. (r.) 1432. *Plate 574.*

Washington (D.C.). 16 (MELLON COLLECTION). 'Goldman' Annunciation. *Plate 557.* 336, 337 (KRESS COLLECTION 414, 415). Two panels: Annunciation.

MASTER OF ARTE DELLA LANA CORONATION

Follower of Niccolò di Pietro Gerini. Possibly an early phase of Lorenzo di Niccolò.

Altenburg. 68. Madonna and Child with four Angels and SS. Anthony Abbot and Julian.

Arezzo. S. FRANCESCO, CHAPEL R. OF CHOIR. Triptych: *Madonna della Cintola*, with SS. Sebastian, John Gualbert, Lawrence and Francis. Pinnacles: Christ blessing and Annunciation.

Florence. ACCADEMIA. 8578. Madonna and Child with six Angels and SS. Lawrence, John Baptist, Anthony Abbot and James.

    PALAZZO DELL'ARTE DELLA LANA, TABERNACLE. Lunette (above Madonna by Jacopo del Casentino): Coronation of the Virgin. *Plates 382–383.*

    MUSEO NAZIONALE DEL BARGELLO, CARRAND COLLECTION. 2010. Madonna and Child with eight Angels and SS. John Baptist and Stephen.

Leningrad. 269. Madonna and Child with four Angels and four Saints. *Plate 384.*

Limoges. MUSÉE ADRIEN-DUBOUCHÉ 4 (CAMPANA 121–124). Four predella panels: S. Lawrence distributing Alms, converting his Jailor, brought before Valerianus, and indicating the Poor as the Treasure of the Church.

Paris. 1316. Madonna and Child with eight Angels. (Companion to Rouen).

Prague. D0796. Madonna and Child enthroned with four Angels and eight Saints.

Rome. VATICAN PINACOTECA. 10. Madonna nursing the Child, with two Angels and four female Saints. Predella: Pietà. *Plate 385.*

Rouen. MUSÉE (CAMPANA 102, 103). Wings of an altarpiece: SS. Bernardino and John Baptist with male Donor, SS. John Evangelist and Louis of Toulouse with female Donor. (Companions to Paris).

MASTER OF THE BAMBINO VISPO

Designation for a painter active in earlier decades of fifteenth century, pupil perhaps and certainly follower of Lorenzo Monaco, close to Giovanni dal Ponte, Rossello di Jacopo Franchi and Bicci di Lorenzo. No other Italian artist came so near to the Franco-Flemish, Valencian and German painters practising before the triumph of the Van Eycks.

Allentown (Pa.). MUSEUM OF ART, KRESS COLLECTION. K 260. Madonna and Child in Glory with SS. Clement and Julian.

Altenburg. 26. Madonna and Child with two Angels.

    41. Cassone panel: Battle of Saracens. *Plate 482.*

Amsterdam. 1896-D1, D2. Two panels (from the frame of an altarpiece): Two Prophets.

Assisi. MRS. F. M. PERKINS. Panel from an altarpiece: S. Lawrence. (Companion to Boston 20.1855).

Baltimore (Md.). WALTERS ART GALLERY. 724. Wings of an altarpiece: S. Christopher, Crucifixion. (?)

Berlin. 1111. Two panels: Annunciation.

(BERLIN–OST). 1123 (DEP. BONN). Left wing (of Orsini triptych from Florence, Duomo, Cappella di S. Lorenzo, 1423?): SS. Mary Magdalen and Lawrence with a Donor. (Companion to Stockholm, and probably to three fragments of a central panel at Dresden, London ex-Carmichael, and Rotterdam). *Plate* 476.

Bonn. 123. See Berlin.

Bordeaux. 131. Crucifixion.

Borgo alla Collina (Casentino). S. DONATO. Marriage of S. Catherine, with S. Francis, Tobias and the Angel, SS. Michael and Louis of Toulouse. Pinnacles: Three Angels. Predella: S. Francis before the Sultan, Raphael appearing to the Parents of Tobias, Martyrdom of S. Catherine, S. Michael parting the Sea before a Pilgrim, S. Louis ministering to the Poor (st.). d. 1423.

Boston (Mass.). 20.1855a, b. Two panels: SS. Vincent and Peter Martyr. (Companions to Assisi).

20.1856, 1857. Two predella panels: Isaiah with two Angels, Jeremiah with two Angels.

Cambridge (Mass.). 1920.1. *Madonna della Cintola* (fr., companion to Philadelphia 13). *Plate* 470.

Chicago (Ill.). 33.1017. Predella panel: Dormition of the Virgin. (Companion to London 3926).

Compton Wynyates (Warwicks.). MARQUESS OF NORTHAMPTON. Nativity.

Douai. 35. Predella panel (to Orsini triptych from Florence, Duomo, Cappella di S. Lorenzo, 1423?): Adoration of the Magi. (Companion to Rome, Colonna and Visconti Venosta). *Plate* 477.

Dresden. 30. Head of the Virgin (fr., see Berlin 1123). *Plate* 476.

El Paso (Texas). MUSEUM OF ART (KRESS COLLECTION 526). S. Nicholas. (Companion to Rotterdam 2649). (?)

Florence. GALLERIE. 6270. Madonna of Humility (r.).

ACCADEMIA. 441. Madonna and Child in Glory with four Angels and SS. John Baptist and Nicholas.

476, 477. Two panels: SS. Catherine and Francis.

478, Madonna and Child with two Angels and SS. Anthony Abbot, John Baptist, Lawrence and Peter. Pinnacle: Crucifixion with SS. Sebastain and Julian (p.).

3149. Crucifixion with two Angels, Virgin, S. Francis and Donor. (?)

MUSEO DEL BIGALLO. Madonna and Child.

MUSEO HORNE. 99. Madonna of Humility crowned by two Angels.

Florence (contd.). s. croce, museo dell'opera. Fresco: Raising of Lazarus (fr.).
(Environs) s. andrea a brozzi, 1st altar r. Triptych: Annunciation, with SS. Eustace and Anthony Abbot. Pinnacles: Christ blessing and two Angels (r.). (?)
— la quiete, coro delle monache. Reliquary: Madonna and four Saints.

Frankfurt am Main. 1177. Three pinnacles: *Salvator Mundi*, Annunciation. *Plate* 481.

Genoa. viezzoli collection. Predella panel: Adoration of the Shepherds. *Plate* 480.

Helsinki. ateneum. Madonna and Child with six Angels.

Kansas City (Mo.). 48.1952 (kress collection 1135). Predella panel: Adoration of the Magi.

London. 3926. Predella panel: Beheading of a female Saint. (Companion to Chicago).
lord carmichael (ex). Head of an Angel (fr., see Berlin 1123). *Plate* 476.
viscount rothermere (ex). Madonna and Child enthroned with Angels. *Plate* 473.

Los Angeles (Cal.). a.5731.47-1. Predella panel: S. Augustine (?) and S. Lawrence. *Plate* 472.

Lucca. 287, 288. Wings of an altarpiece: SS. Michael, James and John Baptist; SS. John Evangelist, Peter and Paul.

Lugano. thyssen collection. 251. Madonna and Child with SS. Anthony Abbot, Mary Magdalen, Lucy and Francis.

Lyons. edouard aynard (ex). Nativity. Pinnacle: Crucifixion (st.).

Munich. 10201. Last Judgement. 1415? *Plate* 469.

New Haven (Conn.). 1943.216. Left wing of an altarpiece: Two martyr Deacons.

Oxford. christ church library. 20. Madonna of Humility crowned by two Angels.

Paris. musée de cluny. 1666. Annunciation.

Parma. 440. Coronation of the Virgin.

Philadelphia (Pa.). museum of art. 43.40.45. Madonna and Child (fr.). (?)
— johnson collection. 12. Madonna and Child enthroned.
   13. Dormition of the Virgin (fr., companion to Cambridge). *Plate* 470.
john d. mcilhenny (ex). Madonna of Humility crowned by two Angels.

Pisa. 160. Madonna and Child with SS. Lucy, Julian, Anthony Abbot and Mary Magdalen (st.).

Radicondoli (Siena). s. simone, altar r. Assumption and Nativity.

Rome. galleria doria pamphilj. Triptych: Madonna and Child with four Angels and SS. Anthony Abbot, Peter, John Baptist and Matthew. Pinnacles: Annunciation (st.).
museo di palazzo venezia. The Prophet Hosea (fr.).
principe colonna. Predella panel: Martyrdom of S. Lawrence (see Douai). *Plate* 479.
marchesa visconti venosta. Predella panel: S. Zenobius raising a young Man to Life (see Douai). *Plate* 478.

Rotterdam. 2557. Two music-making Angels (fr.). (See Berlin 1123). *Plate 476.*
    2649. S. Anthony Abbot. (Companion to El Paso.) (?)
Stia (Casentino). PROPOSITURA DI S. MARIA ASSUNTA, CHAPEL L. OF CHOIR. *Madonna della Cintola* (the Apostles, st.).
Stockholm. 2678. Right wing of an altarpiece: SS. Zenobius and Benedict. (See Berlin 1123.) *Plate 476.*
Subiaco. SACRO SPECO. Frescoes: Life of S. Benedict (st.). (?)
Vienna. LEDERER COLLECTION (EX). Madonna of Humility. *Plate 471.*
Würzburg. MARTIN VON WAGNER MUSEUM. 89. Triptych: Madonna and Child with six Angels and SS. Margaret, Andrew, Peter and Mary Magdalen. *Plate 475.*
Homeless. Predella panel: Man of Sorrows. *Plate 474.*
    Predella (three roundels): Man of Sorrows, Virgin and S. John.

MASTER OF THE BARBERINI PANELS

He must have been a fellow-pupil with Piero della Francesca under Domenico Veneziano and come under other Florentine influences, particularly of Agostino di Duccio and Brunelleschi. He shows affinities with Giovanni di Francesco.

Boston (Mass.). 37.108. (Formerly Barberini). Presentation of the Virgin in the Temple. (Companion to New York). *Plates 696, 697.*
New York. 35.121. (Formerly Barberini). Visitation and Birth of the Virgin. (Companion to Boston). *Plates 698, 699.*
Washington (D.C.). 329 (KRESS COLLECTION 407). Annunciation. *Plate 695.*

MASTER OF THE CARRAND TRIPTYCH
see Giovanni di Francesco

MASTER OF THE CASTELLO NATIVITY

Designation for a group of works by an anonymous artist, whose development steers a course from Fra Angelico to the early Botticelli, between Fra Filippo Lippi, Baldovinetti and Domenico Veneziano.

Baltimore (Md.). WALTERS ART GALLERY. 467. Madonna adoring the Child. L.
    1163. Madonna and Child. *Plate 875.*
Cambridge. M14. Madonna adoring the Child.
Cambridge (Mass.). 1943.1840. Madonna and Child with two Angels.

Cherbourg. 8. Predella panel: S. Augustine meditating in a Garden. E. (?)

Faltugnano (Val di Bisenzio). SS. GIUSTO E CLEMENTE. Madonna and Child with SS. Justus and Clement. (Predella panels at Philadelphia and possibly London). *Plate* 876.

Florence. ACCADEMIA. DEP. 171. 'Castello Nativity': Madonna adoring the Child with Infant S. John. Predella: Four Prophets (r.). *Plate* 871.

    4632. Annunciation. L.

    BADIA, CHIOSTRO DEGLI ARANCI.* Ten frescoes: Scenes from the Life of S. Benedict. [Departure of S. Benedict for Rome, Miracle of the broken Sieve, Investiture of S. Benedict, S. Benedict in the Sacro Speco and the Priest at his Easter Meal, S. Benedict blessing the poisoned Wine, Punishment of a disobedient Monk, Miraculous Recovery of a Scythe from a Lake, Miraculous Rescue of S. Placidus, Miracle of the Raven and the poisoned Bread, The Bewitched Stone, Raising of a Monk from the Ruins of Montecassino]. (?). *Plate* 868–9.

    S. FELICITA, SACRISTY. *Pietà* with SS. Mary Magdalen and John Evangelist. 1470.

    S. GIOVANNINO DEI CAVALIERI, R. WALL. Annunciation. L. *Plate* 878.

    BERENSON COLLECTION. Madonna and Child. *Plate* 872.

Göttingen. 103 (FROM BERLIN). Madonna and Child with a Bird.

Hanover. 161. Madonna and Child.

Leghorn. MUSEO CIVICO. Madonna adoring the Child with Infant S. John (r.).

London. 3648. Predella panel (to Faltugnano altarpiece?): Nativity. *Plate* 879.

    COURTAULD GALLERIES. Roundel: God the Father blessing. (?)

Munich. 645. Annunciation.

    MARCZELL VON NEMES (EX). Madonna adoring the Child with two Angels.

New Haven (Conn.). 1943.222. Madonna and Child with two music-making Angels.

New York. ROBERT LEHMAN. Profile Portrait of a Lady (r.). *Plate* 870.

Paris. 1657A. Madonna and Child with four Angels. *Plate* 874.

    1661A. Madonna and Child with a Bird.

Philadelphia (Pa.). MUSEUM OF ART, JOHNSON COLLECTION. 23. Nativity.

    24, 25. Two predella panels (to Faltugnano altarpiece): Multiplication of the Grain of Volterra by SS. Justus and Clement, Lifting of the Siege of Volterra through the Prayers of SS. Justus and Clement. *Plate* 877.

Pisa. 107. Madonna and Child with two music-making Angéls.

San Giovanni Valdarno. CONSERVATORIO DELLE AGOSTINIANE. Madonna and Child.

San Marino (Cal.). HUNTINGTON MUSEUM. Madonna adoring the Child with Infant S. John. [*Plate* 163].

Sands Point (L.I.). MRS. HANNAH RABINOWITZ. Madonna and Child.

Vienna. LANCKORONSKI COLLECTION (EX). Madonna and Child.

Homeless. Madonna adoring the Child with Infant S. John. *Plate* 873.

    Madonna adoring the Child. *Dedalo* xii, 833.

MASTER OF THE JARVES CASSONI
see Apollonio di Giovanni

MASTER OF THE LATHROP TONDO

Active in the late fifteenth and early sixteenth centuries. Lucchese Follower of Domenico Ghirlandajo and Filippino Lippi.

Barcelona. MUSEO DE ARTE, CAMBÓ BEQUEST. Madonna and Child with SS. Peter and Paul.

Lucca. PINACOTECA. Madonna and Child with SS. Augustine, Monica, Anthony of Padua and Jerome (from S. Agostino). *Plate 1176.*

Polyptych: Madonna and Child with two Angels and SS. John Baptist, Catherine, Lucy and Joseph. Lunette: God the Father, Annunciation.

MARCHESE MAZZAROSA. Wings of an altarpiece: S. Blaise and a male Donor, S. Lucy and a female Donor. *Plate 1175.*

New York. FRANCIS LATHROP (EX). Tondo: Madonna nursing the Child, with SS. Jerome and Catherine and a Donor (Michele Guinigi?). *Plate 1173.*

Rome. S. PAOLO FUORI LE MURA. Madonna and Child with SS. Peter and Paul.

Sarasota (Fla.). 19. *Madonna della Cintola. Plate 1177.*

Homeless. SS. Jerome and Joseph with a Donor. *Plate 1174.*

MASTER OF THE RINUCCINI CHAPEL

A painter between Orcagna and Giovanni del Biondo, active in the third quarter of the fourteenth century.

Florence. ACCADEMIA. 6134. S. Michael with SS. Bartholomew and Julian. (?)

8463. Triptych: Vision of S. Bernard, with SS. Benedict, John Evangelist, Quentin and Galganus. Pinnacles: Christ blessing, Annunciation. Predella: Miraculous Rescue of S. Placidus, S. John and the poisoned Wine, S. Bernard and his Brothers, S. Bernard preaching at Sarlat, Beheading of S. Quentin, S. Galganus adoring his Sword in the Rock. *Plates 282–284.*

S. CROCE, SACRISTY, RINUCCINI CHAPEL. Frescoes (below the frescoes by Giovanni da Milano). Left wall: Presentation of the Virgin, Marriage of the Virgin. Right Wall: *Noli me tangere*, A Prince discovering his lost Wife and Child through the intercession of S. Mary Magdalen. *Plates 279–281, 381.*

Raleigh (N.C.). MUSEUM OF ART, KRESS COLLECTION. K 1171. SS. Cosmas and Damian. Predella: Dream of the Deacon Justinian, Beheading of SS. Cosmas and Damian. *Plate 285.*

Rome. VATICAN, PINACOTECA, MAGAZINE. Predella panels: Man of Sorrows with the Virgin, the twelve Apostles and S. Francis (st.).

MASTER OF S. CECILIA

Close follower of the youthful Giotto; attractive in small figures, but less so in larger ones.

Assisi. S. FRANCESCO, UPPER CHURCH, NAVE, LEFT WALL. Frescoes: Three scenes from the Legend of S. Francis [XXVI. Healing of Giovanni of Ylerda, XXVII. Confession of a Woman raised from the Dead, XXVIII. Liberation of Pietro of Alifia]. This artist may also be responsible for part of the execution of Scenes I (Homage of the Simpleton) and XXI–XXV, according to Giotto's design. *Plates 81–85.*

Brussels. JACQUES STOCLET. Madonna and Child with four Angels and SS. Paul, John Baptist, John Evangelist and Peter.

Budapest. 10. Madonna and Child with two Angels, four Saints and two Donors (r.).

Cracow .V. 233. Portable triptych: Madonna and Child with two Bishop Saints. Wings: Annunciation, Nativity, Flagellation, Crucifixion (p).

Detroit (Mich.). 53.386. Portable triptych: Madonna and Child with SS. Lucy, Margaret, Mary Magdalen and Catherine. Wings: Archangel Michael, Crucifixion, six Saints.

Florence. UFFIZI. 449. S. Cecilia enthroned and eight Scenes from her Life [Marriage of S. Cecilia, Conversion of Valerian, Valerian crowned with Flowers by an Angel, S. Cecilia preaching to Valerian and Tiburtius, Baptism of Tiburtius, S. Cecilia preaching, S. Cecilia before Almachius, Martyrdom of S. Cecilia]. E. *Plates 86–88.*

MUSEO HORNE. 19. Triptych: Madonna and Child with two female Saints (r.). L. 35. Madonna and Child enthroned with SS. Peter and Lucy (st.).

S. GIORGIO ALLA COSTA (SS. GIORGIO E MASSIMILIANO). Madonna and Child enthroned with two Angels (r.).

S. SIMONE, 1ST ALTAR R. S. Peter enthroned with two Angels. d. 1307. *Plate 90.*

CONTINI BONACOSSI COLLECTION. Madonna and Child (r.).

CHARLES LOESER (EX). Madonna and Child with two Angels (st.).

(Environs) CALDINE, S. MARIA MADDALENA, HIGH ALTAR. Madonna and Child enthroned with six Angels. (Annunciation in spandrels by Bicci di Lorenzo). L.

— S. MARGHERITA A MONTICI, HIGH ALTAR. Madonna and Child enthroned with two Angels, S. Margaret and another Saint. *Plates 89, 91–92.*

— — L. TRANSEPT. S. Margaret and Scenes from her Life. [S. Margaret rejecting Olybrius' Proposal, S. Margaret before Olybrius, S. Margaret subduing the Dragon, Flagellation of S. Margaret, Martyrdom of S. Margaret, S. Margaret carried to Heaven by Angels]. *Plate 93.*

— VICCHIO DI RIMAGGIO, S. LORENZO. Madonna and Child enthroned with two Angels (st. or c.).

Oxford. CHRIST CHURCH LIBRARY. 6. S. John Baptist enthroned (st.).

Pescia. MUSEO (BIBLIOTECA COMUNALE). 10. Madonna and Child enthroned.

Venice. CONTE VITTORIO CINI. Two panels: SS. Mary Magdalen and Margaret (st.).

MASTER OF SAN MINIATO ALTARPIECE

Active second half of fifteenth century. Follower of Filippo Lippi and the young Botticelli; influenced by Cosimo Rosselli.

Amsterdam. 1538–S 1. Madonna and Child. L.

Arundel Castle (Sussex). DUKE OF NORFOLK (EX). *Pietà* with SS. Bartholomew, Nicholas of Tolentino, Francis and John Baptist. d. 1460. (?). *Plate 1056.*

Assisi. MRS. F. M. PERKINS. Madonna and Child with two Angels.

Bologna. 346. Predella panel: Adoration of the Magi.

Boston (Mass.). 03.562. Madonna adoring the Child, with two Angels (st.).
  17.3223. Madonna adoring the Child with an Angel.

Budapest. FRIEDRICH GLÜCK (EX). Madonna and Child.

Buenos Aires. PELLERANO COLLECTION. Madonna adoring the Child with Infant S. John.

Capesthorne Hall (Ches.). LT. COL. SIR W. H. BROMLEY-DAVENPORT. Madonna and Child.

Cortona. PALAZZONE, CONTE PASSERINI. Madonna adoring the Child.

Cracow. 118. Madonna and Child.

Detroit (Mich.). 89.18. Madonna and Child with two Angels.

Dijon. 1473. S. Anthony Abbot (?) recommending a Pilgrim to S. James. E.

Esztergom. KERESTÉNY MÜZEUM. Octagon: Madonna and Child with Infant S. John and another young Saint. L.

Fiesole. MUSEO BANDINI. II, 3. Madonna and Child. Lunette: Crucifixion with SS. Francis and Jerome (r.).

Florence. MUSEO BARDINI. 1128. Madonna and Child with two Cherubim.

  MUSEO DEL BIGALLO. Madonna and Child.

  OGNISSANTI, L. TRANSEPT. Madonna and Child with SS. Francis, Matthew, Louis of Toulouse and Clare. d. 1493.

  SPEDALE DI ORBATELLO.* Christ blessing, and SS. Andrew and Dionysius. (Surrounding a Madonna and Child by Mainardi).

  VIA ROMANA 27R. Fresco lunette (over door): Madonna and Child with two Angels (r.).

  ACTON COLLECTION. Madonna and Child with SS. Dominic, Mary Magdalen, Catherine and two other Saints. Predella: Five Saints.

Florence. ACTON COLLECTION (contd.). Madonna and Child.
  Madonna and Child against a Hedge of Roses.
  Madonna and Child with Infant S. John.
  RICHARD MAYO. Madonna adoring the Child with Infant S. John.
  SERRISTORI COLLECTION. Madonna and Child with Infant S. John and S. Mary
    Magdalen.
  (Environs) BRUCIANESI, MADONNA DI FATIMA. Madonna and Child enthroned with
    two Angels (fr.).
Gaviserri (Stia, Casentino). S. ANDREA CORSINI, ALTAR L. Madonna and Child with
  SS. John Baptist, Clement, Bartholomew and Anthony Abbot. *Plate* 1045.
Greenville (S.C.). BOB JONES UNIVERSITY GALLERY. Madonna and Child with S. Paul
  and a Bishop Saint.
Hartford (Conn.). 42.417. Virgin Annunciate.
Highnam Court (Glos.). GAMBIER-PARRY COLLECTION. Madonna and Child with
  Infant S. John.
Le Mans. 407. Madonna and Child.
London. 4868C. Predella panel (to Pesellino, London 727): S. Zeno exorcizing the
  Daughter of Emperor Gallienus (with Filippo Lippi). 1458–60. *Plate* 838.
  BRITISH MUSEUM, HARLEY MS. 1340. Prophecies of Joachim of Flora. Thirty illumina-
    tions: Popes.
  PETER HARRIS. Madonna and Child with S. James and an Evangelist. *Plate* 1055.
  W. H. WOODWARD (EX). S. Nicholas enthroned, with SS. Catherine, Lucy, Margaret
    and Apollonia. *Plate* 1053.
Lwow. PRINCE PININSKI (EX). Nativity with Infant S. John.
Lyons. See Paris, Musées Nationaux.
Minneapolis (Minn.). INSTITUTE OF ARTS (EX). 14.18. Madonna and Child with two
  Angels.
Montefioralle (Chianti). PIEVE. Trinity with SS. Stephen, James, Anthony Abbot
  and a Bishop Saint.
Naarden (Holland). DR. R. WETZLAR. Portrait of a young Man.
New Haven (Conn.). 1959.15.9. Eight fragments from a Man of Sorrows with the
  Virgin and S. John and Symbols of the Passion. (?)
New York. W. R. HEARST (EX). Madonna and Child with two Angels. *Plate* 1051.
  FELIX WARBURG (EX). Adoration of the Shepherds with Infant S. John and four
    Angels.
  STAMFORD WHITE (EX). Madonna and Child with two Angels.
Oxford. CAMPION HALL. Madonna adoring the Child with Infant S. John and an Angel.
Paris. MUSÉES NATIONAUX (CAMPANA 92, DEP. TOULON). Madonna and Child with
  eight Saints.
  — (CAMPANA 312, DEP. LYONS). Deposition. *Plate* 1054.
  JEAN DOLLFUS (EX). Madonna and Child with SS. Peter, John Baptist, James and
    Blaise.

Pavia. 141. Madonna and Child.

Philadelphia (Pa.). MUSEUM OF ART, JOHNSON COLLECTION. 37. Madonna and Child. JOHN D. MCILHENNY (EX). Madonna adoring the Child with Infant S. John.

Pittsfield (Mass.). MRS. LAWRENCE K. MILLER. Predella panel: Burial of S. Catherine of Siena. (Companion to Rome, Vatican 327). *Plate 1046.*

Pomino (Pontassieve). PARROCCHIALE. Madonna and Child with SS. Romuald and Sebastian (r., two more Saints below, added later). *Plate 1047.*

Rome. ACCADEMIA DI S. LUCA. Madonna and Child with SS. John Baptist and Nicholas.

> VATICAN, PINACOTECA. 284, 288. Two predella panels: S. Barbara directing the Construction of a third Window in her Tower, Cripples and Paupers at the Tomb of S. Barbara. *Plate 1048.*

> 294. Madonna and Child with SS. Bartholomew and Stephen.

> 327. Predella panel: S. Catherine of Siena exorcizing a possessed Girl. (Companion to Pittsfield).

Rotterdam. 2550. Lamentation, with SS. Francis and Jerome. E.

San Miniato al Tedesco (Pisa). S. DOMENICO, CHAPEL R. OF CHOIR. Madonna and Child with SS. Sebastian, John Baptist, Roch and a Bishop Saint and the donor with his wife and child. *Plate 1049.*

> CAPPELLA DELLA MISERICORDIA. Madonna and Child surrounded by a panel representing God the Father and four Angels, and SS. Bartholomew, Cosmas, Lucy, Damian and Sebastian. *Plate 1052.*

Sens (Yonne). MUSÉE 132 (CAMPANA 206). Madonna and Child.

Toulon. See Paris, Musées Nationaux.

Upton House (Banbury, Oxon.). NATIONAL TRUST. Madonna and Child.

Zagreb. 55. Madonna and Child.

Homeless. Madonna and Child. *Dedalo* xii, 827.

> Madonna and Child with SS. Francis and Julian. *Plate 1050.*

MICHELANGELO BUONARROTI

1475–1564. Pupil of Ghirlandajo and Bertoldo; influenced by the antique, by the Pisani and Jacopo della Quercia, by Donatello and Signorelli.

Florence. ACCADEMIA. 1570. Venus and Cupid. (By Pontormo on a lost cartoon by Michelangelo of 1533). *Plate 1224.*

> UFFIZI. 1456. 'Doni' tondo: Holy Family.

> CASA BUONARROTI. Holy Family with Infant S. John and six other figures. (By Condivi on Michelangelo's cartoon, British Museum 1895–9–25–15–518; u.).

Holkham Hall (Norfolk). EARL OF LEICESTER. Bathers surprised at the Battle of Cascina (*grisaille* c. of Michelangelo's lost cartoon of 1504–06). *Plate 1212.*

London. 790. Deposition (u.).

    809. Madonna and Child with Infant S. John, called the 'Manchester Madonna' (st., u.). *Plate* 1231.

    1868. Leda (c. after Michelangelo's lost picture of 1530). Cf. *Plate* 1225.

Rome. VATICAN, CAPPELLA PAOLINA. Frescoes: Conversion of S. Paul, Martyrdom of S. Peter. 1542–50. *Plate* 1128.

— SISTINE CHAPEL, VAULT. Frescoes: Scenes from the Old Testament [God separating Light from Darkness, Creation of the Sun and Moon and Plants, God separating Sky from Water, Creation of Adam, Creation of Eve, Fall of Man, Sacrifice of Noah, Deluge, Drunkenness of Noah] framed by twelve Prophets and Sibyls and by couples of 'Ignudi' holding ten monochrome medallions. Spandrels: David and Goliath, Judith and Holofernes, The Brazen Serpent, Esther and Haman, eight groups of Ancestors of Christ. Lunettes: Twenty-eight Ancestors of Christ. 1508–12. [*Plates* 142, 235–238]. *Plates* 1213–21.

— — ALTAR WALL. Fresco: Last Judgement. 1534–41. [*Plate* 239.] *Plates* 1226–7.

Homeless. *Noli me tangere.* (By Pontormo on a lost cartoon by Michelangelo of 1531). *Plate* 1434.

SCULPTURE

Bologna. S. DOMENICO. *Arca di S. Domenico:* S. Proculus, S. Petronius and an Angel with Candelabrum. 1494.

Bruges. NOTRE-DAME. Madonna and Child. Before August 1506.

Florence. ACCADEMIA. David. 1504.

    S. Matthew (u.). 1503–08.

    Four 'Slaves', for the tomb of Julius II (u.). *Plate* 1223.

    Terra-cotta model for a 'River', for the Medici tombs. 1521–34.

    'Palestrina' *Pietà* (u., p.). L.

    CASA BUONARROTI. Bas-relief: *Madonna della Scala.* 1490–92.

    Bas-relief: Battle of the Centaurs and Lapiths. 1490–92.

    MUSEO NAZIONALE DEL BARGELLO. Bacchus. E.

    Bas-relief tondo: Madonna and Child. E.

    Apollo.

    Bust of Brutus.

    PALAZZO VECCHIO, SALONE DEL CINQUECENTO. Victory (u.).

    S. LORENZO, NEW SACRISTY. Madonna and Child. Tombs of Lorenzo de' Medici, Duke of Urbino, and of Giuliano de' Medici, Duke of Nemours (u.). 1521–34.

    S. MARIA DEL FIORE (DUOMO), L. TRANSEPT, 5th CHAPEL. *Pietà* (left u. in 1556). *Plate* 1230.

Leningrad. HERMITAGE. Crouching Boy (st.).

London. BURLINGTON HOUSE, DIPLOMA GALLERY. Bas-relief tondo: Madonna and Child. E.

VICTORIA AND ALBERT MUSEUM. 7560–1861. Cupid.

4117–1854. Wax models for 'Slaves'.

Milan. CASTELLO SFORZESCO. 'Rondanini' *Pietà* (u.). L.

Paris. LOUVRE. Two 'Slaves', for the tomb of Julius II. *Plate 1222.*

Rome. S. MARIA SOPRA MINERVA. Christ with the Cross. 1519 (finished by other hand 1521).

S. PIETRO, 1ST CHAPEL R. *Pietà* ('Madonna della Febbre'). 1499.

S. PIETRO IN VINCOLI, R. TRANSEPT. Tomb of Julius II: Moses. E. Rachel, Leah. L.

MICHELANGELO, Anonymous Early Follower of

(The following paintings are related to London 809)

New York. S. H. KRESS FOUNDATION. K 1569. Madonna and Child with Infant S. John. *Plate 1233.*

Rome. GALLERIA NAZIONALE (PALAZZO BARBERINI). F.N.948. *Pietà* (u.).

Vienna. ACADEMY. 1134. Tondo: Madonna and Child with Infant S. John. *Plate 1232.*

Homeless. Madonna and Child. *Plate 1234.*

MICHELE DI RIDOLFO

1503–1577. Pupil of Lorenzo di Credi, Michele Tosini was assistant and follower of Ridolfo Ghirlandajo (hence his name) and possibly collaborated with Sogliani.

Bergamo. 551. Madonna and Child. E. (?)

Berlin. 263. Assumption.

Dijon. See Paris.

Eastnor Castle (Hereford). HON. MRS. HERVEY BATHURST. Madonna and Child with SS. Michael, Peter, Paul and Mary Magdalen. *Plate 1296.*

Fiesole. MUSEO BANDINI. Holy Family with Infant S. John. *Plate 1300.*

Florence. GALLERIE. 3472. *Madonna della Cintola* with SS. Francis, John Baptist, Ursula and Elizabeth of Hungary.

8640. Madonna and Child in Glory with SS. James, Francis, Clare, Lawrence and a Donor. *Plate 1297.*

ACCADEMIA. 5862. S. Barbara.

6070. Oval: Head of Woman.

6072. Profile of Woman with Helmet.

PITTI. 28. Portrait of a Woman with a Book. *Plate 1294.*

180. Holy Family.

Florence (contd.). S. CROCE, MUSEO DELL'OPERA. See Sogliani.

S. FELICE, 6th ALTAR R. Madonna and Child with SS. Peter, Sebastian, Paul and another Saint. Lunette: God the Father.

S. SPIRITO, 5th ALTAR L. Madonna and Child with S. Anne and SS. Dominic, Mary Magdalen, Catherine, Vincent Ferrer and Thomas Aquinas.

— L. TRANSEPT, 1st ALTAR L. Way to Calvary.

S. TRINITA, 2nd CHAPEL L. Annunciation.

(Environs) CERTOSA DEL GALLUZZO. Madonna and Child with SS. Joseph, Lucy and two other Saints.

— LA QUIETE. Marriage of S. Catherine, with SS. James, Dominic, Thomas Aquinas, Ursula and John Evangelist.

— S. MARIA A SAN MARTINO ALLA PALMA. Assumption with SS. John Baptist, Sebastian, Benedict, a fourth Saint and two Brothers of the Misericordia.

— S. MARTINO A GANGALANDI, 2nd ALTAR R. Triptych: Madonna and Child with S. Stephen and an Archangel.

Fucecchio (Valdarno). COLLEGIATA (S. GIOVANNI BATTISTA) Madonna and Child with SS. John Baptist, Mark, Andrew and Peter. Above: Baptism of Christ.

— SACRISTY. Annunciation, with SS. Andrew and Francis. *Plate 1295*.

Greenville (S.C.). BOB JONES UNIVERSITY. Annunciation. (?)

Panzano (Chianti). S. MARIA, 1st CHAPEL R. Annunciation.

Paris. MUSÉES NATIONAUX (CAMPANA 420). Assumption with SS. Francis, Clare, Catherine and Anthony of Padua.

Passignano (Val di Pesa). BADIA. Nativity. *Plate 1302*.

The Three Archangels. *Plate 1303*.

Prato. S. SPIRITO. See Sogliani.

Rome. GALLERIA BORGHESE. 323. Leda. *Plate 1298*.

GALLERIA COLONNA. 54. Allegory of Night. (Free copy after Michelangelo's figure on Tomb of Giuliano de' Medici). *Plate 1299*.

69. Venus and Cupid. (Copy of Michelangelo's lost cartoon or Pontormo, Florence, Accademia 1570).

San Gimignano. MUSEO DELLA COLLEGIATA. Madonna and Child with SS. Michael, Augustine, Monica and Lucy.

San Marino (Cal.). HUNTINGTON MUSEUM. Madonna and Child with Infant S. John.

Templecombe (Somerset). LADY THEODORA GUEST (EX). Madonna and Child with SS. Jerome and Catherine.

Tynninghame (Prestonkirk, Haddington, East Lothian). EARL OF HADDINGTON. Madonna and Child with Infant S. John. *Plate 1301*.

NARDO di Cione

Active ca 1343–1366. Probably a pupil of Maso; influenced by his brother Andrea Orcagna.

Ajaccio (Corsica). 174. Pentecost.
188. A Bishop Saint enthroned.
Altenburg. 39. Roundel: Head of a Saint. (?)
Balmville (Newburgh, N.Y.). MISS TESSIE JONES. Madonna and Child. *Plate* 203.
Berne. 885. Roundel: Christ blessing.
Dublin. 841. Ecstasy of S. Mary Magdalen.
Florence. ACCADEMIA. DEP. 132. Madonna of Humility (execution by Jacopo di Cione). *Plate* 223.

8464. Triptych: Trinity with SS. Romuald and John Evangelist. Pinnacles: *Agnus Dei* and two censing Angels. Predella: S. Romuald's Vision of S. Apollinaris, S. Romuald chastened by a Hermit and molested by Devils, Dream of S. Romuald (g.p.). d. 1365. *Plates* 206–208.

UFFIZI. 454. Lamentation with two female Donors and their patron Saints. E. (?). [*Plate* 121.] *Plates* 192–193.

3515. Crucifixion. Predella: Five Saints (p).

CASSA DI RISPARMIO (Via Bufalini). Fresco (from Tabernacle of Via del Leone): Madonna and Child with eight Angels and SS. John Baptist and Romuald. E. (?). *Plate* 191.

BADIA, GIOCHI AND BASTARI CHAPEL.* Frescoes: Flagellation, *Ecce Homo*, Way to Calvary, Suicide of Judas and fragments of decoration (fr.). *Plate* 201.

S. CROCE, SACRISTY. Triptych: Madonna and Child with S. Gregory and Job. Predella: Scenes from the Story of Job (with Jacopo di Cione). d. 1365. *Plate* 225.

S. MARIA NOVELLA, STROZZI CHAPEL. Frescoes. Left wall: Paradise. Altar wall: Last Judgement. Right wall: Inferno. Pilasters: SS. Dominic and Peter Martyr. (See also Jacopo di Cione and Giovanni del Biondo). [*Plates* 122–123.] *Plates* 194–200.

— CHIOSTRINO DEI MORTI, STECCUTI CHAPEL. Frescoes: Scenes from the Life of the Virgin [Annunciation to Joachim, Meeting at the Golden Gate, Birth of the Virgin, Presentation in the Temple, SS. Thomas Aquinas, John Evangelist, Luke and Dominic]. (r.). *Plate* 202.

OGNISSANTI, REFECTORY. Fresco: S. Benedict (fr.).
Fresco: Miraculous Rescue of S. Placidus (r.).

SS. STEFANO E CECILIA, L. WALL. Two panels: SS. Peter Apostle and Peter Martyr.

BERENSON COLLECTION. S. Anthony Abbot (fr).
Predella panel: S. Benedict receiving SS. Maurus and Placidus. *Plate* 205.

(Environs) S. ANDREA A CERCINA, REFECTORY. Madonna and Child with SS. Peter and Andrew.

London. 581. SS. John Evangelist, John Baptist and James.

    VICTORIA AND ALBERT MUSEUM. C.A.I.104. Coronation of the Virgin.

Munich. W.A.F. 1027, 1028. Wings of an altarpiece: SS. Julian, Romuald, Peter, a Bishop and a Deacon; SS. John Baptist, Benedict, Gerard of Villamagna, Paul and Catherine.

New Haven (Conn.). 1871.13–14. Two panels from an altarpiece: SS. Peter and John Baptist.

New York. HISTORICAL SOCIETY. B–3. Madonna and Child with SS. Zenobius, John Baptist, John Evangelist and Reparata.

Prague. 0.2376–2385. 'Palfy' polyptych: Madonna and Child with SS. James, Jerome, John Baptist and Raynerius. Predella: Man of Sorrows with the Virgin and S. John, and eight Saints.

Stockholm. 2259. S. Benedict.

Washington (D.C.). 372 (KRESS COLLECTION 478). Triptych: Madonna and Child. Pinnacle: Man of Sorrows. Wings: SS. Peter and John Evangelist. *Plate 204.*

NERI DI BICCI

1419–91. Pupil and close follower of his father Bicci di Lorenzo; influenced by Fra Angelico, Fra Filippo, Domenico Veneziano and Pesellino.

Altenburg. 154. Predella panel: Nativity.

Ancona. 7. Polychrome gesso relief: Madonna and Child.

Arezzo. 27. *Madonna della Misericordia* with SS. Michael, Nicholas and kneeling Bernardino da Siena. Predella: S. John Baptist, S. Bernardino da Siena leads a procession to Fonte Tecta, has the pagan shrine destroyed, preaches for the erection of S. Maria delle Grazie, S. Bartholomew. d. 1456. *Plate 913.*

    S. FRANCESCO, CHAPEL R. OF CHOIR. Annunciation, with SS. Jerome and Francis and the Prophets Isaiah and David.

    S. MICHELE. Madonna and Child with SS. Benedict, George, John Baptist and Romuald. d. 1466.

Badia a Rusti (Chianti). S. PIETRO, HIGH ALTAR. Coronation of the Virgin with SS. Bartholomew, Peter, Benedict, Romuald, Paul and James. Lunette: Annunciation. Pilasters: Eight Saints. Predella: S. Benedict sending S. Maurus to the Rescue of S. Placidus, Rescue of S. Placidus, Nativity, Temptation of S. Romuald.

Bagno di Romagna. S. MARIA DEL FIORE, CHOIR. Triptych: *Madonna della Cintola* with Angels and SS. Benedict, John Baptist, Peter, Paul, Agnes and Romuald. d. 1468.

Baltimore (Md.). WALTERS ART GALLERY. 675. Coronation of the Virgin, with SS. John Baptist, Augustine, Monica and Nicholas. L.

740. Madonna and Child with SS. Bernardino, John Baptist, Bernard, and Apollonia. E.

Barberino di Mugello (Environs). COLLE BARUCCI, S. MARIA, SACRISTY. Madonna and Child with SS. Bartholomew, Agatha, Francis and James. E.

Barcelona. MUSEO DE ARTE. Predella: S. Lawrence and a Donor, Triumph of S. Michael Archangel, Dormition of the Virgin, Martyrdom of S. Catherine, a Saint and two kneeling Nuns.

Madonna and Child enthroned.

Madonna adoring the Child with Infant S. John, surrounded by a cut-out Baldacchino. *Plate 920.*

Berlin (BERLIN–OST). 1459 (DEP. COLOGNE). Madonna and Child with SS. Anthony Abbot, Peter, and Tobias and the Angel.

Brooklyn (N.Y.). 32.791. Madonna and Child with SS. Paul, Peter, Sigismund, Francis, Tobias and the Angel, and Donor.

Budapest. 1228. Madonna and Child enthroned.

Cambridge (Mass.). 1958.294, 295. Two predella panels: Nativity, Baptism of Christ.

Canneto (Val d'Elsa). S. GIORGIO. Madonna and Child with SS. James, Andrew, John Baptist and Anthony Abbot. Predella: Man of Sorrows, Virgin and SS. John, Bernardino and Francis; Vocation and Crucifixion of S. Andrew. d. 1452.

Castelnuovo (Val d'Elsa). S. MARIA ASSUNTA, HIGH ALTAR. Annunciation.

Castiglione d'Olona. COLLEGIATA, CHOIR (DEP. GALLERIE FIORENTINE 8608). Crucifixion. 1461.

Certomondo (Casentino). S. MARIA ASSUNTA, R. WALL. Central panel of triptych: Annunciation. (Companion to Grenoble). 1466.

Città di Castello. PINACOTECA. Madonna and Child with two Angels.

Claremont (Cal.). POMONA COLLEGE, KRESS STUDY COLLECTION. K 1003. Predella panel: Martyrdom of S. Apollonia.

Cleveland (Ohio). 16. 798. Madonna adoring the Child, with two Angels and two Cherubim.

46.242. Madonna and Child.

Cologne. 456. See Berlin.

Corazzano (San Miniato al Tedesco). S. GIOVANNI. *Madonna della Cintola* with SS. John Baptist and Bartholomew.

Cortona. ACCADEMIA (DEP. GALLERIE FIORENTINE 8696). Predella: Pietà and six Saints.

Denver (Col.). MUSEUM OF ART, KRESS COLLECTION. K 1728. S. Anthony Abbot enthroned. *Plate 921.*

Detroit (Mich.). 26.114. Archangels Michael, Raphael with Tobias, and Gabriel.

Dijon. 1646. Madonna adoring the Child.

Englewood (N.J.). D. F. PLATT (EX). Tobias and the Angel.

Esztergom. KERESTÉNY MUSEUM. Tobias and the Angel, with a Monk.

Fabriano. VESCOVADO. Madonna and Child with SS. Ansanus, Andrew and two Martyr Knights. Predella: Man of Sorrows with the Virgin and S. John (r.). E.

Fiesole. MUSEO BANDINI. I, 17. Madonna adoring the Child with Infant S. John and S. James.

I, 35. Small processional Crucifix: *Christus triumphans*; on back, *Christus patiens*.

S. FRANCESCO, 2nd ALTAR R. Crucifixion with Saints. 1463.

Florence. GALLERIE. 3463. Madonna and Child with SS. Louis of Toulouse, Benedict, Apollonia and Catherine. Predella: Man of Sorrows and six Saints. 1472.

3546. Predella: S. Sebastian, Tobias and the Angel, Lamentation, S. Julian, S. Anthony Abbot.

ACCADEMIA. 13 DEP. Coronation of the Virgin with Angels and twelve Saints. 1460.

480. Annunciation, with SS. Apollonia and Luke, and the Prophets David and Isaiah. d. 1458. *Plate 915.*

3470. Right wing of triptych from SS. Annunziata: SS. Francis, Jerome, Philip, Catherine and a Bishop Saint. (Companion to Oberlin). Soon after 1444.

5888. Tobias and the Angel, S. Benedict, Annunciation.

8618. Coronation of the Virgin, with SS. Michael and Stephen.

8622. Annunciation. d. 1464.

12911. SS. Francis and Catherine.

12912–14. Three small Scenes. E.

MUSEO HORNE. 482. Madonna and Child with two Angels.

6156. Tobias and the Angel, and S. Jerome.

MUSEO STIBBERT. 3538. Madonna adoring the Child with two Angels.

S. CROCE, 1st CHAPEL L. OF CHOIR (TOSINGHI). Predella (to Giovanni del Biondo's triptych): Man of Sorrows and Saints.

— SACRISTY. Trinity, with SS. John Baptist, Benedict, Francis and Bartholomew. 1461.

S. FELICE. 6th ALTAR R. Tabernacle: Resurrected Christ, Angels and SS. Nicholas, John Baptist, Julian and Sigismund. Lunettes: Man of Sorrows, Annunciation. 1467.

S. FELICITA, SACRISTY. S. Felicitas and her seven Sons. *Plate 918.*

— SALA DEL CAPITOLO. Predella (to above): Martyrdom of S. Felicitas and her Sons.

S. GIOVANNINO DEI CAVALIERI, 3rd ALTAR R. Coronation of the Virgin, with SS. James, Mary Magdalen, John Baptist, Sebastian, Nicholas, Zenobius (?), Catherine and Dominic. Predella: SS. Francis, Jerome and another Saint, Feast of Herod, Man of Sorrows, S. Nicholas and the three Maidens, SS. Michael, Lawrence and Margaret.

S. LEONARDO IN ARCETRI. *Madonna della Cintola*, with SS. Peter, Jerome, Francis and John Baptist. 1467.

Panel intended to surround Ciborium: God the Father with six Angels, Annunciation and the Prophets Isaiah and David.

S. MARGHERITA DE' RICCI, HIGH ALTAR. Madonna and Child with SS. Mary Magdalen, Margaret, Agnes and Catherine. Predella: Man of Sorrows and six Saints.

S. MARIA NOVELLA, L. WALL, 2nd BAY. Annunciation. 1455.

S. NICCOLÒ, SACRISTY. Trinity, with SS. Lawrence, John Baptist, Francis and Leonard. 1463.

S. PANCRAZIO, CLOISTER. Fresco: S. John Gualbert enthroned, with eleven other Saints. 1455.

S. SALVATORE AL MONTE, 5th CHAPEL R. *Pietà*, with two Saints.

S. SPIRITO, CHOIR, 4th CHAPEL R. Altar frontal: S. Luke, with two Angels.

S. TRINITA, 3rd CHAPEL R. Madonna and Child with SS. Andrew, Catherine, Barbara and Nicholas. Predella: Man of Sorrows and Saints. After 1475.

— 3rd CHAPEL L. Annunciation.

SPEDALE DEGLI INNOCENTI, PINACOTECA. Coronation of the Virgin, with SS. Lucy, Catherine, Bartholomew and Andrew.

BERENSON COLLECTION. Madonna and S. Lawrence adoring the Child.

Predella panel: Nativity.

CHARLES LOESER (EX). Tobias and the Angel. E.

SERRISTORI COLLECTION. Predella panel: S. Leonard praying for the Safe Delivery of a Queen. *Plate 916.*

(Environs) S. MARTINO A MENSOLA, 1st ALTAR L. Madonna and Child with SS. John Baptist, Francis, Mary Magdalen and a Nun. Predella: Man of Sorrows and Saints.

Foligno. MISERICORDIA. Frescoes: Annunciation, Crucifixion, Coronation of the Virgin. E.

Frankfurt am Main. GEORG HARTMANN. Madonna and Child.

Grenoble. MUSÉE. 503, 504 (CAMPANA 127, 128). Wings of Certomondo altarpiece: SS. Catherine, Anthony of Padua, and John Evangelist, and the Prophet Isaiah; SS. Francis, Lawrence, and Louis of Toulouse, and the Evangelist Mark. 1466.

Lawrence (Kansas). UNIVERSITY OF KANSAS, KRESS COLLECTION. K 1143. Right wing of an altarpiece: SS. Bartholomew and James.

Linari (Val d'Elsa). S. STEFANO, L. WALL. Madonna and Child with SS. Francis, John Baptist, Catherine and Verdiana (S. Verdiana a later replacement or restoration).

Liverpool. 2790, Madonna and Child with SS. Mary Magdalen, John Evangelist, Bartholomew and Barbara.

London. HENRY HARRIS (EX). Predella panel: S. John entering the Wilderness.

VISCOUNT LEE OF FAREHAM (EX). Madonna and Child.

Montecarlo (Valdarno Superiore). S. FRANCESCO, 1st ALTAR L. Coronation of the Virgin with Angels and ten Saints. Predella: Meeting at the Golden Gate, Birth of the Virgin, Marriage of the Virgin, Annunciation, Visitation.

Morrocco (Tavarnelle Val di Pesa). s. MARIA, L. WALL. Madonna nursing the Child, with Tobias and the Angel and SS. Nicholas, Anthony Abbot, Julian and Donnino. 1473.

— R. WALL. Lamentation, with SS. Luke, Margaret, Mary Magdalen, John Evangelist, Catherine and Lucy.

— CHOIR. Two predella panels: Two Donors.

— SACRISTY. Wings of an altarpiece: S. Sebastian and the Virgin, SS. John Evangelist and Roch.

Tabernacle door: Blood of the Redeemer.

Moulins. MUSÉE (CAMPANA 129). Coronation of the Virgin, with S. Anthony Abbot, a Bishop Saint and Tobias and the Angel.

Nantes. 15. Left wing of an altarpiece: S. Anthony Abbot and a Bishop Saint. Pinnacle: Angel of the Annunciation.

New Haven (Conn.). 1871.39. Predella panel: S. Nicholas and the three Maidens.

1871. 40. Annunciation (after Pesellino).

1943.220. Madonna adoring the Child.

1943.221. Madonna and Child with two Angels and SS. Jerome and Mary Magdalen.

New York. HISTORICAL SOCIETY. B–9. SS. Jerome, Francis and Anthony Abbot (after Pesellino).

ERNESTO FABBRI (EX). Small *Pietà*.

R. M. HURD (EX). SS. Sebastian, Zenobius, Ambrose and Apollonia.

ROBERT LEHMAN. Tobias and the Angel.

Oberlin (Ohio). COLLEGE, KRESS STUDY COLLECTION. K 254. Left wing of triptych from SS. Annunziata: SS. Margaret, Bernard, John Baptist, James and an Evangelist. (Companion to Florence, Accademia 3470). Soon after 1444.

Ottawa. 3716. *Madonna della Cintola*. Predella: Eight Angels.

Oxford. CHRIST CHURCH LIBRARY. 31. Archangels Gabriel, Michael and Raphael with Tobias and four Saints.

Palermo. CHIARAMONTE BORDONARO COLLECTION. Tobias and the Angel with SS. Simeon, Thaddeus, Nicholas of Tolentino, Augustine, Monica and James.

Paray-le-Monial. MUSÉE.† Man of Sorrows and Saints.

Paris. 1397. Madonna and Child.

1398. Annunciation. E. (?)

MUSÉE JACQUEMART–ANDRÉ. 1012. Coronation of the Virgin.

HEUGEL COLLECTION (EX?). Predella panels: Baptism of Christ, Miracle of S. Bernardino of Siena.

CHARLES PERRIOLAT (EX). Nativity with Infant S. John.

Parma. 442. Madonna and Child with SS. Francis, Bartholomew, John Baptist and James. E.

Perugia. R. VAN MARLE (EX). Two panels: SS. Francis and Dominic.

Pescia. MUSEO (BIBLIOTECA COMUNALE). Annunciation with SS. Apollonia and Luke and the Prophets David and Isaiah. d. 1459.

Coronation of the Virgin, with SS. Bernard, Paul, Barbara, Catherine, John Baptist and Jerome.

s. francesco, cardini chapel. Fresco: SS. John Baptist, Anthony Abbot and two other Saints with Giovanni and Antonio Cardini as Donors.

Philadelphia (Pa.). museum of art, johnson collection. 27. *Madonna della Cintola*, with SS. George, a Bishop Saint, Margaret and Catherine.

28–33. Six predella panels: Virgin adoring the Child, and twelve Saints.

— w. p. wilstach collection 229 (ex). Madonna and Child with SS. Ambrose, Catherine, Margaret and Francis.

Pisa. 103. Right wing of an altarpiece: SS. Boniface and Romuald.

170. Coronation of the Virgin, with Angels and ten Saints.

Poggibonsi. ss. lorenzo e agostino, 2nd altar r. S. Nicholas of Tolentino with female Worshippers (r.).

Rignano sull'Arno (Environs). miransù, s. lorenzo. Triptych: Madonna and Child with two Angels, SS. Nicholas and Lawrence.

— 2nd altar l. Crucifixion with the Virgin and SS. Gregory, Mary Magdalen, Jerome, John Evangelist, John Baptist and two other Saints. Predella: Tobias and the Angel, SS. Michael, Peter, Bartholomew and Dorothy.

Rome. pinacoteca capitolina. 348. S. Blaise.

vatican, pinacoteca. 100. Predella panel: S. Anthony of Padua giving Alms. E.

Rotterdam. 2540. Predella panel: Triumph of S. Michael (variant of Barcelona). *Plate* 914.

Rouen. musée 686 (campana 342). Madonna and Child with SS. Margaret, John Baptist, Jerome, Sebastian and two Bishop Saints.

†Madonna and Child with Donor.

San Casciano (Val di Pesa). (Environs) s. giovanni in sugana, l. wall. Coronation of the Virgin with four Angels and SS. Paul, John Baptist, Peter, James, Mary Magdalen and a Bishop Saint.

San Diego (Cal.). fine arts gallery. Kneeling Angel.

San Gimignano. 21. Madonna and Child.

Seville. casa de las duenas, chapel. *Madonna della Cintola*, with SS. Mary Magdalen and Catherine.

Siena. pinacoteca. Madonna and Child with SS. Cecilia, Anne, Mary Magdalen and Catherine. Sd. and d. 1482.

Tavarnelle (Val di Pesa). s. lucia al borghetto, chapel l. of choir. Annunciation. d. 1471. *Plate* 919.

Toulouse. 401. Background to Lorenzo Monaco's Crucifix: Virgin, S. John and Magdalen.

Utrecht. archepiscopal museum. nk. 2703. Predella panel: An Angel saving a hanging Man.

Utrecht (contd.). ART INSTITUTE. NK. 1472. Predella panel: An Angel helping two
Cardinals on horseback across a River. (Companion to NK.2703 above).

Vienna (Environs). FANITEUM (OBER S. VEIT). Two panels (pilasters from the frame of
an altarpiece): SS. Peter and Paul, SS. John Baptist and Francis.

Viterbo. S. SISTO. Madonna and Child with SS. Lawrence, Felicitas, Sixtus, John
Baptist, Jerome and Nicholas. E.

Volterra. 6. S. Sebastian, with SS. Bartholomew and Nicholas. d. 1478. *Plate*
923.

    SS. GIUSTO E CLEMENTE. Madonna and Child enthroned.

Worcester (Mass.). 1940.35 a–c. Predella: Tobias and the Angel, SS. Cosmas and
Damian, Nativity, S. Ursula and S. Jerome.

Homeless. S. John Evangelist enthroned, with Tobias and the Angel, and SS. Lucy
and William. *Plate 922.*

    Madonna and Child with SS. James and Andrew. d. 1463. *Plate 917.*

    Madonna and Child (*Dedalo* XII, 853).

NICCOLÒ DI PIETRO GERINI

Active ca 1368–1415. Follower of the Gaddi and Orcagna traditions.

Amsterdam. 979–D1. Crucifixion (g.p.).

Avignon. MUSÉE CALVET 410 (CAMPANA 141). Madonna of Humility with eight
Angels, and Christ blessing.

Baltimore (Md.). MUSEUM OF ART. 51.390. Madonna and Child with two Angels
and SS. Catherine, John Baptist, James and Dorothy (p.).

Berlin. 1112. Predella panel: Adoration of the Magi (g.p.).

Birmingham (Ala.). MUSEUM OF ART (KRESS COLLECTION 1719). Burial of the
Quattro Santi Coronati.

Borgo San Lorenzo (Mugello). S. LORENZO. Madonna and Child.

Boston (Mass.). 16.14. Madonna and Child enthroned.

    ISABELLA GARDNER MUSEUM. S. Anthony Abbot enthroned with four Angels.
Pinnacle: Christ blessing.

Bourges. See Paris, Musées Nationaux.

Brunswick. 1. Madonna and Child with six Angels (p.).

Cambridge. 550. Two panels: Annunciation.

Cambridge (Mass.). MRS. A. KINGSLEY PORTER. Madonna nursing the Child.

Capesthorne Hall (Ches.). LT.-COL. SIR W. H. BROMLEY-DAVENPORT. Predella panel:
Disputation of S. Catherine.

Chicago (Ill.). 37.1003. Madonna and Child.

Colorado Springs (Colo.). FINE ARTS CENTER, KRESS COLLECTION. K 1004. Madonna and Child.

Cracow. 317. Christ in Glory with Angels.

Denver (Col.). MUSEUM OF ART, KRESS COLLECTION. K 17. The *Quattro Santi Coronati* before Lampadius. (Companion to Philadelphia 1163). *Plate 369.*

Detroit (Mich.). MRS. LILIAN HENKEL HAASS. Crucifixion.

Empoli. 4. Three predella panels: Last Supper, Betrayal of Christ, Lamentation.

14. Triptych: Madonna and Child with SS. Anthony Abbot, John Baptist, Gregory and Leonard. Pinnacle: Annunciation. Predella: Man of Sorrows and four Saints (st.).

Fiesole. MUSEO BANDINI. I, 9. Trinity.

I, 21. See Jacopo di Cione.

Florence. ACCADEMIA. 3152. Triptych: Crucifixion, and SS. Paul, Mary Magdalen, Luke, Bartholomew, Catherine and Peter Martyr. Pinnacles: Christ blessing and Annunciation (the Crucifixion mostly by Jacopo di Cione).

4670. Crucifixion. (?)

8468. Triptych: Coronation of the Virgin with four music-making Angels and SS. Felicitas, Andrew, John Baptist, Matthew, John Evangelist, Peter, James, and Benedict. Above: Two Angels and two Prophets (Coronation by Lorenzo di Niccolò on design of Spinello Aretino; predella by Lorenzo di Niccolò). d. 1401. *Plate 386.*

8469. See S. Carlo dei Lombardi.

MUSEO DEL BIGALLO, SALA DEL CONSIGLIO. Fresco: The Brethren of the Misericordia receiving Orphans (with Ambrogio di Baldese). 1386. *Plate 365.*

S. CARLO DEI LOMBARDI, HIGH ALTAR (ACCADEMIA 8469). Entombment and Ascension. *Plate 364.*

S. CROCE, HIGH ALTAR. Central panel of polyptych: Madonna and Child with SS. James and Philip (see Giovanni del Biondo and Mariotto di Nardo).

— CASTELLANI CHAPEL (SACRAMENT CHAPEL). Crucifix. d. 1380. *Plate 363.*

— SACRISTY. Frescoes: Resurrection (g.p.), Ascension (p.). (See also Spinello Aretino.) *Plate 381.*

S. FELICITA, L. TRANSEPT. Fresco: Nativity. (With Lorenzo di Niccolò.)

— SALA DEL CAPITOLO. Frescoes (vault): Christ and the seven Cardinal Virtues (p.). Fresco (over altar): Crucifixion.

ORSANMICHELE, 1st PILLAR. Trinity; below: Pentecost (g.p.). *Plate 380.*

CHARLES LOESER (EX). A King and six other Figures kneeling before a Column.

(Environs) PARADISO DEGLI ALBERTI (EX-MONASTERY OF SS. SALVATORE AND BRIGIDA, also called S. BRIGIDA AL BANDINO, via del Paradiso 86–96). Frescoes. Scenes from the Life of Christ [Washing of Feet, Betrayal of Christ, Christ before Pilate, Way to Calvary, Two fragments of a Crucifixion, Way to Emmaus, Incredulity of S. Thomas, Ascension, Pentecost] (r. assisted by Lorenzo di Niccolò, Mariotto di Nardo and Ambrogio di Baldese). 1398–99. *Plate 379.*

Florence (Environs) (contd.). VINCIGLIATA, S. LORENZO. Madonna and Child.

Greenville (S.C.). BOB JONES UNIVERSITY GALLERY. Polyptych: Madonna and Child with SS. Bartholomew, Mary Magdalen, John Baptist and Francis. Pinnacles: Annunciation and three Prophets. Predella: Ecstasy, Last Communion and Burial of S. Mary Magdalen, and two other Scenes.

London. 569–578. See Jacopo di Cione.

    579. Triptych: Baptism of Christ, and SS. Peter and Paul. Predella: S. Benedict, Annunciation to Zacharias and Birth of S. John, Head of S. John brought to Herod and Herodias, S. Romuald. 1387. *Plates 366–367.*

Montreal. 1059. Coronation of the Virgin with six Angels and SS. Francis, Lucy, Catherine and John Baptist. *Plate 368.*

Mount Browne (Guildford, Surrey). LADY ISABEL PEYRONNET BROWNE (EX). Madonna and Child with two Angels and SS. Catherine, John Baptist, James and Nicholas.

Munich. W.A.F.304. Lunette: Lamentation (st.).

New Haven (Conn.). 1871.18. Trinity with the Virgin and SS. John Baptist, Mary Magdalen and John Evangelist (with Jacopo di Cione).

    1871.21. Annunciation.

    1871.26. Portable triptych: Madonna of Humility. Wings: Annunciation, Six Saints, Crucifixion (p., assisted by Lorenzo di Niccolò).

Oxford. CHRIST CHURCH LIBRARY. 9. Head of the Virgin.

    12. S. Philip.

Paris. MUSÉES NATIONAUX (CAMPANA 113). Right wing of an altarpiece: SS. Catherine, Thomas (or Thaddeus) and Anthony Abbot.

    LOUVRE. 1623. Coronation of the Virgin with two Angels.

Parma. 431. Dormition of the Virgin (p.).

Philadelphia (Pa.). MUSEUM OF ART, JOHNSON COLLECTION. 8. *Pietà* (p.).

    1163. Scourging of the *Quattro Santi Coronati.* (Companion to Denver). *Plate 370.*

Pisa. S. FRANCESCO, SALA DEL CAPITOLO DI S. BONAVENTURA. Frescoes: Scenes from the Life of Christ [Judas receiving the Price of Betrayal, Last Supper, Washing of Feet, Agony in the Garden, Betrayal, Flagellation, Way to Calvary, Crucifixion, Deposition, Entombment, Resurrection, *Noli me tangere*, Ascension, Pentecost, S. John Baptist, S. Lawrence] (r.). 1392. *Plate 377.*

Pistoia. MUSEO CIVICO. Madonna and Child with S. John Baptist and a Bishop Saint (p.).

Prato. S. FRANCESCO, SALA DEL CAPITOLO. Frescoes. Vault: Four Evangelists. Walls: Crucifixion and Scenes from the Lives of SS. Anthony Abbot, Benedict and Matthew [Entrance wall: SS. Clare, Catherine, John Baptist and Bartholomew. Left wall: S. Anthony Abbot distributing his Fortune, Vision of S. Benedict, and another Scene. Altar wall: Crucifixion. Right wall: Calling of S. Matthew, Raising of the King's Child, Death of S. Matthew]. (Assisted by Ambrogio di Baldese and others). *Plates 371–376.*

Rome. PINACOTECA CAPITOLINA. 102. Trinity with three Donors.

    VATICAN, PINACOTECA. 223. *Desco:* S. Barnabas kneeling before S. Paul, Vision of S. Barnabas, Healing of Timon, Martyrdom of S. Barnabas (g.p.).

Strasbourg. 206. Madonna and Child. Pinnacle: Christ blessing. (?)

Verona. 788. Right wing of an altarpiece: SS. Gregory and Bartholomew.

Vienna. LANCKORONSKI COLLECTION. Left wing of an altarpiece: SS. Julian and Bartholomew. Pinnacle: Angel of the Annunciation.

Homeless. Two panels: Annunciation. *Plate 378.*

NICCOLÒ DI TOMMASO (Master of the Convento del T)

Active ca 1343-1376. His identified works show him coming out of Nardo and veering toward Jacopo di Cione and Giovanni del Biondo; influenced by Giovanni da Milano.

Arezzo. 13. Madonna and Child with female Donor. d. 1367. (Destroyed). *Plate 312.*

Assisi. MRS. F. M. PERKINS, Madonna and Child with four Saints (r.). *Plate 320.*

Auxerre. See Paris, Musées Nationaux.

Baltimore. (Md.). 478. Madonna and Child (fr.).

    718. Portable triptych: Coronation of the Virgin with two music-making Angels, two Donors and their Patron Saints. Wings, inside: SS. Nicholas, Peter, Paul, Catherine and four Angels. Wings, outside: SS. Anthony Abbot and Christopher. *Plates 314-315.*

    752. Portable triptych: Madonna and Child with four Saints. Wings: Annunciation, Three Saints, Crucifixion. *Plate 308.*

Besançon. 897.1.149. Wings of a portable triptych: Six Saints, Crucifixion.

Boston (Mass.). 37.409. Madonna of Humility. Predella: S. Nicholas and the three Maidens, Crucifixion, *Noli me tangere.*

Brussels. MLLE. MICHÈLE STOCLET. Madonna nursing the Child. Pinnacle: Christ blessing. d. 1362. (?)

Fiesole. MUSEO BANDINI. I, 24-27. Four predella panels: Nativity, Adoration of the Magi, Circumcision, Massacre of the Innocents (st.).

Florence. GALLERIE. Portable altarpiece: Massacre of the Innocents; below: Nativity, Flight into Egypt (p.).

    ACCADEMIA. 8580. Coronation of the Virgin with Saints and Angels. Pinnacle: Christ blessing. *Plate 321.*

    MUSEO HORNE. 75, 76. Two panels from an altarpiece: S. John Evangelist, S. Paul.

    ACTON COLLECTION. Madonna and Child with two Angels and SS. Anthony Abbot and Catherine.

    (Environs) CAREGGI, NUOVO CONVENTO DELLE OBLATE. Madonna and Child with SS. Peter, Christopher, Lawrence and Paul. Predella: Man of Sorrows, three Saints, *Noli me tangere. Plate 317.*

Kansas City (Mo.). 34.130. Coronation of the Virgin with six Angels and eight Saints.

Leghorn. LARDEREL COLLECTION (EX.). Last Judgement.

Le Mans. 7. Wing of a portable altarpiece: SS. Catherine, Francis and a Bishop Saint (fr., r.).

159. See Paris, Musées Nationaux.

London. 569–578. See Jacopo di Cione.

VISCOUNT ROTHERMERE. Portable triptych: Coronation of the Virgin with two music-making Angels and eight Saints. Pinnacle: Christ blessing. Wings: Annunciation, Adoration of the Magi, Crucifixion.

Naples. MUSEO DI S. MARTINO. Triptych: S. Anthony Abbot enthroned with four Angels and SS. Francis, Peter, John Evangelist and Louis of Toulouse. Sd and d. 1371. *Plates* 316, 318.

New Haven (Conn.). 1943.235. S. James (fr., r.).

1943.236. S. Bridget's Vision of the Nativity (r.).

Paris. MUSÉES NATIONAUX (CAMPANA 60, DEP. AUXERRE, FORMERLY LE MANS 159). Madonna and Child with ten Angels and twelve Saints. Above: Crucifixion. (?)

Parma. CONGREGAZIONE DI S. FILIPPO NERI, PINACOTECA STUARD. 2. Lamentation.

Philadelphia (Pa.). MUSEUM OF ART, JOHNSON COLLECTION. 120. Portable triptych: S. Bridget's Vision of the Nativity. Wings: Annunciation, Four Saints, Crucifixion.

Pisa. 32. Madonna and Child with four Angels and ten Saints (r.).

Pistoia. PALAZZO COMUNALE. Fresco: S. James and a Bishop Saint supporting a structure, with the Madonna and Child and two Angels. d. 1360. *Plate* 309.

EX-CONVENTO DEL T (70 CORSO SILVANO FEDI). Frescoes (vault and walls): Last Judgement, Creation and Fall of Man, The Flood, Jacob and Esau, and other Scenes from the Old Testament (fr., r.). *Plates* 310–311.

Potsdam. NEUES PALAIS. Madonna and Child.

Prague. DO 798. Coronation of the Virgin with Angels and ten Saints.

Rome. PRINCIPE COLONNA. Madonna and Child with four Angels and ten Saints. *Plate* 319.

CONTE GIUSEPPE PRIMOLI (EX). Madonna and Child in Glory.

VATICAN, PINACOTECA. 123. Portable triptych: Crucifixion, Last Supper. Wings: Agony in the Garden, Betrayal of Christ, Christ before Pilate, Mocking of Christ, Flagellation, Robing of Christ (?), Way to Calvary, Lamentation. Predella: Six Saints.

137. S. Bridget's Vision of the Nativity. *Plate* 322.

212, 219. Wings of an altarpiece: SS. Julian and Lucy, SS. Anthony Abbot and John Baptist. *Plates* 323–324.

Turin. GALLERIA SABAUDA, GUALINO COLLECTION. Triptych: Madonna and Child with two Angels and SS. Gaudentius and Catherine. Pinnacles: Christ Blessing, Annunciation (r.).

Venice. CA' D'ORO. Nativity.

Vienna. LANCKORONSKI COLLECTION. Madonna and Child with Seraphim, Cherubim, Angels and Saints.

Homeless. Portable triptych: Madonna and Child with SS. Nicholas, Lucy, Catherine and Anthony Abbot. Wings: Annunciation, Nativity, Crucifixion. *Plate* 313.

ORCAGNA (Andrea di Cione, called)

Active ca 1343/4–1368. As sculptor, pupil of Andrea Pisano; as painter, possibly a pupil of Daddi and certainly a follower of Maso.

Angers. MUSÉE. Crucifix.
Florence. ACCADEMIA. 165 Dep. Triptych: Pentecost. (Execution by Jacopo di Cione).
    3469. Polyptych: Madonna and Child with SS. Nicholas, Philip, John Baptist and John Evangelist (p.). (Wings probably by Jacopo di Cione). *Plate* 210.
    SS. APOSTOLI, R. OF HIGH ALTAR. Madonna and Child (st.).
    S. CROCE, MUSEO DELL'OPERA. Six panels containing detached fresco fragments: Triumph of Death, Inferno. *Plate* 215.
    S. MARIA NOVELLA, STROZZI CHAPEL. Altarpiece: Christ in Glory with SS. Michael, Catherine, the Virgin, Thomas Aquinas, Peter, John Baptist, Lawrence and Paul. Pinnacles: Holy Ghost and four Angels. Predella: Mass of St. Thomas, Calling of S. Peter, Death of the Emperor Henry and Redemption of his Soul by S. Lawrence. Sd and d. 1357. [*Plates* 118–120.] *Plates* 211–214.
    — CHOIR.* Frescoes (soffits of entrance arch): Heads of Prophets (st.).
    CINELLI COLLECTION (EX). Predella panel: Adoration of the Magi (p.).
    (Environs) CERTOSA DEL GALLUZZO. Tondo: Madonna and Child (p.).
New York. ROBERT LEHMAN. *Madonna della Cintola* (fr.).
Oxford. ASHMOLEAN. 306. Predella panel: Birth of the Virgin.
    CHRIST CHURCH LIBRARY. 7. Four music-making Angels (fr.).
Rome. GALLERIA NAZIONALE (PALAZZO BARBERINI). F.N. 700. Coronation of the Virgin with two Angels and fourteen Saints (p.).
Utrecht. ARCHEPISCOPAL MUSEUM. (NK. 1726). Triptych: Madonna and Child with SS. Mary Magdalen and Ansanus. Pinnacle: Christ blessing. d. 1350. *Plate* 209.
Washington (D.C.). 814 (KRESS COLLECTION K 1363). Madonna and Child with eight Angels (with Jacopo di Cione).

SCULPTURE

Florence. ORSANMICHELE. Marble tabernacle: Saints, Virtues and Scenes from the Life of the Virgin. Sd and d. 1359.

PACINO DI BONAGUIDA

Mentioned from 1303 to 1339. Possibly a pupil of the Master of S. Cecilia.

Florence. ACCADEMIA. 8568. Polyptych: Crucifixion, and SS. Nicholas, Bartholomew, Florentius and Luke. Sd and d. 13??. *Plate* 94.
Ponce (Puerto Rico). MUSEO DE ARTE (KRESS STUDY COLLECTION 1262). Crucifix.

FRA PAOLINO

*Pistoiese. ca 1490–1547. Pupil and close imitator of his fellow Dominican Fra Barto-
lommeo, whose designs he repeatedly copied.*

Bibbiena (Casentino). (Environs) S. MARIA DEL SASSO, CHOIR. Assumption. 1519.
— L. WALL. Madonna and Child with SS. Dominic, Antonino, Lucy, Catherine,
Vincent Ferrer and Thomas Aquinas. Sd and d. 1525. *Plate* 1337.
Brussels. 638. Madonna and Child with Infant S. John. (?)
Chambéry. 426. Madonna and Child. (Replica of Modena).
Dijon. 71. Madonna and Child with Infant S. John. (?)
Empoli. 36. Madonna and Child.
38. Assumption with SS. Stephen, Mary Magdalen, Barbara, Onuphrius and a
Donor.
Florence. GALLERIE. 3471. Madonna and Child with seven Saints.
PITTI. 199. Tondo: Madonna and Child with Infant S. John. (?)
MUSEO FERRONI. Annunciation. *Plate* 1333.
S. MARCO (MUSEO), REFETTORIO. Lamentation. 1519. *Plate* 1334.
Holy Family with S. Agnes and an Angel. *Plate* 1335.
Leningrad. 97. Tondo: Madonna and Child with Infant S. John. (?)
1517. Madonna and Child. (?)
Modena. 508. Madonna and Child.
New York. S. UNTERMEYER (EX). Virgin Annunciate.
Notre Dame (Ind.). UNIVERSITY, KRESS STUDY COLLECTION. K 1105. Holy Family
with S. Elizabeth and Infant S. John.
Orleans. MUSÉE. 1110 (CAMPANA 443). Madonna and Child.
Pistoia. MUSEO CIVICO. Madonna and Child with Infant S. John and SS. James,
Agatha, Zenobius and Barbara. (?)
Two panels: Annunciation.
SAN DOMENICO, 2nd ALTAR R. Fresco: *Madonna delle Nevi.* (Destroyed 1943.)
— 2nd ALTAR L. Crucifixion.
— SACRISTY. Adoration of the Magi. 1526. *Plate* 1339.
— — Madonna and Child with SS. Lucy, Dominic, Catherine of Siena, Mary
Magdalen, Peter Martyr and Cecilia.

s. MARIA DELLE GRAZIE (MADONNA DEL LETTO), CHOIR R. Madonna and Child with
   SS. Jerome, Catherine, Infant John Baptist, Mary Magdalen and Sebastian.
s. PAOLO, L. OF ENTRANCE. Madonna and Child with fifteen Saints. Sd and d. 1520.
Rome. CONVITTO NAZIONALE VITTORIO EMMANUELE. Madonna and Child with seven
   Saints. (Replica of Florence, Gallerie).
   GALLERIA DORIA PAMPHILJ. 156. Holy Family with Infant S. John and two Angels.
   GALLERIA NAZIONALE (PALAZZO BARBERINI). F.N. 19217. *Madonna della Cintola*. (?)
San Gimignano. s. AGOSTINO, CHAPEL L. OF CHOIR. Madonna and Child with SS.
   Nicholas, Vincent Ferrer and a female Saint.
(Environs) s. LUCIA, R. WALL. Madonna and Child with SS. Gimignano, Dominic,
   Lucy, Mary Magdalen, and two other Saints. Predella: Visitation, S.
   Catherine of Siena and Tobias and the Angel.
Siena. s. SPIRITO, CLOISTER. Fresco: Crucifixion. d. 1516.
Vienna. AKADEMIE. 507. Madonna and Child (partial copy of Raphael's *Pala Dei*,
   Pitti, 165). (?)
   DIOZESAN MUSEUM. 22. Holy Family with Infant S. John. E.
Vinci (Empoli). ORATORIO DELL'ANNUNCIATA. Annunciation. *Plate* 1336.
Viterbo. s. MARIA DELLA QUERCE, R. TRANSEPT. Coronation of the Virgin.
   Noli me tangere.

PAOLO di Stefano Badaloni, called SCHIAVO

1397–1478. *Pupil of Masolino.*

Altenburg. 80. Marriage of S. Catherine, with S. Gerard of Villamagna. (?)
Arezzo. s. FRANCESCO. Fresco: Crucifixion (r.).
Athens (Georgia). UNIVERSITY OF GEORGIA, KRESS STUDY COLLECTION. K 1188. Cruci-
   fixion. (?)
Berlin. 1136. Annunciation. *Plate* 654.
   (BERLIN-OST). 1123. Two panels: SS. Jerome and Lawrence. (Wings to 1136
   above?). *Plate* 654.
Castiglione d'Olona. COLLEGIATA, APSE. Frescoes: Scenes from the Lives of SS.
   Stephen and Lawrence [Ordination of S. Stephen, Disputation of S. Stephen,
   S. Stephen before the Tribunal, Martyrdom of S. Stephen, S. Lawrence
   giving Alms, S. Lawrence before Decius, S. Lawrence baptizing] (Remaining
   frescoes probably by Vecchietta; see also Masolino).
Florence. MUSEO DEL CASTAGNO (CENACOLO DI S. APOLLONIA). Fresco: Crucifixion
   with adoring Nuns. Sd and d. 1448. *Plate* 653.
   s. MINIATO AL MONTE, R. WALL. Fresco: Madonna and Child with SS. Francis, Mark,
   John Baptist, John Evangelist and Anthony Abbot. Sd and d. 1436. *Plate* 652.
(Environs) BROZZI, s. LUCIA ALLA SALA.* Fresco: Stigmatization of S. Francis (fr.).

Florence (Environs) (contd.). CASTELLO, TABERNACOLO DELL'OLMO. Fresco: Annunciation with SS. Julian and Ansanus.

— MONTICELLI, S. MARIA DELLA QUERCE. Assumption. Sd and d. 1460.

Frescoes: Annunciation, Nativity, Adoration of the Magi (p.).

Minneapolis (Minn.). INSTITUTE OF ARTS (EX). 23.11. The Redeemer. (?)

New Haven (Conn.). 1871.67. Cassone panel: Garden of Love. (?)

New York. S. H. KRESS FOUNDATION. K 216. Flagellation (r.). (?)

Pisa. MUSEO. Crucifix.

San Miniato al Tedesco (Pisa). S. DOMENICO. Fresco: A Deacon Saint (fr.).

San Piero a Sieve (Mugello). TABERNACOLO DELLE MOZZETTE.* Frescoes. Vault: God the Father, *Agnus Dei*, and the four Evangelists. Altar wall: Madonna and Child with SS. Peter and Paul. Left wall: SS. Francis, John Baptist, and another Saint. Right wall: SS. Cosmas, Damian and another Saint (r.). *Plate 655.*

Sarasota (Fla.). 10, 11. Two panels: Annunciation.

Stia (Casentino). (Environs) S. MARIA DELLE GRAZIE, ALTAR R. Crucifixion (r.).

Vespignano (Vicchio di Mugello). S. MARTINO. *Fresco: Madonna of Humility with two Angels (r.). *Plate 656.*

PARRI SPINELLI or DI SPINELLO

Arezzo 1387–1453. Pupil and assistant of his father Spinello Aretino, he became an extreme representative of the late Gothic style in Tuscany.

Arezzo. 21. Madonna of Mercy with SS. Pergentinus and Laurentianus. Predella: Condemnation, Imprisonment, Beheading and Burial of SS. Pergentinus and Laurentianus. Documented 1435–37. *Plate 427.*

Fragments of frescoes from the Tabernacolo della Compagnia della Nunziata presso il Duomo Vecchio: Christ in Glory sending the Angel Gabriel, four music-making Angels, S. Michael, S. Leonard (Annunciation, Charity, and Hope are destroyed).

PALAZZO DEI PRIORI. Fresco: Christ on the Cross between Virgin and S. John Evangelist. L. *Plate 428.*

— FRATERNITA DEI LAICI. Fresco: Madonna of Mercy. (1448?).

CONSERVATORIO DI S. CATERINA. Fresco: Crucifixion. d. 1444.

S. DOMENICO, R. WALL. Fresco: S. Catherine. E.

— R. OF ENTRANCE. Fresco: Crucifixion with SS. Nicholas and Dominic; lunette: two Stories of S. Nicholas. *Plate 426.*

S. MARIA DELLE GRAZIE. Fresco: Madonna of Mercy. (1428?).

PESELLINO (Francesco di Stefano, called)

1422–57. *Follower of Fra Angelico, Masaccio, and Domenico Veneziano, but chiefly of Filippo Lippi. Between 1453–56 he was in partnership with Piero di Lorenzo Pratese and Zanobi di Migliore, and these or other members of his studio may have been responsible for the numerous copies of his and Filippo Lippi's works which are listed under the name of 'pseudo-Pier Francesco Fiorentino' (q.v.).*

Berea (Ky.). COLLEGE, KRESS STUDY COLLECTION. K 528. Madonna and Child with four Angels. (st.).

Bergamo. 511, 512. Two cassone panels (front and *testata*): Story of Griselda (Decameron X, 10). *Plate 826.*

Berlin. 1651. Crucifixion.

  HERR BRACHT (EX). Madonna and Child. (Version of Boston).

Birmingham (Ala.). MUSEUM OF ART, KRESS COLLECTION. K 540, 541. Two panels: Seven Liberal Arts; Seven Virtues (st.).

Boston (Mass.). ISABELLA GARDNER MUSEUM. Madonna and Child with a Bird.

  Two cassone panels: Triumphs of Petrarch. *Plate 824–5.*

Cambridge (Mass.).1909.32. Madonna and Child with four music-making Angels (st.).

  1916.495. Construction of the Temple of Jerusalem. (Companion to Kansas City and Le Mans).

  1927.198. Madonna and Child with a Pomegranate (c.).

Cetica (Casentino). S. ANGELO, ALTAR R. Madonna and Child with a Pomegranate. L.

Chantilly. 12. Predella panel: Adoration of the Magi (r.). (?)

Corsham Court (Wilts.). LORD METHUEN. Madonna and Child with two Angels and SS. Julian and Francis.

Denver (Col.). MUSEUM OF ART, KRESS COLLECTION. K 485. Madonna and Child.

Dresden. 7A. Madonna and Child with a Pomegranate.

Esztergom (Hungary). KERESTÉNY MÜZEUM. Pinnacle of an altarpiece: Crucifixion. *Plate 821.*

  Madonna and Child. (Version of Boston). *Plate 835.*

Florence. UFFIZI. 8355. Three predella panels (to Lippi, Uffizi 8354): Martyrdom of SS. Cosmas and Damian, Nativity, S. Anthony of Padua and the Miser's Heart. (Companions to Paris). *Plate 829–30.*

  S. MARGHERITA DE' RICCI, 1st ALTAR R. Predella: Scenes from the Life of S. Margaret (p.).

  BERENSON COLLECTION. Madonna and Child with two music-making Angels (st.).

Fontanellato (Parma). CASTELLO. Madonna and four Angels (c.).

Highnam Court (Glos.). GAMBIER-PARRY COLLECTION. Diptych: Annunciation. *Plate 822.*

Kansas City (Mo.). 32.82. David dancing before the Ark. (Companion to Cambridge and Le Mans).

Le Mans. 14, 15. Two panels: Penitence of King David, Death of Absalom. (Companions to Cambridge and Kansas City 32.82).

Lockinge House (Wantage, Berks.). CHRISTOPHER LOYD. Two cassone panels: Five Episodes from the early Life of David, Triumph of David and Saul. *Plate* 827–8.

London. 727 (and 3162, 3230, 4428, and a fragment loaned by H.M. the Queen). Trinity with two Angels and SS. Zeno, Jerome, James the Great and Mamas. (Completed after Pesellino's death, in the studio of Filippo Lippi; predella by Lippi, Fra Diamante and Master of San Miniato). 1455–60. *Plate* 833.

    BUCKINGHAM PALACE, ROYAL COLLECTION. B.P.447. Coronation of the Virgin. Spandrels: Annunciation (g.p.; r.). L.

Lyons. EDOUARD AYNARD (EX). Madonna and Child. *Plate* 834.

Milan. MUSEO POLDI-PEZZOLI. 436. Lunette: Annunciation.

New Haven (Conn.). 1871.40. Annunciation (c. by Neri di Bicci).

New York. 06.1048. Madonna and Child with S. John Baptist and another Saint. (?)

    50.145.30. 'Holford' Madonna and Child with SS. Anthony Abbot, Jerome, a Bishop Saint, George and two female Saints. *Plate* 823.

    HISTORICAL SOCIETY. B–9. S. Jerome between S. Anthony Abbot and S. Francis (c. by Neri di Bicci).

Paris. 1414. Two predella panels (to Lippi, Uffizi 8354): Stigmatization of S. Francis, Dream of the Deacon Justinian. (Companions to Florence, Uffizi 8355.) *Plate* 832.

    1661. Madonna and Child with a Bishop Saint, SS. John Baptist, Anthony Abbot and Francis (g.p.).

Philadelphia (Pa.). MUSEUM OF ART, JOHNSON COLLECTION. 35. Madonna and Child with SS. Jerome and John Baptist. *Plate* 820.

    36. Madonna and Child (c.).

    55. Three Saints (g.p.).

Rome. GALLERIA DORIA PAMPHILJ, PRIVATE APARTMENTS. Two predella panels: S. Silvester before Constantine, S. Silvester and the Dragon. (Companions to Worcester). [*Plate* 162.]

Seebenstein (Austria). LIECHTENSTEIN COLLECTION (EX). Four panels: Quadrivium (st.).

Toledo (Ohio). 44.34. The 'Hainauer-Pratt' Madonna and Child with Infant S. John and two Angels. [*Plate* 161.]

Venice. BIBLIOTECA MARCIANA. Cod. 4519. Full-page miniature: Mars.

Verona. MUSEO DI CASTELVECCHIO. 2148. Predella panel: Man of Sorrows. (?)

Washington (D.C.). 220 (KRESS COLLECTION 230). Crucifixion with SS. Jerome and Francis.

Worcester (Mass.). 1916.12. Predella panel: S. Silvester raising the Bull. (Companion to Rome, Doria Pamphilj).

Zagreb. 18, 19. Two predella panels: S. Francis, S. Martin (c. by Neri di Bicci?).

    1(44). Marriage of S. Catherine (c.).

PIER FRANCESCO FIORENTINO

Dated works 1474–97. Follower of Benozzo Gozzoli; influenced by Neri di Bicci, Andrea del Castagno and Baldovinetti.

Assisi. MRS. F. M. PERKINS. S. Nicholas of Tolentino.

Bayonne. 968. Madonna and Child with an Angel.

Castelnuovo (Val d'Elsa). S. BARBARA, HIGH ALTAR, Madonna and Child with SS. Lawrence, Barbara, Gregory and James. L.

Frescoes: Christ blessing and four Evangelists, *Pietà*, SS. Ansanus, Verdiana, Catherine, Anthony Abbot, Two Prophets.

— IST ALTAR R. Fresco: Madonna and Child with two Angels (or Saints) (r.).

Certaldo (Val d'Elsa). PALAZZO DEI PRIORI, ATRIUM. Fresco: Incredulity of S. Thomas, with S. Jerome. d. 1490. *Plate* 911.

— SALA DELLE UDIENZE. Fresco: Lamentation (r.). d. 1484.

— CAMERA DEI FORESTIERI. Fresco: Madonna and Child (r.) d. 1495.

CAPPELLA DEL PONTE DELL'AGLIENA. Frescoes: Tobias and the Angel; S. Jerome. L. (Destroyed).

Colle Val d'Elsa. MUSEO CIVICO. Madonna and Child with SS. Anthony Abbot, Onuphrius, Catherine, Mary Magdalen, Bernardino and Lawrence (fr.).

S. MARIA IN CANONICA. Madonna and Child with SS. John Baptist, Lawrence, Nicholas and Mark. Predella: S. John Evangelist, Preaching of S. John Baptist, Martyrdom of S. Lawrence, Adoration of the Magi, Martyrdom of S. Mark, S. Nicholas and the three Maidens, S. Luke. Pilasters of frame: Six Saints.

VIA GOZZINA. Fresco in tabernacle: Madonna and two Bishop Saints. (Destroyed).

VIA DELLA PIEVE DEL PIANO. Frescoes in tabernacle: Annunciation and various fragments. (Destroyed).

Empoli. 22. Madonna and Child with SS. Matthew, William, Barbara and Sebastian. 1474. *Plate* 907.

30. Madonna and Child.

Figline. S. FRANCESCO (MISERICORDIA), CLOISTER. *Fresco lunette: Madonna and Child with SS. Sebastian and Bartholomew (r.).

Florence. MUSEO DEL CASTAGNO (CENACOLO DI S. APOLLONIA). Detached fresco: S. Eustace and four Scenes from his Legend [S. Eustace hunting the Stag, Vision of S. Eustace, Children of S. Eustace carried off by Beasts, Martyrdom of S. Eustace]. d. 1462. (?)

London. VICTORIA AND ALBERT MUSEUM. 196–1869. Fresco: SS. John Baptist and Dorothy.

Montefortino (Amandola, Marche). PINACOTECA. Madonna and Child with Tobias and the Archangels Raphael and Michael. Sd and d. 1497.

New York. MICHAEL DREICER (EX). Madonna and Child with two Angels.

Paris. MUSÉES NATIONAUX (CAMPANA 162, DEP. PERPIGNAN). Madonna and Child with SS. Lawrence, Peter Martyr, John Evangelist and Blaise.

Perpignan. 116. See Paris, Musées Nationaux.

San Gimignano. 27. Detached fresco: Man of Sorrows. d. 1497.

    28. Madonna and Child with SS. Justus and Thomas Aquinas. d. 1477.

    29. Madonna and Child with SS. Bartholomew and Anthony Abbot. Predella: Man of Sorrows and four Dominican Saints. d. 1490.

    30. Fresco: Trinity, surrounded by six small Scenes [Annunciation, *Pietà*, SS. James and Ansanus, Way to Calvary, Madonna and Child with S. Anne, Tobias and the Angel with SS. John Baptist and Sebastian]. 1497.

    Fresco: Madonna and Child.

    COLLEGIATA, NAVE. Monochrome fresco decoration: Putti with garlands and twelve roundels with Apostles. 1474–75.

    — TRIUMPHAL ARCH. Fresco: Man of Sorrows. 1474–75.

    — L. AISLE. Fresco lunettes (above arches): Abraham and six Prophets.

    S. AGOSTINO, 1ST ALTAR R. Madonna and Child with SS. Stephen, Peter Martyr, Bartholomew, Martin, Augustine, Andrew, Vincent Ferrer, Lawrence and Donor. Pilasters: Eight Saints. Predella: S. Bartolo, S. Catherine of Siena, Ascension, Man of Sorrows, Resurrection, S. Margaret of Hungary and S. Fina. Sd and d. 1494. *Plate* 912.

    S. JACOPO, PILLAR R. Fresco: S. James.

    (Environs) S. LUCIA. Fresco: Crucifixion.

    — S. MARIA ASSUNTA A PANCOLE, HIGH ALTAR. Fresco: Madonna nursing the Child.

Siena. 149–152. Four panels: Triumphs of Petrarch.

    209. Madonna adoring the Child with SS. Francis and Dominic.

Ulignano (Val d'Elsa). PIEVE. Madonna and Child with SS. Bartholomew and Stephen.

Villamagna (Volterra). MADONNA DELLE NEVI. Fresco: Madonna and Child.

Volterra. PALAZZO DEI PRIORI, STAIRCASE. Fresco: Crucifixion with SS. Francis and John Baptist (r.).

    — ANTICAMERA SINDACALE. Fresco: Crucifixion (r.).

Zagreb. 26. Madonna and Child with two Cherubim. (?)

Homeless. Madonna and Child with Tobias and the Angel, S. Anthony Abbot and a Bishop Saint. d. 1477. *Plate* 910.

'Pseudo PIER FRANCESCO FIORENTINO'

A craftsman of considerable skill, particularly as a flower painter, who made a business of copying and piecing together figures from Fra Filippo, Pesellino and their followers. It is barely conceivable that, left to his resources, he designed and painted the crude works due to the real Pier Francesco Fiorentino. (The four principal prototypes of these works were the Pesellino designs best represented at Boston, Toledo, and formerly in the Aynard collection at Lyons, and the Lippi Adoration at Berlin. These were combined in various ways. Where a relationship to one of these pictures is mentioned below, it is intended to refer only to the figures of the Madonna and Child. If more than one prototype is indicated, the first-named refers to the Madonna and Child and those which follow to subsidiary figures such as S. John Baptist and Angels).

Ajaccio (Corsica). 189. Madonna adoring the Child, with Infant S. John and two Angels. (Based on Lippi, Berlin 69 and Pesellino at Toledo).

Altenburg. 97. Madonna adoring the Child with Infant S. John. (Based on Lippi, Uffizi 8350).

Arezzo. MUSEO CIVICO. (INV. OGGETTI D'ARTE 467). Tondo: Madonna and Child with Infant St. John.

Balcarres (Fife. Scotland). EARL OF CRAWFORD AND BALCARRES. Madonna and Child. (Based on Pesellino at Boston).

Baltimore (Md.). WALTERS ART GALLERY. 511. Madonna and Child against a Hedge of Roses. (Based on Aynard Pesellino).

637. Madonna adoring the Child with Infant S. John. (Based on Lippi, Berlin 69).

695. Madonna and Child with a Bird. (Based on Pesellino at Boston).

726. Madonna and Child with a Cherry. (Based on Aynard Pesellino).

1028. Madonna and Child with a Bird against a Hedge of Roses. (Based on Pesellino at Boston).

Bergamo. 513. SS. Francis and Jerome in the Wilderness (c. after Lippi at Altenburg).

Berlin. 71A. Madonna and Child against a Hedge of Roses. (Based on Aynard Pesellino). (Destroyed 1945.)

Brooklyn (N.Y.). 33.3. Madonna and Child with Infant S. John and five Angels. (Based on Pesellino at Toledo).

Brussels. PHILIPPE STOCLET. Madonna and Child with a Bird against a Hedge of Roses. (Based on Pesellino at Boston).

Budapest. 2539. Madonna and Child with Infant S. John and an Angel. (Based on Pesellino at Boston and Toledo and Lippi, Berlin 69).

50.752. Madonna adoring the Child, with Infant S. John, S. Catherine and five Angels. (Based on Lippi, Uffizi 1598 and Munich 647). *Plate 841.*

Cambridge (Mass.). 1904.17. Madonna and Child with Infant S. John. (Based on Pesellino at Boston).

Cambridge (Mass.) (contd.). 1943.109. Madonna adoring the Child with Infant S. John and two Angels. (See Cleveland).

Castell' Arquato (Piacenza). MUSEO PARROCCHIALE. Madonna adoring the Child. (Based on Lippi, Berlin 69).

Castiglion Fiorentino. PINACOTECA. Madonna adoring the Child with Infant S. John.

Cleveland (Ohio). 16.802. Madonna adoring the Child with three Angels. (Versions at Cambridge, 1943.109; Florence, Museo Horne; New Haven, 1943.226; New York, formerly Hurd; Philadelphia, Johnson Collection, 40; and Zurich). *Plate* 840.

Columbus (Ohio). GALLERY OF FINE ARTS. Madonna and Child with Infant S. John. (Based on Pesellino at Boston).

Detroit (Mich.). 89.14. Madonna and Child with Infant S. John and an Angel. (based on Pesellino at Boston and Toledo and Lippi, Berlin 69).

Dijon. 1313. Madonna adoring the Child with Infant S. John and an Angel. (Based on Lippi, Berlin 69).

Edinburgh. 1250. Madonna and Child with Infant S. John. (Based on Aynard Pesellino).

Florence. ACCADEMIA. 8158. Madonna adoring the Child. (Based on Lippi, Berlin 69).

UFFIZI. 486. Madonna and Child with three Angels. d. (on back) 1459. (Based on Pesellino at Toledo). *Plate* 836.

PITTI. Tondo: Madonna with Infant S. John.

MUSEO BARDINI. 1131. Madonna adoring the Child with Infant S. John. (Based on Lippi, Berlin 69).

1286. Madonna and Child with Infant S. John. (Based on Aynard Pesellino; figure of S. John a later addition).

1290. Madonna adoring the Child with Infant S. John. (Based on Lippi, Berlin 69).

MUSEO NAZIONALE DEL BARGELLO, CARRAND COLLECTION. 15. Madonna and Child with Infant S. John.

MUSEO HORNE. 62. Madonna adoring the Child with three Angels. (See Cleveland.)

PALAZZO RICCARDI, CAPPELLA MEDICI. Nativity with Infant S. John (c. after Lippi, Berlin 69).

ORATORIO DELLE STIMMATE (S. LORENZO). Madonna and Child.

S. GIOVANNINO DEI CAVALIERI, SACRISTY. Madonna and Child.

(Environs) VILLA SCHIFANOIA. Tondo: Madonna adoring the Child with Infant S. John and two Angels. (Based on Lippi, Uffizi 8350).

Frankfurt am Main. 1089. Madonna and Child with Angels.

Glasgow. 914. Madonna and Child with three Angels. (Based on Pesellino at Toledo).

Göttingen. 142. Annunciation (c. after Filippo Lippi, Galleria Doria Pamphilj, Rome).

Gubbio. 49. Madonna adoring the Child with Infant S. John. (Based on Lippi, Berlin 69).

Highnam Court (Glos.). GAMBIER-PARRY COLLECTION. Madonna and Child with Infant S. John. (Based on Pesellino at Boston).

Madonna adoring the Child with two Angels. (Version at New Haven, 1871.43).

Lille. 21. Madonna and Child with an Angel.

Liverpool. 2797. Head of a Woman (possibly c. of lost portrait of Lucrezia Buti by Fra Filippo; cp. Munich 647).

2890. Madonna and Child with Infant S. John and three Angels. (Based on Pesellino at Boston and Toledo and Lippi, Berlin 69).

London. 1199. Tondo: Madonna and Child with Infant S. John and an Angel. (Based on Aynard Pesellino).

VICTORIA AND ALBERT MUSEUM. C.A.J.99. Madonna and Child with a Cherry. (Based on Aynard Pesellino).

W. E. GRAY (EX). Madonna adoring the Child with Infant S. John. (Based on Lippi, Berlin 69).

Lugano. THYSSEN COLLECTION. 327. Madonna adoring the Child with Infant S. John and three Angels. (Based on Lippi, Berlin 69 and Pesellino at Toledo).

Maidenhead (Berks.). SIR THOMAS MERTON. Madonna and Child against a Hedge of Roses. (Based on Pesellino at Toledo).

Madonna and Child against a Hedge of Roses. (Based on Pesellino at Boston).

Melun. See Paris, Musées Nationaux.

Nancy. MUSÉE. 9 (CAMPANA 146). Madonna and Child. (Based on Aynard Pesellino).

Narbonne. 431. Tondo: Madonna adoring the Child with Infant S. John, two Angels and God the Father. (Based on Lippi, Berlin 69).

New Haven (Conn.). 1871.43. Madonna adoring the Child with S. Catherine and four Angels (perhaps after a lost Fra Filippo; version at Highnam Court).

1943.225. Madonna and Child with two Angels. (Based on Pesellino at Toledo).

1943.226. Madonna adoring the Child with Infant S. John and two Angels. (See Cleveland).

New York. 41.90.9. Madonna adoring the Child with Infant S. John and two Angels. (Based on Lippi, Berlin 69, and Pesellino at Toledo).

41.116.1. Madonna and Child. (Based on Pesellino at Boston).

S. H. KRESS FOUNDATION. K 57. Madonna adoring the Child with Infant S. John (r.). (Based on Lippi, Berlin 69).

JULES S. BACHE (EX). Madonna adoring the Child with Infant S. John and three Angels. (Based on Lippi, Berlin 69).

R. M. HURD (EX). Madonna and Child with two Angels. (Based on Pesellino at Toledo).

Madonna adoring the Child with Infant S. John and an Angel. (See Cleveland).

HENRY LUCE. Madonna and Child against a Hedge of Roses. (Based on Pesellino at Toledo).

Palermo. CHIARAMONTE BORDONARO COLLECTION. Madonna adoring the Child with two Angels.

Paris. MUSÉES NATIONAUX (CAMPANA 224). Tondo: Madonna and Child with Infant S. John and three Angels. (Based on Pesellino at Toledo).

LOUVRE. 1695. Madonna and Child. (Based on Pesellino at Boston).

MUSÉE JACQUEMART-ANDRÉ. 899. A Hedge of Roses. (Painted background to stucco relief of the Madonna and Child).

1037. Madonna and Child with Infant S. John, two Angels and God the Father blessing. (Based on Pesellino at Boston and Toledo, and Lippi at Berlin 69).

Philadelphia (Pa.). ACADEMY OF FINE ARTS. Madonna and Child. (Based on Aynard Pesellino).

MUSEUM OF ART, JOHNSON COLLECTION. 40. Madonna adoring the Child with two Angels.

41. Madonna and Child against a Hedge of Roses. (Based on Aynard Pesellino.)

Richmond (Surrey). COOK COLLECTION (EX). 26. Tondo: Madonna and Child with Infant S. John and three Angels.

San Marino (Cal.). HUNTINGTON MUSEUM. Madonna and Child with Infant S. John. (Based on Pesellino at Boston).

Santa Barbara (Cal.). UNIVERSITY OF CALIFORNIA, FRANCIS SEDGWICK COLLECTION. Madonna and Child. (Based on Pesellino at Boston). *Plate 837.*

Sao Paulo. 126. Tondo: Madonna and Child with Infant S. John and an Angel. (Based on Lippi, Munich 647).

Sinalunga (Val di Chiana). S. MARTINO, SACRISTY. Madonna adoring the Child with Infant S. John and an Angel. (Based on Lippi, Uffizi 8350).

Todi. 151. Madonna and Child.

Tulsa (Okla.). PHILBROOK ART CENTER, KRESS COLLECTION. K 321. Madonna and Child with a Bird against a Hedge of Roses. (Based on Pesellino at Boston).

Venice. CA' D'ORO. Madonna adoring the Child (c. after Filippo Lippi).

Washington (D.C.). 646 (WIDENER COLLECTION). Madonna and Child against a Hedge of Roses. (Based on Aynard Pesellino).

Zagreb. 23. Madonna and Child with Infant S. John and God the Father blessing. (Based on Pesellino at Boston).

Zurich. 1625. Madonna adoring the Child with Infant S. John and Angels. (See Cleveland).

Homeless. Madonna and Child with Infant S. John, another Saint and Angels. (Based on Pesellino at Boston). *Plate 839.*

PIERO DI COSIMO

1462–1521. *Pupil of Cosimo Rosselli. Influenced by Verrocchio, Leonardo, Signorelli, Filippino Lippi and Lorenzo di Credi.*

Amsterdam. 1875 B–1. Profile portrait of Francesco Giamberti. *Plate* 1194.
   1875 B–2. Portrait of Giuliano da San Gallo.
Assisi. MRS. F. M. PERKINS. Tondo: Nativity. (?)
Beaumesnil. M. FÜRSTEMBERGER. Invention of the Flute. (?)
Berlin. 107. Venus, Mars and Cupid. *Plates* 1188–9.
   90A. Madonna and Child. (?). (Destroyed 1945.)
   204. Adoration of the Shepherds. (Destroyed 1945.) *Plate* 1191.
Borgo San Lorenzo (Mugello). ORATORIO DEL CROCIFISSO DEI MIRACOLI (EX).
   Madonna with SS. John Baptist and Thomas. L.
Cambridge (Mass.). 1940.85. Misfortunes of Silenus (u.; companion to Worcester).
   SYDNEY J. FREEDBERG. Two cassone panels: Tritons and Naiads (r.).
Cape Town (South Africa). ROBINSON COLLECTION. Cassone panel: Arrival at
   Colchis and Jason before Aeetes (landscape by Bartolomeo di Giovanni; com-
   panion to Bartolomeo di Giovanni at Cape Town). d. 1487.
Chantilly. 13. Profile Portrait of Simonetta Vespucci, called 'La Bella Simonetta'.
   [*Plate* 189.]
Dresden. 20. Tondo: Holy Family with Infant S. John and two Angels. *Plate* 1187.
Dulwich (London). 258. Portrait of a young Man.
Edinburgh. 1633. Lunette: Two censing Angels holding a Crown.
Fiesole. S. FRANCESCO, L. WALL. Immaculate Conception. L.
Florence. PITTI. 370. Head of a Saint.
   604. Profile Portrait of a Woman.
   UFFIZI. 506. Immaculate Conception, with SS. John Evangelist, Dominic, Cather-
   ine, Margaret, Antoninus and Peter. *Plate* 1201.
   1536. Perseus freeing Andromeda. L. *Plate* 1204.
   3885. Madonna and Child with two Angels (c. of Venice, Cini).
   MUSEO HORNE. 31. Tondo: S. Jerome in the Wilderness.
   32. Tondo: Rest on the Flight into Egypt (c.).
   5062. Virgin and SS. John Evangelist, John Baptist and Jerome adoring the
   Cross (r.). (?)
   PALAZZO DAVANZATI. 509, 510, 514. Three panels: Sacrifice for the Liberation of
   Andromeda, Perseus freeing Andromeda, Phineas at the Wedding of Perseus
   and Andromeda. L.
   SPEDALE DEGLI INNOCENTI, PINACOTECA. Madonna and Child with six Angels and
   SS. Peter, Catherine, John Evangelist and another female Saint.
   Madonna of the Pomegranate.
   S. LORENZO. Nativity with SS. Julian and Francis (r.). L.

Hartford (Conn.). 32.1. Fall of Vulcan. (Companion to Ottawa). [*Plate* 188.]

Honolulu (Hawaii). ACADEMY OF ARTS, KRESS COLLECTION. K 1433 S. John
   Evangelist (p.; r.).

Leningrad. 29. Tondo: Madonna and Child with Infant S. John (c. of Rome,
   Borghese).

London. 698. Death of Procris.

   895. Portrait of a Man in Armour. After 1504.

   4890. Cassone panel: Battle of the Centaurs and Lapiths. *Plate* 1190.

   WALLACE COLLECTION. 556. Triumph of Love. Not after 1488. (?)

Milan. DUCA GALLARATI SCOTTI. Tondo: Madonna and Child.

Munich. 8973. Story of Prometheus. (Companion to Strasbourg 225.)

New Haven (Conn.). 1871.72. Portrait of a Woman with a Rabbit. L.

New York. 22.60.52. Profile Head of the young S. John Baptist.

   75.7.1, 75.7.2. Two panels: The Hunt, Return from the Hunt. *Plate* 1196.

Oakly Park (Shrops). EARL OF PLYMOUTH. Portrait of a young Man.

Ottawa. 4287. Vulcan and Aeolus. (Companion to Hartford.) *Plate* 1195.

Oxford. ASHMOLEAN. 328. A Forest Fire. *Plate* 1197.

   CHRIST CHURCH LIBRARY. 56. Tondo: *Pietà*.

Paris. 1274. Profile Head of the young S. John Baptist.

   1662. Madonna and Child with a Book and a Dove. *Plate* 1193.

Perugia. 67D. *Pietà*.

Philadelphia (Pa.). MUSEUM OF ART. JOHNSON COLLECTION. 76. Madonna and Child
   (fr.).

Rome. GALLERIA BORGHESE. 343. Tondo: Madonna adoring the Child with Infant
   S. John and two Angels.

   GALLERIA NAZIONALE (PALAZZO BARBERINI). F.N. 10045. Portrait of a Woman as
   S. Mary Magdalen.

Saint Louis (Mo.). 1.40. Madonna and Child with SS. Peter, Dominic, Nicholas
   and John Baptist. Predella: S. Dominic and the Miracle of the Book, Meeting
   of the young Christ and S. John, S. Nicholas commanding the Felling of a
   Tree sacred to Diana.

San Diego (Cal.). FINE ARTS GALLERY. Tondo: Madonna and Child with Infant S.
   John and four Angels.

São Paulo. 127. Tondo: Madonna and Child with Infant S. John and an Angel.
   Plate 1198.

Sarasota (Fla.). 22. Building of a Palace. (?)

Stockholm. 1738. Tondo: Madonna and Child with Infant S. John (c.).

   ROYAL PALACE. Madonna and Child. (Version of Filippino Lippi, New York,
   49.7.10). *Plate* 1192.

Strasbourg. 224. Tondo: Madonna and Child with Infant S. John, and SS. Jerome
   and Bernard in the background.

   225. Story of Prometheus. (Companion to Munich). *Plate* 1202.

Toledo (Ohio). 37.1. Tondo: Madonna adoring the Child.

Vaduz. LIECHTENSTEIN COLLECTION. 264. Madonna and Child with Infant S. John. *Plate* 1200.

— (EX). Tondo: A Landscape.

Venice. CONTE VITTORIO CINI. Madonna and Child with two Angels. *Plate* 1203.

Vienna. LANCKORONSKI COLLECTION. Tondo: Madonna and Child with Infant S. John and two Angels.

Washington (D.C.). 271 (KRESS COLLECTION 307). An Allegory.

443 (KRESS COLLECTION 1057). Apollo and Marsyas. (?)

454 (KRESS COLLECTION 1086). Visitation, with SS. Nicholas and Anthony Abbot. [*Plate* 187.]

464 (KRESS COLLECTION 1096). Tondo: Nativity with Infant S. John and an Angel.

Worcester (Mass.). 1937.76. Discovery of Honey. (Companion to Cambridge 1940.85). *Plate* 1199.

PIETRO DI MINIATO

1366–ca 1450. Documented 1409–27, mainly active in Prato. Follower of Agnolo Gaddi.

Florence (Environs). S. MARTINO A TERENZANO, R. WALL. SS. Martin, John Baptist and Lawrence. (?)

— VICCHIO DI RIMAGGIO, S. LORENZO. Marriage of S. Catherine, with SS. Anthony Abbot, Nicholas, Donatus of Fiesole, Margaret. Below: SS. Francis, Andrew, Peter, Lawrence and female Saint (enlarged and r.). (?)

Pistoia. S. FRANCESCO, SACRISTY. Large fresco lunette: Nativity, Crucifixion, Lamentation. (?) *Plates* 397–8.

Prato. PINACOTECA. Polyptych (from Convent of S. Matteo): Coronation of the Virgin, SS. Matthias and Matthew, SS. Peter and Paul. Two predellas: Epiphany and nine Scenes from the Lives of the above mentioned Saints. Documented 1412. *Plate* 399.

CONVENT OF S. MATTEO. Fresco: S. Dominic's Meal.

DUOMO, FIRST CHAPEL L. OF CHOIR (CAPPELLA MANASSEI). Frescoes by Agnolo Gaddi (partly executed by Pietro di Miniato).

POLLAJUOLO, Antonio and Piero

The elder brother, Antonio, 1429–98, sculptor, goldsmith and painter, developed under the influence of Donatello, Andrea del Castagno and Baldovinetti. The younger brother, Piero, ca 1441–96, pupil of Baldovinetti, chiefly worked on Antonio's designs. Where the authorship can be clearly distinguished as by either of the brothers separately, the fact is indicated.

Assisi. S. FRANCESCO, TREASURY. Embroidery: Sixtus IV kneeling before S. Francis; on the border, Madonna and Child and fourteen Saints (probably on Piero's design). *Plate 781.*

Berlin. 73. Annunciation. (Piero). *Plates 769, 773.*

    73A. David. (Antonio). [*Plate 165.*]

    1614. Profile portrait of a Woman. (Piero). E.

Boston. ISABELLA GARDNER MUSEUM. Profile portrait of a Woman. (Antonio). *Plate 777.*

Colle Val d'Elsa. PALAZZO VESCOVILE. Communion of S. Mary Magdalen (from Staggia). (Executed by Piero on Antonio's design). *Plate 768.*

Florence. UFFIZI. 495. Hope (st.). 1470.

    496. Justice (st.). 1470.

    497. Temperance (st.). 1470.

    498. Faith (Piero). 1470.

    499. Charity (st.; on verso, Antonio's design). 1469.

    738. Profile portrait of Gian Galeazzo Sforza (Antonio). *Plate 776.*

    1478. Hercules and Antaeus. (Companion to 8268; by Antonio). ca 1460. [*Plate 166.*]

    1491. Profile portrait of a Woman (Piero; r.).

    1610. Prudence. (Companion to 495–99 above and to Botticelli, Uffizi 1606; by Piero). 1470. *Plate 780.*

    1617. SS. Eustace, James and Vincent. (By Piero on Antonio's design; from S. Miniato al Monte). 1467. *Plate 772.*

    3388. Miniature: Profile portrait of a Woman. (Piero).

    8268. Hercules and the Hydra. (Companion to 1478 above; by Antonio). ca 1460. *Plate 765.*

    MUSEO BARDINI. 1010. S. Michael (r.).

S. MARIA DEL FIORE (DUOMO), MUSEO DELL'OPERA. Embroideries on Antonio's design: twenty-seven scenes from the Life of S. John the Baptist. ca 1466–80. *Plates 783–784.*

S. MINIATO AL MONTE, CAPPELLA DEI PORTOGHESI. Fresco around window: Two Angels drawing aside curtains (Antonio). 1467. *Plate 771.*

S. NICCOLÒ, SACRISTY. Lunette fresco: *Madonna della Cintola* (r.; by Piero). E.

(Environs) TORRE DEL GALLO. Frescoes: Dancing nudes (r.; by Antonio). *Plate 770.*

London. 292. Martyrdom of S. Sebastian. (Antonio). 1475. [*Plate* 167.] *Plates* 785, 786.

928. Apollo and Daphne (Antonio). *Plate* 766.

Milan. MUSEO POLDI PEZZOLI. 157. Profile portrait of a Woman (Piero). E. *Plate* 775.

New Haven (Conn.). 1871.42. Rape of Dejaneira (Antonio, r.). Before 1467. *Plate* 767.

New York. 50.135.3. Profile portrait of a Woman (Piero).

Pistoia. S. DOMENICO. Fresco: S. Jerome (fr.). *Plate* 782.

San Gimignano. S. AGOSTINO, HIGH ALTAR. Coronation of the Virgin with SS. Fina, Nicholas of Bari, Augustine, Gimignano, Jerome and Nicholas of Tolentino. Sd by Piero and d. 1483. *Plate* 787.

Staggia. S. MARIA ASSUNTA. See Colle Val d'Elsa.

Strasbourg. 219. Madonna and Child (Piero; destroyed by fire in 1950). *Plate* 779.

Turin. 117. Tobias and the Archangel. *Plate* 778.

West Orange (N.J.). NILS B. HERZLOFF. Profile portrait of a Woman (Piero). E. *Plate* 774.

SCULPTURE (by Antonio)

Florence. MUSEO NAZIONALE DEL BARGELLO. Bronze: Hercules and Antaeus.
Terracotta: Bust of a young Warrior.
Marble: Bust of a Man. d. 1495.
S. MARIA DEL FIORE (DUOMO), MUSEO DELL'OPERA. Silver Crucifix.

Rome. VATICAN, GROTTE VATICANE. Bronze: Tomb of Sixtus IV. Sd and d. 1493. *Plate* 788.

— S. PIETRO, L. NAVE. Bronze: Tomb of Innocent VIII. 1492–98.

PONTORMO (Jacopo Carrucci)

1494–1556. Pupil of Andrea del Sarto; influenced by the graphic art of Dürer, and by Michelangelo.

Amsterdam. 1896 E–2. Portrait of a Woman seated at a Table.

Baltimore (Md.). WALTERS ART GALLERY. 596. Portrait of a Woman with a Child, called 'Maria Salviati and the young Cosimo'. *Plate* 1431.

Bergamo. 561. Portrait of a young Man, called 'Baccio Bandinelli'.

Berlin. S.2. Portrait of a young Man with a Book.

Bordeaux. PIERRE CHAPANNAN (EX). Portrait of a Man with a Letter.

Borgo San Sepolcro. PINACOTECA COMUNALE. Martyrdom of S. Quentin (g.p.).

Dayton (Ohio). DAYTON ART INSTITUTE. Portrait of a Man with Pen and Book.

Dublin. 103, 104. Predella: *Pietà* and SS. Francis, Lawrence, Peter, Apollonia, Jerome and Benedict. (Companions to Warwick Castle).

Empoli. MUSEO DELLA COLLEGIATA. Two panels (from S. Michele, Pontorme): SS. John Evangelist and Michael. 1518–19.

Florence. GALLERIE. Madonna and Child. E.

　1532. *Desco da parto:* Birth of S. John Baptist.

　ACCADEMIA. 1570. Venus and Cupid (on Michelangelo's cartoon). ca 1533. *Plate* 1224.

　9385. Fresco: *L'Ospedale di S. Matteo*, with a scene from the life of a female Saint. E.

　PITTI. 182. Decimation of the Theban Legion. *Plate* 1429.

　249. Profile portrait of a Man called 'Francesco da Castiglione'.

　379. Adoration of the Magi. ca 1523.

　769. Portrait of a Woman.

　UFFIZI. 743. Portrait of a Musician, called 'Francesco dell'Ajolle'.

　1483. Portrait of a Man.

　1517. Expulsion from Paradise.

　1525. Decimation of the Theban Legion.

　1538. Madonna and Child with SS. Jerome and Francis. *Plate* 1423.

　1556. Leda (after Michelangelo). ca 1533–34. (?)

　3565. Portrait of a Woman, called 'Maria Salviati'.

　3574. Portrait of Cosimo de' Medici, *Pater Patriae*.

　4347. Madonna and Child with Infant S. John (or *Caritas*).

　8379. S. Anthony Abbot.

　8740. Supper at Emmaus (from Certosa del Galluzzo). d. 1525.

　— GABINETTO DEI DISEGNI. 91466. *Chiaroscuro:* Isaac, Jacob and Rebecca. L. *Plate* 1436.

PALAZZO RICCARDI, MUSEO MEDICEO. Profile portrait of Cosimo I as a Boy.

PALAZZO VECCHIO. Fragments of the *Carro della Moneta*: Visitation, Baptism of Christ, SS. John Baptist, Matthew, Zenobius and John Evangelist (r.). E.

— (LOESER BEQUEST). Sibyl.

SS. ANNUNZIATA, FAÇADE. Fresco: Faith and Charity and Coat of Arms of Pope Leo X (r.). 1513–14.

— ATRIUM. Fresco: Visitation. 1516. *Plate* 1419.

— CAPPELLA DI SAN LUCA. Fresco (from S. Ruffillo): Madonna and Child with SS. Lucy, Agnes (?), Zacharias and Michael. E. *Plate* 1418.

S. FELICITA, 1ST CHAPEL R. (CAPPONI). Deposition. 1526–28. [*Plate* 228.] Tondi (in spandrels): Four Evangelists (with Bronzino). Fresco: Annunciation. *Plate* 1426.

S. MARIA NOVELLA, CAPPELLA DEL PAPA (SCUOLA SOTTUFFICIALE CARABINIERI). Frescoes. Lunette: S. Veronica. Vault: God the Father, Putti with Passion Symbols in roundels, Putti with Arms of Leo X in squares. (See also Ridolfo Ghirlandajo). 1515. *Plate* 1417.

S. MICHELE VISDOMINI, 2ND ALTAR R. Holy Family with SS. John Evangelist, Infant John Baptist, Francis and James. d. 1518. *Plate* 1421.

SPEDALE DEGLI INNOCENTI, PINACOTECA. *Madonna della Carità* (p.).

CONTE FERRANTE CAPPONI. Madonna and Child (r.).

CONTINI BONACOSSI COLLECTION. Portrait of a bearded Man.
Portrait of a Boy (on tile.)

GALLERIA CORSINI. 141. Madonna and Child with Infant S. John. *Plate* 1424.

185. Madonna and Child with Infant S. John.

PALAZZO GUICCIARDINI (EX). Portrait of a young Man with a Lute.

(Environs) CARMIGNANO, PIEVE, 2nd ALTAR R. Visitation. *Plate* 1428.

— CERTOSA DEL GALLUZZO. Five frescoes: Agony in the Garden, Christ before
Pilate, Way to Calvary, Lamentation, Resurrection (r.). ca 1522–27. *Plate* 1427.

— POGGIO A CAIANO, VILLA MEDICEA. Fresco lunette: Vertumnus and Pomona. 1521.
[*Plate* 229.]

— VIA DI BOLDRONE. *Tabernacle fresco: Crucifixion, and SS. Julian and Augustine.

Frankfurt am Main. 1136. Portrait of a Woman with a Lapdog. [*Plate* 230.]

Genoa. PALAZZO BIANCO. 262. Portrait of a Man with a Glove.

Gotha. 506. Lady with Book and Flower. (?)

Grey Walls (Henfield, Sussex). LADY SALMOND. Three panels with Episodes from the
Story of Joseph: Joseph sold to Potiphar, Joseph revealing himself to his
Brothers, and the Baker conducted to his Execution. After 1515. *Plate* 1420.

Hamburg. KUNSTHALLE, WEDELLS COLLECTION. Bust of Man writing. (?)

Hanover. 279. Penitent S. Jerome (u.).

Keir (Dunblane, Scotland). LT. COL. WILLIAM STIRLING. Portrait of Bartolomeo
Compagni. d. 1549.

Leningrad. 5527. Holy Family with young S. John.

London. 1131. Joseph in Egypt. After 1515.

3941. A Discussion. *Plate* 1422.

LORD BURTON (EX). Portrait of a young Man with a Book and a Sword.

Lucca. 5. Portrait of a young Man, called 'Giuliano' or 'Alessandro de' Medici'.
Plate 1432.

Lugano. THYSSEN COLLECTION. 332. Portrait of a Woman. (?)

Lwow (Lemberg). MUSEUM. Madonna and Child with Infant S. John. (?)

Milan. CASTELLO SFORZESCO (TRIVULZIO COLLECTION). 547. Portrait of a Boy with a
Book.

Munich. W.A.F.776. Holy Family with two figures in the background (c.). Sd.

New York. CHAUNCEY STILLMAN. Portrait of a young Man, called 'the Halberdier'.
Plate 1430.

Nivaagaard (Copenhagen). HAGE COLLECTION. Portrait of a Boy. E. (?)

Oxford. CHRIST CHURCH LIBRARY. 61. Portrait of a Man with two Statuettes (r.). (?)

Paris. 1240. Madonna and Child with SS. Anne, Sebastian, Peter, Benedict and
Philip.

1516A. Portrait of a Man, called 'Andrea Fausti'.

MUSÉE JACQUEMART-ANDRÉ. 659. Portrait of elderly Lady. L. (?)

Philadelphia (Pa.). MUSEUM OF ART, JOHNSON COLLECTION. 83. Portrait of Alessandro de' Medici (r.). 1534–35. *Plate* 1433.

Rome. DELEGAZIONE PER LE RESTITUZIONI (EX-BARBERINI). Pygmalion. *Plate* 1435.

    GALLERIA BORGHESE. 408. Portrait of Cardinal Marcello Cervini degli Spannocchi. L. (?)

    GALLERIA NAZIONALE (PALAZZO BARBERINI). F.N. 577. Portrait of a Man (r.). (?)

    PALAZZO QUIRINALE. Three tapestries: Jacob's Lament, Joseph and the Wife of Potiphar, Benjamin at the Court of Pharaoh. (Companions to Bronzino, Quirinale, and Florence, Bargello and Palazzo Vecchio). 1546–53. *Plate* 1437–8.

    MAINONI–BALDOVINETTI COLLECTION. Portrait of a Man.

San Francisco (Cal.). DE YOUNG MEMORIAL MUSEUM, KRESS COLLECTION. K 1732. Madonna and Child with two Angels.

Settimo (Pisa). S. BENEDETTO, HIGH ALTAR. S. Peter and Bd. Philip Benizzi. L.

Turin. 122. Portrait of a seated Woman. (?)

Vaduz. LIECHTENSTEIN COLLECTION. 12. S. John Baptist. E. (?).

Varramista (Pisa). PIAGGIO COLLECTION (S.A.P.I.). Madonna and Child with Infant S. John.

Venice. CONTE VITTORIO CINI. Two young Men with a Letter. *Plate* 1425.

Vienna. 48. Portrait of an Old Woman with a Book. L.

Warwick Castle. EARL OF WARWICK. Two predella panels: S. Peter and a Bishop Saint. (Companions to Dublin).

Washington (D.C.). 480 (KRESS COLLECTION 1127). Holy Family with S. Elizabeth and Infant S. John.

    647 (WIDENER COLLECTION). Portrait of Lady with lapdog.

    1609 (KRESS COLLECTION 2154). Allegorical Portrait of Dante.

    1635 (KRESS COLLECTION 1902). Portrait of Monsignor Giovanni della Casa. L.

Homeless. *Noli me tangere.* (On Michelangelo's cartoon.) 1531. *Plate* 1434.

PUCCIO DI SIMONE

Follower of Bernardo Daddi, active in the middle of the XIV century.

Florence. ACCADEMIA. 8569. Polyptych: Madonna and Child with SS. Lawrence, Onuphrius, James and Bartholomew (r.). Sd. *Plates* 188–190.

PULIGO, Domenico

1492–1527. Pupil of Ridolfo Ghirlandajo, influenced by Fra Bartolommeo and close follower of Andrea del Sarto.

Alnwick Castle (Northd.). DUKE OF NORTHUMBERLAND. Portrait of a Man with a
    Letter. (?)
Anghiari (Borgo San Sepolcro). COLLEGIATA, R. TRANSEPT. Deposition.
Baltimore (Md.). WALTERS ART GALLERY. 652. Vision of S. Bernard. *Plate* 1401.
Barberino di Mugello. COMPAGNIA DEI SS. SEBASTIANO E ROCCO. S. Sebastian (r.).
Bari. 26. Holy Family with S. Peter Martyr.
Berlin. 239. Portrait of a Man. *Plate* 1405.
Boughton House (Northants.). DUKE OF BUCCLEUCH. Madonna and Child.
Bowood (Calne, Wilts.). MARQUESS OF LANSDOWNE. Portrait of Pietro Carnesecchi.
    Plate 1404.
Brussels. MUSÉE. Madonna and Child.
Budapest. 54. Holy Family. E.
    LEDERER COLLECTION (EX). Cleopatra. *Plate* 1411.
Chianciano (Chiusi). COLLEGIATA. Madonna and Child with Infant S. John.
Cincinnati (Ohio). MR. and MRS. IRWIN SIGNER. Lucretia. *Plate* 1410.
Città di Castello. PINACOTECA. Madonna and Child.
Columbus (Ohio). GALLERY OF FINE ARTS. Holy Family with Infant S. John.
Coral Gables (Fla.). UNIVERSITY OF MIAMI, JOE AND EMILY LOWE ART GALLERY. KRESS
    COLLECTION. K 427. Bust of Lady.
Dubrovnik. BISKUPSKA PINAKOTEKA. Madonna and Child with an Angel.
Dumfries House (Ayrshire). MARQUESS OF BUTE. Madonna and Child with Infant
    S. John.
Firle Place (Lewes, Sussex). VISCOUNTESS GAGE. Portrait of a young Man writing.
    d. 1523.
    Portrait of a Man, called *il Fattore di San Marco. Plate* 1407.
Florence. PITTI. 39. S. Mary Magdalen.
    145. Madonna and Child with a Saint.
    146. Madonna and Child with S. Lawrence and Infant S. John.
    169. Holy Family with Infant S. John.
    184. Portrait of Pietro Carnesecchi as a Youth (1508–1567). *Plate* 1406.
    242. Madonna and Child with Infant S. John.
    294. Holy Family.
    486. Holy Family.
    UFFIZI. 1480. Portrait of a Woman with a Basket of Bobbins.
    1489. Portrait of Piero Carnesecchi. ca 1527.
    S. MARIA MADDALENA DEI PAZZI, 4th CHAPEL R. Madonna and Child with SS. John
    Baptist, Bernard, and four other Saints. L. *Plate* 1415.

Florence (contd.). CENACOLO DI SAN SALVI (MUSEO). 2149. Portrait of a Woman. *Plate* 1402.

    SPEDALE DEGLI INNOCENTI, PINACOTECA. 107. Madonna and Child with Infant S. John.

    GALLERIA CORSINI. Madonna and Child with Infant S. John and two Angels.

    VIA S. ZANOBI AND VIA DELLE RUOTE. Tabernacle fresco: Marriage of S. Catherine, with S. Peter Martyr (r.). 1526.

Genoa. PALAZZO BIANCO, MAGAZINE. 287. S. Mary Magdalen (r.; originally Cleopatra). (?)

Grenoble. 516. Madonna and Child with Infant S. John. (?)

Hampton Court. 1276. Portrait of a Woman in a Turban. (?)

Leningrad. 1477. Portrait of a Woman as S. Barbara. *Plate* 1412.

London. SIR WILLIAM FARRER (EX). Madonna and Child.

    HENRY HARRIS (EX). S. John Baptist preaching (fr.). (?)

    EARL OF NORTHBROOK (EX). Portrait of a Man.

    HON. MRS. DONNEL POST (EX). 'Graham' Madonna and Child.

    SAUNDERS COLLECTION (EX). Madonna and Child with two Angels. *Plate* 1409.

Milan. GIULIO FERRARIO. Madonna and Child with Infant S. John. (?)

Modena. 509. Madonna and Child.

Montpellier. 728. Madonna and Child, with Infant S. John in background. E. *Plate* 1397.

Muncie (Indiana). BALL STATE TEACHERS COLLEGE. Portrait of a Woman (replica of Florence, S. Salvi 2149).

Nantes. MUSÉE 125 (CAMPANA 465). Holy Family with Infant S. John.

Naples. DUCA DI MONTALTINO (EX). Madonna and Child with Infant S. John. E. *Plate* 1399.

New Haven (Conn.). 1871.81. Adoration of the Magi (r.). (?)

Norton Hall (Glos.). SIR MICHAEL AND LADY POLLEN. Apollo and Daphne, and Narcissus (version of Andrea del Sarto, Florence, Corsini). (?)

Oakly Park (Shropshire). EARL OF PLYMOUTH. Portrait of a young Monsignore. *Plate* 1403.

Ottawa. 567. S. Mary Magdalen.

Paris. 1241. Portrait of an Engraver of Precious Stones.

Philadelphia (Pa.). MUSEUM OF ART, JOHNSON COLLECTION. 82. S. Mary Magdalen (r.). E.

Pisa. 198. Madonna and Child with SS. John Baptist and Catherine.

Rome. GALLERIA BORGHESE. 328. S. Mary Magdalen.

    331. Madonna and Child with Infant S. John and two Angels (c. of Andrea del Sarto, Wallace Collection). (?)

    338. Madonna and Child, with Infant S. John in background. *Plate* 1398.

    432. Holy Family with Infant S. John.

    468. Tondo: Madonna and Child with two Angels.

GALLERIA COLONNA. 163. Madonna and Childwith Infant S. John and two Angels.

MUSEO DI PALAZZO VENEZIA (HERTZ COLLECTION). F.N.19209. Madonna and Child with an Angel. E. *Plate* 1400.

PINACOTECA CAPITOLINA, MAGAZINE. S. Mary Magdalen.

Salisbury (Wilts.). JULIAN SALMOND. Portrait of a Woman with a Music-Book and a Volume of Petrarch. *Plate* 1414.

San Miniato al Tedesco (Empoli). CAPPELLA DEL LORETINO. Six panels surrounding an image of the Virgin: Annunciation, two Angels, and two Saints.

Sarasota (Fla.). 28. Madonna and Child with SS. Quentin and Placidus. *Plate* 1416.

Seville. MUSEO (ABREU BEQUEST). Portrait of a young Man (r.). (?)

Stockholm. G. STENMAN. Portrait of a Woman (r.).

Toulon. MUSÉE (CAMPANA 464). Portrait of a Man (?)

Venice. SEMINARIO. 44. Deposition (after Perugino's of 1517 at Città della Pieve).

45. Madonna and Child with Infant S. John. (?)

Vienna. AKADEMIE. 252. Madonna and Child. (Destroyed). *Plate* 1408.

CZERNIN COLLECTION (EX). 20. Madonna and Child with Infant S. John and two Angels.

Homeless. Female Martyr. *Plate* 1413.

RAFFAELLINO DEL GARBO
(Raffaele dei Carli, or dei Capponi)

This list includes the two previous lists of Raffaellino del Garbo and Raffaele dei Carli. I used the two names to designate two different artistic personalities. Garbo's work betrayed the pupil of Botticelli, influenced by Filippino Lippi, Ghirlandajo, Perugino and Raphael. Carli seemed to start under the influence of Cosimo Rosselli, Ghirlandajo and Credi and later became almost Umbrian. I noticed a close contact between the two personalities in the years around 1505, which I now think marks the transition from the earlier and better to the later phase of the same artist. Documentary proof also confirms that the three names Garbo, Carlo (Croli) and Capponi refer to the same Raffaele (1466–1524). 'E.' marks the work by the personality I used to call Garbo.

Amalfi. DUOMO. Pietà with SS. Augustine and Andrew.

Baltimore (Md.). WALTERS ART GALLERY. 6441. Madonna and Child in Glory with S. Nicholas and another Bishop Saint.

480, 485, 490. Three cassone panels: Story of Susanna. *Plate* 1156.

Berea (Kentucky). COLLEGE, KRESS COLLECTION. K 1616. Cassone panel: Episodes from the Life of Moses. (Companion to Lewisburg).

Berlin. 78. Portrait of a young Man. E.

90. Tondo: Madonna and Child with two music-making Angels. E. *Plate* 1157.

Berlin (contd.). DR. PAUL BONN. Madonna and Child with Infant S. John. E. *Plate* 1162.

KAUFMANN COLLECTION (EX). Three Tondi with Busts of SS. Peter, Dominic and Bernardino.

Beverley Hills (Cal.). MISS MARION DAVIES (EX). Tondo: Madonna and Child with Infant S. John and Angels against landscape. *Plate* 1169.

Budapest. 1154. Tondo: Holy Family with an Angel.

Cambridge (Mass.). 1943.121, 122. Two panels: Tobias and the Angel, and S. Catherine; SS. Stephen, Genesius and Apollonia. (r.).

Cappiano (Valdarno Superiore). S. LORENZO. Madonna and Child with SS. Sebastian, Francis, another Saint and Tobias and the Angel.

Chilston Park. VISCOUNTESS CHILSTON (EX). Fresco tondo: Madonna and Child (r.). E. *Plate* 1164.

Dresden. 21. Tondo: Madonna and Child with SS. Jerome and Francis.
— (EX). 22. Madonna and Child with Infant S. John. E. (?)

Dublin. HON. JAMES MURNAGHAN. Tondo: Madonna and Child with Infant S. John and SS. Mary Magdalen and Lucy. (?)

Düsseldorf. AKADEMIE. 120. Madonna and Child.

Faulkner (Md.). LOYOLA RETREAT HOUSE, KRESS STUDY COLLECTION. K 1028. Madonna adoring the Child with two Angels. (r.).

Fiesole. S. FRANCESCO, HIGH ALTAR. Annunciation.

VILLA DOCCIA, CHAPEL IN PARK. Fresco: S. Francis receiving Stigmata.

Florence. GALLERIE. 3165. Madonna and Child with S. Francis, a Bishop Saint and two Donors. Sd (*Raphael de Caponibus*) and d. 1500. *Plate* 1166.

ACCADEMIA. 561. Four Evangelists (above triptych n. 3152 by Jacopo di Cione and Niccolò di Pietro Gerini). (?)

8363. Resurrection. E. *Plate* 1161.

MUSEO NAZIONALE DEL BARGELLO, SALA DEI BRONZI. Fresco: *Pietà*. (?)

S. AMBROGIO, 4th ALTAR L. S. Anthony Abbot enthroned, with Tobias and the Angel, and S. Nicholas. Lunette: Annunciation.

SS. ANNUNZIATA, L. TRANSEPT, CHAPEL L. SS. Blaise, Ignatius, and Erasmus (r.).

S. GIUSEPPE, 2nd CHAPEL L. Madonna and Child with a Lily.

S. MARIA MADDALENA DEI PAZZI, 4th CHAPEL L. Lateral panels of tabernacle with statue of S. Sebastian: SS. Ignatius and Roch.

— OLD REFECTORY. Fresco: Multiplication of the Loaves. 1503.

S. MICHELE A S. SALVI, SACRISTY. Reliquary: *Pietà*.

S. PROCOLO, ALTAR R. Visitation.

S. SPIRITO, L. TRANSEPT, 2nd ALTAR L. Madonna and Child with SS. John Evangelist, Lawrence, Stephen and Bernard. Predella: S. John in the Cauldron of boiling Oil, Martyrdom of S. Lawrence, Man of Sorrows with two Angels, Stoning of S. Stephen, Vision of S. Bernard. d. 1505. *Plate* 1170.

— — 3rd ALTAR L. Madonna and Child with two Angels, SS. Bartholomew and Nicholas and two Donors. Predella: Man of Sorrows. *Plate* 1155.

— — 1ST ALTAR R. Madonna and Child with two Angels and SS. Bartholomew and John Evangelist and a small Crucifixion inset below the throne.

(Environs) S. ANDREA A BROZZI, R. WALL. Fresco lunette: SS. Albert Siculus and Sigismund. d. 1520.

— CERTOSA DEL GALLUZZO. Two panels: SS. Peter Martyr and George.

— ROVEZZANO, VIA DEL GUARLONE E VIA DEL RONDININO. Tabernacle fresco: Madonna and two flying Putti (fr., r.).

Glasgow. 1015. Tondo: Madonna and Child with Infant S. John and two Angels. E.

Hoe Hall (Dereham, Norfolk). MRS. JOSEPH BARCLAY (EX). Annunciation.

Houston (Texas). 44.554. Profile Portrait of a Woman. E.

Le Mans. 19. Madonna and Child with Cherubim. E.

Lewisburg (Pa.). BUCKNELL UNIVERSITY, KRESS COLLECTION. K 1617. Cassone panel: Episodes from the Life of Moses. (Companion to Berea.)

Locko Park (Derbys.). J. PACKE DRURY LOWE. Deposition. Baptist.

London. 4902. Tondo: Madonna and Child with two music-making Angels (r.; replica of Berlin 90).

4903. 'Pucci' Tondo: Madonna and Child with SS. Mary Magdalen and Catherine. E. *Plate* 1165.

MRS. FRANCIS P. NASH (EX). Tondo: Mystic Marriage of S. Catherine with Magdalen and Infant S. John.

Lucca. PINACOTECA. S. Barbara. (?)

Milan. MUSEO POLDI PEZZOLI. 158. Tondo: Madonna and Child with Infant S. John.

Montepulciano. 20. Tondo: Madonna and Child.

Munich. W.A.F. 801. Lamentation, with SS. John Baptist and James. E. [*Plate* 218.] *Plate* 1163.

Naples. 43. Tondo: Madonna and Child with Infant S. John. E. [*Plate* 217.]

New York. S. H. KRESS FOUNDATION. K 1028. Madonna adoring the Child with two Angels (r.).

K 1137. Madonna and Child in Glory. (Stolen 1940.)

W. R. HEARST (EX). 'Benson' Tondo: Madonna and Child with Infant S. John and two Angels. E. *Plate* 1158.

R. M. HURD (EX). 'Holford' Tondo: Madonna and Child with an Angel. E.

PERCY S. STRAUS (EX). 'Sciarra' Madonna and Child with SS. Leonard and John Evangelist. (?)

Olantigh Towers (Wye, Kent). MR. SAWBRIDGE-ERLE-DRAX (EX). *Pietà*, with SS. Benedict and Francis. L. *Plate* 1172.

Orleans. MUSÉE. 1192 (CAMPANA 255). Madonna and Child with two Angels and SS. John Evangelist and Catherine of Siena. E.

Oxford. ASHMOLEAN. 175. Predella panel: *Pietà*.

CHRIST CHURCH LIBRARY. 36. Tondo: Madonna adoring the Child with Infant S. John and SS. Lawrence and Mary Magdalen. E.

Oxford. (contd). 42. S. Mary Magdalen (replica of Tewin Water). E. *Plate* 1159.

Paris. 1303. Coronation of the Virgin with SS. Benedict, John Gualbert, Bernardo degli Uberti and a Bishop Saint.

  E. RICHTEMBERGER (EX). Tondo: Madonna and Child with two Angels. L.

  BARONNE EDOUARD DE ROTHSCHILD. Profile Portrait of a Woman. E. *Plate* 1160.

Pisa. 171. Madonna and Child with two Angels, four Saints and worshipping Nun. Predella: Adoration of the Magi and Massacre of the Innocents.

  Christ and the Virgin as Intercessors (r.). (?)

Pistoia. MUSEO CIVICO (DEP. GALLERIE FIORENTINE 5057). Annunciation.

Poggibonsi. (Environs). S. LUCCHESE, R. WALL. *Noli me tangere.* Predella: S. Francis, Madonna and Child with SS. Mary Magdalen and another Saint, S. Anthony Abbot. (Destroyed 1944.)

Prato. 23. Tondo: Madonna and Child with Infant S. John.

Rome. SIMONETTI COLLECTION (EX). Madonna and Child and young S. Joseph holding a flowering Rod with a Dove.

San Francisco (Cal.). DE YOUNG MEMORIAL MUSEUM, KRESS COLLECTION. K 1299. 'Corsini' Madonna and Child with two Angels and SS. Jerome and Bartholomew. Sd (*Raphael de Krolis*) and d. 1502. *Plate* 1168.

San Vivaldo (Gambassi, Val d'Elsa). S. MARIA IN CAMPORENA, CHAPEL R. Madonna and Child in Glory with SS. John Baptist, Francis, Vivaldo and Jerome. Predella: Man of Sorrows.

Sarasota (Fla.). 23. Mass of S. Gregory. Sd (*Rafael Karli*) and d. 1501.

Siena. S. MARIA DEGLI ANGELI, HIGH ALTAR, Madonna and Child in Glory with SS. Bernardo degli Uberti, Mary Magdalen, John Evangelist and a Bishop Saint. Lunette: God the Father. Predella: S. Jerome, S. Mary Magdalen, Adoration of the Magi, S. Catherine of Siena, S. Bernardine. Sd (*Raphael de Florentia*) and d. 1502.

Staggia (Poggibonsi). S. MARIA ASSUNTA, CHAPEL R. *Grisaille* window: S. Mary Magdalen. E.

Tewin Water (Welwyn, Herts.). SIR OTTO BEIT (EX). S. Mary Magdalen. (See also Oxford, Christ Church 42). E.

Toledo (Ohio). JOHN N. WILLYS (EX). Tondo: Madonna and Child with Infant S. John and an Angel. E.

Vallombrosa. ABBAZIA, SACRISTY. S. John Gualbert enthroned with SS. Mary Magdalen, John Baptist, Bernardo degli Uberti and Catherine. d. 1508. *Plate* 1171.

Venice. ACCADEMIA. 55. Madonna and Child with two Angels and SS. Lucy and Peter Martyr.

Volterra. 26. Madonna and Child with two Angels and SS. Bartholomew and Anthony Abbot. Lunette: God the Father. Predella: Flaying of S. Bartholomew, Man of Sorrows, Temptation of S. Anthony.

  PALAZZO DEI PRIORI, ANTICAMERA SINDACALE. Fresco: Madonna and Child enthroned.

Worcester (Mass.). 1940.44. Madonna and Child with Infant S. John.
Zagreb. 28. Tondo: Madonna and Child with Infant S. John and an Angel.
Homeless. Tondo: Madonna and Child with SS. Jerome and Francis. *Plate* 1167.

ROSSELLI, Cosimo

1439–1507. *Pupil of Neri di Bicci; influenced by Giovanni di Francesco, Baldovinetti and Benozzo Gozzoli.*

Ajaccio (Corsica). 192. Madonna and Child with Infant S. John.
Amsterdam. 2056 B–1. Tondo: Holy Family with Infant S. John and two Angels.
  OTTO LANZ (EX). Madonna and Child with SS. Jerome and Anthony of Padua.
Baltimore (Md.). WALTERS ART GALLERY. 518. Madonna and Child.
Barberino di Mugello (Environs). BADIA DI VIGESIMO. Assumption with SS.
  Benedict and Anthony Abbot and a Donor (assisted by a follower of
  Ghirlandajo who painted the Saints). L.
Berlin. 63 (DEP. HALLE). Tondo: Madonna and Child with Infant S. John and S.
  Francis (st.). (Destroyed.)
  71. Entombment.
  (BERLIN-OST). 59. Madonna and Child in Glory with Angels and Saints. L.
  59A. Madonna and Child with S. Anne and SS. George, Catherine, Mary
  Magdalen and Francis. d. 1471. *Plate* 1000.
  1075 (DEP. COLOGNE). Madonna and Child with four Angels and SS. John
  Baptist, Augustine, Dominic and Peter, and *Innocenti* (r.).
Birmingham (Ala.). MUSEUM OF ART, KRESS COLLECTION. K 1083. Madonna and
  Child. [*Plate* 186]
Boston (Mass.). 22.651. Deposition.
Breslau. 171. Holy Family with Infant S. John.
Cambridge. 556. Madonna and Child with two Angels and SS. John Baptist,
  Andrew, Bartholomew and Zenobius. d. 1443 (*sic*; 1473?).
Castelfiorentino (Val d'Elsa). (Environs). S. MARIA LUNGO TUONO, SACRISTY.
  Madonna and Child with SS. Verdiana, Clare, Anthony Abbot and Francis
  (r.). d. 1471.
Cleveland (Ohio). 44.91. Expulsion of Hagar.
Cologne. See Berlin 1075.
Columbia (S.C.). MUSEUM OF ART, KRESS COLLECTION. K. 1002. Nativity with SS.
  John Baptist and Jerome (r.).
Edinburgh. 1030. S. Catherine of Siena enthroned with SS. Stephen, Dominic,
  Peter Martyr, Tobias and the Angel, and Dominican Nuns.
Empoli. 32. Nativity with Infant S. John.

Fiesole. DUOMO, CHAPEL R. (SALUTATI). Frescoes. Vault: Four Evangelists. Wall: SS. Leonard and John Baptist. Window embrasure: *Salvator Mundi*, a Sibyl and a Prophet.

— CHAPEL L. Coronation of the Virgin with Saints and Angels (st.).

Florence. GALLERIE. 489. Madonna and Child with two Angels. E.

494. Adoration of the Magi. E. *Plate* 999.

ACCADEMIA. 1562. Madonna and Child with Infant S. John and SS. James and Peter. 1492. *Plate* 1022.

8632, 8633. Four predella panels: Noah, David, Moses and Abraham.

8634. Madonna adoring the Child with Infant S. John (p.).

8635. S. Barbara, with SS. John Baptist and Matthias. E.

UFFIZI. 466. Interstices between pinnacles of Lorenzo Monaco's Adoration: Annunciation and two Prophets. *Plate* 1021.

MUSEO STIBBERT. 11582. S. Michael.

PALAZZO VECCHIO, SALA DI CLEMENTE VII. 'Radda' altarpiece: Madonna and Child with SS. Euphrosynus and John Baptist and Bartolomeo Canigiani as Donor. Predella: Funeral of S. Euphrosynus, Nativity, Baptism of Christ. L. *Plate* 1023.

S. AMBROGIO, 3rd ALTAR L. Madonna and Child in Glory with four Angels and SS. Ambrose and Francis. Predella: Confirmation of the Franciscan Order, Stigmatization of S. Francis, Death of S. Francis. 1498–1501.

— CHAPEL L. OF CHOIR (CAPPELLA DEL MIRACOLO). Frescoes. Vault: Four Doctors of the Church. Left wall: Miracle of the Holy Blood. Wall around tabernacle: Angels. 1486. *Plate* 1010–11.

SS. ANNUNZIATA, ATRIUM. Fresco: Vocation of Bd. Philip Benizzi. 1476. *Plate* 1006.

S. MARCO (MUSEO), CELL 32. Lamentation, with Saints. E.

S. MARIA MADDALENA DEI PAZZI, 2nd CHAPEL L. Coronation of the Virgin, with Angels and Saints. ca 1505.

S. SPIRITO, L. TRANSEPT, 3rd CHAPEL R. Madonna and Child with two Angels and SS. Thomas and Augustine (later altered to represent Peter). Predella: Incredulity of S. Thomas, Annunciation, S. Ambrose preaching to SS. Augustine and Monica. d. 1482.

CONTINI BONACOSSI COLLECTION. An Angel withdrawing a Curtain (fr.). (?)

VIA RICASOLI, TABERNACOLO DELLE CINQUE LAMPADE. Fresco: Madonna and Child with two Angels, and two Saints. *Plate* 1001.

Gazzada (Varese). VILLA CAGNOLA. Predella panel: Annunciation. *Plate* 1013.

Habana (Cuba). OSCAR CINTAS. Pietà. E.

Halle. See Berlin 63.

Houston (Texas). 55–88. Portrait of a Man.

Le Mans. MUSÉE (DEP. LOUVRE 1663A). Portrait of a Man, called 'Bartolomeo di Giovanni Berzichelli'.

Liverpool. 2803. S. Lawrence.

London. 1196. Combat of Love and Chastity (companion to Turin). (?)

SIR THOMAS BARLOW. *Madonna della Cintola*. On frame: God the Father and eight Angels. *Plate 1014*.

HENRY HARRIS (EX). Two panels (joined): Disrobing of Christ, Way to Calvary (fr.). *Plate 1012*.

J. S. MAYNARD (EX). Head of S. John Baptist (fr.). Daughters of Jephtha. *Plate 1016*.

Lucca. DUOMO, L. OF ENTRANCE. Fresco: Legend of the True Cross.

Minneapolis (Minn.). INSTITUTE OF ARTS (EX). 23.89. S. Peter (fr.).

New York. 32.100.84. Madonna and Child with two Angels.

50.135.1. Portrait of a Man. [*Plate 185*].

ROBERT LEHMAN. Madonna nursing the Child with Infant S. John.

JACK LINSKY. Portrait of Matteo Sassetti (died 1506). *Plate 1009*.

North Mimms (Herts.). MRS. WALTER BURNS. Madonna and Child with SS. Michael and Sebastian.

Northwick Park (Blockley, Worcs.). CAPT. E. G. SPENCER CHURCHILL. Adoration of the Magi with SS. Benedict, Jerome and Francis. L.

Notre Dame (Indiana). UNIVERSITY, KRESS STUDY COLLECTION, K 1734. Christ on the Cross. L.

Oxford. ASHMOLEAN. 374. SS. Nicholas and Dominic.

Paris. 1656. Annunciation, with SS. John Baptist, Anthony Abbot, Catherine and Peter Martyr. d. 1473.

1657C. Predella panel: Adoration of the Magi. E. (?)

1663A. See Le Mans.

MUSÉE DES ARTS DÉCORATIFS, LEGS PEYRE. Madonna adoring the Child with young S. John and S. Julian.

Philadelphia (Pa.). MUSEUM OF ART, JOHNSON COLLECTION. 60. Madonna and Child. E.

72. Predella panel: Lamentation.

Pistoia. MUSEO CIVICO. Coronation of the Virgin with Angels.

Rome. GALLERIA NAZIONALE (PALAZZO BARBERINI). F.N. 19216. Madonna adoring the Child with an Angel.

VATICAN, SISTINE CHAPEL. Three frescoes: Moses destroying the Tables of the Law, Sermon on the Mount and the Healing of the Leper, Last Supper (but scenes visible through windows, probably by 'Utili'). 1482. *Plates 1007-8*.

San Marino (Cal.). HUNTINGTON MUSEUM, Madonna and Child in Glory (fr.). *Plate 1002*.

Topsfield (Mass.). MRS. EDWARD JACKSON HOLMES. Madonna and Child with an Angel.

Tulsa (Okla.). PHILBROOK ART CENTER, KRESS COLLECTION. K 515. Madonna and Child with two Angels. L.

Turin. 106. Triumph of Chastity (companion to London 1196). (?). *Plate 1015*.

Upton House (Banbury, Oxon.). NATIONAL TRUST. Madonna and Child with an Angel. *Plate 1017*.

Winter Park (Fla.). ROLLINS COLLEGE, KRESS COLLECTION. K 1073. Madonna nursing the Child.

Wroclaw. See Breslau.

Zagreb. 28. Madonna and Child with two Angels.

Homeless. Madonna and Child with Cherubim. *Plate* 1019.

    Madonna and Child in Glory (fr.). *Plate* 1020.

    Two panels: Two Innocents. *Plate* 1003–4.

    S. Lucy (fr.). *Plate* 1005.

    Tondo: Madonna adoring the Child with Infant S. John. L. *Plate* 1018.

ROSSELLO DI JACOPO ('FRANCHI')

ca 1376–1456. *Possibly a pupil of Mariotto di Nardo. Follower of Lorenzo Monaco, later influenced by Gentile da Fabriano. Close to Bicci di Lorenzo, with whom he worked* (1433).

Baltimore (Md.). WALTERS ART GALLERY. 632. Wing of an altarpiece: SS. John Baptist and James.

Barcelona. MUSEU. Madonna and Child with SS. James, John Baptist, Paul and a Bishop Saint. Pinnacle: *Salvator mundi.* Predella: S. Anthony Abbot. *Plate* 536.

Berlin. 1467. Cassone panel: Sports and Games. *Plate* 543.

Borgo San Lorenzo (Mugello). S. LORENZO, ALTAR R. Madonna and Child.

Buffalo (N.Y.). 27.34. Madonna of Humility. (?)

Cambridge. 1129. Madonna and Child with SS. Andrew, John Baptist, James and a Hermit Saint.

Cleveland. (Ohio). 16.814. Madonna and Child (fr.).

Empoli. 17. Triptych: Madonna and Child with two Angels and SS. Sebastian, John Baptist, John Evangelist and Domitilla. Pinnacles: Christ blessing and Annunciation.

    (Environs) PONTORME, S. MARTINO. Wings of an altarpiece: Five male and five female Saints. (?)

Florence. GALLERIE. 4653. Madonna and Child. Pinnacle: Crucifixion.

    4654. Crucifixion. (?)

    6089. Pinnacle: Crucifixion.

    ACCADEMIA. 457. Incredulity of S. Thomas. Spandrels: Two Prophets. E. (?)

    475. Triptych: Madonna and Child with two Angels and SS. John Baptist, Francis, Mary Magdalen and Matthew. Pinnacles: Crucifixion, SS. Peter and Paul.

    3146. Annunciation. E. (?)

    3333. Predella panel: Stigmatization of S. Francis and S. Nicholas saving a Ship at Sea.

8460. Triptych: Coronation of the Virgin with Archangels Michael and Gabriel, six Angels and twenty-four Saints. Pinnacles: *Salvator mundi*, Annunciation, Two Prophets, Seraphim and Cherubim. Left pilaster: Four Saints. Predella: Man of Sorrows with the Virgin, S. John and twelve other Saints. d. 1420. *Plate 535.*

MUSEO DEL BIGALLO, FAÇADE.* Frescoes: S. Peter Martyr consigning the Banner to the *Capitani di S. Maria*, Preaching of S. Peter Martyr (p.; fr., r.). *Plate 549.*

MUSEO NAZIONALE DEL BARGELLO (SALA DI DONATELLO). Cassone: Offering of Banners (*Pali*) on the Piazza del Duomo.

— DIURNO DOMENICALE, COD. H. 74. Resurrection (u., r.). 1412–13. (?)

PALAZZO DAVANZATI. 5068. *Madonna del Parto* with two Angels and two Donors. *Plate 537.*

PALAZZO VECCHIO, QUARTIERE DI ELEONORA. Lunette (over door to *Camera Verde*): Madonna and Child. E.

S. MARIA DEL FIORE (DUOMO), R. WALL, 2nd BAY. S. Blaise enthroned with two Angels. Predella: Martyrdom of S. Blaise. 1408. *Plate 533.*

S. MINIATO AL MONTE, R. WALL. Fresco: S. Lucy and a male Saint. *Plate 541.*

S. SEBASTIANO DEI BINI, HIGH ALTAR. Madonna of Humility. (Stolen 1931.)

SPEDALE DEGLI INNOCENTI, PINACOTECA. Triptych: Madonna of Humility, with SS. Jerome and Catherine. Pinnacles: Crucifixion, Annunciation.

(Environs) S. DOMENICO DI FIESOLE, 1st CHAPEL L. Pilasters on frame of altarpiece by Fra Angelico: Six Saints.

Highnam Court (Glos.). GAMBIER-PARRY COLLECTION. Madonna and Child enthroned with two Angels.

London. MARY DODGE (EX). Adoration of the Magi. (?).

HENRY HARRIS (EX). Madonna of Humility. On frame: SS. Anthony Abbot, John Baptist, Cherubim and Seraphim. Predella: God the Father, and two Prophets.

Wings of an altarpiece: SS. Michael and John Evangelist, S. Lawrence and a Bishop Saint. *Plate 539.*

Madison (Wisc.). UNIVERSITY OF WISCONSIN, KRESS STUDY COLLECTION. K 170. Cassone panel: Court of Love. *Plate 545.*

Moscow. MUSEUM OF FINE ARTS. Madonna and Child with SS. John Baptist, Anthony Abbot and two female Martyrs.

New Haven (Conn.). 1943.219. Madonna and Child in Glory with two Angels and SS. John Baptist and Peter.

1953.26.1. Pilaster of an altarpiece: S. Catherine.

New York. 43.98.5. 'Griggs' Crucifixion. (?). *Plate 547.*

MRS. JESSE ISIDOR STRAUS. Two panels: S. Stephen, and a female Saint. (?)

Ortimino (Val d'Elsa). S. VITO. Madonna and Child.

Paris. MUSÉE DE CLUNY. 1669–72, 1674. Five panels from a polyptych: Madonna and Child, Two Archangels, S. Philip and S. Nicholas (fr., r.).

Pisa. 120. Madonna and Child with two Angels and SS. Anthony Abbot and John Baptist.

Pistoia. MUSEO CIVICO. Wings of a triptych: SS. Nicholas and Julian. (Central panel by Mariotto di Nardo). *Plate 532.*

Rome. MISS VEDDER (EX). Madonna of Humility. *Plate 540.*

San Miniato al Tedesco (Pisa). S. DOMENICO, ALTAR R. OF ENTRANCE. Two panels from an altarpiece: SS. Michael and Catherine.

— ALTAR L. OF ENTRANCE. Frescoes: Twelve Angels.

Sant'Agata (Scarperia, Mugello). PIEVE, CHOIR. Madonna and Child with the two S. Catherines [only S. Catherine of Alexandria now visible over altar right of entrance].

Siena. 608. Coronation of the Virgin with two Angels. Pinnacle: Trinity, and a Prophet. Sd and d. 1439. *Plate 542.*

Staggia (Poggibonsi). S. MARIA ASSUNTA (EX). Madonna and Child enthroned with two Angels. Sd. (Stolen 1920.) *Plate 534.*

Vienna. LANCKORONSKI COLLECTION. Madonna and Child.

CARL MOLL (EX). Madonna and Child enthroned. Pinnacle: God the Father. *Plate 538.*

Zagreb. 16. Triptych: Madonna and Child with two Bishop Saints.

Homeless. Cassone panel: A Tournament. *Plate 544.*

ROSSO FIORENTINO

1494–1540, *Pupil of Andrea del Sarto, influenced by Pontormo and Michelangelo.*

Baltimore (Md.). DR. GEORGE REULING (EX). Dead Christ sustained by Nicodemus. (?)

Berlin. (BERLIN-OST). 1935. Madonna and Child with Infant S. John (c.).

1989. Crucifixion (c. of Pontormo's Boldrone Tabernacle in Florence).

Borgo San Sepolcro. ORFANELLE. Lamentation. 1528. *Plate 1472.*

Boston (Mass.). 58.27. The Dead Christ supported by four Angels. Sd. 1524–27. *Plate 1470.*

Città di Castello. DUOMO, L. TRANSEPT. So-called 'Transfiguration'. 1528–30. *Plate 1471.*

Dijon. 68. S. John Baptist. (?).

Florence. PITTI. 237. *Pala Dei*: Madonna and Child with SS. George, Peter, Catherine, Bernard, James, Sebastian and four other Saints. Sd and d. 1522.

UFFIZI. 1505. Angel playing a Lute.

2151. Moses defending the Daughters of Jethro. [*Plate 242.*] *Plate 1468.*

3190. Madonna and Child with SS. John Baptist, Stephen, Jerome, and a fourth Saint (from S. Maria Nuova). ca 1518. *Plate 1461.*

3245. Portrait of a Woman.

SS. ANNUNZIATA, ATRIUM. Fresco: Assumption. 1517.

S. LORENZO, 2nd ALTAR R. Marriage of the Virgin. Sd and d. 1523. *Plate 1466.*

SPEDALE DEGLI INNOCENTI, PINACOTECA. 119. Deposition. (?)

(Environs) S. BARTOLOMEO A QUARATA. Tobias and the three Angels.

Fontainebleau. GALERIE DE FRANÇOIS I. Fresco and stucco decoration, with thirteen historical, allegorical and mythological scenes [A Sacrifice, Expulsion of Ignorance, Cleobis and Biton, Education of Achilles, The Triumphal Elephant, Unity of the State, Battle of the Centaurs and Lapiths, Shipwreck of Ajax, Burning of Catania, Fountain of Youth, Death of Adonis, Venus reproving Cupid, Danaë] (r.). 1534–37. *Plates 1474–6.*

Frankfurt am Main. 952. Madonna and Child with Infant S. John. E.

Leningrad. 111. Madonna and Child in Glory with Cherubim. *Plate 1469.*

Liverpool. 2804. Portrait of a Man with a Helmet. Sd. *Plate 1463.*

Los Angeles (Cal.). A.6488.54–2. Madonna and Child with S. Anne, Infant S. John and two Angels. *Plate 1462.*

Naples. 112. Portrait of a young Man seated on a Table. *Plate 1464.*

Paris. 1485. *Pietà.* 1537–40. *Plate 1473.*

1486. Challenge of the Pierides. (?)

Pisa. 201. Rebecca at the Well (c.).

Rome. S. MARIA DELLA PACE, 2nd ALTAR R. Frescoes (lunette): Creation of Eve and the Fall of Man. d. 1524.

Siena. 469. Portrait of a young Woman (r., st.).

Turin. ARMERIA REALE. f. 3. Buckle with Wars of Jugurtha and Marius (on his design?).

Vienna. 155–160. Six tapestries (after Fontainebleau): Cleobis and Biton, Unity of the State, Battle of Centaurs and Lapiths, Fountain of Youth, Death of Adonis, Danaë. *Plate 1477.*

Villamagna (Volterra). PIEVE, 1st ALTAR L. Madonna and Child with SS. John Baptist and John Evangelist. Sd and d. 1521.

Volterra. 1. Deposition. Sd and d. 1521. *Plates 1465, 1467.*

Washington (D.C.). 1611 (KRESS COLLECTION 1735). Portrait of a Man. (?)

SELLAJO, Jacopo del

Ca 1441–1493. Pupil of Filippo Lippi; slightly influenced by Andrea del Castagno. He freely imitated his Florentine contemporaries, especially Botticelli, Filippino Lippi and Domenico Ghirlandajo.

Acquapendente (Viterbo). S. FRANCESCO, SACRISTY. Madonna adoring the Child.

Ajaccio (Corsica). 54. Tondo: Adoration of the Shepherds.

Altenburg. 105. Tondo: Madonna and Child with Infant S. John and Tobias and the Angel (r.).

150. S. Jerome.

Amsterdam. ERNST PROEHL. Cassone panel: Story of Cupid and Psyche. (Companion to Cambridge.) *Plate* 1105–6.

Arezzo. 29. Madonna and Child.

Athens. BENAKIS MUSEUM. Madonna and Child (r.).

Balcarres (Fife, Scotland). EARL OF CRAWFORD AND BALCARRES. A Wilderness, with the young Christ and S. John, Penitent S. Jerome and S. Mary Magdalen.

Baltimore (Md.). WALTERS ART GALLERY. 631. Madonna adoring the Child (r.).

754. Madonna adoring the Child with Infant S. John.

Bergamo. ACCADEMIA CARRARA. 995. Bust of Christ with Instruments of Passion.

Berlin. 94. Meeting of the young Christ and S. John.

1055. *Pietà* with S. Jerome and a Bishop Saint. ca 1483. (Destroyed 1945.) *Plate* 1100.

1132, 1133. Two panels: Assassination of Julius Caesar. (Destroyed 1945.) *Plate* 1110.

1139 (DEP. BONN). S. Jerome in the Wilderness, and SS. Sebastian and Tobias and the Angel. (Destroyed 1945.)

(BERLIN–OST). III. 97. In a Wilderness, Entombment, S. Mary Magdalen, S. Augustine and the Christ Child, and the Vision of S. Bernard. (Companion to Göttingen).

Birmingham (Ala.). MUSEUM OF ART, KRESS COLLECTION. K 424. The Redeemer, with Instruments of the Passion. *Plate* 1112.

Bordeaux. 48. The Redeemer.

Boston (Mass.). 12.1049. Cassone panel: Story of Cupid and Psyche.

Brandenburg. 65. Adoration.

Breslau. 189. S. Jerome in the Wilderness, with Tobias and the Angel and Infant S. John.

Brooklyn (N.Y.). 25.95. Story of Nastagio degli Onesti (*Decamerone* v, 8; p.; version of Botticelli, Madrid 2838). (Companion to Philadelphia 64?).

Budapest. 1221. S. Jerome.

1369. S. Jerome in the Wilderness (r.).

2537. Cassone panel (*testata*): Esther before Ahasuerus. (Companion to Paris, Louvre 1657D.)

5957. S. John Baptist turning to tree with axe at the root.

Buenos Aires. MRS. M. R. VON BUCH. Madonna and Child (r.).

Caen. MUSÉE. 58 (CAMPANA 313). Madonna and Child with Infant S. John and an Angel (r.).

Cambridge. M 75. Cassone panel: Story of Cupid and Psyche. (Companion to Amsterdam.)

Cambridge (Mass.). 1957.61. Tondo: Holy Family with Infant S. John and an Angel. (?).

Castiglion Fiorentino. PINACOTECA. Cassone panel: Pool of Bethesda (st.).

Last Judgement and another Scene (st.).

Scenes from Lives of SS. Nicholas and Bernardino (st.).

Charlottesville (Va.). MRS. JOHN T. WESTLAKE. Madonna adoring the Child (r.).

Chicago (Ill.). 33.1029, 1030. Two cassone panels: Story of Susanna.

Cleveland (Ohio). 42.646. Cassone panel: Tarquinius and Tanaquil entering Rome.

Dublin. 110. Cassone panel: Story of Lucretia.

Edinburgh. 1538. Cassone panel: A Triumphal Procession.

    1941. Entombment, with Tobias and the Angel and S. Sebastian.

El Paso (Texas). MUSEUM OF ART, KRESS COLLECTION. K 1158. S. Jerome in the Wilderness and Stigmatization of S. Francis.

Empoli. 29. Madonna adoring the Child with Infant S. John.

    33. Madonna and Child in Glory with SS. Nicholas and Peter Martyr.

Fiesole. MUSEO BANDINI, II, 1. SS. John Baptist, the young Christ, Jerome and Mary Magdalen in the Wilderness.

    II, 4. Madonna adoring the Child with Infant S. John (r.).

    II, 6–8. Four panels: Petrarch's *Trionfi.*

Florence. GALLERIE. 5071. Coronation of the Virgin.

    6213. S. Sebastian.

    S. Julian and Scenes of his Life.

    ACCADEMIA. 5069. *Pietà* with SS. James, Francis, Mary Magdalen and Michael.

    8456. Madonna and Child.

    8628. *Pietà.*

    8655. Entombment.

    PITTI. 364. Tondo: Madonna adoring the Child with Infant S. John. *Plate* 1104.

    UFFIZI. 491–93. Three panels: Story of Esther.

    LUNGARNO SODERINI. *Fresco Tabernacle of Torrino di S. Rosa: *Pietà.* (?)

    MUSEO DEL BIGALLO. Tondo: Holy Family with two Angels and S. Peter Martyr.

    MUSEO HORNE. 93. Predella panel: S. Jerome in the Wilderness.

    PALAZZO VECCHIO, SALA D'ERCOLE. Tondo: Madonna adoring the Child with Infant S. John.

    S. FREDIANO, SACRISTY. Crucifixion with the Virgin and S. John and SS. Frediano, Catherine, Sebastian, Tobias and the Angel, Mary Magdalen and Lawrence. *Plate* 1102.

    S. JACOPO SOPRARNO, SACRISTY. Pietà.

    S. LUCIA DEI MAGNOLI (TRA LE ROVINATE), 1st ALTAR L. Two panels: Annunciation. ca 1473.

    S. SPIRITO, L. TRANSEPT, 2nd CHAPEL L. Altar frontal: S. Lawrence distributing the Treasure of the Church.

    GALLERIA CORSINI. Madonna and Child. *Plate* 1114.

    MARCHESA BEATRICE ROSSELLI DEL TURCO. Madonna and Child with SS. Lawrence, Peter, Jerome and a Bishop Saint.

    (Environs) CASTELLO, CHIESA PARROCCHIALE. Madonna and Child.

    — S. MARTINO A GANGALANDI, 3rd ALTAR R. Madonna and Child; Eternal in lunette (r.).

    — SETTIMO, BADIA DI S. SALVATORE. 1st ALTAR R. Entombment. (?)

Göttingen. 164. Wilderness with Temptation of S. Anthony, Meeting of Christ and the young S. John, Stigmatization of S. Francis, Tobias and the Angel, Penitent S. Jerome. (Companion to Berlin III.97.)

Hampton Court. 1211. Infants Christ and S. John embracing (fr.).

Highnam Court (Glos.). GAMBIER-PARRY COLLECTION. Head of an Angel (fr.).

Indianapolis (Ind.). 24.4. Madonna adoring the Child.

Kiev. 44. Cassone panel: Story of Orpheus and Eurydice. (Companion to Rotterdam and Vienna, Lanckoronski.) *Plate* 1107–8.

Leningrad. 4125, 4127. Two panels: The Virgin and S. John.

    5512. Man of Sorrows with the Virgin. *Plate* 1103.

Lille. 995. Madonna adoring the Child.

Litchfield (Conn.). STANLEY MORTIMER. Madonna adoring the Child.

London. 916. Allegory of Abundance (or Venus and three Putti?).

    2492. Tondo: Holy Family with three Angels.

Lugano. THYSSEN COLLECTION. 388. S. John Baptist (r.).

    Madonna and Child with Angels, two Saints and worshipping Monk.

Marseilles. MUSÉE. 802 (CAMPANA 236). Madonna and Child with an Angel.

Memphis (Tenn.). BROOKS MEMORIAL ART GALLERY, KRESS COLLECTION. K 316. Adoration of the Magi.

Milan. CONTESSA RASINI. Wilderness with penitent S. Jerome, Job, Meeting of the young Christ and S. John, and S. Mary Magdalen. *Plate* 1099.

Munich. 1352. Matyrdom of S. Sebastian.

Nantes. 157. Madonna and Child (fr.). (?)

    158. Madonna and Child.

New Haven (Conn.). 1871.44. S. Jerome in the Wilderness and Stigmatization of S. Francis. (?)

    1871.45. Madonna adoring the Child, with S. Francis, Tobias and the Angel, young S. John and S. Jerome in the background.

    1871.46. Madonna and Child in Glory with four Cherubim.

    1871.47. S. Sebastian. d. 1479. *Plate* 1098.

    1871.48. Cassone panel: Death of Actaeon (fr.; companion to 1952.37.1).

    1871.49. Creation of Adam and of Eve.

    1946.314. Nativity with S. Onuphrius, Meeting of SS. Francis and Dominic, S. John Evangelist, S. Jerome in the Wilderness and another Saint. (?)

    1952.37.1. Cassone panel: Story of Actaeon (fr.; companion to 1871.48).

New York. 41.100.10. Madonna adoring the Child with Infant S. John.

    JOHN BASS. Portrait of a young Man (r.).

    MRS. ROBERT MINTURN. Tondo: Madonna and Child with Infant S. John and an Angel.

Oxford. CHRIST CHURCH LIBRARY. 32. Madonna adoring the Child.

Palermo. CHIARAMONTE BORDONARO COLLECTION. Tondo: Nativity.

Paris. MUSÉES NATIONAUX (CAMPANA 413, DEP. TOULOUSE). SS. Leonard and James (fr.)

LOUVRE. 1299. Venus and three Putti.

    1300A. Madonna and Child with two Angels (c. after lost Botticelli).

    1657D. Cassone panel (*testata*): Coronation of Esther. (Companion to Budapest 2537.)

    1658. S. Jerome in the Wilderness, with the Infant Christ appearing to S. Augustine and the Meeting between Christ and S. John in the background.

Pavia. 180. Madonna and Child (r.).

Philadelphia (Pa.). MUSEUM OF ART, JOHNSON COLLECTION. 51. David.

    52. Madonna adoring the Child.

    53. Madonna and Child with young S. John and an Angel.

    54. Cassone panel: Reconciliation between the Romans and the Sabines.

    64. Banquet of Nastagio degli Onesti. (*Decamerone*, v, 8; p.; version of Botticelli, Madrid 2840). (Companion to Brooklyn?)

Poitiers. MUSÉE 102 (CAMPANA 191). Madonna and Child.

Princeton (N.J.). L6.48. S. Jerome in the Wilderness.

Rome. COLLEGIO DEGLI SCOZZESI. Lunette: God the Father and two Angels.

    GALLERIA COLONNA. Massacre of Innocents. L.

Rotterdam. 2563. Cassone panel: Story of Orpheus and Eurydice. (Companion to Vienna, Lanckoronski and to Kiev.)

San Giovanni Valdarno. 13, 14. Annunciation. Predella: Nativity, SS. Martin and Sebastian. d. 1472. *Plate* 1097.

Sarasota (Fla.). 17. S. Jerome in the Wilderness.

Stockholm. 2366. Wilderness, with S. Jerome, S. Augustine and the Christ Child, and the Temptation of S. Anthony.

Toulouse. 404. See Paris, Musées Nationaux.

Vaduz. LIECHTENSTEIN COLLECTION. A.1122. Tondo: Madonna and Child with six Angels holding Lilies (version of Botticelli's Raczynski Tondo, Berlin 102A).

Venice. CA'D'ORO. Tondo: Madonna adoring the Child with Infant S. John.

    PALAZZO GRASSI, CINI LOAN. *Pietà*.

Vienna. AKADEMIE. 1099. Madonna and Child with S. John Baptist and an Angel.

    LANCKORONSKI COLLECTION. Cassone panel: Orpheus. (Companion to Rotterdam and to Kiev).

    Young Man adoring a crowned Saint.

Washington (D.C.). 394 (KRESS COLLECTION 501). S. John Baptist in the Wilderness. *Plate* 1109, 1478.

Wiesbaden. STAEDTISCHES MUSEUM (EX). 6. Adoration of Magi. (Destroyed?)

Wroclaw. See Breslau.

Zagreb. 49. Tondo: Adoration of the Shepherds (g.p.). L.

Homeless. *Pietà. Plate* 1101.

SOGLIANI, Giovanni Antonio

1492–1544. Pupil of Lorenzo di Credi; greatly influenced by Fra Bartolommeo, Albertinelli; close follower of Andrea del Sarto.

Anghiari (Borgo San Sepolcro). COLLEGIATA, L. TRANSEPT. Last Supper (after Andrea del Sarto's at S. Salvi, Florence). 1531.

Washing of Feet. *Plate* 1345.

Baltimore (Md.). WALTERS ART GALLERY. 524. Tondo: Madonna and Child with Infant S. John.

Berlin. (BERLIN-OST). 250. Christ in the House of Mary and Martha, with Donors. d. 1524. *Plate* 1344.

Brussels. 637. Madonna and Child with Infant S. John. E.

Capesthorne Hall (Chelford, Ches.). LT.-COL. SIR W. H. BROMLEY-DAVENPORT. Two panels: Two adoring Angels (replica at New Haven). *Plate* 1342.

Castelnuovo Garfagnana. DUOMO, SACRISTY. Madonna and Child with SS. James and Andrew.

Castiglion Fiorentino. COLLEGIATA, CHAPEL R. OF HIGH ALTAR. Nativity (only the S. Joseph; the rest by Lorenzo di Credi). E.

Chantilly. 30. S. Mary Magdalen. (?)

31. Madonna and Child with six Saints (reduced c. of Fra Bartolommeo's picture at Besançon, with female instead of male Donor). After 1512.

Copenhagen. ROYAL PALACE OF AMALIENBORG. Madonna and Child with Infant S. John. *Plate* 1343.

Dublin. HON. JAMES MURNAGHAN. Madonna and Child with Infant S. John.

Empoli (Environs). S. MARIA A RIPA, 1ST ALTAR L. Assumption with SS. Jerome and Anselm. L. *Plate* 1347.

Englewood (N.J.). D. F. PLATT (EX). Ecstasy of S. Mary Magdalen (or S. Mary of Egypt.) E.

Florence. GALLERIE. 753. Madonna and Child with Infant S. John.

3202. S. Bridget giving the Rule of her Order. d. 1522.

3212. Predella panel: Flagellation and Way to Calvary.

4647. Trinity, with SS. James, Mary Magdalen and Catherine.

4648. S. Francis.

4649. S. Elisabeth of Hungary.

8642. *Madonna della Cintola*, with SS. John Baptist, James and John Gualbert. d. 1521.

ACCADEMIA. 3203. Disputation of the Immaculate Conception.

ARCHIVIO NOTARILE. Madonna and Child. E.

SS. ANNUNZIATA, CAPPELLA DEGLI SPOSI. Lunette: Nativity.

S. CROCE, MUSEO DELL'OPERA. Immaculate Conception, with SS. Sebastian and Roch (the Virgin by Michele di Ridolfo?).

S. GIUSEPPE, 2nd CHAPEL L. Predella (to altarpiece in Sacristy): Temptation of S. Anthony, Nativity, Martyrdom of S. Sebastian.

— SACRISTY. Annunciation with SS. Anthony Abbot and Sebastian.

S. LORENZO, 5th CHAPEL L. Martyrdom of S. Acacius. Sd. and d. 1521.

S. MARCO (MUSEO), REFECTORY. Fresco: S. Dominic fed by Angels, in the background Crucifixion and SS. Antonino and Catherine of Siena. d. 1536. *Plate* 1349.

S. MARIA DEL FIORE (DUOMO), L. TRANSEPT, 1st CHAPEL. S. Joseph (in the studio of Credi). E.

S. MARIA DEGLI INNOCENTI, HIGH ALTAR. Annunciation (with Albertinelli). d. 15(17?26?).

ORSANMICHELE, 3rd PILASTER L. S. Martin.

S. NICCOLÒ DEL CEPPO. Processional banners: Visitation, S. Nicholas with two Children.

CENACOLO DI S. SALVI (MUSEO). 8666. Madonna and Child with SS. John Gualbert and Bernardo degli Uberti.

S. SEBASTIANO DEI BINI, HIGH ALTAR. Panels formerly surrounding the stolen Madonna by Rossello di Jacopo: Pietà, SS. Peter and Bernard. Predella: Martyrdom of S. Peter, Annunciation, Vision of S. Bernard.

SERRISTORI COLLECTION. Madonna and Child with SS. Bernard and John Baptist. *Plate* 1346.

(Environs) CONVENTO DEL BOSCO AI FRATI (CAFAGGIOLO), 2nd ALTAR L. Annunciation.

— S. DOMENICO DI FIESOLE, 2nd CHAPEL L. Adoration of the Magi (begun by Andrea del Sarto, who laid in background and small figures; finished by Santi di Tito).

Hamburg. GALERIE WEBER (EX). Holy Family with Infant S. John and an Angel.

High Hall, (Wimborne, Sussex). MRS. ISABEL TRACEY. Madonna and Child with Infant S. John. (?)

Lewisburg (Penna.). BUCKNELL UNIVERSITY, KRESS STUDY COLLECTION. K 1146. Madonna against landscape. E. (?)

Liverpool. 2868. Tondo: Madonna and Child with Infant S. John. (?).

London. 645. Madonna and Child.

Modena. 510. Madonna and Child with Infant S. John.

Nancy. 2. Tobias and the Angel. *Plate* 1348.

New Haven (Conn.). 1871.77. Angel in profile to right (replica of Capesthorne Hall).

Palermo. GALLERIA NAZIONALE DELLA SICILIA (FROM OLIVELLA). Madonna adoring the Child with Infant S. John and an Angel (on Lorenzo di Credi's design). E. *Plate* 1341.

Paris. MUSÉES NATIONAUX, CAMPANA COLLECTION (DEP. TOULON.194). Madonna and Child with Infant S. John.

Pisa. 204, 206. Two oval panels: Angels (fr.; see Duomo, Choir.)

205. SS. Anthony Abbot, Nicholas and Andrew (fr.; see Duomo, Choir).

DUOMO, 3rd ALTAR R. Madonna and Child with SS. Francis, Jerome and Bartholomew.

— R. TRANSEPT, 1st CHAPEL R. Madonna and Child with SS. John Baptist, Peter, Paul, Catherine, Barbara, Mary Magdalen, Francis and George.

— CHOIR, Madonna and Child (fr. of an altarpiece which included the three fragments in the Museo Civico.)

Sacrifice of Noah.

Sacrifice of Cain.

Sacrifice of Abel.

Prato. S. SPIRITO, 2nd ALTAR R. Madonna and Child with SS. Anne, Roch and James (after Fra Bartolommeo's 'S. Marco' altarpiece; with Michele di Ridolfo?).

Rome. PINACOTECA CAPITOLINA. 100. Tondo: Madonna and Child with two Angels. E.

San Godenzo (Mugello). BADIA DI S. GODENZO, CHAPEL L. (BAPTISTERY). Annunciation (st.).

Toulon. 185. Madonna and Child with Infant S. John.

Turin. 139. Madonna and Child with Infant S. John.

Vienna. LANCKORONSKI COLLECTION. Lady with a Unicorn.

Volterra. 53. S. Joseph.

SPINELLO ARETINO

ca 1350–1410. *Probably a pupil of Agnolo Gaddi; principally influenced by the Orcagna school, and to a lesser degree by Luca di Tommè. Assisted in his late years by his son, Parri.*

Allentown (Pa.). ART MUSEUM, KRESS COLLECTION. K 174. Panel of polyptych: four Saints (fr.).

Altenburg. 67. Madonna and Child with two Angels and SS. John Baptist and Anthony Abbot (with Lorenzo di Niccolò).

Arezzo. 7. Fresco: Trinity (r.).

8. Fragment of fresco with Lucifer's Fall, from S. Michele Arcangelo (st.; companion to London 1216 a, b). L.

S. AGOSTINO. Fresco: Madonna and Child with SS. James, Anthony Abbot, and kneeling Warrior. d. 1377. *Plate* 400.

SS. ANNUNZIATA, OVER ENTRANCE. Tabernacle fresco: Annunciation. *Plate* 401.

S. BERNARDO. Fresco: Madonna nursing Child (fr.).

S. DOMENICO, L. OF ENTRANCE. Fresco: SS. James and Philip, Marriage of S. Catherine, Martyrdom of S. Catherine, S. James healing Cripples, Beheading of S. James, S. Philip exorcizing the Temple of Hierapolis, Crucifixion of S. Philip. L. *Plate* 425.

— L. WALL. Fresco: Madonna and Child and Scenes from the Life of S. Christopher.
[S. Christopher and the Devil disguised as a Knight, S. Christopher and the
Hermit, Attempted Martyrdom of S. Christopher with Arrows, S. Christo-
pher before the King of Lycia, and two other Scenes.] (st., r.).

Fresco: Madonna and Child enthroned with two Saints and a Donor (st.)

Fresco: Annunciation (st.).

S. FRANCESCO, R. WALL. Frescoes: S. Michael in niche, with kneeling Donor,
Annunciation, S. Joseph and the Christ Child. *Plate* 402, 421.

— CHAPEL R. OF CHOIR. Frescoes: Scenes from the Legends of SS. Giles and Michael.
[Left wall: S. Giles giving Alms, S. Giles discovered by Huntsmen, Miraculous Absolution of Charles Martell through the Prayer of S. Giles. Right
wall: Christ enthroned with Saints and Angels, Triumph of S. Michael,
Apparition of S. Michael on Castel S. Angelo. Pilasters: S. Nicholas and
two other Saints] (r.). *Plate* 403.

— CHAPEL L. Frescoes (pilasters): S. Peter and a female Saint (r.).

— L. WALL. Frescoes: Two Scenes from the Life of S. Francis, Pentecost (r.).

S. MARIA MADDALENA. Fresco: Madonna and Child (fr.).

S. MARIA DELLA PIEVE, CHOIR, IST PILLAR L. Fresco: SS. Francis and Dominic.

Budapest. 36. Left wing of Monteoliveto altarpiece: SS. Nemesius and John Baptist. Above: A Prophet. Predella: Beheading of S. Nemesius, A Saint, Feast
of Herod. (Companion to Cambridge 1915.12 a–c and Siena 119 and 125).
1385.

Cambridge (Mass.). 1905.1. Madonna and Child with eight Angels.

1915.12a, b, c. Right wing of Monteoliveto altarpiece: SS. Benedict and Lucilla.
Above: a Prophet. Predella: Death of S. Benedict, S. Augustine, Martyrdom
of S. Lucilla (see Budapest). d. 1385. *Plate* 408.

1917.3. Madonna and Child with nineteen Angels. Sd.

1930.201. Predella panel: Adoration of the Magi.

Capesthorne Hall (Ches.). LT.-COL. SIR W. H. BROMLEY-DAVENPORT. Left wing of an
altarpiece: SS. John Baptist and Michael.

Chicago (Ill.). 33.1031. Confirmation of the Franciscan Rule (g.p.).

Città di Castello. PINACOTECA. Madonna and Child enthroned. *Plate* 420.

Copenhagen. 1749. Madonna and Child.

Cortona. S. FRANCESCO, ENTRANCE ARCH TO APSE. Frescoes: Saints.

Enschede. RIJKSMUSEUM TWENTHE. NK. 1404, 1405. Two panels: SS. Elizabeth of
Hungary and Catherine.

Florence. ACCADEMIA. 8461. Triptych: Madonna and Child with four Angels and
SS. Paulinus, John Baptist, Andrew and Matthew. Above: Two Prophets.
Sd and d. 1391. *Plate* 416.

8468. Triptych: Coronation of the Virgin with four music-making Angels and
SS. Felicitas, Andrew, John Baptist, Matthew, John Evangelist, Peter, James

and Benedict. Above: Two Angels and two Prophets (central panel only, with Lorenzo di Niccolò; side panels by Niccolò di Pietro Gerini; predella by Lorenzo di Niccolò). d. 1401. *Plate* 386.

UFFIZI. 464. Crucifixion (st.).

S. BARNABA, L. WALL. Frescoes: S. Michael, and a Pope (fr.). (?)

S. CROCE, SACRISTY. Frescoes: Way to Calvary, Crucifixion (with Lorenzo di Niccolò; see also Niccolò di Pietro Gerini). *Plate* 381.

— MUSEO DELL'OPERA. Fresco lunette: Madonna and Child with S. Michael and a Bishop Saint. (?)

S. MARIA MAGGIORE, CHOIR. Monochrome frescoes: Judgement of Solomon, Massacre of the Innocents (st., r.).

S. MARIA NOVELLA, 2nd CHAPEL R. OF CHOIR (BARDI). Frescoes: Scenes from the Life of S. Gregory [Miraculous Discovery of S. Gregory attempting to escape the Papacy, S. Gregory enthroned as Pope, Death of S. Gregory, and three other Scenes]. Saints and Prophets in medallions (g.p.; r.). *Plate* 422.

S. MINIATO AL MONTE, R. WALL. Fresco: S. Andrew, S. Miniato with female Donor, and S. Nicholas.

— SACRISTY. Frescoes. Vault: Four Evangelists. Walls: Scenes from the Life of S. Benedict [Upper register, beginning on wall opposite entrance: Departure of S. Benedict for Rome, Miracle of the broken Sieve, Investiture of S. Benedict and S. Benedict in the *Sacro Speco* at Subiaco, The Priest sharing his Easter Meal with S. Benedict, Temptation of S. Benedict, S. Benedict elected Abbot and the Blessing of the Poisoned Wine, S. Benedict leaving the Monastery, SS. Maurus and Placidus entrusted to S. Benedict. Lower register, beginning on wall opposite window: Raising of a Monk from the Ruins of Monte Cassino, S. Benedict reforming a lax Monk, Miraculous Recovery of the Scythe from the Lake, Miraculous Rescue from Drowning of S. Placidus, The Bewitched Stone, Totila before S. Benedict, Prophecy of Totila's Death, Death of S. Benedict] (g.p.). 1386–87. [*Plate* 129.] *Plates* 409–410.

(Environs) ANTELLA, ORATORIO DI S. CATERINA. Frescoes. Vault: Four Evangelists. Walls: Scenes from the Life of S. Catherine [Right wall: S. Catherine consulting with the Hermit, S. Catherine baptized by the Hermit, Mystic Marriage of S. Catherine, S. Catherine refusing to worship Idols. Left wall: Disputation of S. Catherine, Martyrdom of the converted Philosophers, Conversion of the Empress and others, Martyrdom of the Empress and her Companions. Altar wall: S. Catherine led from Prison and beheaded, Translation of her Body to Mount Sinai, S. Anthony Abbot, S. Catherine. Pilasters: SS. Francis and Louis of Toulouse. Soffits and dadoes: *Agnus Dei*, twelve Apostles and twelve Prophets]. ca 1387. *Plates* 411–414.

— S. MARIA A QUINTO, L. WALL. Triptych: Madonna and Child with SS. Peter, Philip, Lawrence and James. Pinnacles: Christ blessing, Annunciation (with Lorenzo di Niccolò). d. 1393. *Plate* 415.

Lewisburg (Penna.). BUCKNELL UNIVERSITY, KRESS STUDY COLLECTION. K 256. Madonna and Child with two music-making Angels, SS. John Baptist, Anthony Abbot and two female Saints (st.).

Liverpool. 2752, 2753. Two fresco fragments: Head of Salome, Infant S. John and three Women (see Pisa, Camposanto).

London. 276. Fresco fragment: Heads of two mourning Saints (see Pisa, Camposanto).

1216 A, B. Three fragments from fresco of Lucifer's Fall in S. Michele Arcangelo, Arezzo: S. Michael and other Angels, two decorative borders (st.). L.

VISCOUNT ROTHERMERE (EX). S. James.

Montepulciano. I. Coronation of the Virgin with eleven Angels (Angels above entirely painted and those below begun by Luca di Tommé).

New York. 13.175. Processional banner: S. Mary Magdalen enthroned with eight music-making Angels and four Flagellants. On back: Flagellation of Christ (see Rome, Camposanto Teutonico). *Plates 404–405.*

41.190.203. S. Margaret.

MORGAN LIBRARY. Illuminated Initials from Antiphonary: Last Supper, Ascension, Trinity, and Abraham visited by the three Angels, Saints and Prophets. (?)

— (ex). Angel of the Annunciation.

ROBERT LEHMAN. S. Philip.

Oxford. CHRIST CHURCH LIBRARY. 8. Madonna and Child. Pinnacle: Christ blessing. (g.p.).

Paris. ÉCOLE DES BEAUX ARTS. Triptych: Annunciation, with S. Catherine and a Pope. Pinnacles: Christ blessing and two Angels (p.). (?)

Parma. 430, 439, 452. Three predella panels: Adoration of the Magi, Head of S. John brought to Herod, S. Benedict giving the Rule to his Monks (st.).

454, 457. Wings of an altarpiece: SS. Philip and Chrysanthus, SS. Daria and James the Less.

Pavia. 192. Fresco fragment: S. John Baptist. (See Pisa, Camposanto.)

Pisa. 129. Right wing of triptych (see Duomo): SS. John Baptist, James and Anthony Abbot (with Lorenzo di Niccolò).

133. Madonna and Child enthroned (fr.).

CAMPOSANTO. Three frescoes: Scenes from the Life of S. Ephysius [S. Ephysius before Diocletian, Conversion of S. Ephysius in Battle, Apparition of the Angelic Warrior and Rout of the Pagans, Condemnation and Martyrdom of S. Ephysius]. 1391–92. *Plates 418–419.*

Six fresco fragments: Head of S. Elizabeth, Zacharias writing the Name of John, Head of S. John Baptist, Heads of two Angels, Head of a Lutist, Head of an Apostle. (Companions to Liverpool 2752–53, London 276, Pavia and Rotterdam).

DUOMO, SALA DEL CAPITOLO. Left wing of triptych (see Pisa 129): SS. Raynerius, Silvester and Michael (with Lorenzo di Niccolò).

Pisa. DUOMO (contd.). OPERA PRIMAZIALE. Central panel of triptych (see Pisa 129): Coronation of the Virgin with four music-making Angels (with Lorenzo di Niccolò).

Polesden Lacey (Surrey). CHRISTOPHER NORRIS. Fresco roundel: Head of an Angel.

Poughkeepsie (N.Y.). VASSAR COLLEGE. S. Thaddeus (st.).

Providence (R.I.). 16.243. S. Anthony Abbot enthroned with two Angels and two Donors. Pinnacle: Christ blessing. (?)

Rome. CAMPOSANTO TEUTONICO. Head of Christ (fr. from the New York Flagellation). *Plate 405.*

VATICAN, PINACOTECA. 186. Madonna and Child with music-making Angels.

Rotterdam. 2538. Fresco fragment: A Woman. (See Pisa, Camposanto.)

Saint Louis (Mo.). 48.27. Madonna and Child enthroned with two Angels. *Plate 417.*

Siena. 117, 118. Two predella panels: S. Paul preaching before the Areopagus, S. Paul led to Martyrdom. E. (?)

119. Pinnacle: Coronation of the Virgin with Angels. (See Budapest.) *Plate 406.*

125. Predella panel: Dormition of the Virgin. (See Budapest.) *Plate 407.*

PALAZZO PUBBLICO, SALA DI BALIA. Frescoes: Scenes from the Life of Pope Alexander III. [Right wall: Coronation of Alexander, Alexander consigning the Sword to the Venetian Doge, Foundation of Alexandria, Submission of Barbarossa. Wall opposite entrance: Canonization of SS. Canute and Thomas of Canterbury, Congress of Venice, Alexander entering Rome. Window wall: Alexander at Anagni, Pardon of Barbarossa. Entrance wall: Alexander and Louis VII, Alexander's Flight from Rome, Venetian Conquest of Barbarossa's Fleet at Punta Salvore. Above center arch: Lateran Synod, Burning of the Antipopes, Investiture of Antipope Victor IV, Homage to Alexander] (assisted by his son Parri and by Martino di Bartolomeo). 1408–10. *Plates 423–424.*

Vienna. LANCKORONSKI COLLECTION. Left wing of an altarpiece: SS. Marinus and John Baptist.

STROZZI, Zanobi

Painter and miniaturist. 1412–1468. On commission of Cosimo dei Medici, he illuminated twenty codices for the library of S. Marco between 1446 and 1453. The documents specify that he painted the figures inside the letters while the ornaments were done by Filippo di Matteo Torelli. Paintings by him on panel are documented in 1436 and in 1448. In 1463, with Francesco di Antonio del Chierico, he started illuminating antiphonaries for the Duomo of Florence.

Florence. MUSEO DI S. MARCO. Antiphonary D (inv. 518). Letter P: Young Man in a landscape, blessed by God the Father. Documented 1446. *Plate 627.*

PRINCIPE TOMMASO CORSINI. Antiphonary from S. Gaggio: Marriage of S. Catherine. Documented 1447. *Plate 628.*

'TOMMASO'

*Temporary name for an artistic personality parallel to Lorenzo di Credi, but at times close to
Piero di Cosimo. He is not identical with Tommaso di Stefano, and might be Giovanni
Cianfanini (1462–1542) who worked with Botticelli in 1480 and with Credi in 1523.*

Amsterdam. 737 B–1. Tondo: Madonna and Child with Infant S. John.

Angers. MUSÉE 316 (CAMPANA 243). Tondo: Madonna and Child with Infant S.
John and a female Saint.

Balcarres (Fife, Scotland). EARL OF CRAWFORD AND BALCARRES (EX). Madonna adoring
the Child with an Angel.

Baltimore (Md.). WALTERS ART GALLERY. 458. Cassone panel: Triumph of Chastity.

Bassano. MUSEO CIVICO. Madonna and Child with two Angels.

Bergamo. 544. Predella panel: Nativity. *Plate* 1186.

Berlin. (BERLIN-OST). 104. Tondo: Madonna and Child with Infant S. John.

Buffalo (N.Y.). 33.97. Tondo: Holy Family.

Cambridge. 125. S. Sebastian.

Castiglion Fiorentino. PINACOTECA. Tondo: Nativity with two Saints. L.

Cracow. 48. Tondo: Madonna adoring the Child with Infant S. John and SS.
Francis and Jerome.

Dijon. T 27. Tondo: Madonna and Child with two Angels.

Dublin. 519. Tondo: Madonna and Child with two Angels.

Dubrovnik. S. DOMENICO. Tondo: Holy Family with Infant S. John.

Edenbridge (Kent). ARCHIBALD WERNER. Cassone panel: Venus asks Cupid to
wound Adonis with the arrow of Love. (Companion to Gosford House).
Plate 1181.

Fécamp. MUSÉE. Tondo: Madonna nursing the Child with Infant S. John and two
Angels.

Florence. PITTI. 354. Tondo: Nativity.

MUSEO HORNE. 1599. Tondo: Holy Family with Infant S. John and an Angel.

SS. ANNUNZIATA, CONVENTO, STAIRCASE. Two monochrome fresco lunettes:
Annunciation.

CENACOLO DI S. SALVI. Female allegorical figure in niche. (?)

S. SPIRITO, CHOIR, 1ST CHAPEL R. Madonna and Child with SS. John Evangelist and
Jerome. E. *Plate* 1185.

(Environs) VILLA SCHIFANOIA. Tondo: Holy Family with Infant S. John.

— VILLA SPARTA (QUEEN MOTHER OF ROUMANIA). Tondo: Madonna and Child with
two Angels.

Gosford House (Longniddry, Scotland). EARL OF WEMYSS AND MARCH. Cassone
panel: Death of Adonis. (Companion to Edenbridge).

Leningrad. 50. Tondo: Madonna and Child with Infant S. John and two music-
making Angels. *Plate* 1183.

Los Angeles (Cal.). A.6050.50–1. Tondo: Madonna adoring the Child with Infant S. John and two Angels. *Plate* 1180.

Luton Hoo (Beds.). SIR HAROLD WERNHER. Madonna and Child with a Saint and two Angels.

Memphis (Tenn.). BROOKS MEMORIAL ART GALLERY, KRESS COLLECTION. K B–I. Tondo: Madonna adoring the Child with Infant S. John and two Angels.

Milan. MUSEO POLDI PEZZOLI. 580. Predella panel: Martyrdom of S. Sebastian. *Plate* 1184.

Modena. 503. Madonna and Child with Infant S. John.

Montpellier. MUSÉE FABRE 48 (CAMPANA 223). Tondo: Nativity with two Angels.

Munich. W.A.F. 191. Tondo: Holy Family with Infant S. John and an Angel.

New Haven (Conn.). 1871.55. Predella panel: Baptism of Christ.

Nijmegen (Holland). (Environs) H. W. JURGENS (EX). Lamentation. *Plate* 1182.

Poughkeepsie (N.Y.). VASSAR COLLEGE. Tondo: Nativity, with Infant S. John. (?)

Rome. GALLERIA BORGHESE. 439. Tondo: Holy Family.

Santa Monica (Cal.). J. PAUL GETTY MUSEUM (FORMERLY MUNICH 7820). Madonna and Child with an Angel. *Plate* 1178.

Seattle (Washington). ART MUSEUM (KRESS COLLECTION 99). Tondo: Holy Family.

Vienna. WITTGENSTEIN COLLECTION (EX). Tondo: Holy Family with Infant S. John.

York. 814. Tondo: Madonna adoring the Child with Infant S. John and SS. Jerome and Francis.

Homeless. Tondo: Madonna and Child with Infant S. John and an Angel. *Plate* 1179.

TOMMASO DI STEFANO LUNETTI

Ca 1490–1564. Pupil of Lorenzo di Credi, later active mostly as painter of 'drapperie' and as architect. Not to be identified with 'Tommaso di Credi'.

Florence. GALLERIA CORSINI. Madonna and sleeping Child, with Infant S. John.
VILLA CAPPONI AD ARCETRI, CHAPEL. Adoration of the Shepherds. Predella: Visitation, Agony in the Garden, Crucifixion with SS. Jerome and John Baptist, Way to Calvary, Meeting of SS. Francis and Dominic. *Plates* 1352–4.

New York. 17.190.8. Portrait of a Man. Sd and d. 1521. *Plate* 1356.

Rome. GALLERIA NAZIONALE (PALAZZO BARBERINI). Madonna and sleeping Child, with Infant S. John (replica of Florence, Corsini). *Plate* 1350.

Tulsa (Oklahoma). PHILBROOK ART CENTER, KRESS COLLECTION. K 212. Portrait of a Man. (?).

Homeless. Nativity. *Plate* 1357.
Portrait of young Man. *Plate* 1355.
Madonna nursing the Child and Infant S. John. (?) *Plate* 1351.

UCCELLO, Paolo

1397–1475. Trained in the studio of Ghiberti. Matured under influence of Donatello and Brunelleschi.

Florence. UFFIZI. 479. Rout of S. Romano. (Companion to London 583 and to Paris 1273).

    S. MARIA NOVELLA, CHIOSTRO VERDE. *Four frescoes: Creation of the Animals and Creation of Adam, Creation of Eve and the Fall of Man, The Flood, Noah's Sacrifice and the Drunkenness of Noah. E. *Plates 659, 660, 663, 664.*

    S. MARIA DEL FIORE (DUOMO), ENTRANCE WALL. Clock-face: Four Heads of 'Prophets'. 1443. *Plate 662.*

    -- L. WALL, 3rd BAY. Fresco: Equestrian Portrait of Sir John Hawkwood. 1436. *Plate 661.*

    — CUPOLA. Two circular windows: Nativity, and Resurrection. 1443.

    S. MARTINO DELLA SCALA.* Fresco: Nativity (r.). (?)

    S. MINIATO AL MONTE, UPPER CLOISTER. Frescoes: Scenes from the Lives of Monastic Saints (fr.). E.

London. 583. Rout of S. Romano. (Companion to Florence, Uffizi, and to Paris 1273). [*Plate 143.*] *Plates 665.*

    6294. S. George and the Dragon. L. *Plate 666.*

Oxford. ASHMOLEAN. 442. A Hunt. L. [*Plate 145.*]

Paris. 1272. Portraits of the 'Founders of Florentine Art': Giotto, Uccello, Donatello, Antonio Manetti and Brunelleschi (r.). L.

    1273. Rout of S. Romano. (Companion to Florence, Uffizi, and to London 583).

    MUSÉE JACQUEMART-ANDRÉ. 1038. S. George and the Dragon. [*Plate 144.*]

Urbino. GALLERIA NAZIONALE DELLE MARCHE (PALAZZO DUCALE). Predella: Profanation of the Host. 1468. *Plates 667, 668, 669.*

'UTILI' (Biagio di Antonio?)

Follower of Verrocchio and Ghirlandajo, frequently active in Faenza. First identified with Andrea Utili da Faenza (1481–1502), then erroneously with Giovanni Battista Utili (doc. 1503–1515), and lately with a Biagio di Antonio da Firenze (doc. in Faenza 1476–1483 and again 1504). So far no documented picture has confirmed either hypothesis. A shadowy entity in life, his artistic personality, however, is consistent and clear.

Ajaccio (Corsica). 193. Tondo: Madonna adoring the Child with Infant S. John and S. Francis.

Allentown (Pa.). ART MUSEUM. KRESS COLLECTION. K 257. Madonna and Child with SS. John Baptist, Jerome, Dominic and three other Saints.

Baltimore (Md.). MUSEUM OF ART. 51.120. Madonna and Child with an Angel.
WALTERS ART GALLERY. 471. Madonna and Child with young S. John.
  536. Madonna and Child. E. (?)
  1040. Tondo: Madonna and Child with Infant S. John and two Angels. L. (?)
Bayonne. 6. Head of the Redeemer.
Belgrade. ROYAL PALACE (EX). 'Demidoff' Tondo: Madonna and Child with two
  Angels. *Plate* 1042.
Berlin. 1823, 1824. Two cassone panels: Story of Cupid and Psyche. E.
Besançon. 896.1.58. Madonna adoring the Child with an Angel.
Birmingham (Ala.). ART MUSEUM, KRESS COLLECTION. K 1722. Madonna adoring
  the Child.
Bremen. 741. Madonna and Child with SS. Francis, Louis of Toulouse, Anthony of
  Padua, Lucy, Bernardo degli Uberti, and another Saint. *Plate* 1043.
Budapest. 1386. Madonna and Child with SS. Peter Martyr, Catherine of Siena,
  Vincent Ferrer, James and a Bishop Saint. E. *Plate* 1028.
Cambridge (Mass.). 1928.169. Cassone panel: Judgement of Paris.
Cracow. 285. Madonna and Child (r.). (?)
Dublin. 842. Madonna adoring the Child.
Eastnor Castle (Hereford). HON. MRS. HERVEY BATHURST. Madonna and Child with
  SS. Peter Martyr, Francis, three other Saints and a young Donor.
Faenza. PINACOTECA. Lunette (from Fossolo): Annunciation.
  Two panels (from Fossolo?): SS. Sebastian and John Baptist.
  Triptych: Madonna and Child with two Angels and SS. Dominic, Andrew,
    John Evangelist and Thomas Aquinas. 1483. *Plate* 1041.
  Madonna and Child with young S. John and S. Anthony of Padua.
  Madonna and Child with SS. John Baptist, Benedict, Romuald, John Evan-
    gelist, Jerome and a Bishop Saint (heads of Baptist and Bishop repainted).
  Madonna and Child with SS. Bonaventura and Bernardino. L.
  Crucifixion (st.).
  Man of Sorrows with two Angels.
  Man of Sorrows with two Angels and Symbols of Passion.
  S. Peter Martyr with view of Florence in background. E.
  Two panels from triptych: SS. Peter Martyr and Dominic (st.).
  DUOMO, LAST CHAPEL R. Madonna nursing the Child.
Fiesole. VIA BENEDETTO DA MAIANO AND VIA DEL SALVIATINO. Tabernacle fresco:
  Madonna and Child with two Angels. Vault: God the Father, David and
  another Prophet, S. John Baptist and another Saint (r.).
Florence. GALLERIE. Madonna and Child. E.
  PALAZZO DI PARTE GUELFA, CONSIGLIATOIO. Justice.
  BARTOLINI SALIMBENI COLLECTION. Archangels Michael, Raphael with Tobias,
    and Gabriel. *Plate* 1029–30.
  BERENSON COLLECTION. Head of the Redeemer.

(Environs) S. MARTINO A STRADA. Madonna and Child with SS. Zenobius, Francis, Nicholas and John Baptist. E.

Liverpool. 2808. Cassone panel: Story of Ulysses.

London. COURTAULD GALLERIES, LEE OF FAREHAM COLLECTION. 58. The Morelli–Nerli cassoni. Fronts: The Gauls defeated by Marcus Furius Camillus, The Schoolmaster of Falerii. *Spalliere:* Horatius holding the Bridge, Ordeal of Mucius Scaevola. *Testate:* Justice, Fortitude, Prudence, Temperance. 1472. *Plate* 1031. Madonna adoring the Child.

HON. MRS. DONNELL POST (EX). Tondo: Madonna and Child with two Angels.

W. H. WOODWARD (EX). Cassone panel (*testata*): Judgement of Paris.

Lyons. MUSÉE. Madonna and Child with Infant S. John.

Milan. MUSEO POLDI–PEZZOLI. 591. Madonna and Child with an Angel. *Plate* 1038.

Montauban. MUSÉE. Head of Christ (r.). L.

Munich. 1069. Archangels Michael, Raphael with Tobias, and Gabriel.

New Haven (Conn.). 1943.223. Adoration of the Magi.

New York. 09.136.1, 2. Two cassone panels: Story of the Argonauts. *Plate* 1033.

32.100.69. Cassone panel: Story of Joseph. (Companion to Homeless). *Plate* 1027.

S. H. KRESS FOUNDATION. K 369. Madonna adoring the Child with an Angel. *Plate* 1026.

K 1139, 1184. Wings of an altarpiece: Tobias and the Angel, S. Jerome.

Oxford. ASHMOLEAN. 444. Cassone panel: Sack of Rome and Flight of the Vestal Virgins.

CHRIST CHURCH LIBRARY. 40. Madonna and Child with young S. John and an Angel.

41. Madonna and Child.

48. Crucifixion. *Plate* 1040.

Paris. MUSÉES NATIONAUX (CAMPANA 247, DEP. PÉRIGUEUX). Lunette: Annunciation.

LOUVRE. 1323. Way to Calvary. *Plate* 1044.

1657B. Madonna and Child with Infant S. John and four Angels.

MUSÉE DES ARTS DÉCORATIFS, LEGS PEYRE. Cassone panel: Meeting of Jason and Medea. 1486–87.

MUSÉE JACQUEMART–ANDRÉ. 1032. Madonna adoring the Child with two Angels (after an early Botticelli).

Périgueux. MUSÉE. See Paris, Musées Nationaux.

Philadelphia (Pa.). MUSEUM OF ART, JOHNSON COLLECTION. 62. Nativity.

63. Madonna and Child. L.

Pisa. SCHIFF COLLECTION (EX). Ascension.

Princeton (N.J.). L 7.48. Madonna and Child with a Cherub.

Ravenna. 55. Madonna and Child with Infant S. John.

Rome. VATICAN, SISTINE CHAPEL. Fresco: Crossing of the Red Sea (probably with Davide Ghirlandajo). 1482. *Plate* 1036–7.

Frescoes (background of Last Supper by Cosimo Rosselli): Agony in the Garden, Betrayal of Christ, Crucifixion. 1482. (?) *Plate* 1007.

San Casciano (Val di Pesa). S. FRANCESCO, 1ST CHAPEL L. Madonna nursing the Child, with SS. Francis and Mary Magdalen.

São Paulo (Brasil). 016. Madonna adoring the Child with an Angel.

Strasbourg. 216. Madonna adoring the Child with two Angels.

Tulsa (Okla.). PHILBROOK ART CENTER, KRESS COLLECTION. K 1088. Nativity, with SS. Dominic, Nicholas of Tolentino, Louis of Toulouse and three Donors. ca 1476.

Venice. CA' D'ORO. Tondo: Madonna and Child with young S. John and a music-making Angel.

Two cassone panels: Story of Lucretia. *Plate* 1035.

Cassone panel: Story of Darius. E.

Vienna. LANCKORONSKI COLLECTION. Predella panel: Martyrdom of a Bishop near a Well.

Washington (D.C.). 264 (KRESS COLLECTION 299). Cassone panel: A Triumph. *Plate* 1034.

290 (KRESS COLLECTION 326). Portrait of a Boy.

York. 819. Two panels: SS. Sebastian and Roch.

Zagreb. 98. Madonna and Child with SS. Francis and Jerome.

Homeless. Cassone panel: Story of Joseph. (Companion to New York 32.100.69). *Plate* 1032.

Madonna and Child. *Plate* 1039.

VERROCCHIO, Andrea

1435–88. *Pupil of Donatello and of Baldovinetti; influenced by Pesellino.*

Berlin. 104A. Madonna and Child. E. *Plate* 929.

108. Madonna and Child. [*Plate* 173.]

Florence. UFFIZI. 8358. Baptism of Christ (assisted by Leonardo). [*Plate* 190.]

Frankfurt am Main. 702. Madonna and Child (p.).

London. 296. Madonna and Child with two Angels. *Plate* 928.

781. Tobias and the Angel (st.; perhaps executed by Botticini on Verrocchio's design).

New York. 14.40.647. Madonna and Child.

Sheffield (Yorks.). RUSKIN MUSEUM. 42. Madonna adoring the Child (p.). [*Plate* 174.]

Washington (D.C.). 502 (KRESS COLLECTION 1282). Madonna and Child (r.; later replica of Berlin 104.A)

1144 (KRESS COLLECTION 1850). Madonna and Child with a pomegranate (st.). *Plate* 934.

SCULPTURE

Amsterdam. RIJKSMUSEUM. Bronze: Candelabrum. d. 1468.

Berlin. 93. Terracotta: Sleeping Youth.
  97A. Terracotta: Entombment.

Florence. MUSEO NAZIONALE DEL BARGELLO. Bronze: David.
  Marble: Bust of a Lady. *Plate* 930.
  Terracotta: Madonna and Child.
  Terracotta relief: Resurrection.
  PALAZZO VECCHIO. Bronze: Putto with a Fish. [*Plate* 171.]
  S. LORENZO, SACRISTY. Tomb of Piero and Giovanni de' Medici. 1472.
  Marble: Lavabo (p.).
  S. MARIA DEL FIORE (DUOMO), MUSEO DELL'OPERA. Silver relief: Beheading of S.
  John Baptist. 1480.
  ORSANMICHELE (Façade on VIA CALZAIUOLI). Bronze: Christ and S. Thomas.
  Finished 1483.

London. VICTORIA AND ALBERT MUSEUM. 7599–L861. Terracotta model for the
  Forteguerri monument (st.).

New York. MRS. N. N. STRAUS. Marble relief: Alexander the Great.

Paris. LOUVRE. Two terracotta reliefs: Angels.

Pistoia. DUOMO, L. WALL. Marble: Monument to Cardinal Niccolò Forteguerri (p., r).

Venice. CAMPO SS. GIOVANNI E PAOLO. Bronze: Equestrian monument to Bartolommeo Colleoni (unfinished at the artist's death and completed by Lorenzo di
  Credi). [*Plate* 172.]

Washington (D.C.). A–16 (MELLON COLLECTION). Terracotta: Bust of Giuliano de'
  Medici.
  A–146 (KRESS COLLECTION K 1277). Terracotta: Bust of Lorenzo de' Medici.

UNIDENTIFIED FLORENTINES, ca 1350–1420

Allentown (Pa.). MUSEUM OF ART, KRESS COLLECTION. K 33. Triptych: Madonna and
  Child enthroned with four Saints, Annunciation, Crucifixion and another Scene.
  K 44. Madonna and Child in Glory with SS. James, Anthony Abbot, Catherine
  and John Evangelist. (Between Jacopo di Cione and Niccolò di Tommaso.)

Assisi. MRS. F. M. PERKINS. Portable triptych: Madonna and Child with two Angels
  and SS. John Baptist and Peter. Wings: Nativity, Crucifixion. (Between the
  S. Cecilia Master and Daddi.)

Balcarres (Fife, Scotland). EARL OF CRAWFORD AND BALCARRES. Crucifixion (close to
  Lorenzo di Niccolò). Predella: Madonna and Child with two Saints (by a later
  hand).

Baltimore (Md.). WALTERS ART GALLERY. 642. Right wing of an altarpiece: SS.
  James and Peter. Pinnacle: Virgin Annunciate. (Follower of Nardo di Cione.)
  729. Madonna and Child with Angels and SS. Bernard, John Baptist, Nicholas
  and Julian. (By Master of 'Straus' Madonna, Houston.)

Berea (Ky.). COLLEGE, KRESS STUDY COLLECTION. K 197. Flagellation. (Close to Daddi).

Berlin. 1113. Predella Panel: Nativity. (Between Agnolo Gaddi and Lorenzo Monaco.)

1522. *Salvator Mundi* and twelve Saints. (Follower of Lorenzo Monaco.)

Brussels. MME. FERON-STOCLET. Predella: Supper in the House of Simon, Christ in the House of Mary and Martha, *Noli me tangere*. Last Communion of S. Mary Magdalen. (Close to Giovanni da Milano.)

Cambridge (Mass.). 1917.213. Annunciation, Nativity, Crucifixion and Entombment. (Follower of Niccolò di Pietro Gerini.)

Claremont (Calif.). POMONA COLLEGE, KRESS STUDY COLLECTION. K 1160. Mourning Virgin.

Dijon. 81. See Paris, Musées Nationaux.

— DONATION DARD. Madonna and four Saints. (Close to Rossello di Jacopo).

Edinburgh. 1539. Predella panel: Baptism and Martyrdom of two Saints. (Companion to York).

Florence. ACCADEMIA. 4635. Madonna and Child with SS. Anthony Abbot, Peter, John Baptist and Julian. Pinnacle: Christ blessing. d. 1416. (Archaizing contemporary of Mariotto di Nardo.)

8465. Portable triptych: Madonna and Child in Glory, with two Donors. Wings: Annunciation, Four Saints, Crucifixion. (Between Jacopo di Cione and Niccolò di Tommaso.) *Plate* 307.

8701, 8702. Two panels from polyptych: S. Augustine, S. Lawrence (r.) (Follower of Maso).

MUSEO NAZIONALE DEL BARGELLO. Cassone: Story of Saladin and Torello. (Distant follower of Maso.)

— CARRAND COLLECTION. Madonna of Humility. (By the same hand as 'Straus' Madonna, Houston.) *Plate* 355.

S. MARIA DEL CARMINE, CLOISTER. Fresco: Madonna and Child with two Donors and SS. Anthony Abbot, Lucy and two other Saints (r.). (Between Maso and Spinello.)

SPEDALE DEGLI INNOCENTI, PINACOTECA. Coronation of the Virgin, with SS. Michael and Mary Magdalen. (Between Giovanni del Biondo and Rossello di Jacopo.)

(Environs) CASTELLO, S. MICHELE. Madonna and Child with two Angels. (Rustic follower of Daddi.)

— IMPRUNETA, COLLEGIATA, BAPTISTERY. Polyptych: Madonna and Child with twelve Angels and SS. Stephen, John Evangelist, Peter and Lawrence. Pinnacles: Four Saints or Prophets (r.). (Follower of Nardo di Cione.)

— S. BRIGIDA ALL'OPACO. Madonna and Child with two Angels. (Close follower of Daddi.)

— S. MARIA A QUINTO. Annunciation. (Between Spinello and Lorenzo di Niccolò.)

— S. MARTINO ALLA PALMA. Madonna and Child with six Angels and Worshippers. (Close follower of Daddi.) *Plates* 185–187.

— VILLA LE CAMPORA, CAPPELLA DI S. ANTONIO. Frescoes: Scenes from the Life of S. Anthony Abbot [Left wall, above: S. Anthony distributing his Fortune, S. Anthony visiting an old Monk. Altar wall, above: Temptation of S. Anthony, Destruction of his Chapel by Devils. Right wall, above: S. Anthony molested by Devils. Left wall, below: S. Anthony instructing his Disciples, An Angel telling S. Anthony of S. Paul. Altar wall, below: Encounter of S. Anthony and the Centaur, Meeting of SS. Anthony and Paul. Right wall, below: SS. Anthony and Paul fed by a Raven, Death of S. Paul. Vault: Four Evangelists. Entrance arch: Twelve Apostles. Pilasters: Two Saints and two Donors] (r.). (Close to Maso.) *Plate* 159–161

Forli. PINACOTECA. Fresco: Adoration of the Magi (?), with SS. Peter, Paul and a third Saint (fr.). (Between Spinello and Agnolo Gaddi.)

Houston (Texas). 44–565. 'Straus' Madonna and Child. (By the so-called Master of the 'Straus' Madonna, a follower of Agnolo Gaddi; see also Baltimore, 729, Florence, Bargello and Homeless.) *Plate* 358.

London. 3894. *Noli me tangere.* (Close to Giovanni da Milano.)

COURTAULD GALLERIES, LEE OF FAREHAM COLLECTION. 6. Predella panel: *Noli me tangere.*

Lucca. PINACOTECA. Frame surrounding statues of the Madonna and Child, S. Michael and a Bishop Saint. [Pinnacles: Christ blessing, Annunciation. Pilasters: Six Saints. Predella: Miracle of the Bull of Gargano, Apparition of S. Michael on Castel Sant'Angelo, S. Lawrence, Nativity, S. Stephen, and two other scenes.] (Between Lorenzo Monaco and Alvaro Portoghese.)

Lugano. THYSSEN COLLECTION. 82. Madonna of Humility with Angels and the twelve Apostles. (By the Master of the Kahn S. Catherine, see New York).

Lyons. MUSÉE. Triptych: Madonna enthroned with Angels and Saints. Pinnacles: Christ blessing, Annunciation. (Between Niccolò di Tommaso and Giovanni da Milano.)

Montgomery (Ala.). HUNTINGDON COLLEGE, KRESS COLLECTION. K 1072. Madonna and Child. (Follower of Orcagna.)

Nashville (Tennessee). G. PEABODY COLLEGE, KRESS COLLECTION. K 1190. Madonna of Humility with Trinity above. Predella: Female Martyr, Angel at Sepulchre, *Noli me tangere.* (Close to Bicci di Lorenzo.)

New Haven (Conn.). 1871–15. Adoration of the Magi. Predella: Annunciation. (Between Jacopo di Cione and Antonio Veneziano.)

— GRIGGS BEQUEST (1943). Scene from Life of S. Barbara. (Close imitator of Giovanni da Milano.)

New York. HISTORICAL SOCIETY. B-10. Wings of a portable altarpiece: Annunciation. Crucifixion and three Saints. (Close to Niccolò di Tommaso.)

B-11. Portable triptych: Madonna and Child with twelve Saints. Pinnacle:

Christ blessing. Wings: Annunciation, Nativity, Crucifixion, S. Christopher. (Close to Nardo di Cione.)

METROPOLITAN MUSEUM. 27.231 (KRESS COLLECTION. M–2, M–3). Two Crucifixes (obverse and reverse of panel).

R. M. HURD (EX). Madonna and Child. (Between Maso and Giovanni del Biondo.)

OTTO KAHN (EX). S. Catherine enthroned with SS. Cosmas and Damian, and Nun and Boy as Donors. (Close to Giovanni del Biondo; see also Lugano; Rome, Vatican 520; Vienna, Bondy.) *Plate 299.*

ROBERT LEHMAN. Predella panel: Madonna and Child appearing to S. Catherine (companion to Worcester 1940.30). (Follower of Giovanni da Milano.)

Ottawa. 2995. The youthful S. John Evangelist. (Between Maso and Jacopo di Cione.)

Paris. MUSÉES NATIONAUX (CAMPANA 74). Polyptych: Crucifixion, with SS. Peter, John Baptist, Jerome and James. Predella: Six Saints. (Close to Giovanni dal Ponte.)

Petrognano (Val d'Elsa). S. PIETRO. Madonna and Child with six Saints. (Follower of Jacopo di Cione.)

Raleigh (N.C.). MUSEUM OF ART, KRESS COLLECTION. K 539. Crucifixion. (Between Maso and Daddi.)

Rome. VATICAN, PINACOTECA. 6. Trinity, with SS. Francis, Mary Magdalen and two other Saints. (Between Jacopo di Cione and Giovanni del Biondo.)

7. S. Margaret and Donor and eight Scenes from her Life. [S. Margaret discovered by Olybrius, arrested, comforted in Prison by a Dove, scourged, devoured by the Dragon, miraculously saved from a boiling Cauldron, beheaded, Healing of Cripples at her Tomb, Man of Sorrows with the Virgin and S. John.] (Between Jacopo di Cione and Lorenzo di Niccolò.)

8. Coronation of the Virgin, with Saints and Angels. Predella: Man of Sorrows with the Virgin and SS. John, Mary Magdalen and Francis. (Between Nardo di Cione and Niccolò di Tommaso.)

79. Ascension. (Close to early Lorenzo Monaco.)

520. *Madonna Madre di Virtù.* (By Master of the 'Kahn' S. Catherine; see New York.)

Vienna. OSCAR BONDY (EX). Portable triptych: Madonna and Child with eight Saints and four Angels. Pinnacle: Christ blessing. Wings: Annunciation, Nativity, Crucifixion. (By Master of the 'Kahn' S. Catherine; see New York).

Worcester (Mass.). 1924.15. A Bishop Saint. (Between Orcagna and Agnolo Gaddi.)

1940.30. Predella panel: Martyrdom of S. Catherine (companion to New York, Lehman). (Follower of Giovanni da Milano.)

York. 727. Predella panel: Man of Sorrows. (Companion to Edinburgh).

Homeless. Madonna and Child. (By Master of 'Straus' Madonna; see Houston.) *Plate 357.*

UNIDENTIFIED FLORENTINES, ca 1420–1465

Allentown (Pa.). MUSEUM OF ART, KRESS COLLECTION. K 54. Madonna and Child. (Between Pollajuolo and Verrocchio).

K 103. Cassone: Story of Helen of Troy.

Amsterdam. 1896–B1. S. Francis, and Tobias and the Angel. (Between Baldovinetti and Bartolommeo della Gatta.)

Argiano (San Casciano Val di Pesa). S. MARIA E ANGIOLO. Crucifixion with SS. Jerome and Anthony Abbot. (Between Andrea del Castagno and Botticini). Plate 763.

Avignon. 411. Wings of an altarpiece: SS. Barbara and Dorothy, SS. John Evangelist and Stephen. (Between Lorenzo Monaco and Masolino.)

Bagnères-de-Bigorre. MUSÉE. SS. John Baptist, Anthony of Padua and a third Saint. (Close to Baldovinetti.)

Balcarres (Fife, Scotland). EARL OF CRAWFORD AND BALCARRES. Thebaid, or Scenes from the Legends of the Hermits ($30\frac{3}{4} \times 89$ in.) (Between Giovanni di Francesco and Neri di Bicci). Plate 681.

Thebaid, or Scenes from the Legends of the Hermits. ($18\frac{3}{4} \times 64\frac{1}{2}$ in.) (Close to Giovanni di Francesco). Plate 680.

Bloomington (Ind.). UNIVERSITY OF INDIANA, KRESS STUDY COLLECTION. K 1187. S. John Baptist in the Wilderness. (Close to Paolo Schiavo.)

Brunswick (Maine). BOWDOIN COLLEGE, KRESS STUDY COLLECTION. K 275. Cassone panel: Mythological subject. (Close to Rossello di Jacopo.) Plate 546.

Cambridge (Mass.). MRS. ARTHUR KINGSLEY PORTER. Madonna and Child. (Close to Masolino.)

Cleveland (Ohio). 54.834. Central panel of triptych (side panels Homeless): Madonna and Child enthroned. Pinnacle: Christ blessing. d. 1419. (So-called Master of 1419, follower of Masolino; see also Florence, Contini Bonacossi and S. Gimignano.) Plate 550.

Cori (Lazio). SS. ANNUNZIATA. Frescoes. Right wall: Resurrection, Descent into Limbo, The Redeemer and SS. John Baptist, Peter and Andrew. Left wall: SS. Bartholomew, Paul and John Evangelist. (Between Giovanni dal Ponte, Masolino and Masaccio.)

Cracow. 1076. Cassone panel: A Banquet, an Assassination, and a Knight received by a Lady. (Follower of Masaccio.)

Detroit (Mich.). 25.145. Trinity. (Between Masolino and Pesellino).

Edinburgh. 1528. Fragment of a Thebaid: Burial of S. Ephraim the Syrian. (See Oxford.)

Florence. ACCADEMIA. 8508. Polyptych: The Seven Joys of Mary, with Donor [Annunciation, Nativity, Adoration of the Magi, Circumcision, Flight into Egypt, Christ among the Doctors, Dormition of the Virgin, Assumption]. (Follower of Fra Angelico; perhaps Zanobi Strozzi.)

Florence (contd.). MUSEO STIBBERT. 936. Madonna and Child, with two Angels. (Between the Master of Castello Nativity and Zanobi Machiavelli.)

S. CROCE, L. WALL. Fresco: S. Anthony Abbot, John Baptist and Anthony of Padua (r.). (Between Uccello and Giovanni di Francesco.)

S. MARIA DEL FIORE (DUOMO), MUSEO DELL'OPERA. Polychrome terracotta lunette: God the Father and two Angels. (Between Giovanni di Francesco and Baldovinetti.)

S. MARIA NOVELLA, CHIOSTRO VERDE, EAST WALL.* Frescoes: Scenes from the Book of Genesis [Third bay: Expulsion from Paradise, Sacrifice of Cain and Abel and Death of Abel. Fourth bay: Lamech slaying Cain and Building of the Ark, Entry into the Ark] (r.). (Close to Uccello.) *Plate 657-658.*

— — SOUTH WALL. Frescoes: Scenes from the Book of Genesis [First bay: Departure of Abraham, God appearing to Abraham. Second bay: Parting of Abraham and Lot, Triumph of Abraham over the Enemies of Lot and Meeting of Abraham and Melchisedech. Third bay: Abraham entertaining the Angels, Destruction of Sodom and Flight of Lot. Fourth bay: Dismissal of Hagar, Sacrifice of Isaac. Fifth bay: Death of Sarah, Departure of Eliezer and Rebecca at the Well. Sixth bay: Marriage of Isaac and Rebecca, Death of Abraham] (r.). (Between Lorenzo Monaco and Bicci di Lorenzo.)

— — WEST WALL. Frescoes: Scenes from the Book of Genesis [First bay: Birth of Jacob and Esau and Sale of the Birthright, Rebecca and Jacob and Jacob's Blessing. Second bay: Jacob and Rachel and Jacob welcomed by Laban, Laban and his Daughters entertaining Jacob and Birth of Reuben. Third bay: Marriage of Jacob with the Serving-maids, Division of the Herds. Fourth bay: Jacob's Flight from Laban, God warning Laban, Encounter of Jacob and Laban and Search for the Household Images. Fifth bay: Angels appearing to Jacob and Messengers sent to Esau, Jacob wrestling with the Angel and Jacob meeting Esau. Sixth bay: Jacob sacrificing and Rape of Dinah, Jacob's Sons avenging Dinah] (r.). (Between Lorenzo Monaco and Bicci di Lorenzo.) *Plate 548.*

S. MINIATO AL MONTE, L. WALL. Fresco: S. Jerome. (Imitator of Andrea del Castagno.)

CENACOLO DI OGNISSANTI. Fresco: Madonna and Child with S. Lucy (fr.). (Follower of Andrea del Castagno.)

CONTINI BONACOSSI COLLECTION (EX). Madonna of Humility. (By Master of 1419; see Cleveland.) *Plate 552.*

Madonna and Child. (Follower of Masaccio.)

(Environs) CERTOSA DEL GALLUZZO. Wings of an altarpiece: S. Jerome and a Warrior Saint, SS. Francis and Onuphrius. Pinnacles: Annunciation. (Between Masolino and Fra Angelico.)

Trinity. (Close to Rossello di Jacopo.)

Granada. ALHAMBRA, SALA DE LOS REJES. Three cupolas with frescoes representing chivalrous subjects. (Hispanized Florentine or Spaniard under Florentine influence.)

Heemstede (Haarlem). BOSCHBECK, F. GUTMANN. Cassone panel: The Siege of Vejo. (Follower of Uccello.)

Highnam Court (Glos.). GAMBIER-PARRY COLLECTION. Predella: Accusation of SS. Quiricus and Julitta, S. Quiricus slapping the Judge, Martyrdom of SS. Quiricus and Julitta. (Between Masaccio, Uccello and Castagno). *Plates* 670, 671.

Predella: Man of Sorrows, with the Virgin and S. John and four other Saints. (Close to Fra Angelico.)

London. CHARLES BUTLER (EX). Madonna and Child. (Close to Pesellino.)

Lucca. PINACOTECA. Madonna and Child (r.). (Older contemporary and close imitator of Masaccio.)

Melbourne. NATIONAL GALLERY OF VICTORIA. S. George and the Dragon. (Between Giovanni di Francesco and Master of the Castello Nativity.)

Milan. DUOMO, TESORO. Madonna and Child with three Angels. (Close to Masolino.)

New Haven (Conn.). 1871.22. Triptych: Madonna and Child with two Angels and SS. Albert, Peter, Paul and Anthony Abbot. Pinnacles: Christ blessing, Annunciation. (By the so-called Baldese).

1871.37. Fragment of a *Thebaid* (See Oxford.)

1871.38. Predella panel: Dormition of the Virgin. (Crude imitator of Andrea del Castagno,)

New York. 30.95.254. Madonna and Child. (Between Fra Angelico and Domenico Veneziano; same hand as San Francisco.) *Plate* 818.

43.98.2. Predella panel: Annunciation (r.). (Between Filippo Lippi and Pesellino.)

HISTORICAL SOCIETY. B-18. *Desco da parto.* d. 1428. (Between Master of Bambino Vispo and Rossello di Jacopo.)

Oxford. CHRIST CHURCH LIBRARY. 21-29. Nine fragments of a *Thebaid* (other fragments at Edinburgh, New Haven, 1871.37, and Zurich). (Between Giovanni di Francesco and Neri di Bicci.)

Pelago (Florence). PIEVE DI RISTONCHI. Triptych: Madonna and Child with six Saints (r.). (Between Rossello di Jacopo and Giovanni dal Ponte.)

Philadelphia (Pa.). MUSEUM OF ART, JOHNSON COLLECTION. 24, 25. Two predella panels with Saintly legend. (Close to Master of Castello Nativity).

34. Profile Portrait of a Woman. (Follower of Domenico Veneziano).

Inv. 2034. Portable triptych: Madonna and Child with an Angel, and six Saints. Wings: Annunciation, Way to Calvary, Crucifixion.

Pisa. 159. S. Jerome in the Wilderness, S. Jerome in his Study, Man of Sorrows. (Follower of Masaccio.)

Rome. VATICAN, PINACOTECA. 283, 285, 287, 289. Four predella panels: Visitation,

Birth of S. John, Dance of Salome, Head of S. John brought to Herod. (Crude follower of Masolino, perhaps Spanish).

San Francisco (Cal.). DE YOUNG MEMORIAL MUSEUM. Predella panel: 'Lanckoronski' Annunciation. (Between Fra Angelico and Domenico Veneziano; same hand as New York 30.95.254.) *Plate* 819.

San Gimignano. 14. Triptych: S. Julian between SS. Anthony Abbot and Martin. Pinnacles: Trinity, Annunciation. Pilasters: Four Saints. (By Master of 1419; see Cleveland.) *Plate* 551.

San Giovanni Valdarno. 15. Tobias and the Angel. (Between Baldovinetti and Bartolommeo della Gatta.)

Scarperia (Mugello). MADONNA DELLE GRAZIE (ORATORIO DELLA COMPAGNIA DI PIAZZA). Madonna and Child (r.). (Provincial follower of Andrea del Castagno.)

Seattle (Wash.). ART MUSEUM, KRESS COLLECTION. K 490. Cassone panel: Scenes from the Myth of Theseus. (Follower of Uccello.)

Siena. 389. Madonna and Child. (Close to Alvaro Portoghese; the so-called Baldese?)

Turin. GALLERIA SABAUDA, GUALINO COLLECTION. Madonna and Child, with SS. John Baptist and Anthony Abbot. (Follower of Domenico Veneziano).
Lunette: Penitent S. Jerome (rustic version of Piero della Francesco in Berlin).

Worcester (Mass.). 1921.58. Madonna and Child. (Close to Rossello di Jacopo; so-called 'Baldese'?)

Zurich. 1455–58, 1661–64. Eight fragments of a *Thebaid*. (See Oxford.)

Homeless. Side panels to Cleveland Madonna: SS. Julian and James. Pinnacle: Angel of the Annunciation. SS. John Baptist and Anthony Abbot (fr.). 1419. *Plate* 550.

UNIDENTIFIED FLORENTINES, ca 1465–1540

Altenburg. 99. Adoration of the Magi. (Between 'Utili' and Sellajo.)

Amsterdam. 1513–D1. Tondo: Holy Family with Infant S. John. (Probably Jacopo dell'Indaco.) ca. 1500.

Baltimore (Md.). WALTERS ART GALLERY. 426. Madonna and Child. (Between Pollajuolo and Leonardo.)
506. Tondo: Holy Family with Infant S. John. (Between Piero di Cosimo, Raffaellino del Garbo and early Granacci; same hand as Paris, Richtemberger.)
DR. G. REULING (EX). Tondo: Holy Family with Infant S. John. (Between Granacci and Mainardi.)

Berlin. 90A. Madonna and Child. (Leonardesque.) (Destroyed 1945.) *Plate* 953.

Brunswick (Maine). BOWDOIN COLLEGE, KRESS COLLECTION. K 1619. Monochrome: Apollo and Daphne. (Companion to Lewisburg.) (Follower of Andrea del Sarto.)

Campi Bisenzio (Florence). PIEVE. Madonna and Child with SS. Lawrence, Bartholomew, John Baptist and Anthony Abbot. (Crude follower of early Botticelli.)

Charleston (S.C.). GIBBES ART GALLERY, KRESS COLLECTION. K 56. Holy Family. (Follower of Sellajo.)

Florence. S. MARIA NOVELLA, CONVENTO. Triptych: S. Catherine of Siena, Tobias and the Angel, S. Vincent Ferrer. (Close to Baldovinetti.)

FAIRFAX MURRAY COLLECTION (EX). Tondo: Holy Family with Infant S. John. (Between Cosimo Rosselli and Piero di Cosimo; same hand as Seattle). *Plate* 1024.

(Environs) POGGIO A CAIANO, VILLA MEDICEA. (GALLERIE 1335). The Virgin with the Holy Children. (Follower of Leonardo.) *Plate* 952.

Highnam Court (Glos.). GAMBIER-PARRY COLLECTION. Madonna and Child. (Between Pollajuolo and Leonardo.)

Lawrence (Kansas). UNIVERSITY OF KANSAS, KRESS COLLECTION. K 1929. The Pazzi Conspiracy. (Follower of Sellajo.)

Lewisburg (Pa.). BUCKNELL UNIVERSITY, KRESS COLLECTION. K 1618. Monochrome: Apollo and Cupid. (Companion to Brunswick.) (Follower of Andrea del Sarto.)

Lucardo (Certaldo). S. MARTINO. Madonna and Child with SS. Peter, Martin, Justus and John Baptist. Predella: Crucifixion of S. Peter, S. Martin and the Beggar, Man of Sorrows, Siege of Volterra lifted by S. Justus, Beheading of S. John. (Between Raffaellino del Garbo and Michele di Ridolfo.)

Memphis (Tennessee). BROOKS MEMORIAL ART GALLERY (KRESS COLLECTION 1723). Madonna suckling the Child.

Paris. EUGÈNE RICHTEMBERGER (EX). Tondo: Holy Family with Infant S. John. (Between Piero di Cosimo, Raffaellino del Garbo and early Granacci; same hand as Baltimore 506.) *Plate* 1025.

Princeton (N.J.). 38. *Madonna della Cintola*, with SS. Peter and Paul. d. 1484.

Rome. GALLERIA BORGHESE. 335. Madonna and Child with SS. Elizabeth and Infant John. (Between Ridolfo Ghirlandajo and Andrea del Sarto.)

MUSEO DI PALAZZO VENEZIA. Fresco frieze: Labours of Hercules. (Crude imitator of Pollajuolo.) *Plates* 789–790.

S. PIETRO IN VINCOLI, L. OF ENTRANCE. Fresco over Pollajuolo's Tomb: Pope Sixtus IV praying for the Cessation of the Plague. (Close to Cosimo Rosselli.)

Romena (Casentino). PIEVE (S. PIETRO). Madonna and Child with SS. Mary Magdalen, John Baptist, Anthony Abbot and Francis (r). (Close to Botticini.) *Plate* 1057.

San Antonio (Texas). WITTE MEMORIAL MUSEUM, KRESS COLLECTION. K 1063. Holy Family. (Between Bugiardini and Piero di Cosimo.)

San Gimignano. 22. *Pietà*, with Saints and Symbols of the Passion. (Follower of Neri di Bicci.)

Seattle (Wash.). HENRY ART GALLERY, UNIVERSITY OF WASHINGTON, KRESS COLLECTION. K 99. Tondo: Holy Family. (Follower of Credi.)

   MUSEUM OF ART, KRESS COLLECTION. K 1049. Tondo: Nativity with Infant S. John. (Between Cosimo Rosselli and Piero di Cosimo; same hand as Florence, Fairfax Murray.)

Toledo (Ohio). 30.214. Madonna adoring the Child, with an Angel. (Probably Raffaele Botticini.)

Vaduz. LIECHTENSTEIN COLLECTION. (EX). Tondo: Madonna adoring Child, and S. Joseph resting on saddle in background. (Between Sellajo and Piero di Cosimo).

Venice. CA' D'ORO. Madonna adoring the Child with two Angels. (Between Domenico Ghirlandajo and Filippino Lippi).

PLATES

1–590

1. CIMABUE: *The crucified Christ (detail of painted cross)*. Arezzo, S. Domenico.

2–3. CIMABUE: *The mourning Virgin, the mourning S. John (details of painted cross).* Arezzo, S. Domenico

4. CIMABUE: Reconstruction of the Artaud de Montor polyptych: *The Baptist*, Chambéry, Musée; *S. Peter*, *The Blessing Saviour*, *S. James*. Washington, National Gallery; *S. Ursula*. ex Paris, Artaud de Montor (woodcut from the catalogue of the collection).

5. CIMABUE: *Madonna and Child enthroned with six Angels.*
Paris, Louvre.

6. CIMABUE: *Four Prophets* (detail of the *Madonna enthroned*). Florence, Uffizi.

7. CIMABUE: *Fresco: Madonna and Child enthroned with four Angels and S. Francis.* Assisi, S. Francesco, Lower Church, Right Transept.

8. CIMABUE: *Fresco: The Evangelist Matthew.* Assisi, S. Francesco, Upper Church, Vault of Crossing.

9. CIMABUE: *Frescoed decoration*. Assisi, Upper Church, Vault of Crossing.

10. View of the meeting of transept and nave, with frescoes (or traces of frescoes) by Cimabue on vault and left wall of right transept, by Cimabue's Studio on right wall, first bay, of the nave (*Annunciation* and *Marriage at Cana*). Assisi, S. Francesco, Upper Church.

11. CIMABUE: *Fresco: Christ the Judge*. Assisi, S. Francesco, Upper Church,
Left Transept.

12. CIMABUE: *Fresco: Angels*. Assisi, S. Francesco, Upper Church, Gallery of Left Transept.

13. CIMABUE: *Frescoes: Annunciation to Joachim, Presentation in the Temple, Madonna flanked by Angels.*
Assisi, S. Francesco, Upper Church, Apse, Left Wall.

14. CIMABUE's Studio: *Fresco: Sacrifice of Isaac*. Assisi, S. Francesco,
Upper Church, Nave, Right Wall, Second Bay.

15. CIMABUE: *Fresco: Crucifixion*. Assisi, S. Francesco, Upper Church, Left Transept, Left Wall.

16. CIMABUE's Studio: *Fresco: Betrayal of Christ*. Assisi, S. Francesco,
Upper Church, Nave, Left Wall, Second Bay.

17. CIMABUE: *Fresco: Crucifixion of S. Peter*. Assisi, S. Francesco, Upper Church, Right Transept,
Window Wall.

18. CIMABUE's Studio: *Fresco: The Virgin in Glory*, Assisi, S. Francesco, Upper Church, Nave.

19. CIMABUE: *Fresco: Angel*. Assisi, S. Francesco, Upper Church, Left Transept.

20. CIMABUE's Studio: *Fresco: Nativity (detail)*. Assisi, S. Francesco, Upper Church, Nave.

21. CIMABUE'S STUDIO: *Fresco: Creation of the World*. Assisi, S. Francesco, Upper Church, Nave.

22. CIMABUE: *Mosaic: Christ enthroned with the Virgin and S. John*. Pisa, Duomo. *1301*.

23. CIMABUE: *Madonna and Child enthroned with two Angels.* Bologna, S. Maria dei Servi.

24. GIOTTO: *Fresco: S. Gregory, Doctor of the Church*. Assisi, S. Francesco, Upper Church, Vault of 4th Bay.

25. GIOTTO: *Fresco: Isaac and Esau*. Assisi, S. Francesco, Upper Church, Right Wall of Nave.

26–28. GIOTTO: *The Mourning Virgin, the mourning S. John, the skull (details of painted cross).*
Florence, S. Maria Novella.

29. GIOTTO: *The crucified Christ (detail of painted cross)*. Florence, S. Maria Novella.

30. GIOTTO: *Fresco: S. Francis giving his cloak to a beggar.* Assisi, S. Francesco, Upper Church,
Right Wall of Nave.

31. GIOTTO: *Fresco: S. Francis instituting the 'Presepio' at Greccio*. Assisi, S. Francesco, Upper Church,
Right Wall of Nave.

32. Assistant of GIOTTO: *The Polyptych from the Badia.* Florence, Opera di S. Croce.

33. GIOTTO: Fragment of fresco: *Pope Boniface VIII proclaiming the Jubilee.*
Rome, S. Giovanni Laterano. *1300*

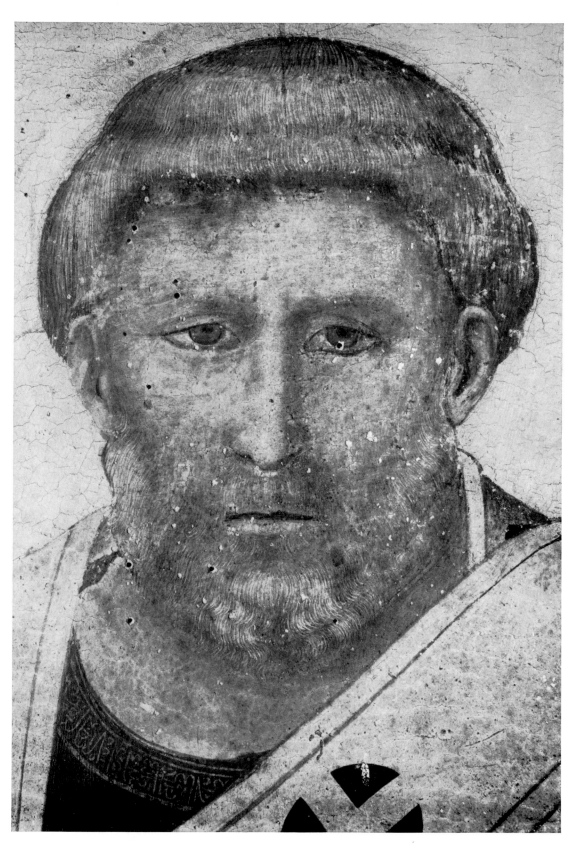

34. Assistant of GIOTTO: *Head of S. Peter* (*detail of Badia Polyptych*). Florence, Opera di S. Croce.

35. Giotto: The interior of the Cappella degli Scrovegni in Padua seen from the door.

36. GIOTTO: *Fresco: Meeting at the Golden Gate*. Padua, Cappella degli Scrovegni. *ca 1305/6.*

37. GIOTTO: *Fresco: Adoration of the Magi*. Padua, Cappella degli Scrovegni. *ca 1305/6.*

38. GIOTTO: *Fresco: Detail of the Nativity*. Padua, Cappella degli Scrovegni. *ca 1305/6*.

39. GIOTTO: *Fresco: Detail of the Lamentation*. Padua, Cappella degli Scrovegni. *ca 1305/6.*

40. GIOTTO: *Fresco: Detail of the Circumcision*. Padua, Cappella degli Scrovegni. *ca 1305/6*.

41. GIOTTO: *Fresco: Detail of the Betrayal of Christ.* Padua, Cappella degli Scrovegni. *ca 1305/6.*

42. GIOTTO: *Fresco: Detail of the Last Judgement.* Padua, Cappella degli
Scrovegni. *ca 1305/6.*

43, 44. GIOTTO: *Monochrome frescoes in the dado: Hope* (right wall, on the side of the *Elect*) and
Despair (left wall, on the side of the *Damned*). Padua, Cappella degli Scrovegni. *ca 1305/6.*

45. GIOTTO: The interior of the Cappella degli Scrovegni seen from the altar.

46. *Angel (mosaic) from the frame of Giotto's 'Navicella'.*
Boville Ernica, S. Pietro Ispano.

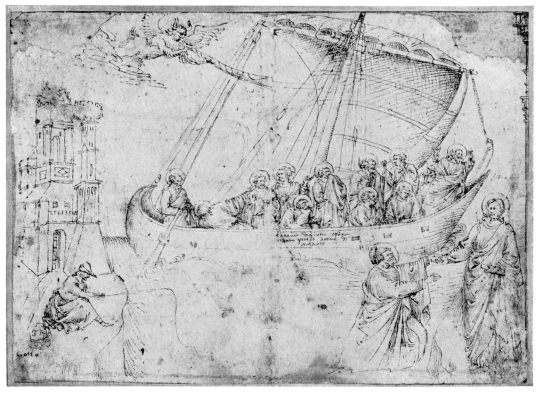

47. PARRI SPINELLI: *Drawing after Giotto's 'Navicella'.* New York, Metropolitan Museum of Art.

48. GIOTTO: *Painted Cross.*—*The crucified Christ*, Rimini, S. Francesco; *the top-finial with the Blessing Saviour*, formerly London, Lady Jekyll; *the side-finials and the bottom, lost. Before 1313.*

49. GIOTTO and Assistants: *Fresco: The Magdalen with Teobaldo Pontano.* Assisi, S. Francesco, Lower Church, Cappella della Maddalena.

50. GIOTTO and Assistants: *Fresco: The Raising of Lazarus.* Assisi, S. Francesco, Lower Church,
Cappella della Maddalena.

51. Assistant of GIOTTO: *Fresco: Lazarus and his sister landing at Marseilles.* Assisi, S. Francesco,
Lower Church, Cappella della Maddalena

52. GIOTTO and Assistants: *Dormition (detail)*. Berlin, Staatliche Museen.

53. GIOTTO's Studio: *Entombment*. Florence, Berenson Collection.

54. GIOTTO: *Madonna and Child (central panel of polyptych)*. Washington, National Gallery of Art, Kress Collection.

55. GIOTTO: *Fresco: S. John on Patmos (detail).* Florence, S. Croce, Cappella Peruzzi (after cleaning).

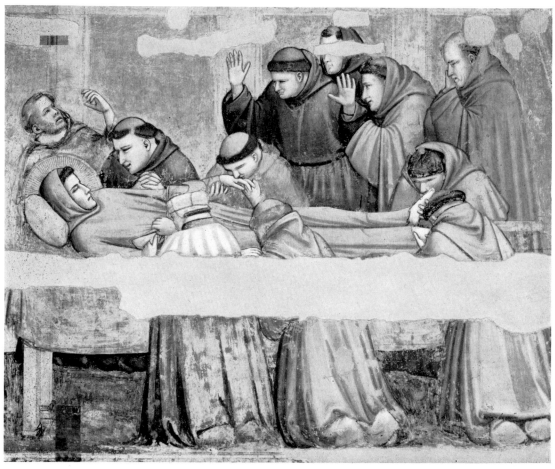

56. GIOTTO: Central Group in the *Death of S. Francis.* Florence, S. Croce, Bardi Chapel (after cleaning).

57. GIOTTO: *Fresco: S. Francis renouncing his inheritance.* Florence, S. Croce, Bardi Chapel (after cleaning).

58. GIOTTO: *Fresco: Raising of Drusiana.* Florence, S. Croce, Peruzzi Chapel (before cleaning).

59–61. GIOTTO: *Details of frescoes: A Virtue* in the Vault; *An ornamental Head; The Hawk* in the *Stigmatisation of S. Francis*. Florence, S. Croce, Cappella Bardi (after cleaning).

62. Giotto: *Fresco: The Ordeal by Fire (detail)*. Florence, S. Croce, Cappella Bardi (after cleaning).

63. GIOTTO's Studio: Reconstruction of the central panel of the Baroncelli altarpiece:
the *Coronation*, still in Florence, S. Croce, Cappella Baroncelli;
the *Pinnacle*, in San Diego (Cal.), Fine Arts Gallery.

64, 65. Assistant of GIOTTO: *The Stefaneschi Polyptych:* Front: *Christ enthroned with Angels and Cardinal Stefaneschi as Donor; Martyrdoms of S. Peter and S. Paul;* in predella, *Madonna with two Angels and twelve Apostles.* Back: *S. Peter, enthroned with Angels, is offered the Stefaneschi Polyptych; SS. James, Paul, Mark and John;* in fragmentary predella, *Saints.* Rome, Vatican.

66. Assistant of GIOTTO: Detail from Stefaneschi Polyptych. Rome, Vatican.

67, 68. Assistant of GIOTTO: *Frescoes: Allegory of Obedience (detail); Marriage of S. Francis and Poverty (detail).*
Assisi, S. Francesco, Lower Church, Vault of Crossing.

69. Assistant of GIOTTO: *Fresco: Allegory of Chastity* (detail). Assisi, S. Francesco, Lower Church, Vault of Crossing. *ca 1335/40.*

70. Assistant of GIOTTO: *Fresco: Miracle of S. Francis.* Assisi, S. Francesco, Lower Church, Right Transept.

71. Assistant of GIOTTO: *Frescoes: Visitation, Nativity, Adoration of the Magi, Circumcision, Crucifixion.* CIMABUE: *Fresco: Madonna with Angels and S. Francis.* Assisi, S. Francesco, Lower Church, Vault of Right Transept.

72. GIOTTO's Studio: *Madonna and Child with six Saints and Seven Virtues.* Homeless.

73–76. Contemporary of GIOTTO: *Annunciation*—Homeless; *Nativity*—Brussels, Mme. Feron-Stoclet; *Crucifixion*—Florence, Berenson Collection; *Lamentation*—Homeless.

77. Assistant of GIOTTO: Polyptych: *Madonna and Child, SS. Peter, Gabriel, Michael and Paul; in predella Man of Sorrows, and four Saints.*
Bologna, Pinacoteca. *After 1330.*

78. Contemporary of GIOTTO: *Polyptych: Man of Sorrows and SS. Francis, Peter, Paul and Philip*. Capesthorne Hall, Lt.-Col. Sir W. H. Bromley Davenport.

79. Contemporary of GIOTTO: *Kneeling Donor in Painted Cross*. Florence, S. Marco.

80. Contemporary of GIOTTO: *Painted Cross, with two Donors at the bottom.*
Florence, S. Marco.

81. MASTER OF ST. CECILIA: *Fresco: Confession of a woman raised from the Dead* (*detail*). Assisi, S. Francesco, Upper Church, Nave, Left Wall.

82. MASTER OF S. CECILIA: *Fresco: Liberation of Pietro of Alifia* (*detail*). Assisi, S. Francesco, Upper Church, Nave, Left Wall.

83. MASTER OF S. CECILIA: *Fresco: Healing of Giovanni of Ylerda (detail)*.
Assisi, S. Francesco, Upper Church, Nave, Left Wall.

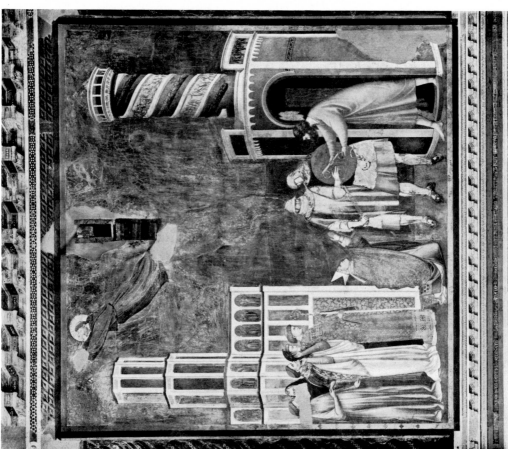

84, 85. Master of S. Cecilia: *Frescoes: Liberation of Pietro of Alifia; Confession of a woman raised from the Dead.* Assisi, S. Francesco, Upper Church, Nave, Left Wall.

86, 87. MASTER OF S. CECILIA: *Martyrdom of S. Cecilia, S. Cecilia preaching (details from S. Cecilia and Scenes of her Life)*. Florence, Uffizi.

88. Master of S. Cecilia: *S. Cecilia and Scenes of her Life.* Florence, Uffizi.

90. MASTER OF S. CECILIA: *S. Peter enthroned and two Angels.*
Florence, S. Simone. *1307.*

89. MASTER OF S. CECILIA: *Madonna with S. Margaret and another Saint.*
Florence, S. Margherita a Montici.

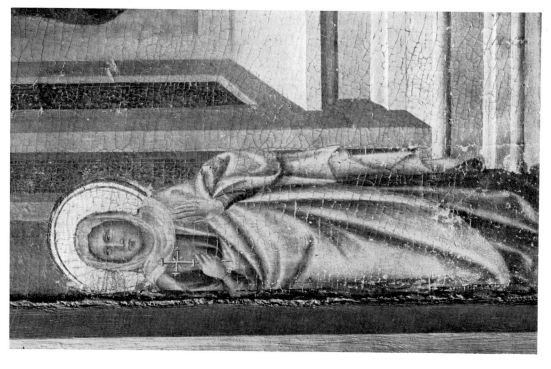

91, 92. MASTER OF S. CECILIA: *An Angel, a female Saint (details of Madonna with S. Margaret and another Saint)*. Florence, S. Margherita a Montici.

93. MASTER OF S. CECILIA: *S. Margaret and Scenes of her Life*. Florence, S. Margherita a Montici.

94. Pacino di Bonaguida: *Centre panel of polyptych from S. Firenze.* Florence, Accademia.
Signed and dated 131 . .

95, 96. LIPPO DI BENIVIENI: *Two panels from the Bartolini–Salimbeni–Vivai Polyptych:*
Madonna—Florence, Acton Collection; *S. John Evangelist*—Ottawa, National Gallery of Canada.

97. LIPPO DI BENIVIENI: *The Alessandri Polyptych, from S. Piero Maggiore: Madonna, SS. Zenobius, Peter,*
Paul, Benedict (detail). Florence, Conte Cosimo degli Alessandri. *Signed.*

98. Jacopo del Casentino: S. *Catherine and Scenes of her Life.* Formerly New York, W. R. Hearst.

100. JACOPO DEL CASENTINO: *The Madonna with six Angels and two Saints*, from S. Maria della Tromba. Florence, Arte della Lana.

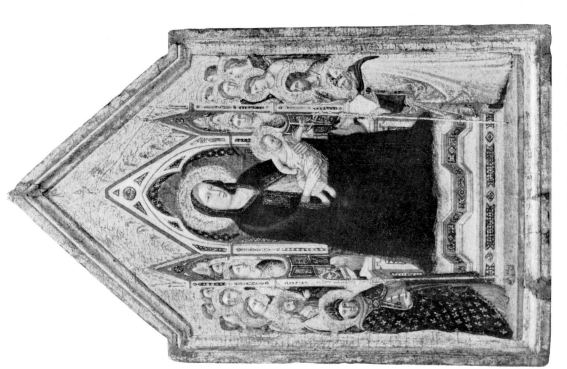

99. JACOPO DEL CASENTINO: *The Loeser Madonna with fourteen Angels and four Saints*. Ann Arbor (Michigan), Museum of Art.

101. Jacopo del Casentino: *Annunciation*. Florence, Charles Loeser (ex).

102. JACOPO DEL CASENTINO: *The Cagnola Triptych*. Florence, Uffizi. *Signed*.

103. JACOPO DEL CASENTINO: *Circumcision (detail)*.
Kansas City, Museum, Kress Collection.

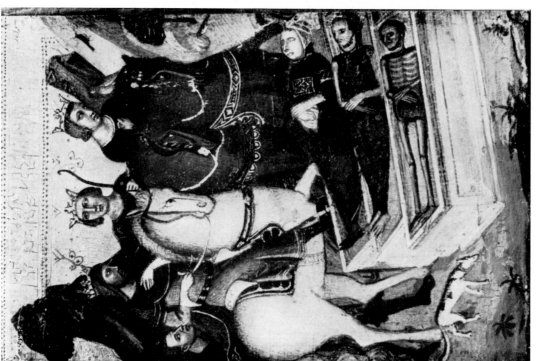

104, 105. JACOPO DEL CASENTINO: *The three dead Kings and the three living Kings; Nativity (details of wings of triptych)*. Berlin, Museum.

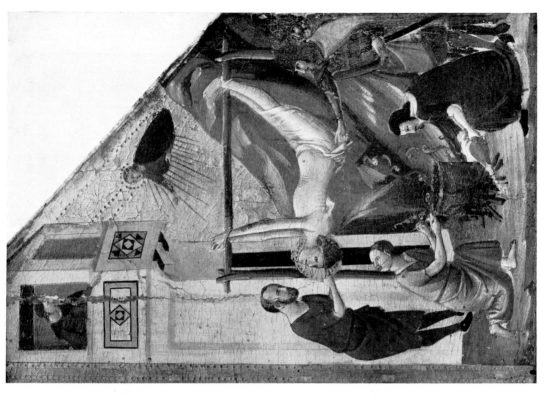

106, 107. JACOPO DEL CASENTINO: S. Miniato and the Leopard, S. Miniato tortured over a fire (details of altarpiece). Florence, S. Miniato al Monte.

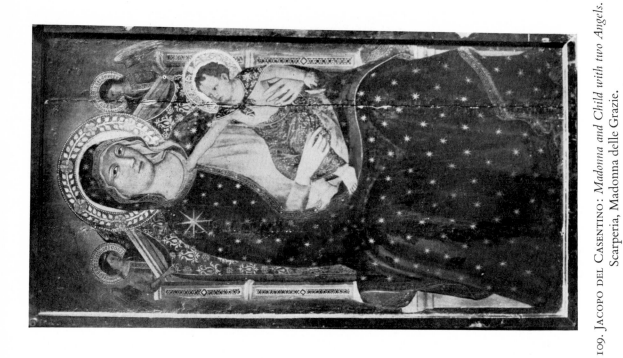

109. JACOPO DEL CASENTINO: *Madonna and Child with two Angels.*
Scarperia, Madonna delle Grazie.

108. JACOPO DEL CASENTINO: *S. Miniato and Scenes of his Life.*
Florence, S. Miniato al Monte.

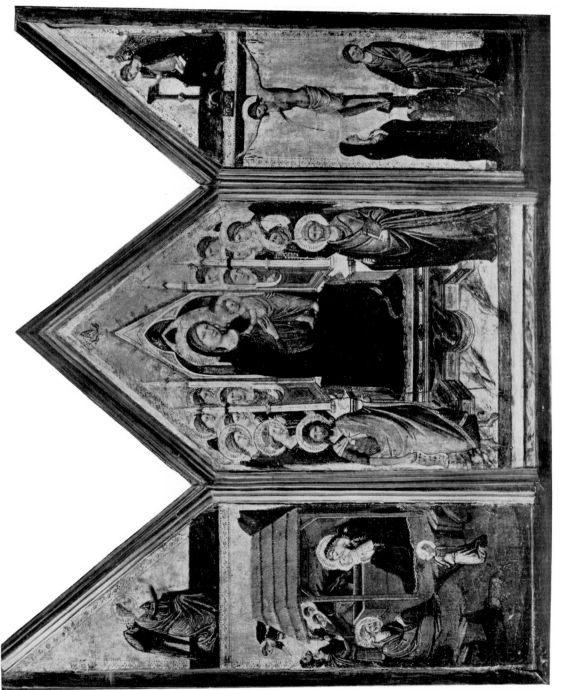

110. Jacopo del Casentino: *Portable Triptych*. Vienna, Oscar Bondy (ex).

111. GIOTTO's Studio: *Detail of the Baroncelli Polyptych*. Florence, S. Croce.

112. Taddeo Gaddi: *Fresco lunette over Baroncelli Tomb: Madonna and Child.*
Florence, S. Croce. *1327–8.* See plate 118.

113. Taddeo Gaddi: *Death of the Knight of Celano (from the cupboard doors in the Sacristy of S. Croce).*
Munich, Alte Pinakothek.

114, 115. TADDEO GADDI: *S. Francis institutes the 'Presepio' at Greccio; Adoration of the Magi (from the cupboard doors in the Sacristy of S. Croce)*. Florence, Accademia.

116. TADDEO GADDI: *Portable Triptych (open): Madonna and Child with two Donors and fourteen Saints; S. Nicholas rescuing Adeodatus from the service of the Persian King and restoring him to his Parents; Nativity; Crucifixion.* Signed and dated 1334. Berlin, Staatliche Museen.

117. TADDEO GADDI: *Portable Triptych* (closed); *S. Margaret and S. Catherine; Christ recommending the Virgin to S. John; S. Christopher carrying Jesus across the stream.* Berlin, Staatliche Museen. *1334.*

118. View of the Cappella Baroncelli with frescoes by Taddeo Gaddi before the Baroncelli Polyptych was brought back. Florence, S. Croce.

119, 120. TADDEO GADDI: *Frescoes: Hope and Faith.* Florence, S. Croce. Vault of the Cappella Baroncelli. *1332–38.*

121. TADDEO GADDI: *Frescoes: Annunciation and Visitation*. Florence, S. Croce. Altar-wall of the Cappella Baroncelli. *1332–38*.

122. TADDEO GADDI: *Fresco: David with the head of Goliath*. Florence, S. Croce.
Pilaster of the Cappella Baroncelli. *1332–38*.

123. TADDEO GADDI: *Fresco: Marriage of the Virgin (detail)*. Florence, S. Croce. Cappella Baroncelli, left wall. *1332–38*.

124. TADDEO GADDI: *Frescoes on the left wall*. Florence, S. Croce. Cappella Baroncelli. *1332–38*.

125. TADDEO GADDI: *Fresco: Entombment with female Donor.* Florence, S. Croce, Cappella Bardi di Vernio.

127. TADDEO GADDI (partly): *Fresco: S. Francis in Glory*. Pisa, S. Francesco, Vault of the Choir. *1342*.

126. TADDEO GADDI: *Fresco: Saint*. Florence, S. Miniato al Monte. Vault of the Crypt. *1341–42*.

128. TADDEO GADDI: *Fresco: S. Bonaventure's Vision of the Crucifixion flanked by Stigmatisation of S. Francis, S. Louis of Toulouse ministering to the sick and the poor, S. Benedict in the Sacro Speco and the Priest at his Easter Meal, Feast in the House of Simon. Below, Last Supper. Florence, S. Croce, Refectory.*

129. Taddeo Gaddi: *Polyptych*. Pistoia, S. Giovanni Fuorcivitas. *1353*.

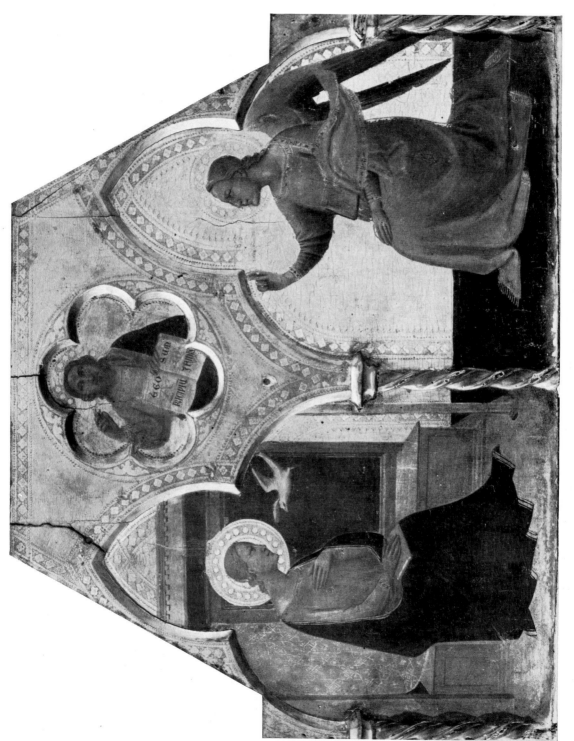

130. Taddeo Gaddi: *Annunciation (detail of polyptych)*. Pistoia, S. Giovanni Fuorcivitas. *1353*.

131. TADDEO GADDI: *Head of S. James (detail of polyptych)*. Pistoia, S. Giovanni Fuorcivitas. *1353*.

132. TADDEO GADDI: *Madonna and Child holding a Goldfinch, with Blessing Christ above.*
Formerly Venice, Mariano Fortuny.

133. MASO: *Madonna della Cintola*. Berlin, Museum.

134. MASO: *Portable Triptych*. Brooklyn (New York), Museum.

135. MASO: *Coronation*. Budapest, Museum.

136. MASO: *Dormition*. Chantilly, Musée Condé.

137–139. MASO: *Frescoes: Coronation of the Virgin; S. Stanislaus raising a man who testifies to his honesty; Dismembering of S. Stanislaus.* Assisi, S. Francesco, Lower Church.

140. MASO: *Fresco: Crucifixion with SS. Louis of Toulouse, Paul, the mourning Virgin, S. Francis, S. Clare, the mourning S. John, SS. Peter and Anthony of Padua.* Assisi, S. Francesco, Sala del Capitolo.

141–143. MASO: *Panels from dismembered polyptych: Madonna and Child*—Berlin, Museum; *SS. John the Baptist and Anthony Abbott*—formerly Berlin (destroyed).

144. MASO: *Fresco: Madonna and Child with SS. Clare, John the Baptist, George and Francis (detail).*
Assisi, S. Chiara, Cappella di S. Giorgio.

145. MASO: *Fresco: Annunciation (fragment).* Assisi, Educatorio di S. Giuseppe.

146. MASO: *Polyptych: The Saviour with S. John Evangelist, the Virgin, S. Francis and S. John the Baptist.*
Raleigh (N.C.), Museum of Art, Kress Collection.

147. MASO (?): *The Blessing Saviour*. Homeless.

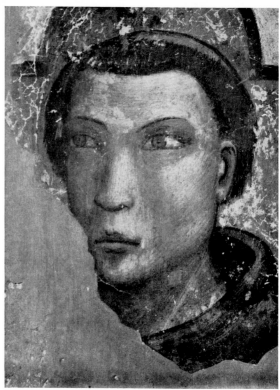

148–151. MASO: *Fragments of frescoes: Four decorative Heads*. Naples, Castelnuovo, Cappella Palatina.
1329–32.

152. MASO: *Fresco: Coronation of the Virgin*. Florence, Museo dell'Opera di S. Croce.

153. MASO: *Fresco: Flaying of St. Bartholomew (detail)*. Florence, Badia, Cappella Covoni.

154. View of the Cappella Bardi di Vernio with family tomb and frescoes. By MASO: *Resurrection of a member of the Bardi family; two Prophets and two roundels with Angels, in soffit; two roundels with Prophets above the arch and, to the right, the Dream of Constantine.* By TADDEO GADDI: *Entombment, with Man of Sorrows and two Prophets in roundels above.* Florence, S. Croce.

155. MASO: *Angel holding symbols of Passion (detail of fresco over Bardi di Vernio Tomb)*. Florence, S. Croce.

156. MASO: *Fresco: Miracle of S. Sylvester—the Raising of the Bull (detail)*. Florence, S. Croce, Cappella Bardi di Vernio.

157. Maso: *Fresco: Miracle of S. Sylvester—the Raising of two Pagan Priests.* Florence, S. Croce, Cappella Bardi di Vernio.

158. MASO: *Fresco: Miracle of S. Silvester—the Raising of the Bull (detail).* Florence, S. Croce, Cappella Bardi di Vernio.

159–161. Follower of MASO: *Frescoes: S. Anthony Abbot instructing his Disciples, SS. Anthony and Paul fed by a raven; Death of S. Paul.* Florence, Villa Le Campora, Cappella di S. Antonio.

162. Daddi: *S. Paul and worshippers*. Washington, National Gallery, Mellon Collection. *Dated 133(3?)*.

163. DADDI: *Triptych: Madonna and Child with SS. Peter and Paul (detail).*
Parma, Pinacoteca. *Early work.*

164. DADDI: *Triptych: Madonna and Child with SS. Matthew and Nicholas (detail)*. Florence, Uffizi.
Signed and dated 1328.

165. DADDI: *Madonna del Magnificat flanked by SS. Catherine and Zenobius, with Blessing Christ above and two female Donors below.* Florence, Opera del Duomo, *Dated 1334.*

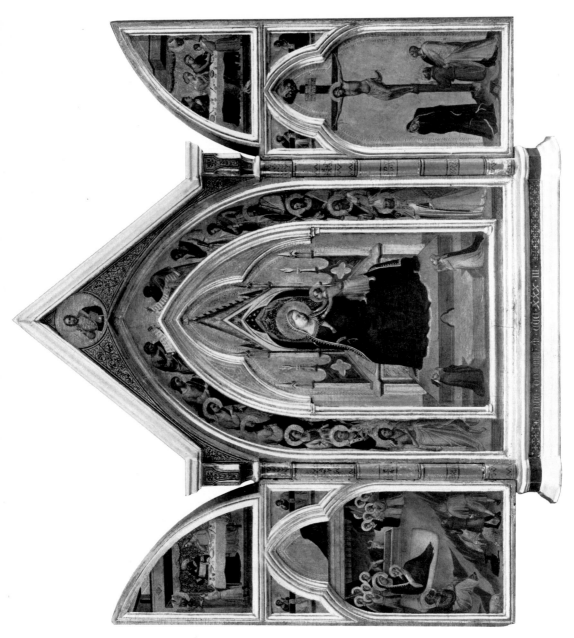

166. DADDI: *Portable Triptych* (open). Florence, Museo del Bigallo. *Dated 1333.*

168. DADDI: *Fragment of a Crucifixion.* Homeless.

167. DADDI: *S. Nicholas rescuing Adeodatus from the service of the pagan king* (detail of Plate 166).

169. Daddi: *Left leaf of Diptych: Madonna and Child with SS. Bernard (?), Francis, Augustine and John Baptist.*
Naples, Capodimonte.

170. DADDI: *Centre of portable triptych: Madonna and Child with eight Angels and eight Saints.*
London, Count Seilern. *Dated 1338.*

171. DADDI: *Adoration of the Magi (detail of portable triptych, when closed)*. London, Count Seilern. *1338*.

172-175. DADDI: *Four Stories of Dominican Saints*, presumably from a predella of an altarpiece painted for S. Maria Novella, signed and dated 1338. *S. Dominic's Vision of SS. Peter and Paul*—New Haven, Yale University, Art Gallery; *S. Thomas Aquinas resisting seduction with the aid of Angels*—Berlin, Staatliche Museen; *Preaching of S. Peter Martyr*—Paris, Musée des Arts Décoratifs; *S. Dominic saving a ship at sea*—Poznan, Museum.

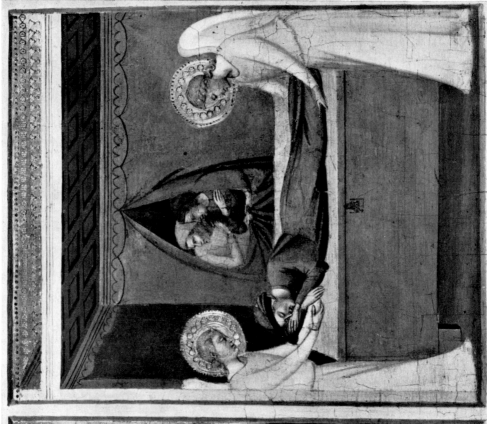

176. DADDI: *Michele Dagomari's journey to Italy with the Holy Girdle, Dagomari moved by Angels in his Sleep (detail of predella once in the Cappella del Sacro Cingolo at Prato.)* Prato, Pinacoteca.

177. DADDI: *The Polyptych from S. Pancrazio. Florence, Uffizi.*

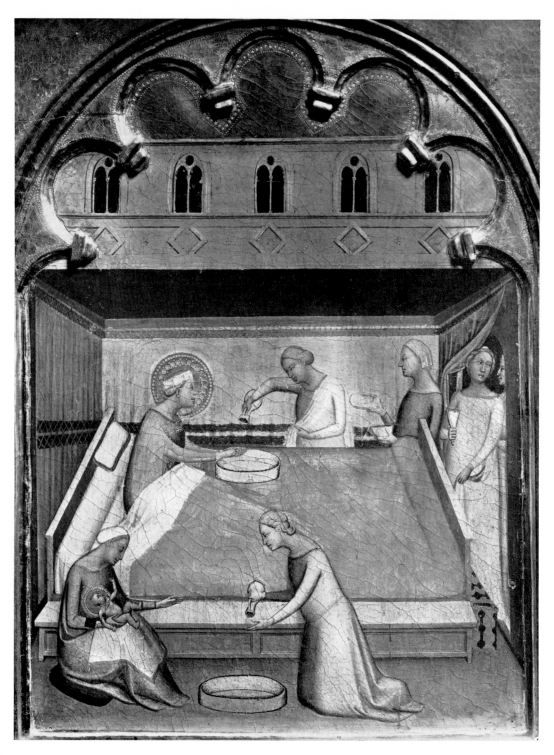

178. DADDI: *Birth of the Virgin (detail of predella to the Polyptych from S. Pancrazio)*. Florence, Uffizi.

179. DADDI: *Nativity (detail of predella to the Polyptych from S. Pancrazio)*. Florence, Uffizi.

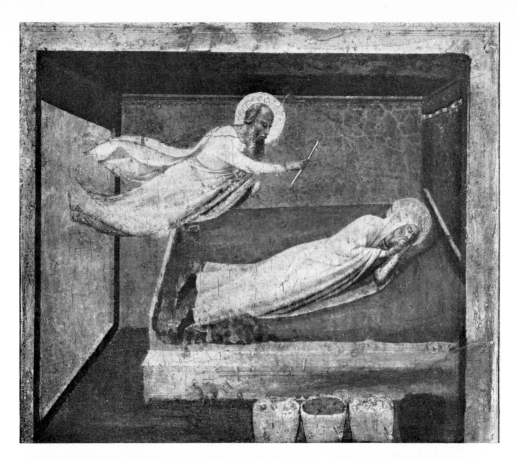

180, 181. DADDI: *Two predella panels: S. Gamaliel appears to S. Lucian in his dream; Burial of S. Stephen with S. Lawrence* and *Exorcism of the Emperor's Daughter*. Rome, Pinacoteca Vaticana.

182. DADDI: *Madonna and Child with a Goldfinch*. Florence, Berenson Collection.

183. DADDI: *Polyptych: Crucifixion, SS. Lawrence, Andrew, Bartholomew, George, Paul, Peter, James and Stephen; in pinnacles, Christ and the Evangelists.* Highnam Court, Gambier-Parry Collection. *Signed and dated 1348.*

185. Close Follower of DADDI: *Madonna and Child with Angels and Worshippers.* Florence, S. Martino alla Palma.

184. DADDI: *Madonna and Child with eight Angels.* Florence, Orsanmichele. 1347.

186, 187. Close Follower of DADDI: *Two details of the Madonna and Child with Angels and Worshippers.*
Florence, S. Martino alla Palma.

188. Puccio di Simone: *Polyptych: Madonna of Humility, SS. Lawrence, Onuphrius, James Major and Bartholomew.* Florence, Accademia. *Signed.*

189, 190. Puccio di Simone: *S. Lawrence, S. Bartholomew* (details of Plate 188).

191. Early NARDO DI CIONE (?): *Fresco: Madonna and Child with eight Angels, the Baptist and S. Romuald (from a Tabernacle in Via del Leone).* Florence, Cassa di Risparmio.

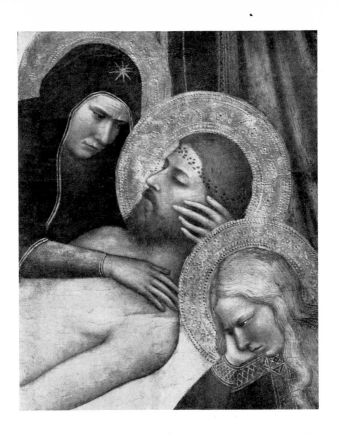

192, 193. Early NARDO DI CIONE (?): *Two details of the Lamentation from S. Remigio*. Florence, Uffizi.

194. NARDO DI CIONE: *Fresco: Paradise*. Florence, S. Maria Novella, Cappella Strozzi.

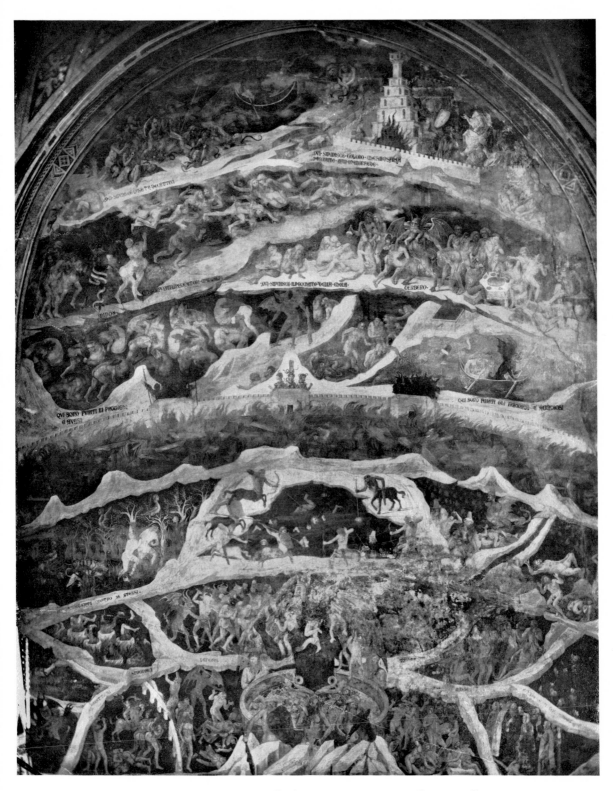

195. Nardo di Cione: *Fresco: Hell.* Florence, S. Maria Novella, Cappella Strozzi.

196. Nardo di Cione: *Fresco: Detail from the Elect*. Florence, S. Maria Novella, Cappella Strozzi.

197. NARDO DI CIONE: *Fresco: Detail from the Elect.* Florence, S. Maria Novella, Cappella Strozzi.

198. NARDO DI CIONE: *Fresco: Last Judgement (upper part)*. Florence, S. Maria Novella, Cappella Strozzi.

199. NARDO DI CIONE: *Fresco: Last Judgement* (*The Elect*). Florence, S. Maria Novella, Cappella Strozzi.

200. NARDO DI CIONE: *Fresco: Detail of the Damned.* Florence, S. Maria Novella, Cappella Strozzi.

202. Nardo di Cione: *Fresco: Presentation in the Temple.* Florence,
S. Maria Novella, Chiostrino dei Morti, Cappella Strozzi.

201. Nardo di Cione: *Fresco: Suicide of Judas.* Florence, Badia,
Cappella Giochi e Bastari.

203. NARDO DI CIONE: *Madonna and Child*. Balmville, Mrs. Tessie Jones.

204. NARDO DI CIONE: *Portable triptych: Madonna and Child with S. Peter and S. John Evangelist.*
Washington, National Gallery of Art, Kress Collection.

205. NARDO DI CIONE: *Predella panel: S. Benedict receiving Maurus and Placidus.*
Florence, Berenson Collection.

206, 207. NARDO DI CIONE and Assistants: *S. Romuald's Vision of S. Apollinaris, Dream of S. Romuald*
(details of plate 208).

208. NARDO DI CIONE and Assistants: *Triptych: Trinity, S. Romuald, S. John Evangelist;* in pinnacles, *Agnus Dei and two censing Angels;* in predella, *Life of S. Romuald.* Florence, Accademia. *Dated 1365.*

209. ANDREA DI CIONE called ORCAGNA: *The Baronci Triptych: Madonna suckling the Child, Mary Magdalen and S. Ansanus.* Utrecht, Archepiscopal Museum. *Dated 1350.*

210. ANDREA DI CIONE called ORCAGNA, and Assistants: *Polyptych from S. Maria Maggiore: Madonna and Child with music-making Angels, SS. Nicholas, Philip, John Baptist and John Evangelist* (*Wings probably by* JACOPO DI CIONE). Florence, Accademia.

211. ANDREA DI CIONE called ORCAGNA: *Christ calling to S. Peter on the Lake of Galilee* (*from the predella to the Strozzi altarpiece*). Florence, S. Maria Novella. *Signed and dated 1357.*

212. Andrea di Cione called Orcagna: *SS. Michael and Catherine
(detail of the Strozzi altarpiece).* Florence, S. Maria Novella. *1357.*

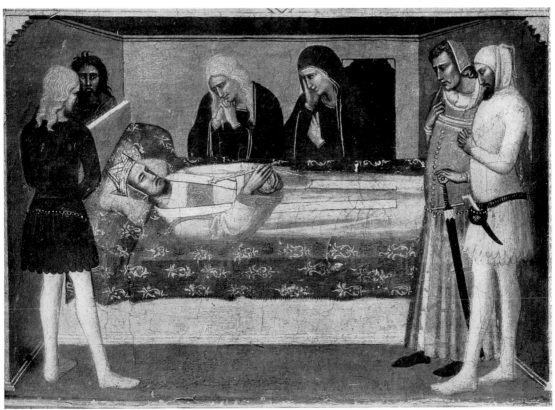

213, 214. ANDREA DI CIONE, called ORCAGNA: *Death of the Emperor Henry and Redemption of his Soul by S. Lawrence (from the predella to the Strozzi altarpiece)*. Florence, S. Maria Novella. *1357*.

215. ANDREA DI CIONE, called ORCAGNA: *Fragments of fresco with Triumph of Death*. Florence, Opera di S. Croce.

216. Early JACOPO DI CIONE: *Fresco: Crucifixion (detail)*. Florence, S. Maria Novella, Chiostrino dei Morti, Cappella Strozzi.

217, 218. Early Jacopo di Cione: *Heads of Virgin and of Angel (two details from fresco of Nativity)*. Florence, S. Maria Novella, Chiostrino dei Morti, Cappella Strozzi.

220. Early JACOPO DI CIONE: *Annunciation.* Calenzano (Prato), S. Niccolò.

219. Early JACOPO DI CIONE: *A Shepherd (detail from fresco of Nativity).* Florence, S. Maria Novella, Chiostrino dei Morti, Cappella Strozzi.

222. Early Jacopo di Cione: *Portable triptych*. Bayonne, Musée, Bonnat.

221. Early Jacopo di Cione: *Annunciation*.
Rosano (Pontassieve), Chiesa Parrocchiale.

224. Jacopo di Cione: *Madonna and Child with six Angels.*
Budapest, Museum.

223. Jacopo di Cione (on Nardo's design): *Madonna of Humility.*
Florence, Accademia.

225. NARDO and JACOPO DI CIONE: *Triptych: Madonna and Child, SS. Gregory and Job;* in predella, *Three Scenes from the Life of Job.* Florence, S. Croce. *Dated 1365.*

226. JACOPO DI CIONE: *Triptych of the Arte del Cambio at Orsanmichele: S. Matthew and four Scenes of his Life.* Florence, Uffizi. *1367–68.*

227. JACOPO DI CIONE and Assistants: *Flight into Egypt (predella panel of the Triptych from S. Pier Maggiore)*. Rome, Pinacoteca Vaticana. *1370–71*.

228. JACOPO DI CIONE: *S. Matthew subduing the dragons (detail of the Triptych of the Arte del Cambio at Orsanmichele)*. Florence, Uffizi. *1367–68*.

229. JACOPO DI CIONE: *Prophet* in spandrel of the Coronation.
Florence, Accademia. *1373.*

230. JACOPO DI CIONE: *Angels from Coronation*. London, National Gallery. *1371.*

231. Jacopo di Cione: *Coronation of the Virgin with ten Saints and two Prophets in spandrels.*
Florence, Accademia. *1373.*

232. JACOPO DI CIONE: *Detail from the Coronation*. Florence, Accademia. *1373*.

233. JACOPO DI CIONE: *Fragment of circular fresco with the Expulsion of the Duke of Athens from Florence.* Florence, Palazzo Vecchio.

234. JACOPO DI CIONE: *Adoration of the Magi (from predella of polyptych).* Florence, Accademia. *1383.*

235. View of the Cappellone degli Spagnuoli towards the altar and the left wall: *polyptych* (1344) by DADDI and *frescoes* (1366–68) by ANDREA DA FIRENZE. Florence, S. Maria Novella.

236. View of the Cappellone degli Spagnuoli towards the altar and the right wall: *polyptych* (1344) by DADDI and *frescoes* (1366–68) by ANDREA DA FIRENZE.

237. View of the Cappellone degli Spagnuoli towards the ceiling, with frescoes (1366–68) by ANDREA DA FIRENZE. Florence, S. Maria Novella.

238. Andrea da Firenze: *Fresco: Christ on the way to Calvary.* Florence, S. Maria Novella, Cappellone degli Spagnuoli, Altar wall. *1366–68.*

240. ANDREA DA FIRENZE: *S. Domitilla (detail)*. Florence, Accademia.

239. ANDREA DA FIRENZE: *Fresco: Virtue in the Triumph of S. Thomas Aquinas.*
Florence, S. Maria Novella, Cappellone degli Spagnuoli. *1366–68.*

242. ANDREA DA FIRENZE: *Mary Magdalen.*
Formerly Berlin, Von Beckerath Collection.

241. ANDREA DA FIRENZE: *Fresco: Geometry, Astronomy and Music*
(detail from the *Triumph of S. Thomas Aquinas*).
Florence, S. Maria Novella, Cappellone degli Spagnuoli. *1366–68.*

243. ANDREA DA FIRENZE: *Fresco: Detail from the 'Via Veritatis'*. Florence, S. Maria Novella,
Cappellone degli Spagnuoli.

244. ANDREA DA FIRENZE: *The Blessed Peter Petroni of Siena*. Berkeley (Cal.),
W. H. Crocker Loan to the Episcopal Student Center.

245. ANDREA DA FIRENZE; *Fresco: Two Horsemen in the Crucifixion*. Florence, S. Maria Novella,
Cappellone degli Spagnuoli. *1366–68.*

246. ANDREA DA FIRENZE: *Triptych: Madonna and Child with a Deacon Martyr and S. Dorothy.*
Cracow, Czartoryski Museum.

247. ANDREA DA FIRENZE: *Fresco: S. Raynerius's pilgrimage to the Holy Land (detail).* Pisa, Camposanto.

248. ANDREA DA FIRENZE: *Fresco: S. Raynerius tormented and uplifted by Devils*. Pisa, Camposanto.

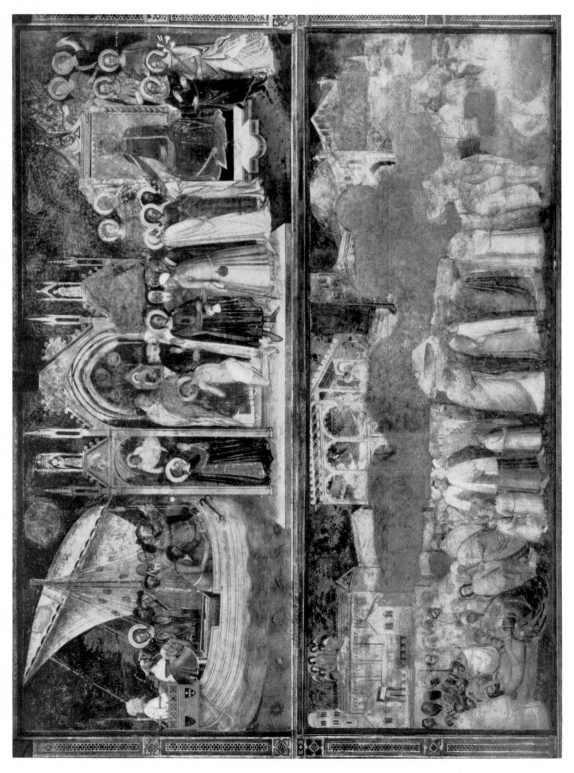

249. Frescoes by ANDREA DA FIRENZE (upper row: *S. Raynerius goes to the Holy Land, gives up his riches, has a vision of the Virgin enthroned*—1377) and by ANTONIO VENEZIANO (lower row: *Death of S. Raynerius, his soul being carried to Heaven, his body to the Duomo of Pisa, and Miracles of S. Raynerius*—1384–86). Pisa, Camposanto

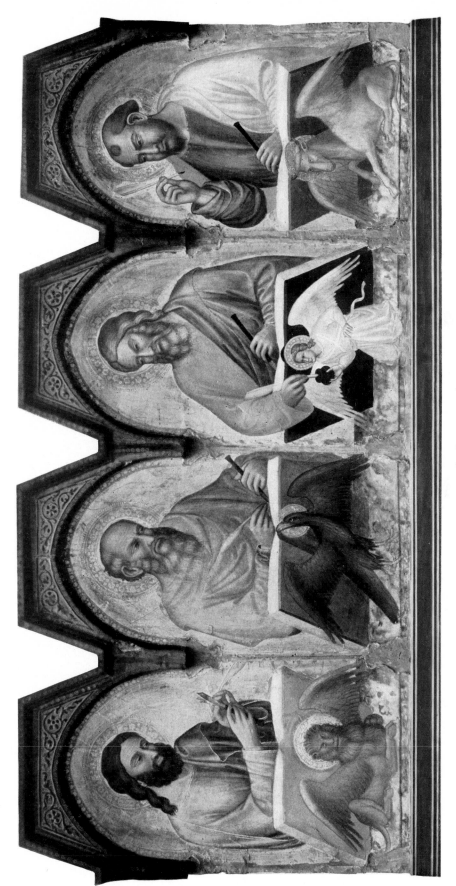

250. ANTONIO VENEZIANO: *The four Evangelists.* Siena, Pinacoteca.

251. ANTONIO VENEZIANO: *Coronation of the Virgin*. Formerly New York, Mrs. Franklin Lawrence.

252. ANTONIO VENEZIANO: *Ruined frescoes of Tabernacle: Christ and Evangelists* in Vault, *Deposition*, on Wall. Florence, Torre degli Agli.

253. ANTONIO VENEZIANO: *S. Matthew*. Homeless.

254. ANTONIO VENEZIANO: *Fresco: S. Raynerius performs the miracle of the Wine and Water.*
Pisa, Camposanto. *1384–86.*

255, 256. ANTONIO VENEZIANO: *Frescoes: S. Raynerius heals the Archbishop Villani; S. Raynerius laid out on the bier and the dropsical Woman at his feet.* Pisa, Camposanto.

258. ANTONIO VENEZIANO: *Right wing of altarpiece:
Apostles watching an Assumption.* Altenburg, Lindenau Museum.

257. ANTONIO VENEZIANO: *Assumption.* Pisa,
Convento di S. Tommaso. *ca 1387.*

259. ANTONIO VENEZIANO: *Flagellation and panel with the list of the Members of the Confraternita di S. Niccolò (detail).* Palermo, Museo Diocesano (formerly S. Niccolò Reale). *Signed and dated 1388.*

260–263. ANTONIO VENEZIANO: *Side panels of polyptych: SS. Peter and Paul*—formerly Florence, Charles Loeser; *S. Andrew*—Homeless; *S. Bartolomew*—formerly Vienna, Hermann Eissler.

264. ANTONIO VENEZIANO: *Madonna and Child (central panel of polyptych)*. Boston, Museum of Fine Arts.

265. GIOVANNI DA MILANO: *Madonna and Child;* in predella, *Man of Sorrows with S. Dominic, Virgin, Magdalen and S. Catherine.* Florence, Opera di S. Croce.

266. GIOVANNI DA MILANO: *Polyptych: Madonna and Child, SS. Catherine, Bernard, Bartholomew and Barnabas;* double predella with *Beheading of S. Catherine, Vision of S. Bernard, Annunciation, Flaying of S. Bartholomew, Martyrdom of S. Barnabas, Nativity, Adoration of Magi, Circumcision, Agony in the Garden, Betrayal of Christ, Way to Calvary.* Prato, Pinacoteca. *Signed.*

267, 268. GIOVANNI DA MILANO: *Nativity, Betrayal of Christ* (*from predella of polyptych*).
Prato, Pinacoteca.

269. GIOVANNI DA MILANO: *Christ enthroned with four Angels.*
Florence, Contini Bonacossi Collection.

270, 271. GIOVANNI DA MILANO: SS. *Stephen and Lawrence, SS. Catherine and Lucy (details of polyptych)*. Florence, Uffizi.

272. GIOVANNI DA MILANO: *Predella panel: Incredulity of S. Thomas.* Formerly Sutton Place, Duke of Sutherland.

273. GIOVANNI DA MILANO: *Fresco: S. Francis (detail from Plate 274)*. Florence, S. Croce, Cappella Rinuccini
(after cleaning).

274. View of the left wall of the Cappella Rinuccini, with frescoes by Giovanni da Milano (above) and by the Rinuccini Master (below). Florence, S. Croce (before cleaning).

275. GIOVANNI DA MILANO: *Fresco: Christ in the House of Mary and Martha.* Florence, S. Croce, Cappella Rinuccini, Right Wall. *Before* 1365. (After cleaning.)

276. GIOVANNI DA MILANO: *Fresco: Birth of the Virgin*. Florence, S. Croce, Cappella Rinuccini, Left Wall. *Before 1365*. (After cleaning.)

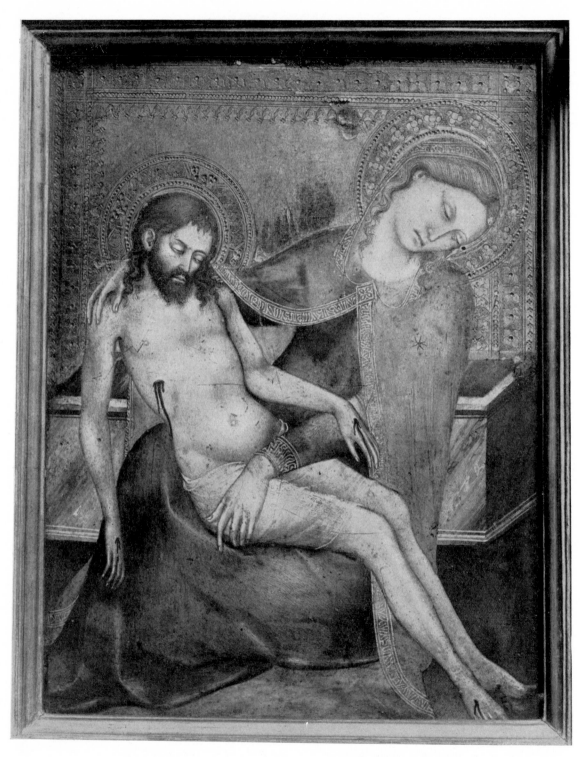

277. GIOVANNI DA MILANO: *Pietà*. Formerly Paris, Martin Le Roy.

278. Giovanni da Milano: *Lunette: Madonna and Child with Donors*. New York, Metropolitan Museum.

279. Master of the Rinuccini Chapel: *Fresco: Presentation in the Temple (detail)*.
Florence, S. Croce, Cappella Rinuccini.

280, 281. MASTER OF THE RINUCCINI CHAPEL: *Frescoes: Marriage of the Virgin* (detail) and *Mary Magdalen helps a Prince to find his Wife lost at sea* (detail). Florence, S. Croce, Cappella Rinuccini.

282. MASTER OF THE RINUCCINI CHAPEL: *Vision of S. Bernard* (*detail*). Florence, Accademia.

283. MASTER OF THE RINUCCINI CHAPEL: *Triptych: Vision of S. Bernard, SS. Benedict, John Evangelist, Quentin, Galganus, and Scenes of their Lives.* Florence, Accademia.

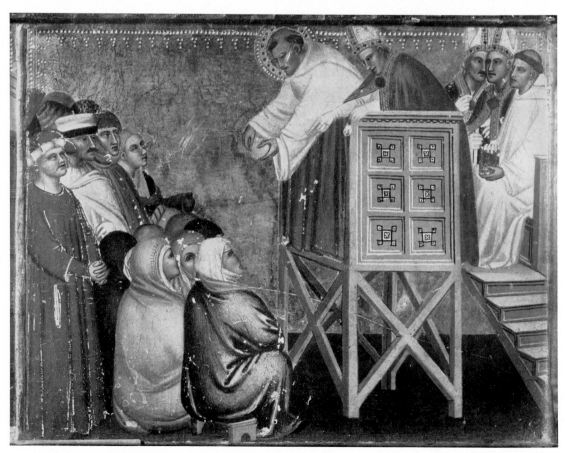

284. MASTER OF THE RINUCCINI CHAPEL: *S. Bernard preaching at Sarlat (detail from Plate 283).* Florence, Accademia.

285. MASTER OF THE RINUCCINI CHAPEL: *SS. Cosmas and Damian, with Scenes of their Lives.*
Raleigh, N.C., Museum of Art, S. H. Kress Collection.

286. GIOVANNI DEL BIONDO: *SS. Ambrose and Gregory (detail of polyptych)*. Florence, S. Croce, High Altar.
Dated 1363.

287. Giovanni del Biondo: *Fresco on entrance arch to the Strozzi Chapel: S. Gregory.*
Florence, S. Maria Novella.

288, 289. Giovanni del Biondo: *Circumcision and Feast of Herod (details of triptych)*.
Florence, Accademia. *Dated 1364*.

290. GIOVANNI DEL BIONDO: *S. John Baptist and Scenes of his Life*. Florence, Contini Bonacossi
Collection.

291. GIOVANNI DEL BIONDO: *The Plague (detail of S. Sebastian and Scenes of his Life).*
Florence, Opera del Duomo.

292. GIOVANNI DEL BIONDO: *The Vices under the feet of S. John Evangelist (detail).*
Florence, Gallerie Fiorentine.

293. GIOVANNI DEL BIONDO: *Martyrdom of S. Sebastian*
(*centre of triptych*). Florence, Opera del Duomo.

294. GIOVANNI DEL BIONDO: *Triptych: Coronation of the Virgin with Guglielmo Geri de Spinis, prior of Peretola, as Donor. Formerly Richmond, Cook Collection. Dated 1372.*

295. GIOVANNI DEL BIONDO: *Madonna and Child with Angels. Montreal, Museum.*

296. GIOVANNI DEL BIONDO: *Coronation. San Donato in Poggio, Baptistery. Dated 1375.*

297. GIOVANNI DEL BIONDO: *Madonna, and Crucifixion above. Siena, Pinacoteca. Signed and dated 1377.*

298. GIOVANNI DEL BIONDO: *Madonna and Child with Saints; Annunciation above,
'Imago Mortis' below*. Rome, Pinacoteca Vaticana.

299. Florentine close to Giovanni del Biondo (MASTER OF THE KAHN S. CATHERINE): *S. Catherine enthroned with SS. Cosmas and Damian and nun and boy as donors.* Formerly New York, O. H. Kahn.

300. Giovanni del Biondo: *Polypytch: Madonna and Child surrounded by Theological and Cardinal Virtues, between SS. Francis, Baptist, Evangelist, Magdalen; six half-length figures of Saints; Crucifixion and Doctors of the Church; Stigmatization of S. Francis, Baptism of Christ, Adoration of Magi, S. John on Patmos, Ecstasy of Magdalen. Florence, S. Croce, Cappella Rinuccini. Dated 1379.*

301. GIOVANNI DEL BIONDO: *S. Francis receiving Stigmata (detail of polyptych).*
Florence, S. Croce, Cappella Rinuccini. *1379.*

302. GIOVANNI DEL BIONDO: *S. Michael and the Bull of Gargano (predella panel).* Philadelphia,
Johnson Collection.

303. Giovanni del Biondo: *Triptych: Annunciation, SS. Nicholas and Anthony Abbot.* Florence, Spedale degli Innocenti. 1385.

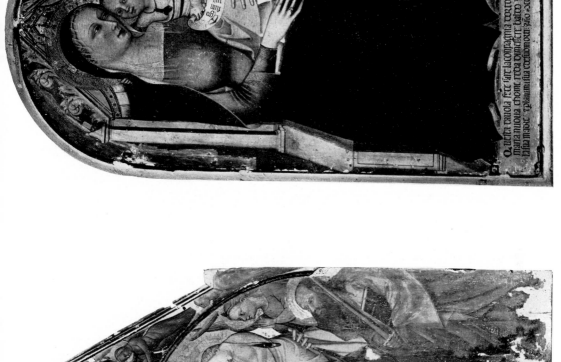

305. GIOVANNI DEL BIONDO and Assistants: *Madonna and Child.*
Figline, S. Francesco. *Signed and dated 1392.*

304. GIOVANNI DEL BIONDO: *Madonna and Child with
Angels, Saints and Donor. Romena, Pieve di S. Pietro. 1386.*

306. GIOVANNI BONSI: *Polyptych: Madonna and Child, SS. Onuphrius, Nicholas, Bartholomew and John Evangelist.* Rome, Pinacoteca Vaticana. *Signed and dated 1371.*

307. Florentine between Jacopo di Cione and Niccolò di Tommaso: *Portable triptych: Madonna and Child in Glory with two Donors, Annunciation, Saints, Crucifixion,* Florence, Accademia.

308. NICCOLÒ DI TOMMASO: *Portable triptych: Madonna and Child with four female Saints; Annunciation, three Saints, Crucifixion.* Baltimore, Walters Art Gallery.

309. NICCOLÒ DI TOMMASO: *Fresco: S. James and S. Zeno supporting a structure with a Madonna and Child.*
Pistoia, Palazzo Comunale. *Dated 1360.*

310, 311. NICCOLÒ DI TOMMASO: *Two frescoes: Creation, Adam and Eve forced to work.*
Pistoia, ex-Convento del T.

312. Niccolò di Tommaso: *Madonna and Child with kneeling Nun*
(from the Convent of S. Margherita). Arezzo, Pinacoteca.
Dated 1367. (Destroyed).

313. NICCOLÒ DI TOMMASO: *Portable triptych: Madonna and Child with SS. Nicholas, Lucy, Catherine and Anthony Abbot; Annunciation, Nativity, Crucifixion.* Homeless.

314. Niccolò di Tommaso: *Portable triptych (open): Coronation of the Virgin with two music-making Angels,
two Donors and their Patron Saints; SS. Nicholas, Peter, Paul and Catherine with Angels.*
Baltimore, Walters Art Gallery.

316. NICCOLÒ DI TOMMASO: *Central panel of triptych:*
S. Anthony Abbot. Naples, Museo di S. Martino.
Signed and dated 1371.

315. NICCOLÒ DI TOMMASO: *Portable triptych (closed):*
SS. Anthony Abbot and Christopher.
Baltimore, Walters Art Gallery.

318. Niccolò di Tommaso: *Right panel of triptych:
SS. John Evangelist and Louis of Toulouse.*
Naples, Museo di S. Martino. 1371.

317. Niccolò di Tommaso: *SS. Peter
and Christopher (detail from altarpiece).*
Florence, Convento delle Oblate.

320. NICCOLÒ DI TOMMASO: *Madonna and Child with four Saints.*
Assisi, Mrs. F. M. Perkins.

319. NICCOLÒ DI TOMMASO: *Madonna and Child with four Angels
and ten Saints.* Rome, Principe Colonna.

321. Niccolò di Tommaso: *Coronation of the Virgin with Saints and Angels (detail)*. Florence, Accademia.

322. Niccolò di Tommaso: *S. Bridget's Vision of the Nativity.* Rome, Pinacoteca Vaticana.

323, 324. NICCOLÒ DI TOMMASO: *Wings of altarpiece: SS. Anthony Abbot and John Baptist, SS. Julian and Lucy.* Rome, Pinacoteca Vaticana.

325. CRISTIANI: *S. John Evangelist and eight Scenes from his Life.* Pistoia, S. Giovanni Fuorcivitas.
Signed and dated 1370.

326. CRISTIANI: *Crato's Followers destroying their Patrimony (detail of S. John Evangelist and
Scenes from his Life).* Pistoia, S. Giovanni Fuorcivitas. *1370.*

327. CRISTIANI: *S. John Evangelist enthroned (detail of S. John Evangelist and Scenes from his Life)*.
Pistoia, S. Giovanni Fuorcivitas. *Signed and dated 1370*.

328. CRISTIANI: *S. Lucy enthroned with six Angels*. New Haven, Yale University.

329, 330. CRISTIANI: *S. Lucy distributing her Fortune, S. Lucy standing fast against the Oxen.*
New York, Metropolitan Museum.

331. CRISTIANI: *Triptych: Madonna and Child with Angels; SS. James, Baptist, Anthony Abbot and Bishop Saint; Annunciation, S. Ursula and S. Margaret.* Florence, Acton Collection.

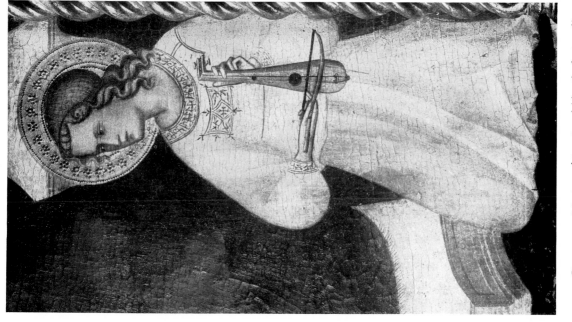

333. CRISTIANI: *Music-making Angel (detail of triptych)*.
Florence, Acton Collection.

332. CRISTIANI: *Salvator Mundi*. Homeless.

334. CRISTIANI: *Madonna and Child with S. Anthony Abbot, S. James and Donor.* Florence, S. Ambrogio.

335. CRISTIANI: *Madonna and Child with six Angels*. Pistoia, Museo Civico. *Signed*.

336. AGNOLO GADDI: *Centre panel of altarpiece: Madonna and Child
with Angels.* Florence, Contini Bonacossi Collection;
Two Stories of S. Michael. New Haven, Yale University.

337, 338. AGNOLO GADDI: *Wings of altarpiece: S. Nicholas with kneeling Donor and two Scenes of his Life; S. Julian and two Scenes of his Life.* Munich, Alte Pinakothek.

339, 340. Agnolo Gaddi and Assistants: *Predella panels: Crucifixion, Hermogenes brought to S. James and Beheading of S. James.* Paris, Louvre.

341. AGNOLO GADDI: *Painted Cross*. Florence, S. Martino a Sesto.

342. AGNOLO GADDI: *Fragment of fresco: Martyrdom of S. Sebastian and Donor*. Florence, S. Ambrogio.

343. View of the Choir of S. Croce in Florence, with frescoes by Agnolo Gaddi; above entrance to first chapel left of choir, *fresco of Assumption*, by Agnolo Gaddi; above entrance to first chapel right of choir (Cappella Bardi) *fresco of S. Francis receiving Stigmata*, by Giotto.

344. AGNOLO GADDI: *Fresco: Theft of the True Cross by King Cosroes.* Florence, S. Croce, Choir, Left Wall. *ca 1385/95.*

345. AGNOLO GADDI: *Fresco: Detail from the Recovery of the Wood and the Manufacture of the Cross. Florence, S. Croce, Choir, Right Wall. ca 1385/95.*

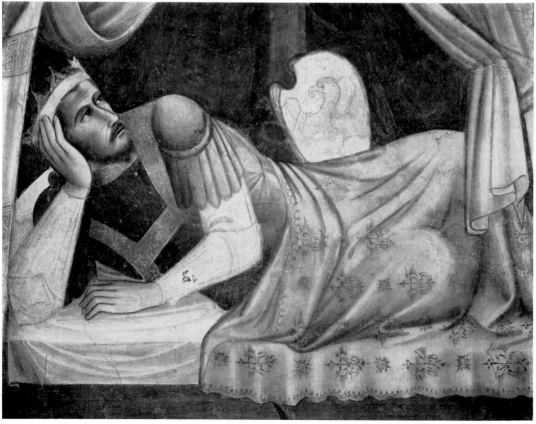

346, 347. AGNOLO GADDI: *Frescoes: detail from the Beheading of Cosroes; detail from the Dream of Heraclius.*
Florence, S. Croce, Choir, Left Wall. *ca 1385/95.*

348. AGNOLO GADDI: *Fresco: The Evangelist Mark*. Florence, S. Croce, Vault. *ca 1385/95*.

349. AGNOLO GADDI: *Triptych from S. Caterina all'Antella: Madonna and Child with SS. Philip and Lawrence; Christ blessing, Annunciation; in predella, Miracle of S. Philip, Dead Christ with Virgin and S. John Evangelist, Martyrdom of S. Lawrence.* Florence, Gallerie Fiorentine.

350. AGNOLO GADDI: *Coronation of the Virgin*. Washington, National Gallery of Art, Kress Collection.

351. AGNOLO GADDI: *Fresco: S. John on Patmos.* Florence, S. Croce, Cappella Castellani.

352. AGNOLO GADDI: *Fresco: S. James baptising Hermogenes.* Prato, Duomo, Cappella Manassei.

353. AGNOLO GADDI: *Fresco: Voyage of Michele Dagomari to Prato*. Prato, Duomo, Cappella del Sacro Cingolo. *1394/96* (during cleaning).

354. AGNOLO GADDI: *Fragments of the Armadio del Crocifisso di S. Giovanni Gualberto*. Florence, S. Miniato al Monte, Cappella del Crocifisso. Left unfinished in 1396.

355. MASTER OF THE STRAUS MADONNA:
Madonna of Humility. Florence, Bargello.

356. AGNOLO GADDI: *Madonna of Humility*.
Formerly New York, H. I. Pratt.

357. MASTER OF THE STRAUS MADONNA:
Madonna. Homeless.

358. Florentine 1350–1420: *The 'Straus Madonna'*.
Houston (Texas), Museum.

359. CENNI DI FRANCESCO: *Fresco: Madonna and Child with the Cardinal and the Theological Virtues (detail)*. San Miniato al Tedesco, Palazzo Comunale. *Dated 1393.*

360. CENNI DI FRANCESCO: *Fresco: St. Helena taking the Cross to Jerusalem.* Volterra, S. Francesco.

361. CENNI DI FRANCESCO: *Madonna and Child*. Lawrence, University of Kansas, Kress Collection.

362. CENNI DI FRANCESCO: *Fresco: Seth planting a branch of the Tree of Knowledge on Adam's grave*.
Volterra, S. Francesco.

363. NICCOLÒ DI PIETRO GERINI: *Painted Cross*. Florence, S. Croce,
Cappella Castellani. *Dated 1380.*

364. NICCOLÒ DI PIETRO GERINI: *Entombment and Ascension*. Florence, S. Carlo dei Lombardi.

365. NICCOLÒ DI PIETRO GERINI and AMBROGIO DI BALDESE: *Fresco: The Brethren of the Misericordia receiving Orphans*. Florence, Bigallo.

366. NICCOLÒ DI PIETRO GERINI: *Triptych: Baptism of Christ, SS. Peter and Paul.*
London, National Gallery. *1387.*

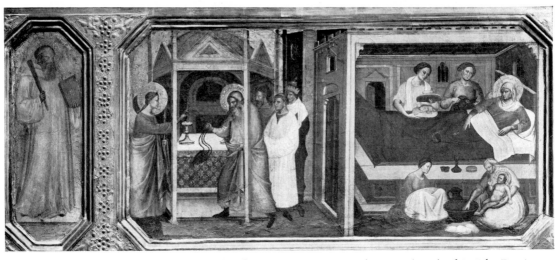

367. NICCOLÒ DI PIETRO GERINI: *S. Benedict, Annunciation to Zacharias and Birth of S. John Baptist*
(from predella to triptych above).

368. Niccolò di Pietro Gerini: *Coronation of the Virgin with six Angels and SS. Francis, Lucy, Catherine and John Baptist*, Montreal, Museum.

369, 370. Niccolò di Pietro Gerini: *The four crowned Martyrs appear before Lampadius.* Denver, Museum, Kress Collection. *Flagellation of the four crowned Martyrs.* Philadelphia, Johnson Collection.

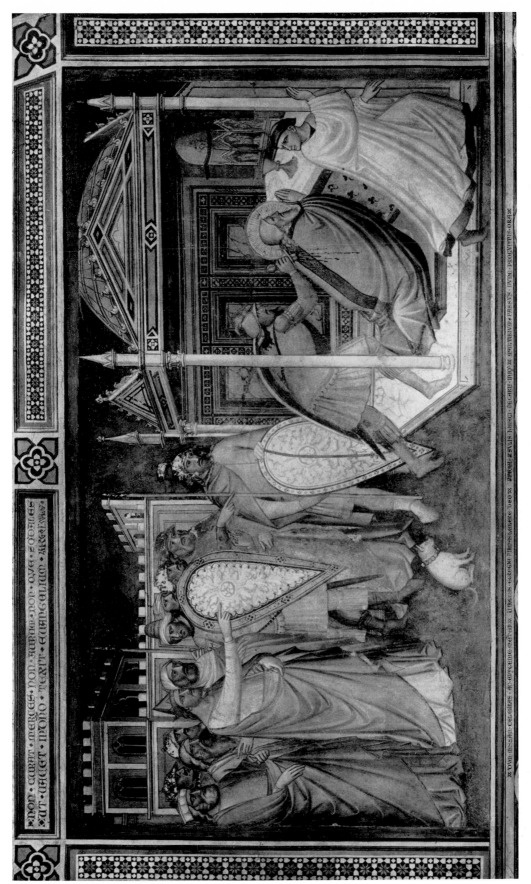

371. Niccolò di Pietro Gerini and Assistants: *Fresco: Death of S. Matthew.* Prato, S. Francesco, Sala del Capitolo.

372, 373. Niccolò di Pietro Gerini and Assistants: *Frescoes: Vision of S. Benedict* (*detail*), *Crucifixion* (*detail*).
Prato, S. Francesco, Sala del Capitolo.

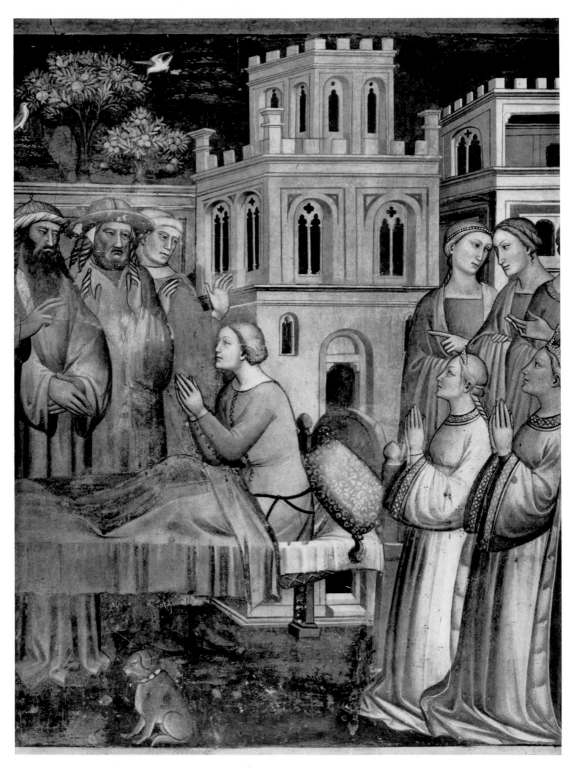

374. Niccolò di Pietro Gerini and Assistants: *Fresco: Raising of the King's Child (detail).*
Prato, S. Francesco, Sala del Capitolo.

375, 376. NICCOLÒ DI PIETRO GERINI and Assistants: *Frescoes: Calling of S. Matthew* (*detail*), *S. Anthony distributing his fortune* (*detail*). Prato, S. Francesco, Sala del Capitolo.

377. NICCOLÒ DI PIETRO GERINI: *Fresco: Ascension (detail).* Pisa, S. Francesco, Capitolo
di S. Bonaventura. *1392.*

378. NICCOLÒ DI PIETRO GERINI: *Annunciation.* Homeless.

380. Niccolò di Pietro Gerini and Assistants: *Trinity*. Florence, Orsanmichele. *1408/09*.

379. Niccolò di Pietro Gerini and Assistants: *Fresco: Pentecost*. Florence, Paradiso degli Alberti. *1398/99*.

381. View of the Sacristy of S. Croce in Florence with frescoes by NICCOLÒ DI PIETRO GERINI and Assistants (*Resurrection, Ascension*), and by SPINELLO ARETINO (*Way to Calvary, Crucifixion*). On the left, the Cappella Rinuccini with frescoes by GIOVANNI DA MILANO above and by the RINUCCINI MASTER below and with polyptych by GIOVANNI DEL BIONDO.

382. *Detail from Coronation*. Florence, Arte della Lana.

383. *Detail from Coronation*.
Florence, Arte della Lana.

384. MASTER OF ARTE DELLA LANA CORONATION: *Madonna and Child with Saints and Angels*. Leningrad, Hermitage.

385. MASTER OF ARTE DELLA LANA CORONATION: *Madonna and Child with Saints and Angels.*
Rome, Pinacoteca Vaticana.

386. Niccolò di Pietro Gerini, Spinello Aretino and Lorenzo di Niccolò: *Triptych: Coronation of the Virgin, Angels, Saints and Prophets*. Florence, Accademia. Dated 1410.

387. LORENZO DI NICCOLÒ: Triptych: S. Bartholomew enthroned and Scenes from his Life. San Gimignano. Museo. Dated 1401.

388. Lorenzo di Niccolò: S. Gregory, S. Fina and Scenes from the Life of S. Fina. San Gimignano, Museo.

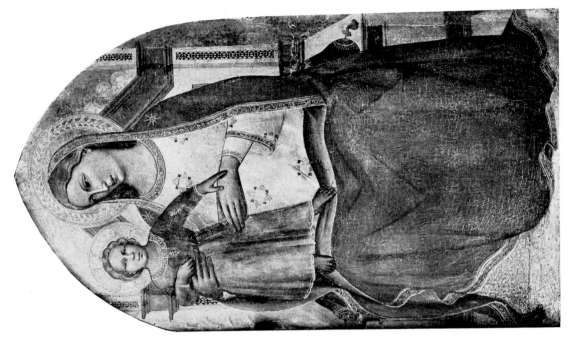

390. LORENZO DI NICCOLÒ: *Madonna and Child (central panel of triptych)*. Florence, S. Leonardo in Arcetri.

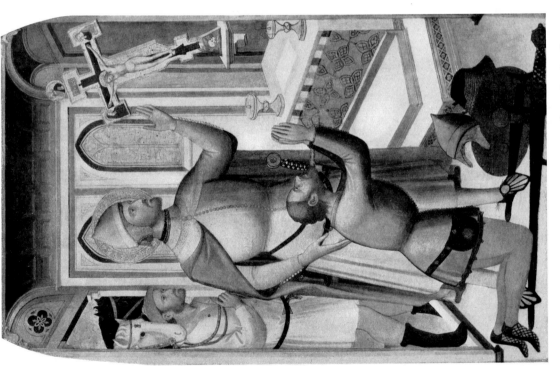

389. LORENZO DI NICCOLÒ: *Conversion of S. John Gualbert*. New York, Metropolitan Museum.

391. LORENZO DI NICCOLÒ: *Triptych: Madonna and Child, SS. Martin and Lawrence.*
Terenzano (Florence), S. Martino. *Signed and dated 1402.*

392. LORENZO DI NICCOLÒ: *Two panels of polyptych: SS. Clement and Lucy.*
Terenzano (Florence), S. Martino.

393. LORENZO DI NICCOLÒ: *Polyptych of the Coronation of the Virgin (detail of central panel).*
Cortona, S. Domenico. *1402.*

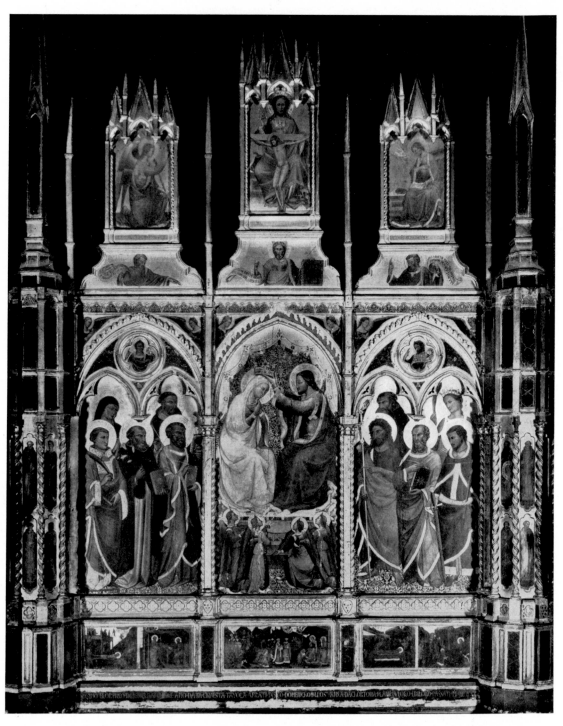

394. Lorenzo di Niccolò: *Polyptych of the Coronation of the Virgin*. Cortona, S. Domenico. *1402*.

395. LORENZO DI NICCOLÒ: *Triptych: Madonna and Child with Saints*. Saint Louis, City Art Museum.

396. LORENZO DI NICCOLÒ: *Triptych of the Coronation of the Virgin*. Florence, S. Croce.

397–398. Pietro di Miniato (?): *Nativity and Lamentation* (*details of frescoed lunette*). Pistoia, S. Francesco.

399. PIETRO DI MINIATO: *Polyptych of the Coronation of the Virgin, from the Convent of S. Matteo. Prato, Pinacoteca. 1412.*

400. SPINELLO ARETINO: *Fresco: Madonna and Child blessing a kneeling Warrior, with SS. James and Anthony Abbot. Arezzo, S. Agostino. Dated 1377.*

402. SPINELLO ARETINO: *Fresco: S. Michael with Donor. Arezzo, S. Francesco.*

401. SPINELLO ARETINO: *Fresco: Annunciation in Tabernacle over Entrance. Arezzo, SS. Annunziata.*

403. Spinello Aretino: Fresco: *Apparition of S. Michael over Castel Sant'Angelo in Rome*. Arezzo, S. Francesco, Chapel right of Choir.

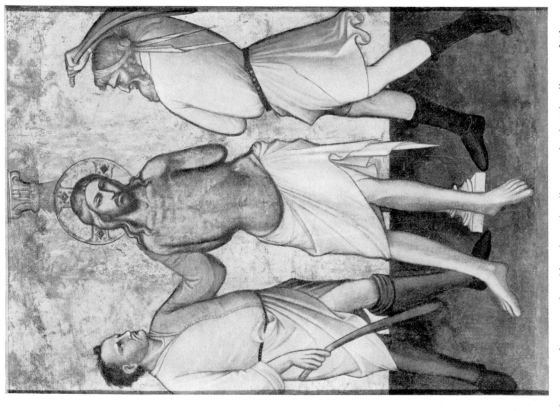

404, 405. SPINELLO ARETINO: *Processional banner: S. Mary Magdalen enthroned with music-making Angels and kneeling Flagellants; on back, Flagellation of Christ.* New York, Metropolitan Museum (the Flagellation has been completed with the Head of Christ, now at the Camposanto Teutonico in Rome).

406, 407. SPINELLO ARETINO: *Coronation and Dormition of the Virgin* (pinnacle and predella from the dismembered polyptych of Monteoliveto). Siena, Pinacoteca. *1385*.

408. Spinello Aretino: *SS. Benedict and Lucilla and predella with Death of S. Benedict and Martyrdom of S. Lucilla* (from the dismembered polyptych of Monteoliveto). Cambridge (Mass.), Fogg Art Museum. *Dated 1385.*

409, 410. SPINELLO ARETINO: *Frescoes: Temptation of S. Benedict in the Wilderness; King Totila before S. Benedict.*
Florence, S. Miniato, Sacristy.

411. SPINELLO ARETINO: *Detail of Fresco: S. Catherine, in prison, has a vision of Christ*. Florence, Oratorio di S. Caterina all'Antella. *ca 1387*.

412. SPINELLO ARETINO: *Fresco: Mystic Marriage of S. Catherine*. Florence, Oratorio di S. Caterina all'Antella.
ca 1387.

413, 414. Spinello Aretino: *Frescoes: Translation of the body of S. Catherine to Mount Sinai; S. Catherine baptized by the Hermit (detail).* Florence, Oratorio di S. Caterina all'Antella. *ca 1387.*

415. SPINELLO ARETINO and LORENZO DI NICCOLÒ: *Triptych: Madonna and Child, SS. Peter, Philip, Lawrence and James*. Florence, S. Maria a Quinto. *Dated 1393*.

416. SPINELLO ARETINO: *Triptych: Madonna and Child, SS. Paulinus, John Baptist, Andrew and Matthew*. Florence, Accademia. *Signed and dated 1391*.

417. SPINELLO ARETINO: *Madonna and Child with two Angels*.
Saint Louis (Missouri), City Art Museum.

418. SPINELLO ARETINO: *Fresco: Condemnation and Martyrdom of S. Ephysius. Pisa, Camposanto. 1391/92.*

419. Spinello Aretino: *Fresco: Conversion of S. Ephysius in Battle (detail)*. Pisa, Camposanto. 1391/92.

420. SPINELLO ARETINO: *Madonna and Child*. Città di Castello, Pinacoteca.

421. SPINELLO ARETINO: *Fresco: Annunciation (detail)*. Arezzo, S. Francesco.

422. SPINELLO ARETINO: *Fresco: Life of S. Gregory (detail)*. Florence, S. Maria Novella, Cappella Bardi.

423, 424. SPINELLO ARETINO with his son PARRI and MARTINO DI BARTOLOMEO: *Frescoes:
Submission of Barbarossa to Pope Alexander III and detail from the Pope's journey to Rome.*
Siena, Palazzo Pubblico, Sala di Balìa. *1408/10.*

425. SPINELLO ARETINO: *Fresco: SS. James and Philip with Scenes from their Lives; Mystic Marriage of S. Catherine and her Martyrdom* in lunette above. Arezzo, S. Domenico.

426. PARRI SPINELLI: *Fresco: Crucifixion with S. Nicholas and S. Dominic;* in lunette *two Stories of S. Nicholas.*
Arezzo, S. Domenico.

427a–b. PARRI SPINELLI: *Madonna of Mercy with SS. Pergentinus and Laurentianus; in predella
Life of SS. Pergentinus and Laurentianus (detail).* Arezzo, Pinacoteca. *1435/37.*

428. Parri Spinelli: *Fresco: Crucifixion*. Arezzo, Palazzo dei Priori. *Late work*.

429. Lorenzo Monaco: *Madonna and Child*. Amsterdam, Rijksmuseum.

430, 431. LORENZO MONACO: *Illuminated initials: S. Jerome* (Corale n.5, 1394); *S. Romuald* (Corale n.8, 1395).
Florence, Biblioteca Laurenziana.

432. LORENZO MONACO: *Betrayal of Christ* (*from the predella of the Agony in the Garden*).
Florence, Accademia.

433. Lorenzo Monaco: *Madonna of Humility (central panel of triptych)*. Empoli, Pinacoteca.
Dated 1404.

434. LORENZO MONACO: *Madonna and Child with Angels* (*detail*). Vaduz, Liechtenstein Collection.

435. LORENZO MONACO: *Illuminated initial: Madonna and Child.* Florence, Bargello, Codex E 70.

436. LORENZO MONACO: *Predella panel: Flight into Egypt.* Altenburg, Lindenau Museum.

437. LORENZO MONACO: *Portable Triptych: Madonna of Humility, the Baptist, S. Nicholas, Annunciation, a Bishop Saint*. Siena, Pinacoteca.

438. LORENZO MONACO: *Portable altarpiece: Madonna and Child with two Angels, the Baptist and S. Peter.*
Florence, Accademia. *Dated 1408.*

439. LORENZO MONACO: *Lamentation*. Prague, National Gallery.

440. LORENZO MONACO: *King David*.
Formerly New York, Guggenheim Museum.

441. LORENZO MONACO: *Noah*.
Formerly Parcieux, Henri Chalandon.

442, 443. LORENZO MONACO: *Two illuminated initials with Prophets*. Florence, Biblioteca Laurenziana, Corale 3. *1409*.

444. Lorenzo Monaco: *Triptych from the Badia Fiorentina: Annunciation; SS. Catherine, Anthony Abbot, Proculus and Francis.* Florence, Accademia.

446. LORENZO MONACO: *Virgin of Annunciation.*
Formerly Vaduz, Liechtenstein Collection.

445. LORENZO MONACO: *Annunciation.*
Brussels, Mme Feron-Stoclet.

447. LORENZO MONACO: *Coronation with Angels and sixteen Saints* (*detail*) (from S. Benedetto
fuori Porta a Pinti). London, National Gallery.

448. LORENZO MONACO: *Coronation with Angels and twenty Saints:* in pinnacles, *Blessing Saviour and Annunciation;* in predella, *Life of S. Benedict;* in pilasters, *Saints and Prophets* (from S. Maria degli Angeli). Florence, Uffizi. *Signed and dated 1413 (new style 1414).*

449. LORENZO MONACO: *Madonna of Humility.*
Washington, National Gallery, S. H. Kress
Collection. *Dated 1413.*

450. LORENZO MONACO: *Virgin of Annunciation*
(detail of Pl. 448). Florence, Uffizi. *1414.*

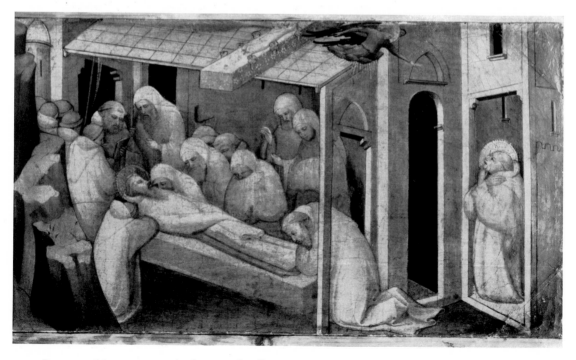

451. LORENZO MONACO: *Death of S. Benedict* (from predella of *Coronation*). London, National Gallery,
Lennard Loan.

452, 453. LORENZO MONACO: *Blessing Saviour; Miraculous rescue of Placidus, and S. Benedict detained by S. Scholastica* (details of Pl. 448). Florence, Uffizi. *1414.*

455. LORENZO MONACO: *Death of S. Francis.* Rome, Palazzo Rospigliosi, Pallavicini Collection.

454. LORENZO MONACO: *S. Francis receiving Stigmata.* Amsterdam, Rijksmuseum.

456, 457. LORENZO MONACO: *Cut-out figures of mourning Virgin and John Evangelist*. Florence, S. Giovannino dei Cavalieri.

458. Lorenzo Monaco: *Cut-out Crucifix*. Budapest, Museum.

459. LORENZO MONACO: *Detail from Adoration of the Magi* (possibly same as the S. Egidio altarpiece, paid 1420/22). Florence, Uffizi.

460. LORENZO MONACO: *Detail from Adoration of the Magi.* Florence, Uffizi.

461. LORENZO MONACO: *Detail from Adoration of the Magi.* Florence, Uffizi.

462. LORENZO MONACO: *Fresco: Marriage of the Virgin (detail).* Florence, S. Trinita, Cappella Bartolini.
1422/25.

463. LORENZO MONACO: *Altarpiece: Annunciation; Prophets in pinnacles; Life of Virgin in predella; Saints in pilasters of frame.* Florence, S. Trinita, Cappella Bartolini. *1422/25.*

464. LORENZO MONACO: *Adoration of the Magi* (*from predella of Annunciation*). Florence, S. Trinita, Cappella Bartolini. *1422/25*.

465. LORENZO MONACO: *Predella panel: S. Nicholas saving a ship at sea.* Florence, Accademia.

466. ALVARO PORTOGHESE: *Triptych: Madonna and Child with Goldfinch; SS. Nicholas, John Baptist, Christopher, Michael; Heads of SS. Cosmas and Damian in pinnacles. Volterra, Duomo. Signed and dated 1423.*

467. ALVARO PORTOGHESE: *Madonna and Child with eight Angels. Pisa, S. Croce a Fossabanda. Signed.*

468. ALVARO PORTOGHESE: *Portable triptych: Madonna and Child with SS. John Baptist and Anthony Abbot; Annunciation, Crucifixion, Resurrection. Signed and dated 1434. Brunswick, Herzog Anton Ulrich Museum.*

469. MASTER OF THE BAMBINO VISPO: *Last Judgement*, from the Colegio Raimondo Lulo in Majorca.
Munich, Alte Pinakothek. *1415?*.

470. MASTER OF THE BAMBINO VISPO: *Dormition and Assumption of the Virgin* (photomontage).
Lower half—Philadelphia, Johnson Collection; upper half—Cambridge, Fogg Art Museum.

471. MASTER OF THE BAMBINO VISPO: *Madonna of Humility.*
Formerly Vienna, Lederer Collection.

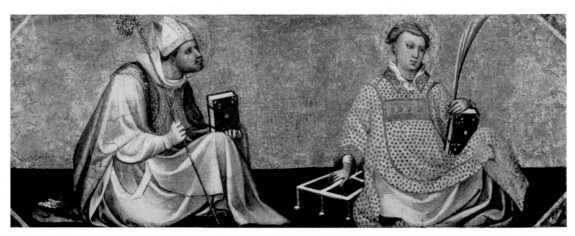

472. MASTER OF THE BAMBINO VISPO: *Predella panel: S. Augustine (?) and S. Lawrence.*
Los Angeles, County Museum.

473. MASTER OF THE BAMBINO VISPO: *Madonna and Child with twelve Angels.*
Formerly London, Viscount Rothermere.

474. MASTER OF THE BAMBINO VISPO: *Man of Sorrows, Virgin and S. John (detail of predella,
companion to Plate 472).* Homeless.

475. MASTER OF THE BAMBINO VISPO: Triptych: Madonna and Child with six Angels, SS. Margaret, Andrew, Peter and Mary Magdalen. Würzburg, Martin von Wagner Museum.

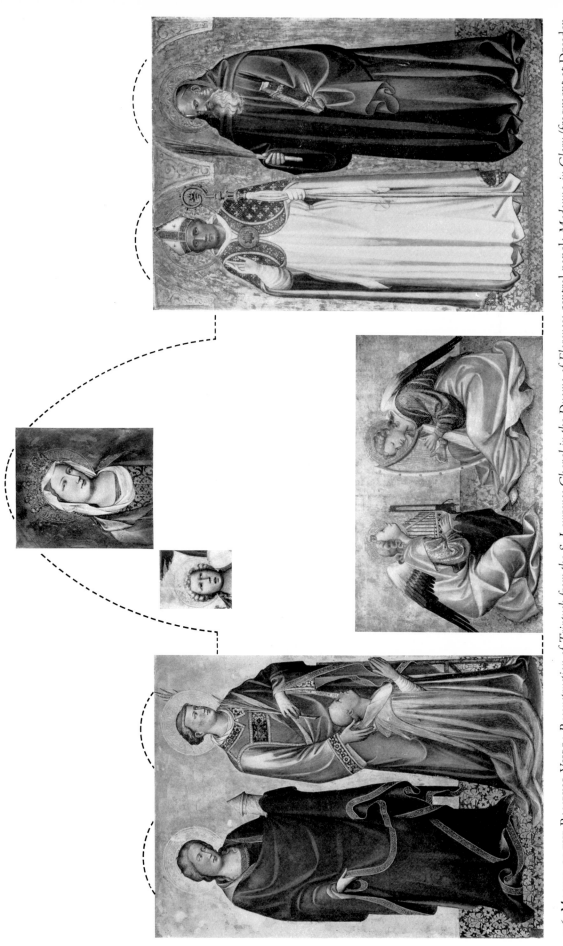

476. MASTER OF THE BAMBINO VISPO: *Reconstruction of Triptych from the S. Lawrence Chapel in the Duomo of Florence*: central panel: *Madonna in Glory* (fragment at Dresden, Gemäldegalerie) *and Angels* (fragments at Rotterdam, Boymans–Van Beuningen Museum and formerly London, Lord Carmichael); side-panels: *Mary Magdalen and S. Lawrence with Cardinal Pietro Orsini* (Berlin-Ost, Staatliche Museen), *SS. Zenobius and Benedict* (Stockholm, National Museum). *1422 or later.*

477. MASTER OF THE BAMBINO VISPO: *Adoration of the Magi* (from the predella of the Triptych of the S. Lawrence Chapel in the Duomo at Florence). Douai, Musée. *1422 or later.*

478. MASTER OF THE BAMBINO VISPO: *Miracle of S. Zenobius* (from the predella of the Triptych of the S. Lawrence Chapel in the Duomo at Florence). Roma, Marchesa Visconti Venosta. *1422 or later.*

479. MASTER OF THE BAMBINO VISPO: *Martyrdom of S. Lawrence* (from the predella of the Triptych of the S. Lawrence Chapel in the Duomo at Florence). Roma, Principe Colonna. *1422 or later.*

480. MASTER OF THE BAMBINO VISPO: *Predella panel: Adoration of the Shepherds.* Genoa, Viezzoli Collection.

481. MASTER OF THE BAMBINO VISPO: *Two pinnacles: Annunciation*. Frankfurt, Staedelsches Institut.

482. MASTER OF THE BAMBINO VISPO: *Cassone panel: Battle of Saracens*. Altenburg, Lindenau Museum.

483. GIOVANNI DAL PONTE: *Triptych: Coronation of the Virgin, SS. Anthony Abbot, Louis of Toulouse, male Saint, Peter, John Baptist, Blaise, Nicholas and Thomas; in pinnacles, Annunciation; in pilasters, Abraham, Moses and six Angels. Chantilly, Musée Condé. Dated 1410.*

484. GIOVANNI DAL PONTE: *Triptych: Coronation of the Virgin, SS. Francis, John Baptist, Ives and Dominic; in pinnacles, Annunciation, Descent to Limbo.* Florence, Accademia.

486. GIOVANNI DAL PONTE: *Allegorical Couple (fragment of 'spalliera').*
Formerly Ashburnham Place (Sussex), Lady Ashburnham.

485. GIOVANNI DAL PONTE: *Dante and Petrarch (fragment).*
Cambridge (Mass.), Fogg Art Museum.

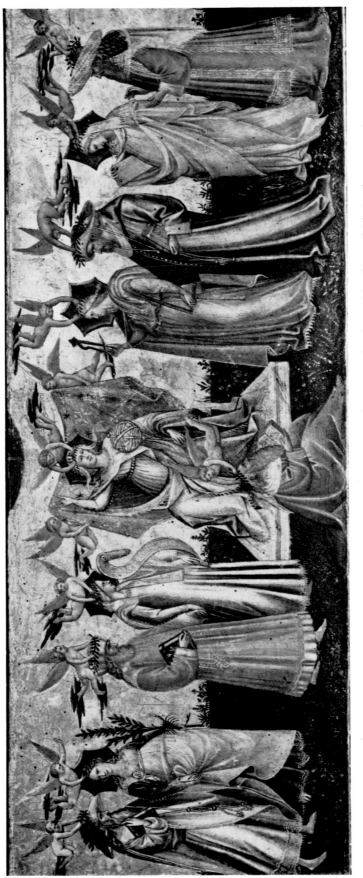

487. Giovanni dal Ponte: *Front panel of a cassone: The seven Liberal Arts (detail)*. Madrid, Prado.

489. GIOVANNI DAL PONTE: *Portable altarpiece: Madonna nursing the Child with SS. Lucy, John Baptist, Francis and Catherine. Oakly Park, Earl of Plymouth.*

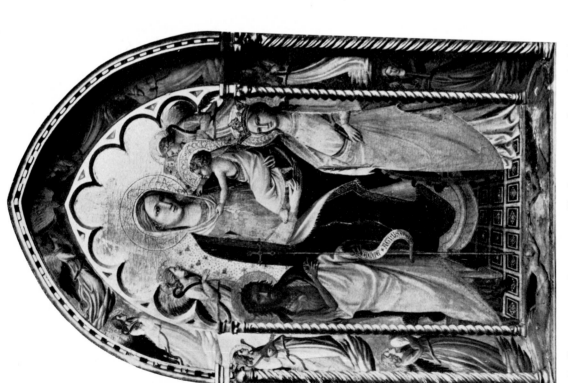

488. GIOVANNI DAL PONTE: *Portable altarpiece: Madonna and Child with SS. John Baptist, Catherine and Angels. Homeless.*

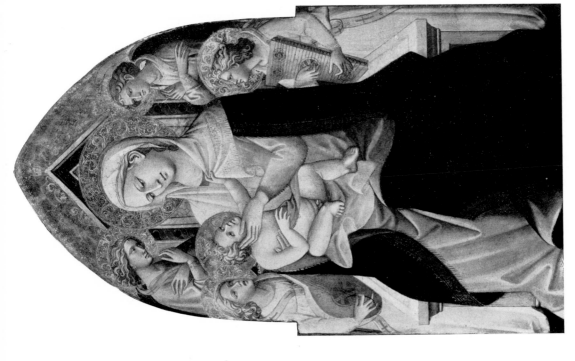

491. GIOVANNI DAL PONTE: *Madonna and Child with four Angels.*
San Francisco, De Young Memorial Museum, Kress Collection.

490. GIOVANNI DAL PONTE: *Madonna and Child.*
Florence, Certosa del Galluzzo.

492. GIOVANNI DAL PONTE: *Marriage of S. Catherine with Angels and two Donors; eight Saints in pilasters;*
Life of S. Catherine in predella. Budapest, Museum.

493, 494. GIOVANNI DAL PONTE: *Two predella panels: Liberation and Martyrdom of S. Peter.*
Florence, Uffizi.

496. GIOVANNI DAL PONTE: *Fresco: Flaying of S. Bartholomew.*
Florence, S. Trinita, Cappella Scali. *1434/35.*

495. GIOVANNI DAL PONTE: *Annunciation (central panel of triptych).*
Rosano, SS. Annunziata. *Dated 1430.*

497. Bicci di Lorenzo: *Fresco: S. Cecilia arrested while giving alms, S. Cecilia preaching, Baptism of two Converts by Urban. Florence, Carmine, Sacristy.*

498. BICCI DI LORENZO: *Triptych: Annunciation; SS. Michael, James the Less, Margaret and John Evangelist;*
in pinnacles, Cherubs and Crucifixion; in predella, S. Michael and the Bull of Gargano, Nativity,
S. John Evangelist in the cauldron of boiling oil. Stia, S. Maria Assunta. *Dated 1414.*

499. BICCI DI LORENZO: *Predella to triptych by Daddi: S. Salvi healing the plague-stricken, Nativity, S. Bernardo degli Uberti defending Rome.* Berlin, Staatliche Museen (destroyed). *Dated 1423.*

500. BICCI DI LORENZO: *Triptych: Marriage of S. Catherine, with SS. Agnes and Elizabeth of Hungary; SS. Anthony of Padua, John Evangelist, Louis of Toulouse, Herculanus, Lawrence and Constantius; in spandrels, Stigmatization of S. Francis, Annunciation, SS. Jerome, Onuphrius and another Saint in the Wilderness; in predella, Noli me tangere, Martyrdom of S. Agnes, S. Elizabeth of Hungary ministering to the Poor, Baptism of Christ.* Perugia, Pinacoteca.

501. BICCI DI LORENZO: *Frescoed Tabernacle: Madonna and Child with S. Paul, S. Jerome and Donor.*
Florence, via dei Serragli and via S. Monaca. *Dated 1427.*

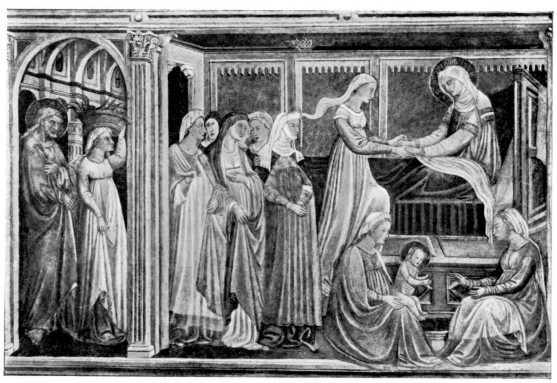

502. BICCI DI LORENZO: *Fresco: Birth of the Virgin.* Pescia, S. Francesco.

503. BICCI DI LORENZO: *Madonna nursing the Child
with S. Anne and Angels.* Greenville (S.C.),
Bob Jones University Gallery.

504. BICCI DI LORENZO: *Triptych (detail).*
Vertine (Chianti), S. Bartolomeo.
Dated 1430.

505. BICCI DI LORENZO: *Frescoed Lunette: Madonna and Child with S. George and S. Leonard.*
Florence, Porta S. Giorgio. *Dated 1430.*

506. BICCI DI LORENZO: *Triptych: Madonna and Child with Angels* (Parma, Pinacoteca); *SS. Benedict and Nicholas* (Grottaferrata, Badia), *Baptist and Evangelist* (New York, R. Lehman). *Dated 1433.*

507. BICCI DI LORENZO: *Predella panel: S. Nicholas raising the three Youths in the barrels.*
New York, Metropolitan Museum.

508. BICCI DI LORENZO: *Fragment of altarpiece: Visitation;* in spandrel, *King David.*
Velletri, Museo del Duomo. *Dated 1434.*

509. BICCI DI LORENZO: *Nativity*; in predella, *Circumcision, Trinity, Adoration of Magi*. Florence, S. Giovannino dei Cavalieri. *Dated 1435*.

510. BICCI DI LORENZO: *Fresco: Pope Martin V consecrating the Church of S. Egidio in 1420. Florence, Spedale di S. Maria Nuova. After 1424.*

511. BICCI DI LORENZO: *Triptych: Madonna nursing the Child; SS. Hippolytus, John Baptist, James and Christopher;* in pinnacles, *Head of Christ, Annunciation, Pentecost, Crucifixion, Resurrection;* in pilasters, *Saints and Angels;* in predella, *Martyrdom of S. Hippolytus, Baptism of Christ, Nativity, Beheading of S. James, Martyrdom of S. Christopher, Two Saints.* Bibbiena, Pieve di S. Ippolito. *Dated 1435.*

512. BICCI DI LORENZO: *S. Blaise enthroned.*
Indianapolis, Herron Art Institute.

513. BICCI DI LORENZO: *S. Nicholas of Tolentino
defending Empoli from the Plague.*
Empoli, Collegiata. *1445.*

514. BICCI DI LORENZO: *Annunciation.* Legnaia (Florence). S. Arcangelo. *Dated 1440.*

515. MARIOTTO DI NARDO: *Fragmentary polyptych: Madonna and Child with two Angels and twelve Saints;*
in pinnacles, *Annunciation;* in predella, *Man of Sorrows, Mourning Virgin and S. John, four Saints.*
Florence, S. Donnino di Villamagna. *ca 1394/95.*

516. MARIOTTO DI NARDO: *Predella: Life of the Baptist (detail).* San Miniato al Tedesco, S. Domenico.

517. MARIOTTO DI NARDO: *Triptych: Madonna della Cintola; SS. Jerome and John Evangelist;* in pinnacle,
Christ holding the crown. Fiesole, Oratorio di Fontelucente. *Formerly dated 1398.*

519. MARIOTTO DI NARDO: *Madonna and Child with two Donors.*
Assisi, Mrs. Perkins. *Dated 1404.*

518. MARIOTTO DI NARDO: *Madonna and Child with Saints and Angels.*
Formerly Parcieux, Henri Chalandon.

520. Mariotto di Nardo: *Triptych: Coronation of the Virgin with Angels; SS. Lawrence, Stephen, Baptist and Evangelist; Angels in pinnacles, Saints in pilasters.* Formerly London, Hatton Garden Church. *Dated 1408.*

521. MARIOTTO DI NARDO: *Pinnacle: S. James*. Homeless.

522. MARIOTTO DI NARDO: *Predella panel: Ordination of S. Stephen, Exorcism of a possessed Woman*.
Formerly Munich, Erwin Rosenthal.

523, 524. MARIOTTO DI NARDO: *Two predella panels: Circumcision and Baptism of Christ.*
Balcarres, Earl of Crawford and Balcarres.

525. MARIOTTO DI NARDO: *Triptych*. Formerly Florence, Compagnia del Bigallo. *1415–16*.

526. MARIOTTO DI NARDO: *Madonna and Child with Angels and Saints*. Formerly Berlin, Kaufmann.

527. MARIOTTO DI NARDO: *Desco da Nozze: Garden of Love*. Vaduz, Liechtenstein Collection.

528. MARIOTTO DI NARDO: *Predella panel: Dormition of the Virgin*. Florence, Accademia.

529. MARIOTTO DI NARDO: *Frescoes: Judas receiving the money, Last Supper, Washing of the Feet.*
Florence, Farmacia di S. Maria Novella.

530. MARIOTTO DI NARDO: *Triptych (detail)*.
Panzano, S. Leonino. *Dated 1421*.

531. MARIOTTO DI NARDO: *Coronation of the Virgin*.
Florence, Acton Collection. *Dated 1431*.

532. MARIOTTO DI NARDO (*Annunciation*) and ROSSELLO DI JACOPO (*Saints*): *Triptych*. Pistoia, Museo.

534. ROSSELLO DI JACOPO: *Madonna and Child enthroned.*
Staggia, S. Maria Assunta (stolen in 1920). *Signed.*

533. ROSSELLO DI JACOPO: *S. Blaise enthroned.*
Florence, Duomo. *1408.*

535. ROSSELLO DI JACOPO: *Coronation of the Virgin*; in pinnacles, *Saviour, Annunciation, two Prophets, Cherubs*; in pilasters, *Saints*; in predella, *Man of Sorrows, Saints*. Florence, Accademia. *Dated 1420*.

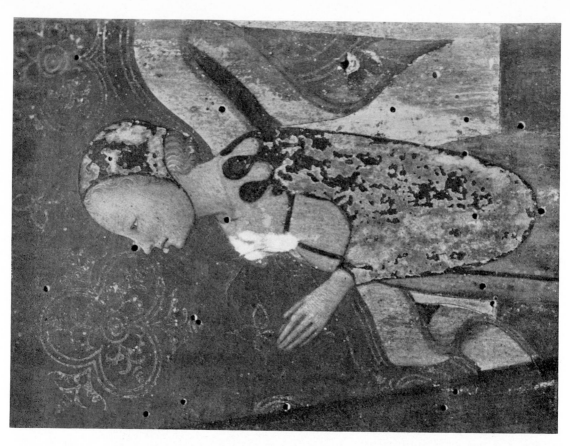

537. Rossello di Jacopo: *Female Donor* (*detail of the Madonna del Parto*). Florence, Palazzo Davanzati.

536. Rossello di Jacopo: *Madonna and Child in Glory* (*detail of Tabernacle*). Barcelona, Museo.

540. ROSSELLO: *Madonna of Humility.*
Formerly Rome, Miss Vedder.

539. ROSSELLO: *SS. Michael and John Evangelist.*
Formerly London, H. Harris.

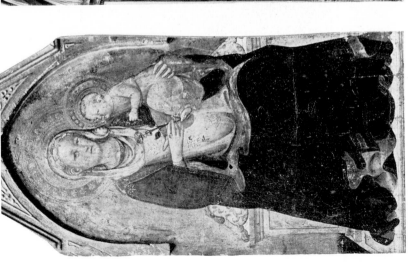

538. ROSSELLO: *Madonna and Child enthroned.*
Formerly Vienna, Karl Moll.

541. ROSSELLO DI JACOPO: *Fresco: A Male Saint and S. Lucy.* Florence, S. Miniato al Monte.

542. ROSSELLO DI JACOPO: *Coronation of the Virgin, with Trinity and Prophet above.* Siena, Pinacoteca. *Signed and dated 1439.*

544. ROSSELLO DI JACOPO: *Cassone: A tournament (detail)*. Homeless.

543. ROSSELLO DI JACOPO: *Cassone: Sports and Games (detail)*. Berlin, Staatliche Museen.

545. Rossello di Jacopo: *Cassone: Court of Love*. Madison, University of Wisconsin, Kress Study Collection.

546. Florentine close to Rossello di Jacopo: *Cassone: Mythological Subject*. Brunswick (Maine), Bowdoin College, Kress Study Collection.

547. ROSSELLO DI JACOPO: *The 'Griggs' Crucifixion*. New York, Metropolitan Museum.

548. Florentine ca 1430/40: *Fresco: Jacob's Flight from Laban (detail)*. Florence, S. Maria Novella, Chiostro Verde, West Wall.

549. ROSSELLO DI JACOPO: *Fresco: Preaching of S. Peter Martyr (detail)*. Florence, Bigallo.

550. Florentine close to MASOLINO (Master of 1419): *Dismembered and fragmentary Triptych from Casa Giugni: Madonna and Child enthroned*, in pinnacle, *Saviour*—Cleveland, Museum of Art; *SS. Julian and James*, in pinnacle, *Angel of Annunciation*—Homeless; *SS. John Baptist and Anthony Abbot* (cut at top, through the Virgin of Annunciation)—Homeless. *Dated on central panel 1419.*

551. Florentine close to MASOLINO (Master of 1419): *Triptych: S. Julian enthroned between SS. Anthony Abbot and Martin;* in pinnacles, *Trinity and Annunciation;* in pilasters, *four Saints.* San Gimignano, Pinacoteca.

552. Florentine between GIOVANNI DAL PONTE and MASOLINO: *Madonna of Humility*.
Formerly Florence, Contini Bonacossi Collection.

553. MASOLINO: *Madonna of Humility*. Bremen, Kunsthalle. *Dated 1423.*

554–556. MASOLINO: *Fragments of Carnesecchi Triptych: Madonna and Child* (formerly Novoli, S. Maria),
S. Julian (Florence, Seminario Maggiore), *S. Julian murdering his parents* (Montauban, Musée). *ca 1424/25.*

557. MASOLINO: *Annunciation*. Washington, National Gallery, Mellon Collection. *ca 1423/25*.

558. MASOLINO: *Frescoed lunette: Madonna and Child with two Angels*. Empoli, S. Stefano. *1424*.

559. MASOLINO: *Fresco: Preaching of S. Peter* (*detail*). Florence, Carmine, Cappella Brancacci. *ca 1425*.

560. MASOLINO: *Fresco: Fall of Man*. Florence, Carmine, Cappella Brancacci. *ca 1425*.

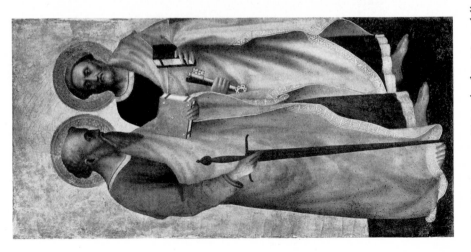

561–563. MASOLINO: *Triptych of S. Maria delle Nevi* (front): *SS. Peter and Paul* (Philadelphia, Johnson Collection), *Assumption* (Naples, Capodimonte), *S. Matthias and a Pope* (London, National Gallery). *ca 1430.*

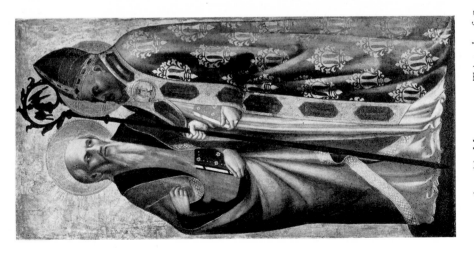

564–566. MASOLINO: *Triptych of S. Maria delle Nevi* (back): *S. Martin and S. John the Evangelist* (Philadelphia, Johnson Collection), *Foundation of S. Maria Maggiore* (Naples, Capodimonte), *S. Jerome and the Baptist* (these last two, by MASACCIO; London, National Gallery). *ca 1430.*

568. MASOLINO: *Madonna and Child with two Saints (detail)*.
Stockholm, Museum. *(1427?)*.

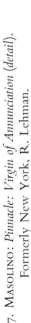

567. MASOLINO: *Pinnacle: Virgin of Annunciation (detail)*.
Formerly New York, R. Lehman.

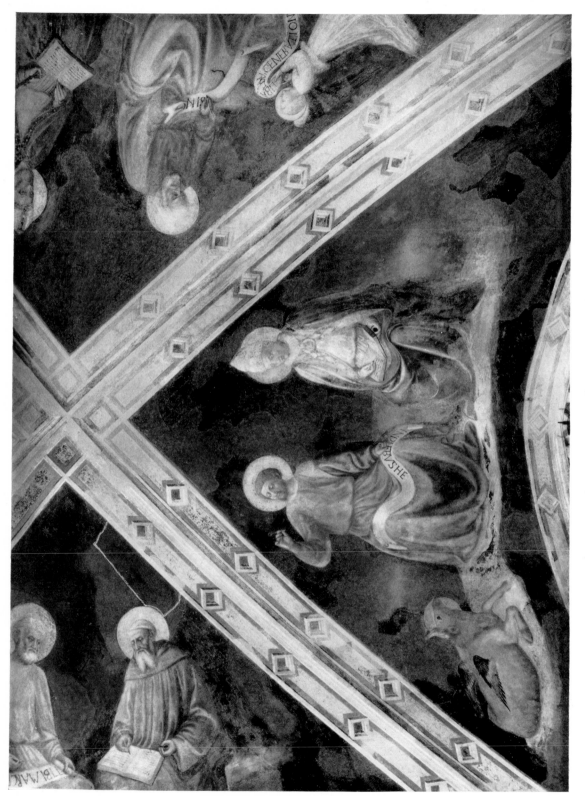

569. Masolino: *Ceiling Fresco: Evangelists*. Rome, S. Clemente. 1428/31.

570. MASOLINO: *Fresco: Life of S. Catherine*. Rome, S. Clemente. *1428/31*.

571. MASOLINO: *Fresco: Annunciation* (entrance arch). Rome, S. Clemente. *1428/31*.

572. MASOLINO: *Fresco: S. Catherine pleads with the Emperor to remove the idols.* Rome, S. Clemente. *1428/31.*

573. MASOLINO: *Fresco: Detail from the Crucifixion.* Rome, S. Clemente. *1428/31.*

574. MASOLINO: *Fresco: Madonna and Child with two Angels.* Todi, S. Fortunato. *1432.*

575. MASOLINO: *Fresco: Coronation* (ceiling). Castiglione d'Olona, Collegiata.

576. MASOLINO: *Fresco: The Baptist preaching, baptising Christ in the river Jordan, appearing before Herod.*
Castiglione d'Olona, Baptistery. *1435.*

577. MASOLINO: *Fresco: S. John's head brought to Salome.* Castiglione d'Olona, Baptistery. *1435.*

578. MASOLINO: *Madonna of Humility*. Munich, Alte Pinakothek. *ca 1425*.

579. MASACCIO: *The S. Ambrogio altarpiece: Madonna and Child with S. Anne and five Angels.*
Florence, Uffizi. *Before 1425.*

580. MASACCIO: *Madonna and Child with four Angels* (central panel of altarpiece from S. Maria del Carmine at Pisa). London, National Gallery. *1426*.

581. MASACCIO: *Crucifixion* (pinnacle of altarpiece from S. Maria del Carmine at Pisa).
Naples, Capodimonte. *1426.*

582. MASACCIO: *Adoration of the Magi (detail)* (predella panel of altarpiece from S. Maria del Carmine at Pisa).
Berlin, Staatliche Museen. *1426.*

583. ANDREA DI GIUSTO on MASACCIO's design: *S. Julian murdering his Parents* (predella panel of altarpiece from S. Maria del Carmine at Pisa). Berlin, Staatliche Museen. *1426.*

584. MASACCIO: *Beheading of the Baptist* (predella panel of altarpiece from S. Maria del Carmine at Pisa). Berlin, Staatliche Museen. *1426.*

585. MASACCIO: *Fresco: Trinity with the Virgin, S. John and two Donors;* below, '*Imago Mortis*'.
Florence, S. Maria Novella.

586. MASACCIO: *Fresco: S. Peter healing the Sick with his shadow while going to the Temple with S. John.*
Florence, S. Maria del Carmine, Cappella Brancacci. *1425/27.*

587. MASACCIO: *Fresco: S. Peter distributing alms and Death of Ananias.* Florence, S. Maria del Carmine, Cappella Brancacci. *1425/27.*

588. MASACCIO: *Fresco: Head of the toll-collector in the Tribute Money*. Florence, S. Maria del Carmine,
Cappella Brancacci. *1425/27*.

589. MASACCIO: *Fresco: Head of S. Peter in the Tribute Money*. Florence, S. Maria del Carmine, Cappella Brancacci. *1425/27*.

590. MASACCIO: *Fresco: Self-portrait* (detail of *S. Peter raising the Son of Theophilus*). Florence, Carmine, Cappella Brancacci.

MADE IN GREAT BRITAIN 1963

PRINTED BY GEO. GIBBONS LTD · LEICESTER

BOUND AT THE PITMAN PRESS · BATH